FROM RABIN TO NETANYAHU: ISRAEL'S TROUBLED AGENDA

Cass Studies in
Israeli History, Politics and Society

ISSN 1368-4795

General Editor: Efraim Karsh

From Rabin to Netanyahu: Israel's Troubled Agenda
edited by Efraim Karsh

Israel at the Polls, 1996
edited by Daniel J. Elazar and Schmuel Sandler
(forthcoming)

Other Books in the Series:

U.S.–Israeli Relations at the Crossroads
edited by Gabriel Sheffer

Between War and Peace: Dilemmas of Israeli Security
edited by Efraim Karsh

The Shaping of Israeli Identity: Myth, Memory and Trauma
edited by Robert Wistrich and David Ohana

Peace in the Middle East: The Challenge for Israel
edited by Efraim Karsh

FROM RABIN TO NETANYAHU
Israel's Troubled Agenda

Edited by
EFRAIM KARSH
King's College London

FRANK CASS
LONDON • PORTLAND, OR

First published in 1997 in Great Britain by
FRANK CASS AND COMPANY LIMITED
Newbury House, 900 Eastern Avenue, London IG2 7HH, England

and in the United States of America by
FRANK CASS
c/o ISBS, Inc.
5804 N.E. Hassalo Street, Portland, Oregon 97213-3644

British Library Cataloguing in Publication Data

A catalogue record for this book is available from the British Library

ISBN 0 7146 4431 0 (cloth)
ISBN 0 7146 4383 1 (paper)

Library of Congress Cataloging-in-Publication Data

From Rabin to Netanyahu : Israel's troubled agenda / edited by Efraim
Karsh.
    p.   cm. -- (Israeli history, politics, and society)
  Includes bibliographical references and index.
  ISBN 0-7146-4831-0 (cloth). -- ISBN 0-7146-4383-1 (pbk.)
  1. Israel --Politics and government--1993- 2. Arab-Israeli
conflict--1993- 3. National characteristics, Israeli. 4. Jews-
Israel--Identity. 5. Rabin, Yitzhak, 1922-   . 6. Netanyahu,
Binyamin. I. Karsh, Efraim. II. Series.
DS128.2.F76   1977
956.9404'4--dc21   97-23517
                                                                CIP

This group of studies first appeared in a Special Issue,
From Rabin to Netanyahu: Israel's Troubled Agenda in Israel Affairs,
Vol.3, Nos.3&4 (Spring/Summer 1997),
published by Frank Cass & Co. Ltd.

Printed in Great Britain by
Antony Rowe Ltd., Chippenham, Wilts.

Contents

Introduction: From Rabin to Netanyahu   **Efraim Karsh**   i

DOMESTIC ISSUES

The Forming of the Netanyahu Government:
Coalition Formation in a Quasi-Parliamentary
Setting   **Gregory S. Mahler**   3

Ideo-Theology: Discourse and Dissonance
in the State of Israel   **Clive Jones**   28

Israeli Identity in Transition   **Lilly Weissbrod**   47

Elections 1996:
The De-Zionization of Israeli Politics   **Danny Ben-Moshe**   66

Towards a New Portrait of the (New)
Israeli Soldier   **Stuart A. Cohen**   77

THE PEACE PROCESS

Peace Despite Everything   **Efraim Karsh**   117

From War to Peace: The Middle
East Peace Process   **Mohammed Z. Yakan**   133

Israel's Peace-Making with the
Palestinians: Change and
Legitimacy   **Yaacov Bar-Siman-Tov**   170

The Potential for Ambiguity
The Case of Jerusalem   **Ira Sharkansky**   187

Attitude Change and Policy Transformation:
Yitzhak Rabin and the Palestinian
Issue, 1967–95   **Hemda Ben-Yehuda**   201

The Golan Heights: A Vital Strategic Asset
for Israel   **David Eshel**   225

Labour, Likud, the 'Special Relationship'
and the Peace Process, 1988–96   **Jonathan Rynhold**   239

ISRAEL AND ITS NEIGHBOURS

Arab Responses to the Assassination of
Yitzhak Rabin   Gil Feiler 265

Rethinking Israel in the Middle East   Elie Podeh 280

Continuity and Change in
Egyptian–Israeli Relations, 1973–97   Kenneth W. Stein 296

Myopic Vision: Whither Israeli–Egyptian
Relations?   Shawn Pine 321

Documents   337

Index   345

For details of past and future contents of this and our other journals please
visit our website at *http://www.frankcass.com/jnls*

In Memory of Robert F. Shafritz
Rabbi, Scholar, Friend

ISRAEL BEFORE THE JUNE 1967 WAR

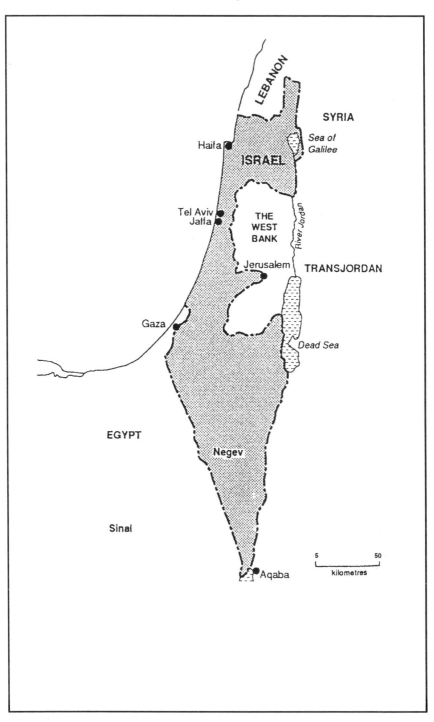

Introduction:
From Rabin to Netanyahu

EFRAIM KARSH

The May 1996 election of Benjamin Netanyahu, the 46-year-old leader of the right-wing Likud Party, as Israel's youngest ever prime minister provides further proof, if such is at all needed, of the volatility of Israeli politics. A couple of years earlier, with public euphoria sky-rocketing following the signing of a Declaration of Principles (DOP) with the Palestine Liberation Organization (PLO) and a fully-fledged peace treaty with Jordan, the standing of the Labour-led government seemed unassailable. Comprehensive peace between Israel and its Arab neighbours, a longstanding expressed objective of the Jewish State, seemed within reach; its promoters were seen as courageous men of vision, its critics – small-minded paranoiacs. Enter a string of suicide bombings across Israel by Islamic militants leaving a long trail of mayhem and blood, and the popularity of Prime Minister Yitzhak Rabin and his government went tumbling down. This trend was reversed overnight by Rabin's assassination on 4 November 1995 at the hands of a Jewish zealot. The first such act in the annals of the Jewish State, the assassination sent an unprecedented tremor throughout the nation, raising a tidal wave of sympathy with the slain prime minister and his quest for peace and revulsion with the perceived culprits of his killing, not least Netanyahu who had spearheaded a fierce campaign against the Labour-led peace process, rife with sharp personal attacks on Rabin and his nemesis-turned-partner, Foreign Minister Shimon Peres. Then came yet another round of atrocities by Islamic militants in late February and early March 1996, killing some 60 Israelis in four suicide bombings within the span of one week. Labour's electoral lead was wiped out once and for all.

More than anything else, then, Netanyahu's hair-breadth electoral victory represents the agonized and convoluted state of mind of the Israeli public. Netanyahu was not elected for his charismatic personality or the depth of his ideas; he was catapulted, or rather bombed to power by an atavistic mixture of fear and hope at an extremely vulnerable moment in the nation's life, to which his simplistic promise of 'peace with security' seemed a panacea.

Efraim Karsh is Professor and Head of the Mediterranean Studies Programme at King's College, University of London.

Some people are born with a silver spoon in their mouth. Such was the extent of Netanyahu's luck that his electoral rival was none other than the veteran politician Shimon Peres. On the face of it, the scales were unequivocally tilted against Netanyahu. As a newcomer to the political scene, he lacked any executive experience and his political record was essentially confined to the diplomatic-representative sphere: Deputy Ambassador to the United States, Israel's Representative to the United Nations, and Deputy Foreign Minister. True, Netanyahu's communicatory skills had made him an international media celebrity; but they had also bought him the unflattering title of 'Mr. Sound-bite', a man of catchy phrases rather than deeds, a poor man's Abba Eban. But then Eban has never become prime minister...

Peres, by contrast, is one of Israel's most accomplished politicians. With a career dating back some 50 years, he served for many years in the Ministry of Defence, becoming Director General in 1953, at the age of 29, and Deputy Minister of Defence in 1959 (when he also became a Knesset member), a position he held until 1965. Since then he went to serve twice as Prime Minister and respectively held the defence, foreign affairs, and finance portfolios, among others. In these capacities Peres played a prominent role in the establishment and the development of Israel's defence industries, including the nuclear reactor in Dimona; in the containment of the country's three-digit inflation in the mid-1980s; in Israel's extrication from the ill-conceived Lebanese adventure; and, most recently, in the promotion of the nascent peace process.

Yet, for all his remarkable achievements, Peres suffers from the same 'malignant disease' that afflicted British politician Neil Kinock: unelectability. For one reason or another, to most Israelis, he has represented the epitome of the professional politician: slick, opportunistic, non-credible. Five times he made his bid for Israel's top spot, never to win. He lost twice to Menachem Begin (in 1977 and in 1981). In 1984, against the backdrop of the hugely unpopular Lebanon War and sky-rocketing inflation, he failed to defeat the lacklustre Yitzhak Shamir and was forced to share a 'national unity' government with Likud (an experience repeated in 1988). Had he headed the Labour Party in the 1992 elections, rather than the late Yitzhak Rabin, Labour would not have returned to power. Similarly, had he relinquished power in favour of a younger successor, such as Chief-of-Staff-cum-Foreign Minister Ehud Barak, Labour would have won the 1996 elections by a comfortable majority, despite the murder of dozens of Israelis at the hands of Palestinian bombers.

But Netanyahu's luck did not end here. Fortunately for him, Peres undermined his own position by two cardinal mistakes. For one thing, he failed to call immediate elections after Rabin's assassination. Whether because of his reluctance to be seen as manipulating the national tragedy for personal gain, or because of the desire to leave his own imprint on the peace process, Peres made no attempt to bring the elections forward, seeking instead to reach an instantaneous Israeli–Syrian declaration of principles on the essence of peace. It was only upon realizing that President Hafiz Asad did not share this sense of urgency and would not reciprocate Israel's readiness to withdraw from the Golan Heights that Peres decided to call general elections. By then, however, the terrorists had dented his personal position beyond repair.

An equally devastating mistake related to the nature of Labour's electoral campaign. Heeding the advice of his chief campaigner, Interior Minister Haim Ramon, Peres decided to run a low-key, indeed an anaemic campaign. Hardly any mention was made of the Rabin assassination, as if this traumatic event had taken place on a different planet, and no personal attacks were launched against Netanyahu for fear of putting him on a par with the incumbent prime minister and of alienating those voters who had not yet made up their minds (the so-called 'fleeting vote'). Even when they encountered each other on television a few days before the elections Peres opted for a laid-back approach, avoiding a frontal assault on Likud's policies and ignoring Netanyahu in a blunt patronizing fashion.

This strategy backfired in grand style. With the national trauma attending the Rabin assassination buried under the fresher shock of Islamic bombings, Likud abandoned the self-imposed restraint adopted in the wake of the assassination and reverted to an aggressive propaganda campaign. Shrewdly distancing himself from this campaign so as to keep a premiership-like gravitas, Netanyahu left the 'hatchet job' to a group of able henchmen who shunned no means to discredit the Peres Government, from the charge that it sacrificed Israeli security (and lives) by handing over responsibility for this vital sphere to Yasser Arafat and his 'bunch of terrorists', to the accusation that Labour would divide Jerusalem by surrendering its eastern part, captured in the 1967 Six Day War, to PLO rule. Peres's emphatic denials of any such intention came too late to influence Israeli public opinion.

Finally, Netanyahu was a net beneficiary of the electoral reform (put into effect for the first time in the 1996 elections), which provided for the direct election of Israel's prime minister independent of, but in tandem with, the election of the country's parliament, the Knesset. Under the old system, it was up to Israel's President to observe the results of the Knesset elections and to appoint the prime minister-designate, who would normally come from the plurality party which usually had the greatest chance of forming a ruling coalition (there had never been a 'majority situation' in which the plurality party controlled on its own more than 50 per cent of the Knesset seats). Had this traditional pattern been followed in the May 1996 elections, Peres would have most probably retained the premiership since Labour emerged as the plurality party, winning 34 seats compared with Likud's 32, while the left-wing bloc (Labour, MERETZ, the Arab lists) kept a clear edge over its right-wing counterpart (Likud, Moledet, MAFDAL), with 52 vs 43 parliamentary seats. As things were, the new electoral system allowed Netanyahu, who won the direct race for premiership by the slimmest of margins (receiving 50.4 per cent of the ballots compared to 49.5 per cent for Peres) to become prime minister despite his party's defeat in the elections.

That Netanyahu's election heralded no public rejection of the peace process is evidenced not only by Labour's and the left-wing bloc's electoral edge but, moreover, by the predication of Likud's election campaign on its (however grudging) commitment to the Oslo Process. This effectively reduced the choice confronting the Israeli public to one of form rather than of substance: not between two mutually exclusive visions of peace but between two vaguely defined paths to the same destination, the only difference being Likud's pledge that its peace would be more 'secure' than Labour's.

It has been suggested that Netanyahu is in fact a die-hard doctrinaire, no less committed to the 'Greater Israel' ideology than former Likud prime ministers Menachem Begin and Yitzhak Shamir, and that his endorsement of the Oslo Process was merely a clever ploy aimed at capturing 'an important part of the Israeli electorate'.[1] Nothing could be further from the truth. It may well be that Netanyahu's endorsement of the Oslo Process stemmed from practical considerations; but this is precisely the fundamental difference between ideological and pragmatic, indeed opportunistic leaders. The former stick to their ideological precepts even in the face of the starkest dissonance between them and the existing reality; the latter adjust their worldview to the vicissitudes in their environment. The former speak their mind and stand by their principles even at the risk of public unpopularity or, still worse, loss of power; the latter subordinate their principles to the expediencies of power.

Begin and Shamir were undoubtedly ideological leaders: both would rather have given up power than surrender parts of the Land of Israel to foreign control (Begin's son, Benny, did indeed resign from the Netanyahu Government following its signing of the Hebron Protocol in January 1997). David Ben-Gurion and his Labourite successors Rabin and Peres have all been pragmatists: though staunch believers in the right of the Jewish People to the entire Land of Israel they have been prepared to partition this land as a means of keeping Israel's Jewish and democratic nature (interestingly enough, Ben-Gurion was already supporting the idea of a Palestinian State in the late 1940s[2] while Rabin and Peres subscribed to the 'Jordanian Option' until the early 1990s and have not openly endorsed the establishment of a Palestinian State to this very day).

Netanyahu, in contrast, epitomizes the new brand of Israeli politicians: the pure opportunist interested more in the attainment and exercise of political power than in the promotion of the 'common good', let alone the furtherance of an ideological vision – the postmodernist manifestation of *l'état c'est moi*.

Whether or not in his hearts of hearts Netanyahu still believes in the idea of 'Greater Israel', upon which he was reared in his father's home, is immaterial. Being the 'political animal' he is, Netanyahu is keenly aware of the hopes, desires and sensitivies of the Israeli public which amount to a deep yearning for normalcy rather than a return to the bad old days of bloodshed and confrontation. He knows full well that he has received a clear mandate from the Israeli electorate to lean more heavily on Yasser Arafat, seen by many Israelis as having systematically evaded his obligations stipulated by the Oslo Accords – but not to renege on the peace process, let alone intensify Jewish settlement activity in the West Bank. And he is all too aware that, for all the hype about settlement over the past three decades, merely two per cent of Israel's Jewish population have chosen to make their home in the occupied territories, and the overwhelming majority of Israelis would not condone an overall confrontation with the Palestinians over the possible expansion of the settlements, now that the two peoples are on the verge of their final, irreversible disengagement.

This is why the issue of Jewish settlements was conspicuously absent from Likud's election campaign, and why Netanyahu chose to embrace the Oslo Process. Running on a 'Greater Israel' platform, with its corollaries of a renewed Palestinian *intifada*, growing international isolation, and a diminishing economic peace dividend, would simply have been an assured recipe for electoral disaster: opinion polls in the wake of the February-March 1996 massacres by Islamic militants revealed clear support for the continuation of the peace process despite widespread dismay with the Labour Government's handling of Palestinian terrorism.

Netanyahu must have suspected that his endorsement of the Oslo Process meant the effective demise of the 'Greater Israel' dream, for no other reason than that this process commits Israel to surrendering most of the West Bank population and much of its territory to Palestinian control well before the completion of the final-status negotiations between the two parties. But if this was the price for realizing his burning ambition to reach the country's top spot – so be it.

And if there remained any doubts about Netanyahu's readiness to shed the 'Greater Israel' ideology, these were dispelled by the Hebron Protocol of 15 January 1997, in which Israel undertook to evacuate some 80 per cent of the City of the Patriarchs and to implement the Interim Agreement, including the completion of military redeployment in (that is, withdrawal from) the West Bank by mid-1998. True, it took the Netanyahu Government some six months to conclude an agreement not dissimilar to that reached by its Labour predecessor; yet there has scarcely been a single issue which Netanyahu, endowed with the potentially disastrous mixture of vanity (if not pomp), inexperience, and deeply-seated suspicion, has failed to bungle: from the appointment of ministers and state officials, to the handling of the economy, to civil–military relations, to relations between religious and secular Jews, to Israel's international relations. Moreover, even the Peres Government had delayed the evacuation of Hebron by several months following the relentless terrorist campaign of early 1996, for fear of denting Labour's electoral chances; hence it was only natural for Netanyahu to take some time to resign himself to the inevitability of this watershed development and to overcome opposition within Likud to it. But when it was eventually concluded, the Hebron Protocol was approved by 87 of the Knesset's 120 members (with 17 opposed and 15 abstentions), compared to 61:50 and 61:59 in the votes on the Oslo I and Oslo II Accords. As the jubilant Arafat told a cheering Palestinian crowd in Hebron on 20 January: 'We have [now] concluded a peace agreement with the entire Israeli people... The 87 Knesset votes in favour of the agreement represent a new reality in the Middle East.'

Israelis have long quipped that only Labour can make war, for it will always enjoy right-wing backing for such a move, while Likud alone can make the necessary territorial concessions for the sake of peace, for it will always receive left-wing support for this endeavour. What this handy quip fails to consider is that while the die-hard doctrinaire is best poised to rally the widest national consensus behind a painful compromise, he will be loathe to do precisely that. Thus, while Menachem Begin was probably the only leader who could, and indeed did, return the entire Sinai Peninsula to Egypt and dismantle the Jewish settlements there, he would never have been able to bring about a comprehensive peace due to his adamant refusal to surrender the West Bank (and the Golan Heights) to foreign control (in the event, Begin was spared of the need to face this stark decision since the PLO, then openly committed to Israel's destruction, rejected President Jimmy Carter's offers to join the Camp David process).[3] Similarly, it was only Yitzhak Rabin's reputation as 'Mr. Security', the man who would not surrender Israel's vital interests, which allowed Labour under his leadership to launch the Oslo Process with the Palestinians and to conclude a peace treaty with Jordan; but then even Rabin's credentials, not to speak of those of his successor, Shimon Peres, would probably not have sufficed to secure the necessary public and/or parliamentary support for a fully-fledged peace agreement with the Palestinians, or even with Syria.

This in turn means that a fox in a wolf's skin, an opportunist heading a right-wing coalition and preaching a nationalist gospel, stands the best chance of uniting the nation behind the painful concessions attending peace with Israel's immediate neighbours. Whether Netanyahu will prove to be such a person and lead Israel to the coveted peace, or continue to muddle through and go down in history as Israel's worst ever prime minister, remains to be seen. To judge by the speed with which he has wasted the domestic and international credit gained by the Hebron agreement, the future seems very bleak indeed.

NOTES

1   Shalom Lapin, 'Netanyahu and the Palestinians: Pragmatism or Ideology?', *Jewish Quarterly*, Winter 1996/97, pp.33–36.
2. See, for example, David Ben-Gurion, *Yoman Ha-milhama* (War Diary), Tel-Aviv, 1982, Vol.III, 18 December 1948, p.885.
3. On Palestinian rebuff of American offers to join the Camp David peace process see Edward Said, 'The Morning After', *London Review of Books*, 21 October 1993, pp.3, 5. As Palestinian intellectual Fayez Sayigh put it, the Palestinians would never accept 'a fraction of rights in a fraction of their homeland'. Cited in Howard M. Sachar, *A History of Israel, Vol. II: From the Aftermath of the Yom Kippur War*, New York, 1987, p.86.

DOMESTIC ISSUES

The Forming of the Netanyahu Government: Coalition-formation in a Quasi-Parliamentary Setting

GREGORY S. MAHLER

Recent electoral system reform has had a significant impact upon Israeli government, often characterized as among the world's more tumultuous democracies. The 12th Knesset (1988–92) enacted a number of reforms in Israel's electoral system that first took effect with the May 1996 election for the 14th Knesset. The single most important change made by these reforms involved the direct election of Israel's prime minister independent of, but chosen at the same time as, the election of Israel's parliament. This essay illustrates the impact of these changes on the coming to power of Israel's youngest-ever prime minister, Benjamin Netanyahu, or – more specifically – on the process of coalition-formation in Israel.

The recent changes distanced Israel's political system from what can be considered to be the basic principle of parliamentary government: that the prime minister comes from, and is responsible to, a majority of the legislature. The concept of responsible government – central to the 'Westminster' parliamentary model – includes the assumption that the prime minister is elected as the leader of a majority (or a majority coalition) in the legislature. The direct election of the prime minister suggests that the 'new' Israeli government should be called 'quasi-parliamentary', or perhaps 'quasi-presidential'; it will have direct implications for public policy in Israel and for the creation and survival of coalition governments in years to come.

Israel saw the results of this new system of government following the elections for the 14th Knesset: a prime minister was elected who did not lead the plurality party in the Knesset. While it was true that Netanyahu was still able to create a majority coalition without the participation of the (plurality) Labour Party, the fact that he was the first prime minister in Israeli political history to have a direct mandate from the voters coloured the coalition-formation process, and will clearly continue to affect the policies coming from his government in the coming months and years.

Gregory S. Mahler is Provost of Kalanazoo College, Michigan.

This essay performs several tasks. First, it describes the new Israeli electoral system and some of its implications for the creation of Israeli coalitions and for cabinet behaviour. Following this, it describes the manner in which the process of coalition-formation in Israel has worked in the past. The results of the May 1996 elections are then described, and analysis is offered of the implications of those results for the coalition-formation process. It then examines in some detail the coalition negotiations that followed the 1996 Knesset/Prime Minister elections, leading to the creation of the Netanyahu Government, as well as some of the coalition machinations during the early days of this government. Finally, some observations are offered about future implications of the contemporary coalition for Israeli public policy.

THE SETTING: THE NEW ELECTORAL SYSTEM

The 12th Knesset (1988–92) enacted much legislation that was significant for the Israeli political system. Among the most significant legislation was that involving the amendment to *The Basic Law: The Government* which changed the electoral system from what could be called a 'purely parliamentary' system (even allowing for uniquely Israeli characteristics in its electoral system) to what can be called a quasi-presidential or quasi parliamentary model.

Elections for the Knesset are described in *The Basic Law: The Knesset* as follows: 'The Knesset shall be elected by general, national, direct, equal, secret and proportional elections'. Citizens (over the age of 18; candidates must be over the age of 21) vote for parties, not individual candidates, and parties receive a number of seats in the Knesset proportional to the number of votes they receive. The vote 'threshold' is 1.5 per cent of the vote;[1] votes cast for parties receiving fewer votes than 1.5 per cent are 'wasted' and are not considered in the awarding of parliamentary seats.

The major change in the new electoral system involved the direct election of the prime minister. In the past, it was up to the president of Israel to observe the outcome of the Knesset election and to decide who should be the prime minister-designate. While the decision was *usually* an easy one to make because one of the two major parties (or blocs) had a plurality in the Knesset and had a greater or lesser mandate to lead from the public, there were occasions when the margin between the two major parties was extremely small. (To take one example, in 1988 the Likud had 40 seats in the Knesset while Labour had 39 seats.)

One of the motivations for electoral reform was the result of past tensions in the creation and survival of political coalitions: this kind of situation gave disproportionate influence to some small parties – usually the orthodox religious parties – whose support could make the difference between a party capable of forming a government and one incapable of doing this. Supporters of electoral reform argued that the direct election of a prime minister would 'free' him/her from this type of constraining or 'blackmailing' influence of smaller parties.

The new electoral law went into effect with the elections to the 14th Knesset in May 1996. Two separate ballots were cast: one for a prime minister, and another for a party list for members of the Knesset. Parties advertised their platforms and (rank ordered) lists of candidates during the campaign period, and voters cast their Knesset votes for the single party they most preferred. Surplus vote agreements were signed by many parties in advance of the elections, in which some parties agreed to pool their surplus votes, or one party promised to 'give' its surplus votes to another party after the election.[2]

The second vote for each voter involved the race for the prime minister. In the period preceding Likud's primary elections, there were several candidates who indicated that they would contest the race for prime minister; Ariel Sharon withdrew his candidacy in December 1995;[3] Rafael Eitan was co-opted into the Likud list early on,[4] and as the deadline approached David Levy agreed to not contest the premiership in exchange for the number two position on the Likud list and a commitment from Benjamin Netanyahu of a cabinet position in the new government should the Likud win,[5] leaving the race a two-candidate event between incumbent Shimon Peres of the Labour Party[6] and Likud's Benjamin Netanyahu.[7]

The new electoral law – actually, changes to the *Basic Law: The Government* – had to provide a number of specifics about how the election would actually work. The law indicated that should no candidate receive more than half of the valid votes, a run-off election would be held between the two candidates with the most votes. In the run-off election, the candidate with the largest number of votes would be declared the winner. Following the elections, the prime minister-elect had 45 days to present a list of ministers to the Knesset and receive a confidence vote for the cabinet from the Knesset. Should the prime minister not successfully present a government to the Knesset within 45 days, special elections for a new prime minister would have to be held within 60 days. The law indicates that should the same candidate be re-elected and not successfully present a government within a second period of 45 days, new elections would have to be held once more but that candidate would not be eligible to run in the third round of elections.

The changes to the *Basic Law: The Government* also described the circumstances under which the Knesset might be dissolved before the expiry of its four-year term and new elections called. Under the new system, new elections for the Knesset would take place[8] if the Knesset rejected the list of ministers proposed by the prime minister; if it expressed no-confidence in the prime minister by a majority of at least 61 MKs; if it failed to adopt the Budget Law within three months after the beginning of the fiscal year; if the Knesset dissolved itself by passing a special law to that effect; or if the prime minister, after notifying the president, resigned and dissolved the Knesset.

There was similar concern about when, under the new system, the popularly-elected prime minister might be 'fired' and new elections called – what would be the functional equivalent of a vote of non-confidence under the 'old' system. Under the new electoral system new elections for prime minister would take place if the Knesset (by a special majority of 80 members) voted to remove the prime minister from office; if the Knesset by a regular majority vote removed the prime minister from office due to a conviction on an offense involving moral turpitude; if the prime minister was unable to appoint the specified minimum of eight ministers to form his government; or if the prime minister died, or was permanently unable to fulfill his functions.

It is clear that while much of the preceding electoral system still exists, there are a number of significant changes in the new model. The most obvious potential change is that the new model would permit a prime minister of one party to be elected who might need to form a coalition headed by a different party to control the Knesset. Moreover, the functional equivalent of a non-confidence vote – the Knesset 'firing' a prime minister – would now require 80 votes, not simply a majority of those MKs present and voting as had been the case in the 'old' system.

As shall be seen later, one of the clearest surprises of the elections to the 14th Knesset was a significant increase in voting for the smaller parties; given this, it is entirely plausible that a Likud candidate for prime minister could win that race, and that the Knesset could be controlled by a Labour-left coalition, or vice versa. What would happen under those circumstances? If this situation had developed, could Benjamin Netanyahu have put together a coalition cabinet that would receive the support of a Labour-dominated Knesset? (As it turned out, of course, he *was* able to receive the support of the Knesset with an opposition-Labour plurality, though it would be saying too much to say that the Knesset was 'Labour-dominated'.) Would the reverse of this have been possible? While analysts were examining a wide range of possibilities leading up to the May 1996 elections, the general consensus was that it *would*, indeed, be possible for Netanyahu to put together a cabinet acceptable to a Labour-led Knesset majority, and it *would* be possible for Peres to put together a cabinet acceptable to a Likud-dominated Knesset majority. On balance, observers felt that the task would probably be easier for Netanyahu than for Peres.

Speculation about how the new electoral system would affect Israeli politics almost reached the point of being a national sport in Israel in the weeks and days leading up to the 1996 elections. There was no shortage of hypotheses dealing with the effect of the changes on the parties, on turnout, on the prime minister's power, on the role of the Knesset, and on everything else from voters' feelings of efficacy (and alienation) to the long-term health of Israeli democracy. As the election returns became clear several days after the voting, it was apparent that the new experiment in electoral institutions would, indeed, have several effects on the political system.

ISRAELI COALITION FORMATION: SOME PAST PATTERNS

An understanding of the existence of government coalitions is central to the study of Israeli politics.[9] Since the time of Israel's independence there has never been a 'majority situation'[10] in Israel's parliament – that is, one in which the party organizing the government has controlled *on its own* more than 50 per cent of the seats in the Knesset. Israel, in fact, has been an oft-cited illustration of a 'minority situation, majority government', one in which a party with *less* than a majority of parliamentary seats joins with other minority parties to *create* a majority government.[11]

This has resulted in coalitions being formed not only *after*, but also *between* Knesset elections. Thus, while elections to Israel's 14th Knesset took place in May 1996, the coalition government created the following month was by one count Israel's *27th* Government.

The study of what has come to be called coalition theory has greatly expanded over time.[12] Indeed, in a recent study political scientists have suggested that coalition theory is now in its third generation. The first generation developed theories of how coalitions work; the second tried to apply the general theories dealing with coalition-formation and behaviour to 'real world' politics to see how well the models predicted what would happen. The third generation seeks to combine the research of both the first and the second generations to make coalition theory a truly predictive model.[13]

There are, of course, a number of problems with broad theories of coalition formation. First, the theories may be more or less valid in one political system than in another. Second, the research may not be transferrable. That is, research done in Japan may not tell us a great deal about how coalitions work in Israel. Third, the distribution of cabinet positions may be explained by many different theories, including the number of seats a party can claim to control, patronage, loyalty to past partners, payment for future support, and a variety of other reasons. Finally, a theory that explains coalition behaviour in Israel at one point in time may not work at all at another time.

Several of these themes must be kept in mind when analyzing the formation of coalitions among Israeli political parties and attempting to discuss the significance of specific coalitions for Israeli politics. First, political parties play an overwhelming role in not only the 'political' but also the social and economic life. They publish newspapers, run medical clinics, sponsor athletic and social events, and, in short, permeate every aspect of life.[14]

Second, one must note the number of parties which are currently active in Israeli politics. As many as 24 political parties presented themselves at elections for the 1st and 2nd Knesset;[15] more recently, 27 parties ran candidates in the 12th Knesset elections in 1988, and 12 won Knesset seats. At one point in the campaign in 1992, according to one report, 67 political parties submitted lists for election including 17 of the 18 parties in the Knesset at the time;[16] in the final analysis, 25 parties were approved by the Central Elections Committee.[17] In the May 1996 elections, 21 parties took part; nine of them were represented in the outgoing Knesset; the others were 'either new parties or ones created by MKs who broke away from their factions'.[18] Thus, the mere *number* of political parties that are active in the political system may affect our ability to theorize about coalition-formation, and in practice certainly makes more difficult anything resembling prediction in the Israeli case.

It has been noted that whereas 12 cabinets had actually formed through 1965, in those 12 cabinets there were 7,873 possible winning coalitions,[19] to say nothing of the number of near-winning or minority coalitions possible. To provide a comparison, in Belgium over a comparable period of time there were 14 actual coalitions with 463 possible winning combinations.[20] Thus the *number* of political parties active in the electoral system is a factor which must be taken into consideration in an analysis of coalition-formation and behaviour.

Third, the regional military balance and national security in general have always been of paramount importance in Israeli politics. War situations, especially in 1967, have greatly influenced the size of coalitions that have been formed in Israel. On several occasions coalitions have been created that were larger than they 'needed' to be and that included parties whose support was not really necessary, in order to demonstrate to the outside world that the government in power at the time had a strong base of support. This factor was of great significance in the 1991 Gulf War period for the Shamir Government, for example, and although Israel was not actually *at war* in 1996, the issues of war and security (and terrorism) were omnipresent in the election campaign.

Fourth, the concept of a 'minimal winning coalition' must be treated carefully in the Israeli context. With the Knesset membership of 120, an absolute majority would be 61 seats. However, on several occasions blocs of representatives have publicly announced that they will systematically abstain on a range of parliamentary votes. On one occasion in which 20 members announced that they would systematically abstain from voting, this had the effect of lowering the active population of the Knesset from 120 to 100, which in turn lowered the effective minimal winning coalition from 61 to 51.

Fifth, imperfect information occasionally increases the size of a coalition. The Israeli party system contains strong and highly disciplined parties – many political scientists argue that the Israeli system is second to none in the relative impotence of the individual members and in the strength of party leaders there.[21] A certain amount of imperfect information remains, however, because of the large number of parties and because of the fact that even though the parties may run for office together in a grand alliance, they will not necessarily be in agreement in all policy spheres.

This means that the party that forms the governmental coalition cannot automatically count on any party's vote. One illustration not all that unusual is the elaborate 'contract' among members of the 18th cabinet-governing coalition, which defined precisely the conditions under which party members and coalition members could 'vote their consciences'; a similar 'contract' was developed for the Begin cabinet in 1977.[22] Labour and Likud signed a similar agreement in 1984 and again in 1988. In 1992 a formal contract was also arrived at following much negotiation for the Rabin Government.[23] And, the same thing happened in June 1996 for the Netanyahu Government because of the rule that all coalition arrangements must be in writing a full 24 hours before the new Government is presented to the Knesset.[24] This will be further discussed in the next section of this essay.

Finally, the history and ideological nature of the Israeli party system must be considered. The party system in Israel has been called over-developed by many, and several political scientists have written that the large number of political parties is not really necessary. The abundance of political parties is usually attributed to the fact that most existed before the state did; 'every one of the political parties represented in the 5th Knesset (August 1961), with the exception of two small Arab lists, had roots in and at least some organizational history going back to the pre-state period.'[25] This history, combined with the proportional representation electoral system that encourages new parties to form by making representation in the Knesset relatively easy, has encouraged the expansion of parties, which has complicated the coalition-formation process.

Moreover, ideological issues in recent Israeli politics, including issues relating to religion and the state, have significantly influenced the complexity of the coalition-formation process. Increasingly the orthodox religious parties have become estranged from the Labour Party, and to the extent that there was a 'natural' coalition constituency for Benjamin Netanyahu following the 1996 elections it was with the religious parties. Some of the small parties would have been willing coalition partners for either of the larger parties. Others were much more clearly aligned with one or the other.

The important consequences of coalition governments for the Israeli political system are several. First, they result in increased party discipline, and thereby less individual legislative freedom, because the Government has to be sure that it can depend upon coalition members to support government policy.

Second, and perhaps more important, coalitions leave the government vulnerable to 'blackmail', a point to be further discussed later. If a given coalition is a 'minimal' one in which the government would lose its majority if a single party withdrew, then a relatively small coalition partner might have considerably greater leverage with the Government than its size alone would suggest. This, of course, is precisely why Israel's religious parties have been able to wield the disproportionate influence over Israeli governments that has been the case in the past. Their influence has rarely reflected a government's ideological commitment to religious issues. Rather, it has often been because the smaller religious parties have issued ultimatums such as 'Pass/Support our policy, or we will withdraw from the government coalition and you will lose your majority and will no longer be prime minister'. Prime ministers have tended, over the years, to be quite responsive to this kind of threat.

The electoral reform that became effective in May 1996, including the direct election of the prime minister, was at least partially in response to this kind of 'blackmail' system. The authors of the electoral reform measures were seeking to insulate the prime minister from this kind of pressure, and felt that direct election of the prime minister was an effective way to do this. As will be shown later, one of the results of the reforms was an unintended one: an *increase* in the representation of the small parties in the Knesset, giving them even *more* influence in the coalition-formation process.

Finally, coalitions have led to a condition termed 'immobilisme' – or an inability to act on a given issue. This occurs when a problem comes up and the government knows that if it acts in a certain direction, one of its coalition partners will get angry and quit the coalition, but if it acts in another direction a different coalition partner will be antagonized and quit the coalition. The only solution, then, is to do nothing.

Indeed, shortly after the outbreak of the 1991 Gulf War, Prime Minister Shamir announced that he would ask the government to 'co-opt' the leader of the right-wing Moledet Party, Rehavam Ze'evi, a former army general, as a minister without portfolio,[26] though it was Shamir's intention that Ze'evi would sit as a member of the ministerial security affairs committee.[27] Ze'evi had been calling for military retaliation against the Iraqi missile attacks. This appointment was made over the objections of several significant Likud ministers, including Foreign Minister David Levy, Defence Minister Moshe Arens, Justice

Minister Dan Meridor, and Health Minister Ehud Olmert. Ze'evi said that he wanted to be in the coalition government for several reasons, but primarily 'because we wanted to be partners in this struggle. The war is not only on the borders of Iraq and Kuwait, and is not limited to missile attacks on Israel. After this war, there will be the fight over the future of the Land of Israel'.

Shamir saw the co-optation of Ze'evi as an opportunity to bring another party in the Knesset into the coalition, 'enabling the prime minister to pass religious and other legislation more easily, and to neutralize the power of Finance Minister Yitzhak Moda'i and his breakaway Liberal faction. It also further diminishes the chances for a unity government'.[28] It meant that Shamir's coalition controlled 66 Knesset seats, which was considered a 'safe' coalition size: it was observed that 'no longer will any but the very largest of the minor parties have the power to bring the Government down'.[29] Further analysis, in fact, suggested that the appointment 'was just one more step in the Likud party's preparations to rebuff the expected pressure from abroad to solve the Palestinian problem, once the Gulf War ends'.[30]

Thus, coalition governments by their very nature inject a note of uncertainly and instability into the Israeli political system. However, it is probably safe to observe that there was *less* instability and uncertainty in the behaviour of the Yitzhak Shamir coalition during the Gulf War than in past war situations – primarily because of the actors in the coalition – or than there would have been with a more ideologically diverse (such as a Government of National Unity) coalition.

THE OUTCOME OF THE NEW ELECTORAL SYSTEM: THE COMING OF NETANYAHU

This is not the place for a detailed analysis of all facets of the 1996 Israeli elections. The focus here is on the coalition-formation process, and of the impact of the new direct elections structure upon the selection of the prime minister and its impact upon the Israeli parliamentary system more broadly construed. Two significant points are important here. First, the direct election of the prime minister was an extremely close vote, far closer than most observers had thought would be the case. It resulted in an elected prime minister who does *not* lead the plurality party in the Knesset. Second, the elections introduced Israel for the first time to the split-vote process. It appears that voters felt freer to vote for small parties with the split-ballot process than they did in the past. Each of these two issues merits discussion here.

The Vote

The actual operation of the electoral system was uneventful. Two names were on the ballot for prime minister, and the Israeli electorate got into the spirit of the campaign quickly. As the time of the elections drew near, it became increasingly obvious that the margin of victory was going to be extremely narrow. Indeed, as noted above, the results of the elections left Israel with a prime minister who was *not* the leader of the plurality party in the Knesset. Much of the blame for this was directed at Netanyahu personally, who had given away seven 'safe' seats to the Tsomet faction, and later another seven 'safe' seats to the Gesher faction, with critics noting that

> They are the sacrificial lambs in Netanyahu's bid for the premiership. The claim that the Likud and Tsomet together will win more Knesset seats than the two of them separately is unproven. What is sure is that Tsomet brings no real dowry to the match... The shrewd [Rafael] Eitan will effortlessly bring in an eight-member faction to the next Knesset, something he could not have hoped to achieve running on his own against the Third Way.[31]

This, of course, would never have happened in the 'old' system, and while Netanyahu was still able to put together a majority coalition in the Knesset, the ultimate effect of this is unclear.

The pre-election phase, it will be recalled, witnessed the posturing of David Levy in the autumn of 1995, with his leaving Likud and announcing that he was going to run for the position of prime minister. This would clearly have created (at least) a three-candidate race, with most of Levy's support coming from the ranks of Likud supporters, thus likely guaranteeing Shimon Peres a victory. Netanyahu, accordingly, had to do whatever was necessary to make sure that Levy (and earlier Rafael Eitan, too) did not run for office; it was clearly in Netanyahu's interest to keep both Eitan and Levy *out* of the race for the position of prime minister. This resulted, as noted earlier, in his promising cabinet positions to Levy and Eitan, and seven 'safe' seats to each Levy's party, Gesher, and Eitan's party, Tsomet. Would Levy have been able to negotiate this arrangement in exchange for his return to the Likud under the 'old' system? It is hardly likely, but it cannot be deemed impossible. The question of whether the new electoral system will always lead to pre-election negotiations to generate a two-candidate race is an interesting one, since that clearly was not the intention of the authors of the plan.

Netanyahu made other deals with small parties, exchanging their endorsement of his candidacy for the premiership for Likud surplus votes.[32] It should be recalled that moving away from small party 'blackmail' was one of the major justifications of the new electoral system. This trading of Knesset seats for support for prime ministerial victory is a manifestation of the idea that the Knesset is strategically less important than the premiership, something that certainly would not have been so obvious under the 'old' system.

These deals had a significant effect upon the election outcome in a variety of ways. Most notably, many longtime Likud candidates were affected, individuals who would certainly have been elected to the Knesset had Netanyahu not given away 14 'safe' positions.[33] Netanyahu's deals with Gesher and Tsomet were justified on the grounds of the 'greater good', that is 'it will be worth it if Bibi captures the premiership and we keep Shimon Peres out of office'.[34] It also clearly kept 14 Likudniks out of the Knesset, and this would have proven to be of significance in the coalition-formation process that would occupy Netanyahu in days to come after the elections.

The Split Ballot

A second issue arising from the direct election of the prime minister that affects the Israeli coalition process involves the idea of 'split-ticket' voting in Israel.[35] Probably the single biggest surprise in the elections was the significant increase in representation of the smaller parties in the Knesset and the corresponding decrease in representation for the larger parties. What appears to be the case is that the split-ballot system was in a sense 'liberating' for Israeli voters. Apparently many voters who traditionally supported Labour or Likud did so because they saw it as a way to influence the election of the prime minister. Under the 'old' system the only way to influence the election of the prime minister was to help one party have more representation in the Knesset than any other party. That party's leader, of course, would become the prime minister.

TABLE 1
PARTY REPRESENTATION IN THE KNESSET

Party	Prime minister candidate %	% Vote 1996	Seats 1996	Seats 1992	Seat Difference
Labour	49.5	26.8	34	44	-10
Likud	50.4	25.1	32	37*	-5
Shas	–	8.5	10	6	+4
Nat'l Rel Party	–	7.8	9	6	+3
Meretz	–	7.4	9	12	-3
Israel Be-aliya	–	5.7	7	–	–
Hadash	–	4.2	5	3	+2
United Torah Judaism	–	3.2	4	4	0
Third Way	–	3.1	4	–	–
United Arab List	–	2.9	4	3	+1
Moledet	–	2.3	2	3	-1

* Includes 32 seats held by Likud and 5 seats held by Tsomet

Sources: Israel Ministry of Foreign Affairs, 'Israel Update: Israel Elections, 1996,' 'Elections in Israel, May 1996,' located at http://www.israel-mfa. gov.il/news/results.html; Consulate General of Israel in New York, The Electoral System in Israel (Consulate General of Israel in New York, New York, 1995).

Under the 'new' system it is now possible to vote for the prime minister directly, and *also* to be able to vote for the Knesset, and one's choice for the former does not necessarily have to be the same as one's choice for the latter. The data show[36] that in practice this happened often in the May elections. While 50.4 per cent of the valid votes were cast for the Likud candidate for prime minister, only 25.1 per cent of the valid votes were cast for the Likud list of candidates for the Knesset. Similarly, while 49.5 per cent of the valid votes were cast for the Labour candidate for prime minister, only 26.8 per cent of the valid votes were cast for the Labour list of Knesset candidates. This means that half of Netanyahu's supporters deserted the Likud Party when it came to voting for Knesset candidates, and virtually half of Peres's supporters deserted the Labour Party when it came to voting for Knesset candidates.

This dimension of the new electoral system had a clear and undeniable impact upon the process of coalition-formation in 1996. While one of the motivating forces for electoral reform in the 12th Knesset was that the small parties had 'too much' power and were able to 'blackmail' the larger parties during coalition-formation periods, what ended up happening under the new electoral system was that the small parties became *bigger*, and had *correspondingly more* power vis-à-vis the large parties in the coalition-formation process. It is to this dimension of the process that we now turn our attention.

COALITION NEGOTIATIONS

The elections demonstrated that the Israeli electorate was as deeply divided as at any time in its history. The campaign was a bitter one, and the fact that results were slow to come in on elections night did nothing to calm voters' frayed nerves; the announcement early on election day that it could be several *days* until the final results would be known greatly contributed to some voters' consternation.[37] By the following day, however, it was clear that Benjamin Netanyahu would be Israel's next prime minister. It was also clear that the small parties[38] – and especially the religious parties[39] – were the big winners in the Knesset elections. While some detractors of Shas blamed its increased success purely on superstition,[40] the fact was that Shas workers had campaigned hard as an alternative to the two major parties, and clearly their campaign work paid off. Similarly, the NRP's representation in the Knesset increased from 6 seats to 9, primarily on the basis of a campaign emphasizing 'values, Judaism, and education'.[41]

Within a few days of the elections, Prime Minister-elect Netanyahu was preparing to begin coalition negotiations. Likud leaders anticipated intense and difficult negotiations, given the increased strength of some of the smaller partners, but still Netanyahu's advisors indicated that he hoped to complete the formation of his new government in ten days.[42] This was not, in fact, to happen. Each of the potential coalition partners sent one representative to a preliminary meeting on coalition-formation strategy. One of the problems that appeared at the outset was one of payoff ratios: while cabinet portfolios-to-Knesset seats has been a common means of measuring returns to political parties for joining coalitions in the past, Netanyahu faced the problem of making sure that he had enough Likud members in his cabinet while at the same time giving his coalition partners an acceptable level of cabinet positions.

The new law limited the maximum size of the cabinet to 18 members. Given that ceiling, it was unclear how Netanyahu could balance the demands of all potential cabinet partners. His initial plan was to give Shas and the NRP two ministers each, to give one minister each to the United Torah Judaism, Israel Be-aliya, and the Third Way, and save the remaining ten cabinet seats for his party list (with himself counting as the 18th slot), although they would have to be divided up among Likud, Gesher, and Tsomet leaders. As soon as the plan was announced, however, it was criticized: Zevulon Hammer of the NRP declared that 'It would be unthinkable that there would be a three-MK-to-one-portfolio ratio for the Likud and a four-MK ratio for the other parties'.[43]

Almost immediately the posturing began, with Netanyahu and his transition spokesman Avigdor Lieberman – who would head the Prime Minister's Office under Netanyahu – indicating to the NRP and Shas (and other small parties) that 'excessive demands' would not be tolerated, that there would be no more than 18 ministers and six deputy ministers in the new government, as stipulated in the law, and that the Likud *would*, in fact, be given preference in the number of portfolios to be awarded.[44] Netanyahu indicated that Likud would receive proportionately more ministers in the cabinet than other parties because he wanted his party to have a majority in the cabinet; this was exacerbated by the fact that Likud was a bloc of three separate parties, each of which wanted an identifiable share of cabinet positions. In a second negotiating position Netanyahu indicated that he planned to give his coalition partners eight positions, saving nine for the three components of the Likud, resulting in the Likud bloc having ten votes at the cabinet table, counting the prime minister.

The potential coalition partners demanded that the ratio of one-portfolio-for-three-seats in the cabinet from past governments be followed, but Netanyahu's spokesmen responded that with a coalition of 66 MPs this would mean a cabinet of 22 members, far more than the law would permit. Nor would he agree to the NRP and Shas each getting three ministers, Israel Be-aliya two, and UTJ and the Third Way one each, since that would give ten of the 18 portfolios to non-Likud actors; taking Netanyahu into consideration that would leave only seven positions for the three Likud factions.

Prior to the elections there had been some discussion suggesting that the religious parties – Shas, NRP, and UTJ – should create a religious bloc to run together. Proponents of this idea argued that they could win as many as 17 to 19 seats if they did so.[45] As things turned out, the parties did not run on a joint list, and they ended up winning 23 seats in any event! Clearly the religious parties as a group were winners in the elections, and they wanted recognition of this fact from the new Prime Minister in the form of cabinet portfolios.

Negotiations began apace. The NRP and Shas met to try to put together a united list of demands of Netanyahu, but were unable to agree on a substantive division of responsibilities. While they did not want to end up submitting conflicting claims to Netanyahu for cabinet portfolios (for example the Religious Affairs portfolio which was demanded by both the NRP and Shas) they were unable to come to a mutually acceptable agreement over cabinet responsibilities, though they were able to agree to communicate to Netanyahu that he should not have one ratio of portfolios-per-MK for the Likud, and another for coalition partners.[46] For several days the three religious parties worked on a joint platform that they would use as a basis of negotiations with Netanyahu, as well as discussing Knesset leadership positions, the religious status quo, and other policy issues.[47]

The religious parties were not the only source of tension for Netanyahu, however. Natan Sharansky's party, Israel Be-aliya, did well in the campaign period, and virtually all election observers were confident that *whoever* won the premiership, Sharansky would be included in the next cabinet. Sharansky and his supporters let it be known[48] that he would not accept a 'toothless' ministry and that he would prefer to have one of the significant economic ministries in the new government.

And, in addition to the demands of the religious parties, Sharansky, and the other potential cabinet partners, one very significant individual was sitting just offstage waiting to hear what his (cabinet) reward would be for his crucial pre-election activities: Ariel Sharon. Even though not all observers were using Sharon's name routinely, he was never far from everyone's mind, and none of the post-election pundits were leaving his name off of the speculative lists.

A week after the elections the 'initial' round of negotiations ended, and the 'serious' bargaining began. In the 'initial' round the potential coalition partners presented their lists of demands to the Likud. The second stage of the procedure consisted of Likud responding to the demands of the potential partners. One of the things that made these particular negotiations different from those of past years involved the direct election of the prime minister. In this case the prime minister was already known, he already had a substantial degree of legitimacy by virtue of his direct election by *all* of the people of Israel, and he had announced that he was prepared to use executive power to an extent not previously used in Israel. So, while the prime minister still had to present a coalition to the Knesset, he had far more negotiating leverage with the Members of Knesset than had past prime ministers-designate. In fact, several observers noted that

> Likud insiders say they have never known a situation in which nothing leaks regarding ministerial appointments. The chief reason is that Netanyahu personally holds all the cards and isn't showing them to anyone. His intentions are a mystery even to some of those closest to him.[49]

When the religious parties released their list of coalition demands, there were few surprises in terms of policy issues included. Their demands included the following:

- Institutionalizing the status quo on religious affairs through a basic law, and rolling back the status quo to what it was prior to the 1992 elections;
- Amending the law on conversion so that Reform conversions cannot be carried out in Israel;
- Drawing up legislation that would bar representatives of the Reform and Conservative movements from serving on Religious Councils in Israel;
- Extending the law preventing the importation of non-kosher meat;
- Amending the Antiquities Law so that there could be no excavations of ancient cemeteries without the consent of the rabbinate;
- Stopping abortions for socio-economic reasons;
- Stopping the running of buses before the Shabbat has ended;
- Enforcing the laws against the opening of businesses on the Shabbat;
- Closing Jerusalem's Rehov Bar-Ilan to traffic on the Shabbat;
- Establishing a religious/haredi radio station;
- Granting a broadcasting license to Channel 7; and
- Making no changes in the electoral system without the consent of the religious parties.[50]

The demands of the religious parties were having an effect on coalition negotiations, however, in terms of the *number* of portfolios to be awarded, in terms of disagreement between Shas and the NRP about the specific ministries to be received, as well as in terms of some of the *policy* questions raised. While Likud negotiators were continuing to tell the religious parties that they simply could not make the level of demands that they were making, the religious negotiators were complaining that Likud negotiators were being 'insensitive' to the religious parties, especially given their remarkable mandate from the people of Israel, far larger than in past years.[51] From the other side, the Third Way and Israel Be-aliya negotiators were demanding that Netanyahu's agents *not* concede too much to the religious parties.

At the beginning of the second week of negotiations Netanyahu's agents told the representatives of the religious parties that they were simply going to have to bring their coalition demands 'down to more realistic levels', specifically to two seats each for Shas and the NRP, and one each for Israel Be-aliya and the Third Way.[52]

The religious parties continued to work on their policy demands; whatever the outcome of cabinet positions, they had a well-developed agenda in terms of policy questions that they wanted adopted by the new Government. During the second week of negotiations the NRP presented a multi-demand list – primarily authored by MK Hanan Porat – which it wanted to serve as the centrepiece of a set of demands of all religious parties. The list included (but was not limited to) such points as:

* There will be no negotiations over the status of Jerusalem;
* No Jewish settlements will be uprooted in any agreements;
* Israel will object to the Palestinian 'right of return';
* Israeli sovereignty will be extended over Greater Jerusalem, including Gush Etzion, Ma'aleh Edumim, Givat Ze'ev, Betar, and Rachel's Tomb;
* The settlement in Hebron will be strengthened;
* The status of Jewish law will be strengthened through a basic law;
* The government will work to stop the erosion of the authority of the religious courts; and
* The government will set up haredi and religious television and radio stations.[53]

As Likud began to circulate its draft guidelines for the new government among its potential coalition partners, it found that *none* of its potential partners was especially laudatory. The Third Way called the Likud's draft 'a watery document, which we cannot accept as it is and will want to amend'. The religious parties refused to meet to discuss the document, since the draft document did not contain any reference to religious issues.[54]

Likud's chiefs worked hard on the religious bloc, to the extent that Lieberman visited Shas's Aryeh Deri in the hospital to seek Shas's help in resolving the coalition problems, specifically trying to 'elicit concessions to placate the sulking National Religious Party'. In particular, it was reported, Likud wanted Shas to relinquish its claim on the Religious Affairs ministry in favour of the NRP; the NRP was also demanding a 'second major ministry', stating that 'This is no bluff. This is no way to treat us. If we don't get another major ministry [in addition to Education], we won't join the coalition. Then we'll see how well the government gets along without us. In four months they will come crawling to us, we won't have to crawl to them'.[55]

As Likud was able to resolve problems with one potential partner, new problems surfaced with others.[56] While Netanyahu was making progress with the NRP, the leaders of Israel Be-aliya broke off coalition talks, claiming that Likud was discriminating against their party in favour of the religious ones. Policy positions acceptable to all parties were difficult to achieve; what pleased the NRP and Shas in terms of adequately endorsing religious orthodoxy offended Israel Be-aliya, which did not want a more stringent religious status quo.

Eventually, as a deadline neared for resolving coalition negotiations, compromises began to appear. After substantial negotiations, a rotation of the Religious Affairs portfolio appeared to be acceptable to both Shas and the NRP. As the deadline neared, marathon meetings took place between leaders of Likud and other leaders. Under the law all coalition arrangements except for the distribution of portfolios within the Likud itself had to be presented in writing a full 24 hours before the Government was presented to the Knesset, and conflicts were being resolved at the end of the day.

Shas received two major portfolios, Interior and Labour and Social Affairs. To convince the NRP that it was equally appreciated, its two ministers were awarded three portfolios, one major (Education), one medium (Transport), and one minor (Energy). (This caused Shas to complain that it was 'unfair that a party with only nine MKs [the NRP] should get three portfolios, while a party with ten MKs [Shas] would be entrusted with only two portfolios'.)[57] Beyond this, the Third Way brought up a new demand which caused problems, asking for a commitment that the Government would support a bill requiring a special Knesset majority and a special referendum majority on any decision to cede territory in the Golan. The Third Way, Israel Be-aliya and United Torah Judaism all continued to fight over the Construction and Housing ministry.

At midnight before the deadline there were still disputes separating the coalition partners. Coalition agreements had been signed between Likud and Shas, the National Religious Party, and the Third Way, but these parties together only brought the coalition to 55 seats in the Knesset. Israel Be-aliya was insisting that it retain full freedom to vote its conscience on any religious issues. UTJ was angry with Likud because the latter had failed to support its requests to restore the *status quo* on religious affairs from prior to the Labour victory in 1992. With Israel Be-aliya's seven seats, Netanyahu would have a coalition large enough for a Knesset majority; the United Torah Judaism faction (with four seats) was dispensable, since it was not sufficient without Israel Be-aliya, and with Israel Be-aliya it was not necessary.[58]

At the last minute Israel Be-aliya signed on to the coalition, receiving two portfolios (Industry and Trade, and Absorption) as well as several other important commitments. The Absorption Ministry was expanded to include the social absorption unit of the Ministry of Education, and the vocational retraining division of the Labour and Social Affairs Ministry. It also received an undertaking from Likud for a NIS 600 million budget for 100 new hostels for immigrants, as well as a commitment for the chairmanship of the Knesset Environment Committee and the Committee on the Status of Women. It was also promised that two of its members would be appointed as ambassadors to CIS countries.[59]

On the day of the presentation of the Netanyahu Government, the situation was still in flux. To a substantial degree, this was a result of the situation with Ariel Sharon and the question of which ministry(ies) would be required to be an acceptable payoff to him. On Sunday, 16 June, he was offered the Housing Ministry, and the following day he notified Netanyahu of his acceptance; it turned out, however, that the Housing Ministry had also been promised to UTJ by Netanyahu just hours before Sharon's positive response, so the situation which had been resolved was again unsettled. Several different options were explored to resolve 'the Sharon problem',[60] but no solution was found before the government was presented to the Knesset for approval.

The Netanyahu Government was approved by the Knesset, and its policy guidelines were laid out in detail for the body. These specifically focused upon peace, security, and foreign relations, Jerusalem, religion and the state, immigration and absorption, economic and social policies, settlements, status of women, quality of government, and education.[61]

THE FIRST DAYS OF THE NETANYAHU GOVERNMENT

The government of Prime Minister Benjamin Netanyahu was presented to the Knesset on 18 June 1996, and was endorsed by a 62 to 50 vote. The ceremony that accompanied the Knesset vote was labelled as 'the strangest transition ceremony the Knesset has ever seen'.[62] The initial coalition presented to the Knesset did not include coalition partner (and foreign minister presumptive) David Levy, nor did it include Ariel Sharon, the *éminence grise* of the Likud Party. Prime Minister Netanyahu announced publicly that he would retain for himself the ministries of Foreign Affairs, Construction and Housing, and Religious Affairs, while some assignments were still pending. After a short break, Netanyahu re-entered the Knesset with David Levy and changed the coalition presented for Knesset vote to include Levy in the Foreign Ministry.

The 'Sharon problem' continued to haunt Netanyahu for days to come. At least part of the problem was caused by Sharon's delay in getting into the cabinet negotiations: it appeared that by the time Netanyahu began to actively search for a position for Sharon there were no 'major' positions remaining unoccupied. The strategy of the Likud leadership now turned to making a new 'super-ministership' for Sharon, a 'Minister of National Infrastructure', with various responsibilities being taken from a number of other positions. The expectation was that it would take about a week to put together the mandate of National Infrastructure, convincing a number of the new cabinet ministers to relinquish some of their jurisdiction to go into a pot for Sharon.

Foreign Minister Levy informed Netanyahu that a week was too long to wait, and threatened that if Sharon were kept out of the government, then he, too, would stay out: 'I will not be a member in a government which does not represent all the forces which brought about its creation. It is inconceivable that we have a government without Arik.'[63] Levy increased the pressure on Netanyahu by adding that his five-man Gesher faction would not support the Government if Sharon were not in it. (It should be noted that this threat did not come from an ideologically disparate coalition partner, but rather from a member faction *within* the central coalition party. It was a testimony to the coherence of Likud's pre-electoral political alliances and, many noted, to David Levy's trustworthiness.[64])

By this time Sharon was clearly in the public eye, and was announcing that 'he would not join the government if the Infrastructure Ministry to be created for him was "a make-believe" portfolio'.[65] He did not sympathize with Netanyahu's plight of having to force his coalition partners to 'yield significant chunks of their ministries' in order to create his new ministry, and indicated that the areas of the Prime Minister's Office over which Netanyahu had direct control which were being discussed in the media were simply not adequate.

At the end of the day a ministry was created for Sharon including parts of housing, energy, water and electricity, airport construction and planning, sea ports, rural development and road building, public works, and several other governmental divisions. The creation of the 'mega-ministry' for Sharon proved to be a major undertaking, with many cabinet members supporting the idea in principle, as long as it did not take any jurisdiction or patronage out of *their* ministry. Yitzhak Levy of the NRP who had jurisdiction over the Energy and Transport ministries said: 'I was given whole portfolios and not parts of portfolios, and I intend to keep my portfolios intact.'[66] This expression was fairly typical of many other cabinet members. Eventually the package *was* assembled, and Sharon did join the cabinet.

The resolution of the 'Sharon problem' did not mean that the Netanyahu cabinet was now on stable ground, because immediately after that issue was resolved a major fracas developed between the NRP and Shas over *which* of the two parties would be the first to occupy the Ministry of Religious Affairs. While the parties had agreed to share the portfolio through a rotation agreement, once the time came to put that compromise into practice both parties proved to be less than cooperative, and both threatened to quit if they could not be the first directors of the ministry.[67]

CONCLUDING OBSERVATIONS

The Netanyahu Government, then, was a 'first' in a number of respects in Israeli political and coalition history. It was the first coalition government formed under the new procedures passed during the 12th Knesset in which the Prime Minister was directly elected by the people and in which he was relatively more powerful in the actual creation of the coalition. It was the first coalition government created following the establishment of the new 'split-ballot' electoral system, in which (apparently) so many Israelis felt freer to vote for small parties than had been the case in the past. And, following on from this, it was the first coalition government in which the orthodox religious parties controlled as many as 23 seats in the Knesset, giving them a significant bargaining tool in the coalition-formation process.

The jury is still out on the impact of the new electoral system on the process of coalition-formation, and on the process of coalition *survival*. Early reports, however, seem to indicate a fluidity and instability in the Netanyahu Government that do not demonstrate the degree of stability of past governments (though it is certainly the case that past coalitions have begun with rocky starts, too). According to one report, within a matter of weeks following the establishment of the Netanyahu Government, 'members of [the] coalition are already forming alliances designed to limit the prime minister's freedom of movement'. Netanyahu's rough beginning in government concerned many of his colleagues; frequently cited here are the offering of the Finance Ministry to Bank of Israel Governor Jacob Frenkel, then giving it to Dan Meridor, and not paying sufficient attention to Ariel Sharon during the early phases of the coalition-formation process.

One response to this has been, apparently, that

> Coalition members have made alliances designed to keep Netanyahu in line. Some of these were forged or strengthened during the cabinet in-fighting – David Levy and Ariel Sharon joined

forces to press for a top place for Sharon, and Meridor and Ze'ev B. (Benny) Begin did the same for each other. Now it is anticipated that Sharon, Rafael Eitan, the NRP's Yitzhak Levy and Begin will link up to oppose an army withdrawal from Hebron, and that a similar constellation of forces will do its best to stop Netanyahu from holding face-to-face talks with Arafat.[68]

It is difficult to say with certainty whether this type of behaviour is caused and/or exacerbated by the new electoral system(s) or simply by Netanyahu's personal style and predilections. It is evident, however, that the Netanyahu Government is off to the same kind of tumultuous start experienced by many previous Israeli administrations. The nature of the Israeli coalition system gives small parties more of an opportunity to vocalize their demands, and then to exert pressure on the larger government-forming party (something the new electoral system was specifically designed to prevent!), and to the extent that prediction is in order, it is not likely that this type of behaviour is likely to stop in the future.

The question to ask at this point is whether the experiences of the Netanyahu Government in assembling a majority coalition in the 14th Knesset support or refute past studies of Israeli coalition behaviour. To a substantial extent they illustrate precisely the same kinds of behaviours that have been seen in the past, though not all of the past principles of coalition-formation can be seen to have been significant in the June 1996 coalition-formation process.

The nature of the electoral system yielded a situation in which there were a substantial number of small political parties, any one of which could prevent the formation of a sufficiently large coalition. While the electoral reforms were intended to reduce the relative influence of the small parties and strengthen the larger parties, in fact – for reasons discussed earlier – the reverse happened, and the smaller parties (and especially the religious parties) were strengthened in the current electoral system. The number of parties in the Knesset left a situation in which a variety of parties *could* have participated in coalition negotiations, though the 'natural' allies of Likud all ended up participating in the coalition. Of the coalition partners only the United Torah Judaism was expendable; the departure of any other single party would bring down the Government.

The process of negotiation was similar to that seen in earlier Knessot, with tensions between and among the religious parties to determine which of them received 'more' and 'better' payoffs for participating in the coalition, and other tensions between and among the religious parties on one hand and the secular parties on the other to determine the general thrust of government policy towards the institutionalization of religious dogma. In this case the Netanyahu team had to worry not only about squabbling between the NRP and Shas (and, to a lesser extent, United Torah Judaism) over which party would control the Religious Affairs Ministry, but also about squabbling between the religious parties that wanted an increased degree of religion in Israeli daily life, and some of the more secular parties that did *not* want precisely this.

One more or less unique variable in the 1996 coalition-formation process was almost a personal factor, the participation of Ariel Sharon in the Government. Sharon has been such a significant actor in the Likud for so many years that perhaps this was an unavoidable conflict, and perhaps Netanyahu should have been calculating a coalition payoff to Sharon from the outset of the coalition-formation process. It appears, however, that he did not do so, and this generated problems resulting from zero-sum games when, later in the process, he tried to find enough 'rewards' to suit Sharon's demands. In the final analysis, a new 'mega-ministry' was created for Sharon and he was brought into the Government.

The coalitional nature of the present government means that for as long as he is Prime Minister, Netanyahu will have to look over his shoulder at his cabinet 'allies'. It is clear that sub-coalitions already exist within the cabinet, and these will be cabinet crises waiting to happen. While Netanyahu cannot be immediately forced out of office by a cabinet crisis in exactly the same way as his predecessors, because he was directly elected and has a direct mandate, he is required to maintain a coalition that receives the support of a majority in the Knesset, so he is not free to disregard cabinet factionalization.

Political prediction is a dangerous game, but some prognostication is relatively safe: Israeli politics in the next several years will continue to have tumultuous. Israeli political parties (and, within the larger parties, political factions) will continue to have cleavages along which political coalitions may break. Religious–secular rifts will continue to cause tension within Israeli civic culture as to the direction in which Israeli society should evolve. And, should all other sources of tension be resolved, issues of parliamentary government, and the general 'decline of parliament' in the Israeli context will continue to cause concern among Members of Knesset. It is within this world that Israeli politics will continue to operate, and it is upon these seas that Israeli coalition governments will endeavour to remain afloat.

NOTES

1. In earlier years this was a 1% threshold.
2. Four examples of this kind of negotiation and outcome are discussed in the following: Herb Keinon, 'NRP, UTJ Sign Surplus Vote Pact', *Jerusalem Post*, 26 April 1996, p.1; Yochi Dreazen, 'Shas: One More and We Have a Minyan'; *JP*, 30 May 1996, p.2; Liat Collins, 'Third Way's Campaign Paying Off', *JP*, 28 May 1996, p.2; and Sarah Honig, 'Likud and Shas Team Up to Bring Voters to Polls', *JP*, 20 May 1996, p.2.
3. See Sarah Honig, 'Sharon Withdraws from Race for PM', *JP*, 22 December 1995, p.4.

Honig wrote: 'Some believe that Sharon and Netanyahu had come to a tacit understanding about the role to be accorded Sharon in any government Netanyahu might form, if he wins the elections. But Sharon's withdrawal from the ring does not leave Netanyahu unchallenged on the political right. He is still dogged by Tsomet's Rafael Eitan and by David Levy, each of whom might force a second round, if not hand victory to Labour's Shimon Peres.'

4. Sarah Honig and Liat Collins, 'Likud, Tsomet to Okay Pact Today', *JP*, 8 February 1995, p.1.

5. This was a long and drawn out affair. The beginning of what could be called its final phase was reported in an article by David Rudge, 'Hundreds Attend David Levy Rally in Kiryat Shmona', *JP*, 7 September 1995, p.2, describing a huge rally in support of MK David Levy in Kiryat Shmona, 'the first such rally since Levy announced his decision to leave the Likud and run for prime minister'. The end of the process was reported by Sarah Honig in an article titled 'Levy, Likud Deal Expected This Week', *JP*, 3 March 1996, p.1, when she wrote that 'The culmination of the process is expected to be a meeting between arch-adversaries Likud chairman Benjamin Netanyahu and Levy. Netanyahu's side sought to arrange a meeting already last week, but to no avail. Levy has been boycotting Netanyahu for the past three years... David Levy will be in the joint ticket's No.2 slot, after Netanyahu and ahead of Tsomet leader Rafael Eitan. If current configurations hold up... Levy is also slated to get the 21st, 30th, 37th and 41st slots.'

6. Labour's Religious Affairs Minister Shimon Shitrit tested the wind for a while, but withdrew in late January when it became clear to him that his challenge was 'hopeless'. See Sarah Honig and Liat Collins, 'Peres is Official Labor PM Candidate', *JP*, 22 January 1996, p.1.

7. Sarah Honig, 'Tsomet and NRP Realign with the Opposition', *JP*, 8 December 1995, p.3. It is interesting to note that Honig wrote: 'Likud chairman Benjamin Netanyahu expressed confidence that "the entire national camp will field one prime ministerial candidate", but his party continues to oppose the notion of primaries across party lines to choose that candidate. The Likud's position is that the right's candidate should be the one chosen by the largest party in the bloc. Throughout the past two years, right-wing primaries were proposed by those who challenged Netanyahu and declared their own candidacy for prime minister, like Eitan.'

8. These guidelines are derived from material provided by the Israeli Ministry of Foreign Affairs, 'Elections in Israel 1996: Background', http:\\www.israel-mfa.gov.il/news/elec1996.html.

9. This has been an extremely popular area of research in recent years. Among the many articles on this subject might be included the following: Gregory Mahler and Richard Trilling, 'Coalition Behavior and Cabinet Formation: The Case of Israel', *Comparative Political Studies*, Vol.8 (1975), pp.200–33; Dan Felsenthal, 'Aspects of Coalition Payoffs: The Case of Israel', *Comparative Political Studies*, Vol.12 (1979), pp.151-68; David Nachmias, 'Coalition Politics in Israel', *Comparative Political Studies*, Vol.7 (1974), pp.316-33; David Nachmias, 'A Note on Coalition Payoffs in a Dominant Party System: Israel', *Political Studies*, Vol.21, No.3 (1973), pp.301-05, and K.Z. Paltiel, 'The Israeli Coalition System', *Government and Opposition*, Vol.10 (1975), pp.396–414.

10. Valerie Herman and John Pope, 'Minority Governments in Western Democracies', *British Journal of Political Science*, Vol.3 (1973), p.191.

11. Ibid. See also Avraham Brichta, 'Forty Years of Struggle for Electoral Reform in Israel: 1948–1988', *Middle East Review*, Vol.21 (1988), pp.18–26; Efraim Torgovnik and Jonathan Mendilow, 'Federal Factions and Federated Host Parties in Israel: Some Ideological and Structural Dimensions', *Publius*, Vol.16, No.2 (1986), pp.113–32; Amnon Rapoport and Eythan Weg, 'Dominated, Connected, and Tight Coalitions in Israeli Knesset', *American Journal of Political Science*, Vol.30 (1986), pp.577–96; and Dan Felsenthal and Avraham Brichta, 'Sincere and Strategic Voters: An Israeli Study', *Political Behavior*, Vol.7 (1985), pp.311–24.

12. A very recent study of coalitions in found in the book by Ian Budge and Hans Kerman, *Parties and Democracy: Coalition Formation and Government Functioning in Twenty States*, London, 1990.

13. Eric Browne and Mark Franklin, 'Editors' Introduction: New Directions in Coalition Research', *Legislative Studies Quarterly*, Vol.11, No.4 (1986), p.471. The entire issue of *Legislative Studies Quarterly* in which this article appears is devoted to the study of coalition theory.

14. The classic article in this regard is by Benjamin Akzin, 'The Role of Parties in Israeli Democracy', *Journal of Politics*, Vol.17 (1955), pp.507–45.
15. 'Knessot' is plural for 'Knesset'. See Akzin, *JP*, p.532.
16. See '67 Lists This Time?', *Jerusalem Post International Edition*, 23 May 1992, p.2.
17. See 'Elections Committee Okays 25 Lists, Bans 5', *JP*, 13 June 1992, p.2. A final description can be found in 'The Electoral Lists', *JP*, 20 June 1992, p.8 of the supplement.
18. Liat Collins, 'CEC Approves 21 Parties Running in Elections', *JP*, 6 May 1996, p.3.
19. Eric Browne, 'Testing Theories of Coalition Formation in the European Context', *Comparative Political Studies*, Vol.3 (1971), p.400.
20. Ibid., p.402
21. One of the classic studies of Israeli politics discusses this issue – Leonard Fein, *Israel: Politics and People*, Boston, 1966, p.222 – as does one of the most recent studies: Gregory Mahler, *Israel: Government and Politics in a Maturing State*, New York, 1990, pp.97–120.
22. See *JP*, 12 March 1974, p.2; and *JP International*, 24 May 1977, respectively.
23. These negotiations were discussed in some detail in 'Smaller Parties Sing the Post-Election Blues', *JP International*, 11 July 1992, p.2, and 'Rabin Forms Narrow Government With Meretz, Shas', ibid., 18 July 1992, p.1.
24. See Sarah Honig, 'Coalition Talks Near Deadline', *Jerusalem Post*, 16 June 1996, p.1.
25. Scott Johnston, 'Party Politics and Coalition Cabinets in the Knesset', *Middle Eastern Affairs*, Vol.13 (1962), p.130.
26. *JP International*, 9 February 1991, p.1.
27. Michal Yudelman and David Makovsky, 'Shamir Intends to Bring Far-Right MK Into Cabinet', *JP International*, 9 February 1991, p.3. Material in this paragraph comes from this source.
28. Ibid.
29. Joel Brinkley, 'Arab-Expulsion Party in Israel's Cabinet', *New York Times*, 4 February 1991, p.A3.
30. Ibid., 'Shamir's Move: Postwar Leverage?', 7 February 1991, p.A18.
31. See Sarah Honig, 'Netanyahu Sacrificed Likud List in His Bid for the Premiership', *JP*, 6 February 1996, p.1.
32. See, among many other articles covering like events, 'Likud, Shas Close to Surplus Vote Pact', *JP*, 29 April 1996, p.1; David Rudge, 'Hadash, UAL Plan Knesset Coordination', *JP*, 17 May 1996, p.3.
33. See Honig, 'Netanyahu Sacrificed Likud List', ibid.
34. See the statement of one Likudnik reported by Sarah Honig and Liat Collins in 'Tsomet to Okay Clause Linking It With Likud', *JP*, 7 February 1996, p.1: 'I will support the agreement because the main issue is increasing the chances of Netanyahu becoming premier.' Similarly, MK Ovadia Eli, who was critical of the deal between the Likud and Tsomet, observed: 'It does not serve the Likud in its main aim of bringing Netanyahu to the prime minister's post.' See Liat Collins, 'Likud, Tsomet MKs Split Over Deal', *JP*, 6 February 1996, p.1.
35. It is not 'split ticket voting' in the same sense that the term is used in the United States, of course, since there are two separate ballots. The term is meant to refer to voters who voted for one party's candidate for prime minister on one ballot, and a different party for the Knesset race, something that would have been impossible in the 'old' system.
36. Israel Ministry of Foreign Affairs, 'Israel Update: Israel Elections, 1996', 'Elections in Israel, May 1996', located at http://www.israel-mfa.gov.il/news/results.html; Consulate General of Israel in New York, *The Electoral System in Israel*, New York, 1995.
37. See Liat Collins, 'Final Election Results May Not Be In Until June 2', *JP*, 23 May 1996, p.1.
38. See Sarah Honig, 'The Small Parties Were the Big Winners', *JP*, 30 May 1966, p.1.
39. See Peter Hirschberg, 'With God on Their Side', *The Jerusalem Report*, 27 June 1996, pp.22–3.
40. This referred to the amulets that were passed out prior to the elections that were blessed by Rabbi Yitzhak Kedourie. The Central Elections Commission ruled that these were not legal electoral material, and their distribution ceased after only a few days. See Herb Keinon, 'SHAS Gets Last Laugh', *JP*, 31 May 1996, p.4.
41. Herb Keinon, 'NRP's Strong Showing Is Good Reason for Party to Celebrate', *JP*, 31 May 1996, p.4.
42. Sarah Honig, 'Netanyahu Begins Coalition Talks Today', *JP*, 2 June 1996, p.1.

43. Ibid.
44. Sarah Honig, 'Netanyahu Lays Down Law to Potential Partners', *JP*, 3 June 1996, p.1.
45. Herb Keinon, 'Victory Lends Sudden Harmony to Religious Parties', ibid., 4 June 1996, p.2.
46. See Sarah Honig, 'Religious Parties Fail to Agree on Portfolios', *JP*, 3 June 1996, p.2.
47. Herb Keinon, 'Religious Parties Work on Joint Platform', *JP*,5 June 1996, p.1.
48. 'Sharansky Expected to Ask Much From Likud', *JP*, 3 June 1996, p.3.
49. Sarah Honig, 'Initial Coalition Talks End; Real Bargaining Begins', *JP*, 5 June 1996, p.2.
50. Herb Keinon, 'Religious Parties Produce Joint Coalition Demands', *JP*, 6 June 1996, p.3.
51. Sarah Honig, 'Coalition Talks Falter Due to Religious Parties' Tough Demands', *JP*, 7 June 1996, p.1.
52. Sarah Honig, 'Coalition Talks Resume Today', *JP*, 9 June 1996, p.2.
53. Herb Keinon, 'NRP Draws Up List of Coalition Guidelines', *JP*, 10 June 1996, p.1.
54. Sarah Honig, 'Likud Issues Guidelines for New Government', *JP*, 11 June 1996, p.1.
55. Sarah Honig and Herb Keinon, 'Netanyahu Pressing Shas to Help Placate NRP', *JP*, 12 June 1996, p.1.
56. Honig and Keinen, 'NRP In As Coalition Talks Seesaw', *JP*, 16 June 1996, p.1.
57. Honig and Keinen, 'Coalition Talks Near Deadline', *JP*, 16 June 1996, p.1.
58. Sarah Honig and David Makovsky, 'Religious Issues Delay Coalition Deal', *JP*, 17 June 1996, p.1.
59. Sarah Honig, 'New PM Finally Gets His Majority', *JP*, 18 June 1996, p.1.
60. Sarah Honig, 'Netanyahu to Present Government Today', *JP*, 18 June 1996, p.1.
61. 'The New Government's Guidelines', *JP*, 18 June 1996, p.3.
62. Liat Collins, 'Netanyahu's New Government Sworn In', *JP*, 19 June 1996, p.1.
63. Sarah Honig, 'Is Ariel Sharon In or Out?', *JP*, 19 June 1996, p.1.
64. It should be noted that at the beginning of the campaign many political observers in Israel did not have a tremendous amount of trust and confidence in David Levy, and indicated that he was willing to sign a deal with Netanyahu only because it was convenient for him at the time. It was necessary to be wary of Levy, they added, predicting that he would double-cross Likud in a minute if it served his personal interests.
65. Sarah Honig, 'Sharon: No Deal If It's "Make-Believe" Portfolio', *JP*, 23 June 1996, p.1.
66. Honig, 'Sharon "Mega-Ministry" Still On Hold', *JP*, 20 June 1996, p.1.
67. Honig, 'Shas, NRP Threaten to Quit Coalition', *JP*, 2 July 1996, p.1.
68. Leslie Susser, 'Coalition Cliques Aim to Keep Netanyahu in Line', *Jerusalem Report*, 11 July 1996, p.6.

Ideo-Theology:
Dissonance and Discourse in the
State of Israel

CLIVE JONES

On 27 October 1995 an article titled 'Forget the Kahanists' was published in the *Jerusalem Post*. The author of the piece, Professor Efraim Inbar, a well-respected political scientist at Bar-Ilan University, focused upon the growing dissent among Israelis over the perceived policy of territorial retrenchment followed by the government of Yitzhak Rabin. The article concluded:

> Constitutionally, Rabin can do whatever he desires as long as he has enough votes in the Knesset. But he should understand that a majority of the public is unimpressed by his negotiation position and his tactics. And many reasonable Israelis are very uncomfortable with the borders Rabin is fashioning for the future, unspecified, and without formal backing. It is not just the lunatics of the far right who question Rabin and are prepared to boo him.[1]

Eight days later, Rabin was assassinated by Yigal Amir, an act motivated according to the assassin 'for the glory of God'. While Inbar may well have been correct regarding the general climate of public dismay over the peace process, active resistance to Israeli concessions in the West Bank, and eventual withdrawal from it, had since September 1993 become synonymous with Israel's religious-nationalists. To that extent, this essay is not concerned with the history or structure of groups and organizations associated with religious-nationalism in Israel such as Gush Emunim.[2] Rather, it concentrates upon how particular interpretations of Judaic texts have come to fashion an environment that regards the universalist interpretations associated with classical Zionism as apostasy. For the most part anti-government demonstrations remained within the boundaries of non-violence; rallies, petitions, the closure of main highways, the occupation of hilltops on the West Bank outside the jurisdiction of official settlements were some of the more ostentatious features of this campaign.[3] Nonetheless, there remained a capacity for violence, a

Clive Jones is Lecturer in Middle Eastern Politics at the Institute for International Studies, University of Leeds.

capacity that was discernible in the language used by a political community whose ideological agenda was mortgaged to a particularist interpretation of theological texts regarding the divinity of *Eretz Israel* (The Land of Israel).

This essay sets out to explore this ideo-theology, a term that encapsulates the fusion of biblical precedence and *halachic* jurisprudence with the belief that Zionism as a largely secular ideology heralds the beginning of the messianic era. It concentrates on the ideas underpinning this world-view, ideas that have increasingly come to accommodate and condone the use of violence as a pro-active means of forestalling any moves that may retard this process. This is not to suggest that ideo-theology can be considered the preserve of one particular grouping. While a consensual base clearly exists among the religious-nationalists regarding the theological legitimacy of Israel's claim to *Judea and Samaria*, this has never been translated into a coordinated programme that delineates clearly the boundaries of political action.

Nonetheless, the language and symbols used in this process are important because they occupy a realm removed from the discourse of mainstream Zionism and, therefore, remain impervious to secular arguments regarding the sagacity of exchanging land for peace.[4] The use of the biblical term *Amalek* to justify the actions of Baruch Goldstein proved one of the more extreme examples where analogical reasoning based on biblical precedent was used to sanctify violence. While the majority of Israeli settlers, as well as religious leaders,[5] condemned the massacre of 29 Palestinian Arabs in Hebron on 25 February 1944, consistent *halachic* rulings had eroded the normative values and laws of the Jewish State among the religious right. Moreover, placards paraded by both the political and religious right in Israel, depicting Rabin either in the uniform of an SS officer or with head wrapped in a Palestinian *keffiyeh*, were expressly meant to de-legitimize the former Prime Minister as a Jew in a religious-national sense. Accordingly Jews, both in Israel and the diaspora, initially shocked at the slaying of Rabin by a fellow Jew, should not have been so surprised.

In exploring these issues, this essay concludes that if the ideo-theological cleavages in Israeli society are to be assuaged, a religious discourse condoning territorial compromise and conciliation has to invade the space now dominated by the religious right. This is not to suggest that extremist individuals can ever be convinced of the acumen of territorial compromise on theological grounds. The importance of such a dialogue lies, nonetheless, in demonstrating to both Israelis and Palestinians that Judaism can, and indeed does, accommodate the demands of territorial compromise.

THE DEVELOPMENT OF IDEO-THEOLOGY

Examining the broader dynamics of ideo-theology remains crucial to understanding the death of Rabin. In so doing, it is necessary to make the clear distinction between what *occasioned* the death of the Israeli premier, and what *caused* his death. This is more than just an exercise in semantics. The former traces the interaction between groups and individuals in what some have suggested was a conspiracy to remove the top echelon of the Israeli cabinet. The latter is concerned with tracing the contours of a debate that came to inform a world-view opposed to the perceived recidivism of trading land for peace.

It was Israel's stunning military victory in June 1967 that first saw the emergence of the religious right as a true force in the politics of the Jewish State, but the contours of their ideo-theology had begun to emerge in the pre-state *Yishuv*. In particular, the ideas of Rabbi Avraham Yitzhak Ha-Cohen Kook (1865–1935), Chief Ashkenazi Rabbi of the Jewish community in British Mandate Palestine, were influential in challenging the rejection of Zionism by the majority of Orthodox Jews. Zionism was regarded as a heterodox creed, a denial of a central tenet of Judaism – that only the coming of the *mashiach* could reunite the Jews with *Eretz Israel*. Throughout this process, Jews were expected to be passive. Indeed, the main debates within Judaism centred on whether Jews could hasten the day of redemption through leading pious lives, or, alternatively, that this day had already been pre-ordained.[6]

As such, Zionism was viewed as a usurpation of God's plan for the Jews. It denied the eschatological reasoning in Ultra-Orthodox thinking, a reasoning that saw Zionism as the anti-thesis of the redemptive process. In this sense, the ideas of Kook were revolutionary. Whereas classical Zionism was largely seen as a secular nationalist movement – the idea of being a Jew was defined on the grounds of ethnicity-nationalism – Kook argued that Zionism heralded the beginning of the messianic era, a view supported by the growing emigration of Jews to Palestine throughout the inter-war period. Ignoring the political realities that largely dictated this population flow, Kook argued that Zionists were in fact the unknowing tools of God, and as such, were hastening the redemptive process by settling once more in *Eretz Israel*. Kook attracted the approbation of the Ultra-Orthodox community by this line of reasoning, investing as he did a largely secular, nationalist, non-observant movement with being the creation of God. As one commentator remarked:

> Kook expressed confidence that the Jewish community in Palestine, the *Yishuv*, would ultimately turn to religious law for governance. The modern Zionist movement was an instrument designed for returning the Jews to the Holy Land, but once in *Eretz Israel* the Jews would be reunited with their divine law by another instrument of God's design.[7]

Although Kook never explicitly delineated the borders of the Jewish State – a process which he felt would be revealed in the fullness of time – his ideas came to be enshrined in Israel's national prayer which makes reference to '*reshit tzmichat geulatenu*', the belief that the establishment of the state heralded the start of the redemptive process.[8] The conviction that Zionism was the necessary precursor to the messianic era found a particular resonance after 1967. The capture of the West Bank and East Jerusalem, the biblical heart of *Eretz Israel,* against apparently overwhelming odds soon acquired messianic overtones. In particular, Rabbi Zvi Yehuda Kook, the son of Rabbi Avraham Kook, placed Israel's military triumph within the continuing evolution of the messianic era. His vision encompassed a preordained Jewish right to settle the newly captured territories, a process that was encouraged by Rabbi Zvi Yehuda Kook among the students of the Yeshivat Merkaz Ha-rav in Jerusalem. They were to spearhead the early settlement drives, leading to the establishment of settlements such as Kiryat Arba next to Hebron.[9] Rabbi Kook used the ideas of his father to add theological legitimacy to the use of force in order to achieve and maintain the unity of *Eretz Israel.* Such ideas found a receptive audience among the wider religious right, offering as they did a *carte blanche* that divorced settlement activity from any moral or humanistic constraints.

Indeed, the real impact of the religious right was to redefine the normative character of Zionism. While never a single cohesive ideology, Zionism was nonetheless an amalgam of ideas drawn from Jewish philosophy, history, and religion on the one hand, and fused with the universal values of freedom, democracy, and justice for its citizens – values identified with Western civilization. First outlined in Theodore Herzl's *Der Judenstaat*, statehood was viewed as a prerequisite for the Jewish people if they were to escape the age old threat of anti-Semitism and be accepted as an equal into the family of nations. While the period 1948–67 never saw the complete synthesis of these ideas – Israel's Arab minority could never accept the Jewish character of the new State – close association with universal values marked the development of an *Israeli,* rather than a *Jewish,* identity. The June 1967 War marked a watershed in this process. Capture of the West Bank and East Jerusalem with its sacred Jewish sites witnessed not only the emergence of the covenantal relationship between 'People, God and promised land', but in the process, the reaffirmation of particularly Jewish, rather than universal, values, in determining the character of the State of Israel.[10] These particularist values increasingly influenced the political agenda in Israel, a process accelerated by the election of the first Likud-led coalition government under Menachem Begin in 1977. The claim that on both security and historical grounds no Israeli government would cede any part of *Eretz Israel* neatly conflated with the developing ideo-theology of the religious right. Indeed, many within Likud argued that

Israel had surrendered enough territory to the Arabs by forfeiting its claim that Jordan formed a historical part of *Eretz Israel*.[11] While it had been Labour-led coalition governments that had set the precedent of settlement on the West Bank, this process was greatly accelerated by Begin on assuming power. Moreover, settlements associated with Gush Emunim were accorded the same status as Kibbutzim and Moshavim, a move that allowed public money to be used in the process of settlement construction. This was significant in both a political and ideological sense: politically, it was a means of undermining two movements deemed to be bastions of support for the Israeli centre-left; ideologically, it suggested that the Gush was the true inheritor of the pioneering ideals behind Zionism that had previously been the preserve of the Kibbutz movement. The sub-text was clear: classical Zionism, with its traditional socialist, secular ethos was morally a spent force, bankrupted by its emphasis upon the material, rather than spiritual well-being of the Jewish people.[12]

This also led the religious-right, influenced by the teachings of Rabbi Zvi Yehuda Kook, to reject the theory of normalization outlined by Herzl and other classical Zionist thinkers. In this respect, the October 1973 War was of particular significance. If the Six Day War was interpreted as signifying divine intervention in hastening the process of redemption, the Yom Kippur War signified the continued rejection by Gentiles of the Jews as a people, and an attempt to negate the process of redemption. This position was put forcefully in an essay written in the aftermath of that conflagration by Rabbi Yehuda Amital. While pouring scorn on Herzlian thinking regarding the process of normalization, Amital went on to declare:

> But there exists another Zionism, the Zionism of redemption, whose great announcer and interpreter was Rabbi [Zvi Yehuda] Kook.... This Zionism has not come to solve the Jewish problem by the establishment of a Jewish state but is used, instead, by the High Providence as a tool in order to move and advance Israel towards its redemption. Its intrinsic direction is not the normalization of the people of Israel in order to become a nation like all the nations, but to become a holy people, a people of living God, whose basis is in Jerusalem and a king's temple is its centre.[13]

From such pronouncements it became clear that maintaining the integrity of *Eretz Israel* was the supreme goal of religious-nationalists and formed *the* core component of their evolving ideo-theology. Clear reference was made to the covenant between God and Abraham regarding the land as an 'everlasting possession', a promise that is repeated by God, according to the book of *Genesis,* to Abraham's son Isaac and to his son Jacob.[14] As long as successive Israeli governments – albeit on security grounds – continued to value Jewish control over the territories captured in 1967, a clear symbiosis of objectives existed with religious-nationalism. As such, submitting to the secular authority of the Jewish State posed little real difficulty. Nonetheless, by regarding the land as central to the redemptive process of the Jewish people, it followed that any attempt to trade land for peace usurped the will of God, and therefore, would be opposed. This position brought to the fore the centrality of *Halacha* – the doctrine, rules, and laws of Judaism that through the centuries had been codified into juridicial law.

But as Ehud Sprinzak has noted, use of the *halacha* in formulating positions over the sanctity of the land proved problematic. *Halacha* traditionally has had little to say regarding the sanctity of land, but rather concerns itself with the moral behaviour of Jews, both as individuals and as communities. Indeed, the imposition of violent sanctions against transgressors was limited to actions of 'idolatry, incestuous relationships, and the shedding of blood'.[15] By using a process of analogical reasoning, Rabbi Kook was to apply the actions of idolatry to a wider political setting by invoking *Pikuach Nefesh*, a term used to define situations of 'mortal danger'. Accordingly, as territory of strategic worth was ceded to the Arabs, relinquishing land deemed holy not only fell under the remit of idolatry, but increased the danger of *pikuach nefesh* to the Jewish people as a nation. The whole issue of *pikuach nefesh* became increasingly salient to the actions of the religious-nationalists as they attempted to resist the implementation of the Oslo Accords by the government of Yitzhak Rabin.

Such views have, however, never been the sole preserve of Israel's religious right. Considerable controversy met the remarks of Brooklyn Rabbi Abraham Hecht, who in June 1995 invoked the idea of *pikuach nefesh* in claiming that Israeli leaders who gave up land were guilty under *halacha* of a sin worthy of death.[16] They were labelled with the *Talmudic* dictum of *moser*, a term applied to Jews who inform on their own people, or Jews who forfeit property to the Gentiles. For the religious right, the question became increasingly one of defining actions permitted under the *Torah, Talmud,* as well as *halachic* jurisprudence, in defending the sanctity of the land. At one level, it was claimed that pronouncements of rabbis opposed to territorial compromise were formal opinions, rather than orders. Indeed, the remarks made by the Brooklyn Rabbi were placed within this context, it being pointed out that Hecht was not a *posek*, a senior rabbi who is qualified to issue religious edicts. But such proclamations clearly circumvented the issue. Opinions provide frameworks in which the latitude for interpretation and action remains broad. Moreover, it becomes all too easy for such 'opinions' to influence groups and individuals – motivated by profound religious beliefs – who seek sanctification for more extreme acts of opposition.

While by no means characteristic of the majority of rabbis associated with Israel's religious-right, the language used was broad enough in its conceptual base to accommodate extreme acts. In the aftermath of Rabin's death it emerged that two influential West Bank rabbis, Dov Lior and Nahum Rabinovich, had issued a religious edict, declaring the Israeli premier to be a *rodef*. Under *halachic* law it is permissable to kill a *rodef* or pursuer if there exists clear evidence that life is endangered. Again, while this ruling originated within the context of Jewish communal life, there existed an all-too-obvious correlation with the idea of *pikuach nefesh*. As such, this edict further redefined the limits of opposition to justify violent acts.[17] Moreover, it became clear that in opposing the policies of Rabin's government, ideo-theology had, among the more radical elements of the religious-right, encompassed the notion of de-legitimizing Rabin as a Jew. The emergence of such a trend was of significance precisely because from a religious perspective it removed the veil of Judaic legitimacy from Rabin, thus placing him in a gentile world that was never to be trusted. The placards at right-wing demonstrations displaying Rabin variously in Nazi regalia or swathed in a *keffiyeh* were the more visible aspects of this process. Nonetheless, this line of reasoning was best illustrated during the course of an interview, broadcast on Israel Television in the aftermath of the assassination, with a member of Eyal, a tiny extremist group initially suspected of complicity in Rabin's assassination. It is worth quoting the interview, conducted by journalist Nitzan Hen, at length:

Hen: Activists of *Eyal* and *Kahane Chai* are more dangerous than those of *Kach*. They hardly meet the media to document their activities. Until a week ago their activity was only against Arabs, but the writing has been on the wall for a long time.
Unidentified Activist: – to kill too.

Hen: Who?
Activist: Whoever I am told.

Hen: Arabs?

Activist: Whether it is a terrorist or just an Arab, everybody.

Hen: If you are told to kill Jews?

Activist: There are Jews who are not Jews in my opinion.

Hen: If you are told to kill Jews, will you kill them too?

Activist: If it is a Jew who is not a Jew, and people can understand to whom I am referring, then yes.[18]

While the sentiments expressed by the activist are indeed disturbing, they are nonetheless the theological legacy of the late Rabbi Meir Kahane, the most radical of thinkers among right-wing religious opinion. Though most Israelis dismissed his ideas as unhinged – his party *Kach*, was banned in 1988 from participating in Knesset elections because of its overtly racist agenda – individuals inspired by Kahane's teachings have been behind some of the bloodiest actions visited upon the Palestinians.[19]

Kahanism is not a coherent ideology but it does contain a clear veneration, if not outright sanctification, of the use of violence in order to maintain the integrity of *Eretz Israel*. Kahanism takes issue with the prevailing view among the religious-nationalists concerning Zionism as the necessary precursor to the messianic era. In a little-read essay, *Hillul Ha-shem*, published in 1976 Kahane maintained that the Jewish State was established not because of the righteousness of the Zionist cause, but rather because God could no longer tolerate the continued persecution of his chosen people by Gentiles. Thus Israel was created by God as a punishment to the Gentiles, not a reward to the Jews. But this also led Kahane to conclude that the newly-born State was virtuous not because Zionists were a pious people – clearly they were not – but because of what a Jewish State 'inflicts upon the Gentiles'.[20]

Building upon this unique interpretation of historical events, Kahanism reinterpreted the *halachic* concepts of *hillul ha-shem*, and *kiddush ha-shem*, placing them within an extreme nationalist milieu. The former refers to the humiliation suffered by God when the Jews, irrespective of moral behaviour and religious adherence, are subject to repression. Conversely, when the Jews are strong, God's power is revealed and his name sanctified – *kiddush ha-shem*. This was a radical departure from accepted orthodoxy surrounding a term that condoned martyrdom as the ultimate act in sanctifying God's name. Instead, Kahanism saw sanctification of God's name in the very act of killing those opposed to the Jewish people. As Kahane went on to explain, *kiddush ha-shem* now represented 'A Jewish fist in the face of an astonished Gentile world that had not seen it for two millennia, this is *Kiddush Ha-shem*'.[21]

In a very real sense, Kahanism views violence as a cleansing process, one that has set the Jewish people free from the persecution and servitude of the diaspora. Kahanism consciously adopted a meta-historical approach which applied the term *amalek* to describe all enemies, past, present, and future, of the Jewish people. The *amalek* were a biblical tribe whose destruction was demanded of the Israelites by God according to the Torah.[22] As such the term was applied by Kahane to include all enemies of the Jewish people in general, and the Palestinians in particular. Therefore, if God's name is to be sanctified, it is incumbent upon the Jews to destroy the *amalek*, thus ushering in the true messianic era. This view was also propagated by the Department of Religious Education, run by rabbis under the auspices of the Ministry of Education. In a booklet written for use by teachers in Israeli schools, a clear correlation was drawn between the Palestinians and the *Amalekites*. This booklet concluded that 'Just as we obeyed the command [of God] by exterminating the ancient *Amalek*, we must now do the same with the modern *Amalek*'.[23] But as one commentator noted:

> Conversely, any weakening of Jewish power or humbling of the Jewish people is a setback to the messianic process – a *hillul ha-shem* – or desecration of God's name. Territorial compromise, according to these principles, is not merely a political tragedy but a cosmic wound, a reversal of the divine plan for the triumph of the Jews over the *amalek*.[24]

The extent to which this 'cosmic wound' was felt among the more extreme elements of the religious-right was demonstrated in October 1995 on the eve of Yom Kippur. Standing outside the Prime minister's residence in Jerusalem, a rabbi associated with the *Kach* movement invoked a sacred curse in Aramaic from the *Mishna*, part of the *Talmud*, known as the *pulsa denura*.[25] Calling the policies of Rabin 'heretical', he demanded in Aramaic that 'the angels of destruction... take a sword to this wicked man ...to kill him ... for handing over the Land of Israel to our enemies, the sons of Ishmael'.[26] While perhaps among the more bizarre forms of religious opposition to the Oslo Accords, such sentiment nonetheless underlined that concessions over territory threatened the religious-right and their explanation of what it actually meant to be an Israeli. In this respect, the language of the religious-right was crucial in creating an environment that not only condoned active civil disobedience, but, through the prism of its ideo-theology, sanctified recourse to violence. As Israeli journalist Hirsh Goodman observed:

> Because they [the religious-right] cannot win through democratic means they have taken the fight to the streets, and it is only a matter of time before this country's democratic institutions are trampled in the gutter and chaos becomes the norm.[27]

IDEO-THEOLOGY: FROM CIVIL DISOBEDIENCE TO VIOLENCE

Ever since the Washington signing of the Oslo Accords on 13 September 1993, extra-parliamentary opposition to the Rabin Government began increasingly to engage in acts of civil disobedience. The Accords presented religious-nationalists with the stark choice between recognizing the temporal authority of a recidivist state, or active opposition based upon the logic of their ideo-theology. Both *Kach* and *Kahane Chai* made known their intent to undertake violent actions against Palestinian Arabs in the hope of provoking an escalating cycle of retaliatory violence. Initially, however, civil disobedience was largely organized and non-violent. New organizations emerged such as *Zo Artzenu* (This is our Land), in reality little more than a front for the *Yesha* Council dominated by Gush Emunim who attempted to set up the nucleus of new, unauthorized settlements all over the West Bank.[28] Far more serious however were *halachic* rulings that aimed to usurp the authority of the state over the Israel Defence Forces. Prominent settler activists had long called for soldiers to disobey orders requiring them to evacuate settlements, but such action had hitherto lacked official rabbinic sanction.[29]

This changed with the *halachic* edict issued on 12 July 1995 by the International Rabbinic Forum for Israel, an organization that included the former Chief Rabbi Avraham Shapira, that prohibited IDF soldiers from enforcing the evacuation of settlements called for under any final settlement. Invoking the great twelfth century Jewish philosopher and Talmudic scholar, Maimonides, who wrote that even the command of a King should be disregarded if it violated the *Torah*, the signatories claimed that evacuation was a threat to life, *pikuach nefesh*, and thus endangered the security of the State. This claim did have some resonance among the wider Israeli public reeling from a succession of bloody suicide bomb attacks claimed by *Izz al-din al-Qassem,* the military wing of HAMAS. In particular, the edict presented a moral dilemma to *Hesder Yeshiva* soldiers, youngsters who combined military service with religious studies in a *Yeshiva* often affiliated to a West Bank settlement. Moreover, while the religious-right made up only 10 per cent of the total population, it provided 40 per cent of all officers in the IDF and incurred 30 per cent of all casualties during Israel's invasion of Lebanon in 1982. The threat of large-scale unrest in the army was a major concern for most Israelis, a concern amplified when it was announced that over 1,000 reserve soldiers had signed a petition refusing in advance any attempt to uproot the settlers. Irrespective of political opinion, the IDF had remained traditionally a sacred cow, an institution whose function had been social and educational as much as strategic in the consolidation of the Jewish State. But dissonance inside the IDF was not a new phenomenon. Both the invasion of Lebanon and the Palestinian *intifada* had seen the emergence of soldiers' organizations such as *Yesh Gvul*, who supported those servicemen who refused to serve in the occupied territories. But such organizations remained relatively small; the fear of unrest among *hesder yeshiva* soldiers was more tangible given their numbers and status accumulated from service in front-line combat units. In a very real sense, the edict of the rabbis challenged the set values of secular Zionism by placing the integrity of *Eretz Israel* over *the* embodiment of Israeli society and national identity.[30]

This uncompromising position was reflected further in the scorn poured upon the reliance of the Rabin Government on the smaller Arab parties in the Knesset. The view that the government had no public mandate because it lacked a Jewish majority in the Knesset was endorsed fully by Likud Party leader Benjamin Netanyahu. On 28 September 1995, in a symbolic riposte to the signing of the Oslo II agreements extending Palestinian self-rule to the main population centres throughout the West Bank, Netanyahu attended a ceremony reaffirming 'loyalty to *Eretz Israel*'. He went on to declare at this ceremony that 'No Jew hitherto ever longed to give up slices of the homeland', and promptly went to Hebron in a deliberate show of solidarity for the militant settlers in the very heart of that ancient city.[31] Such sentiment was echoed by Ariel Sharon, the former Likud Defence Minister and Rehavam Ze'evi, Knesset member for the far-right Moledet party, both of whom were quick to invoke the memory of the Holocaust when accusing the Rabin Government of being accomplices in the 'annihilation' of the Jewish State.

Such emotive statements illustrated not only the growing polarization between the centre-left and the political right, but also the failure by all sides to engage in a common discourse likely to reduce tension. Indeed, the conceptual disparities between the two positions were so marked that one commentator noted that at least in ideological and intellectual terms Israel's body politic was already engaged in a form of internecine conflict.[32] Rabin has been accused of failing to address the security fears of settlers who were encouraged by successive Labour and Likud administrations to move to the occupied territories. Certainly, Rabin's dismissing Likud as collaborators with HAMAS and referring to rabbis who condoned civil disobedience as *ayatollahs* offered little in the way of constructive dialogue or reasoning.[33] But however regrettable such pronouncements by the late Israeli prime minister may have been, the ideo-theology of religious-nationalism remained impervious to any secular argument regarding the sagacity of exchanging land for peace. There was no room for compromise, given the absolutes demanded by the religious-right. In this respect, the failure of the Rabin Government was not the strategy of territorial compromise, but the failure to engage the religious-right on their own terms in justifying the policy of incremental withdrawal from the West Bank and Gaza Strip. Yet the need to puncture this ideo-theology grew more pressing as violence became increasingly a feature of anti-government protests.

While civil disobedience remained the preferred strategy of opposition, there had been early indications among elements of the religious-right of their readiness to engage openly in acts of violence. During what some labelled the beginning of a Jewish *intifada*, groups of armed settlers set up road blocks throughout the West Bank in early

November 1993 in a deliberate attempt to disrupt the flow of Palestinians from the territories seeking work in Israel. More ominous however was reaction to the attempted murder by suspected HAMAS militants of Rabbi Haim Druckman. The ensuing clashes with Palestinians in and around Hebron, a cycle of violence that resulted in further deaths on both sides, was to lead to the fateful events at the Tomb of the Patriarchs/Ibrahimi Mosque on 25 February 1994.[34] Baruch Goldstein was a resident of Kiryat Arba, a settlement generally acknowledged to be a stronghold of Kahanism. Here, the ideas surrounding *hillul ha-shem* found a particular resonance among the settlers. Many regarded the restrictions placed upon rights of access to the Tomb of the Patriarchs, the second holiest shrine in Judaism, as a desecration of God's name and a clear sign of Jewish self-degradation in the face of their nemesis, the Palestinians. Continued tension between Jew and Arab in Hebron was equated with the meta-historical struggle against *amalek*, a confrontation that Kahanist logic embraced if God's glory was to be redeemed; *kiddush ha-shem*. Goldstein's actions were therefore entirely consonant with the most radical interpretation of Kahanist ideo-theology. The community of Kiryat Arba not only felt itself threatened in a physical sense by the overwhelming Palestinian presence in Hebron, but the spiritual atrophy of a secular State had negated the redemptive process. Indeed, it was reported that on 24 February, on the eve of the festival of *Purim*, a crowd of Palestinians approached the Tomb shouting '*Itbah al-yahud*', Death to the Jews, an incident thought to have provoked Goldstein's bloody actions. The massacre has to be understood, therefore, within the context of a Kahanist interpretation of *hillul ha-shem*, and not solely as a brazen attempt to destroy the peace process.[35]

While Goldstein was the subject of vilification by the overwhelming majority of Israelis, the attempt to portray him as a deranged individual belied a widespread empathy for his motives, if not his actions, among West Bank settlements previously considered to be moderate. While rabbis associated with *Yesha* condemned the massacre, others were quick to apportion equal blame on a government that had imposed a siege mentality on the West Bank by abandoning the settlers.[36] Emerging evidence suggested that some settlements were preparing to form a Jewish militia. In November 1993, Rabbi Avraham Toledano, a former member of *Kach*, was arrested trying to smuggle bomb-making equipment into Israel. Such incidents prompted memories of the campaign of terror waged by the so-called Jewish Underground against high-profile Palestinian targets between 1980 and 1984, a campaign that had the tacit support of several leading West Bank rabbis.[37] The clarion call to resist the authority of the secular state remained, nonetheless, a constant theme among the religious right. Synagogues were encouraged to alter prayers asking for God to protect Israel's leaders, to those asking for God to protect the Jewish people from a destructive form of secularism seeking to amputate the very soul of the Jewish State, *Judea* and *Samaria*, from the people.[38] Such views contained an implicit rejection of modernity, an abrogation of the consensual pact between the spiritual and the temporal that had largely forged the settlement drive across the length and breadth of the occupied territories. From being the spiritual and territorial vanguard – the religious heirs to a pioneering tradition – the religious-right saw their chimera of redemption sacrificed to the *amalek* on the alter of political expediency. Influenced by an ideo-theology that refuted normative values in dealing with the Israel–Palestine dispute, the actions of Yigal Amir on 4 November 1995 were in a very real sense pre-ordained.

COUNTERING RELIGIOUS NATIONALISM

The immediate aftermath of Rabin's assassination saw not only the arrest of those suspected of being accomplices to murder, but calls for increased powers of search and arrest to be given to Israel's law-enforcement agencies in the fight against 'Jewish extremism'.[39] The Interior Ministry was given new powers to restrict the entry of suspected Jewish extremists from the diaspora, while measures under further consideration included the closure of the settlers' pirate radio station, *Arutz 7* (Channel 7), and curbs on the press to prohibit the publication of material likely to incite violence.[40] Yet such measures, however inevitable, appear to threaten basic civil liberties without necessarily tackling the underlying cause behind Rabin's assassination. Education and Culture Minister Amnon Rubinstein spoke of 'cancerous cells… made up of thousands of people who believe that God speaks to them and orders them to carry out such acts'.[41] Yet if, to use Rubinstein's analogy, the cancer is to be cured, it is incumbent upon Israel's leadership to engage religious-nationalists in their own language.

Such a process soon began to emerge. In a speech on 22 November 1995 presenting his new government to the Knesset, Prime Minister Peres made explicit reference to the humanistic values to be found in the teachings of Rabbi Avraham Kook, reminding his assembled audience that the rabbi had made the capacity to 'love' a fundamental tenet in the resurrection of the Jews as a nation.[42] This was a symbolic attempt to break the monopoly held by the religious-right over Kook's ideas by placing emphasis upon the humanistic, rather than the particular values of his teaching. But any sustained challenge to the ideo-theology of religious-nationalism has to apply *halachic* jurisprudence and the *Torah*, both in disputing the centrality of the land in the welfare of Israel as a nation-state, and in demonstrating that Judaism as a religion can encompass the demands of regional peace.

There are those who refute the validity of *halacha* in determining any discourse among a largely secular populace. Meron Benvenisti, former deputy mayor of Jerusalem, dismissed *halacha* on historical grounds, the claim being that it emerged as a means of ensuring social and ethnic cohesion and regulating communal life following the dispersion of the Jews in roughly 70AD. Having emerged as a response to the conditions of Jews in the diaspora, *halacha* is, according to Benvenisti, irrelevant to questions regarding the sanctity of land because it never referred to a given territory inhabited by the Jews as a cohesive nation.[43] While a rational argument in a chronological sense, this overtly secular view ignores the reality of a situation where *halacha* has come to exert enormous influence as a commentary on the *Torah* regarding the absolute spiritual value of territory. *Halacha* remains therefore a crucial element in challenging the ideo-theology of the religious-right, demonstrating that the well-being of the people takes precedent over the sanctity of the land. A contemporary of Rabbi Zvi Yehuda Kook, the late Rabbi Shaul Israeli, took issue with the approbation placed upon the requirement to settle all of *Eretz Israel*. Israeli argued that, even if the commandment to conquer and settle God-given land remained relevant to the contemporary age, it was clear that such a commandment applied to the whole nation including the diaspora, not just to Jews living in the State of Israel. Israeli argued that given the enormous responsibility imposed by settlement, requiring great effort and sacrifice, it remained inconceivable that only part of the nation should shoulder such a burden. In his view, if all Jews who were capable were to take up arms in pursuit of redemption, the land could be secured. But with only a small part of the Jewish nation engaged in the process of settlement, the Rabbi invoked the spectre of mortal danger *pikuach nefesh*. Accordingly, Israeli argued that any commandment to settle all *Eretz Israel* remained in abeyance in the absence of any active participation of the Jews as a nation.[44]

The use of *pikuach nefesh* in this context is important because it removes the sanctity of the land as an absolute value from the redemption for the Jewish people and places the latter on a higher plane. This interpretation of *pikuach nefesh* was used by the former Chief Rabbi of Great Britain, Lord Immanuel Jakobovits, when advocating support for an Israeli withdrawal from the occupied territories.[45] Similarly, the epithet *moser* remains problematic under *halachic* jurisprudence given that Rabin did represent a government elected by a majority of Jews, irrespective of its dependency on Arab parties in the Knesset. This view was put most forcefully by Rabbi Yehuda Amital, one-time member of Gush Emunim, whose maximalist views regarding the sanctity of the land underwent a 'Road to Damascus' conversion following the shock registered at the scale of Israel's casualties during the 1982 Lebanon War.[46] Amital made it clear that the use of *halacha* as a prism to interpret reality remained potentially explosive, particularly among those who viewed it as an absolute set of truths, removed from a particular historical and social context.

In the aftermath of Rabin's death, several liberal rabbis spoke of the threat posed by Judaism to the universal values of Israel as a nation-state. Some, such as Rabbi David Hartmann, argue that the command by God for the Jews to be a holy people – the Ten Commandments received by Moses on Mount Sinai – preceded God's command for the Jews to enter the Land of Israel. Using such historical precedent, Hartmann believes it is possible to argue that the law, including the commandment 'Thou shalt not kill', preceded the conquering of the land. This view, however laudable, falls foul of its own historical reasoning. It is all too easy for the religious-right to point to the first book of Genesis where God makes his covenant with Abraham, declaring 'Unto thy seed have I given this land, from the river of Egypt unto the great river, the Euphrates.'[47] Later on in Genesis this covenant is repeated to both Issac and Jacob. There is however, a biblical precedent for the ceding of land in exchange for peace. It is mentioned in Genesis that Abraham gave land to the shepherds of Lot in settling a dispute over grazing rights, a precedent that according to David Hall-Cathala suggests that, 'divine promise cannot be equated with the actual ownership of the land'.[48] Given the shifting nature of the borders that marked the Hebrew Kingdoms of David and Solomon, religious peace organizations such as *Oz ve-Shalom* have concluded that it is impossible for settler groups to claim sanctity over a defined territory.

Accordingly, *Oz ve-Shalom* have placed emphasis on universal values to be found in Judaism, including the belief that all 'human beings were created in God's image and are worthy of being treated with dignity, respect, and compassion'.[49] It follows from this that what sanctifies any territorial space is not the land itself, but rather the quality of a society built upon that land and the treatment of its population. The enforced slavery of the Children of Israel as described in the book of *Genesis* is cited as proof of God's approbation when Jews failed to adhere to such strictures. If Israel is to fulfil the prophetic vision of being a 'light onto the nations', it cannot continue to occupy or dehumanize another people.[50] This contrasts sharply with the apocalyptic vision of the *amalek*, while challenging the normative values represented by the ideo-theology of the religious-nationalism. While conceding that the conceptual basis surrounding the term *amalek* could be located in meta-historical terms, British Chief Rabbi Dr Johnathan Sacks invoked the use of *amalek* with specific reference to the activities of Islamic radicals, rather the crude generalizations applied to all Arabs by Kahanism. Writing in the aftermath of the 4 March 1996 suicide bomb attack in the centre of Tel-Aviv, carried out on the eve of the festival of *Purim*,

Sacks likened the position of the Palestine National Authority to that of the Pharaoh whose hatred of the Jews as described in the book of *Exodus* was at least driven by reason, however ill-founded. Where a rationality behind hate exists, maintained Sacks, such malevolence can be assuaged, a clear reference to the hope of at least partial reconciliation contained within the spirit of the Oslo Accords.[51]

Such arguments are not new to Israeli politics, but their influence has remained secondary to a debate that has concentrated upon the strategic rationale behind Israel's control over the occupied territories. Even after the Shamgar Commission – set up to investigate the Hebron massacre – warned publicly of the potential for settlers and their supporters to engage in acts of terror, concern in Israel remained centred on the strategic threat posed to the security of the state by the autonomy proposals, rather than countering the growing militancy among elements within the religious-nationalist camp.[52] In July 1993, a symposium organized by the United States Institute for Peace on the Israel–Palestine conflict concluded that 'more can be done in advancing peace in areas of conflict through work with religious bodies and communities'.[53] While the conference was aimed at promoting inter-faith dialogue between Jew and Muslim, Rabin's assassination demonstrated that intra-faith dialogue among Israelis had to be accorded at least equal importance.

CONCLUSION

In the formation of his new government, Prime Minister Peres included Rabbi Yehuda Amital in his cabinet as Minister without portfolio. This was seen as an overt attempt by the new premier to bridge the divisions, at least in a symbolic sense, with the religious-nationalists. Up until the spate of suicide bomb attacks in Tel-Aviv, Ashdod and Jerusalem in February–March 1996, support remained strong for the peace process begun at Oslo and for the policies of the Labour-led coalition government, with Peres seemingly set to win comfortably the national elections scheduled for May 1996.[54] But religious-nationalism, quiescent in the aftermath of Rabin's death, remained a potent force that, however unintentional, could only have drawn support from the carnage visited upon Israel's streets throughout February and March. But even before the recent spate of suicide bombings, and as the pace of Israeli withdrawal from the main Palestinian population centres accelerated, rabbis once again issued a *halachic* ruling, condoning the use of firearms by settlers in preventing their evacuation from the occupied territories.

The failure of the main religious parties in Israel, as well as the main national newspaper most closely associated with religious-nationalism, *Ha-tzofeh*, to censure the edict openly, elicited sharp criticism from the new government who condemned it as 'sedition against Israeli democracy'.[55] But such expressions of revulsion are not enough by themselves to confront a world-view that remains impervious to the temporal mandate of a modern state. If moves towards a regional settlement are to progress forward, it remains incumbent upon the Government of Israel to engage the ideo-theology of religious-nationalism on its terms, using its vocabulary. Demonizing religious-nationalists as individuals cannot but fail to undermine their beliefs or heal cleavages in Israeli society; debating whose Judaism, whose interpretations of sacred texts, whose values should apply, a discourse conducted openly at a national level, has to be part of a broader political panacea if the ideo-theology of religious-nationalism is not to become Israel's nemesis. At one level, this questions the sagacity of those located primarily among Israel's centre-left who seek a clear separation between religion and the state. This is not to suggest that a theocratic tradition should become the dominant feature of Israel's political culture. But the fact that both the *Torah and Halacha* can accommodate and actively promote reconciliation between peoples – *Ve-ahavta La-ger* – does suggest that a humane Judaism, re-established firmly within the wider Zionist debate, can provide a constructive force for change, both inside Israel and in the broader context of Middle East politics. As one noted observer of Israel's political scene remarked: 'If [ideo-theology] combatted on its own terms, with interpretations of Jewish tradition that make Judaism the friend of democracy, pluralism and life over land – not the enemy of those values – then Judaism can still save the Jewish State.'[56]

NOTES

1. Efraim Inbar, 'Forget the Kahanists', *Jerusalem Post*, 27 October 1995.
2. Accounts concerning the emergence and influence of the settlers' movement Gush Emunim are numerous. For perhaps the most comprehensive see Ehud Sprinzak, *The Ascendance of Israel's Radical Right*, Oxford, 1991, pp.107–66.
3. For example, on the eve of Rabin's assassination, the settler protest group *Zo Artzenu* was advocating the boycott of the government census, claiming that the Prime Minister had 'usurped democracy'. See Herb Keinon, 'Settler Protesters: In Government We Don't Trust', *JP*, 27 October 1995.
4. For example, one Jewish Orthodox leader in the West Bank was quoted as saying, 'Those who even discuss territorial concessions are committing the sin of "Profanation of God's name"'. See Mark Tessler, 'Religion and Politics in the Jewish State of Israel', in Emile Sahliyeh, ed., *Religious Resurgence and Politics in the Contemporary World*, New York, 1990, p.279.
5. The Chief Sephardi Rabbi, Eliahu Bakshi-Doron, condemned Goldstein's actions outright, declaring 'I am ashamed that a Jew carried out such a villainous and irresponsible act, and I am distressed that it is viewed as the act of a religious person'. Interview with *Israel Television*, 27 February 1994.
6. Tessler, *Religious Resurgence*, p.264.
7. Ibid., p.267.
8. See Ethan D. Bloch, 'Religion, Zionism, and Religious Zionism', *Tikkun*, Vol.11, No.1 (1996), p.61.

9. Ehud Sprinzak, 'Fundamentalism, Terrorism, and Democracy: The Case of Gush Emunim', *New Outlook*, Vol.31, No.9 (1988), p.9.
10. This point is made forcefully by David Hall-Cathala, *The Peace Movement in Israel 1967–87*, Oxford, 1990, pp.4–5.
11. See, for example, Lenni Brenner, *The Iron Wall: Zionist Revisionism from Jabotinsky to Shamir*, London, 1984, pp.72–84.
12. David Newman and Tamar Hermann, 'A Comparative Study of Gush Emunim and Peace Now', *Middle Eastern Studies*, Vol.28, No.3 (1992), pp.509–30.
13. Amital is cited in Ehud Sprinzak, *The Ascendance*, p.116.
14. The covenant between God and Abraham is made in *Genesis*, Chapter 12, Verses 1–3. Abraham is looked upon as the 'father of all'. In *Genesis* Chapter 15, Verse 18, God declares to Abraham: 'Unto thy seed have I given this land, from the river of Egypt unto the great river, the river Euphrates'. In *Exodus*, Chapter 6, Verse 4 it is made to all the Israelites: 'And I have also established my covenant with them, to give them the land of Canaan, the land of their pilgrimage, wherein they were strangers'.
15. Sprinzak, *The Ascendance*, p.113.
16. Joe Sexton, 'Synagogue Debates Dismissing Rabbi Over View on Violence', *New York Times*, 17 November 1995.
17. 'Council of Rabbis Denounces Accusations against Fellow Rabbis as "Blood Libel"', *BBC-SWB*, ME/2461 MED/10–11, 15 November 1995.
18. 'Israel TV Profiles Extreme Jewish "Right-Wing Movements"', *BBC-SWB*, ME/2458 MED/2, 11 November 1995.
19. For example, the slaying of 7 Palestinians by Israeli Ami Popper. Popper, while still in prison serving a life sentence, married the daughter of Benjamin Kahane, son of Meir Kahane and leader of the *Kahane Chai* movement.
20. Ehud Sprinzak, 'Violence and Catastrophe in the Theology of Rabbi Meir Kahane: The Ideologization of Mimetic Desire', in Mark Juergensmeyer, ed., *Violence and the Sacred in the Modern World*, London, 1992, pp.48–9.
21. Ibid., p.50.
22. For the story of Amalek see *Exodus*, Chapter 17, Verse 8–16; *Deuteronomy*, Chapter 25, Verse 17–19. *Amalek*, though a collective name used to describe a warring tribe, was actually the son of Esaw, an opponent of Jacob. Renowned for their underhand methods of combat, the tribe of the *Amalek* were eventually defeated in battle. The grandson of Amalek, Agag was eventually captured by Saul and condemned to death. Saul allowed him to live for one day, during which time, so tradition has it, he impregnated two women, one of whom gave birth to Hanon. Consequently, the enemy of the Jews continued to reproduce and multiply every generation. This story fits in neatly with those who regard Arabs as the modern day *Amalek* who must be destroyed if God's glory is to be revealed. I am grateful to Rabbi Ian Goodhardt of the United Hebrew Congregation Synagogue of Leeds, for explaining the symbolism of *Amalek*.
23. The booklet *Adey Ad* (Forever and Ever) was written by religious educator Dov Ehrlich. His work was the subject of considerable criticism. See the comments of Nili Mandler, *Ha-aretz*, 5 April 1994.
24. Yossi Klein Ha-levi, 'Kahane's Murderous Legacy', *Jerusalem Report*, 24 March 1994, pp.14–15.
25. *Talmud* literally means 'instruction'. It is a compilation of learned rabbinical commentaries on the *Torah* and encompasses rulings on the Jewish social and religious life. There are in fact two *Talmuds*. The first, known as the Jerusalem *Talmud*, was completed in 4AD. The other, more thorough work known as the Babylonian *Talmud* was written in Aramaic between 4–5 AD.
26. Peter Hirschberg, 'Invoking the Spirits', *Jerusalem Report*, 16 November 1995, p.17.
27. Hirsh Goodman, 'The Enemy in the Mirror', *Jerusalem Report*, 2 November 1995, p.56.
28. Herb Keinon, 'Settlers Choose Civil Disobedience as their Best Shot', *Jerusalem Post*, 4 August 1995.
29. For example, see the comments made by Eliyakim Ha-etzni, *Ha-aretz*, 10 September 1993.
30. Herb Keinon, 'The Army Faces Off against a Rabbinical Battalion', *Jerusalem Post*, 14 July 1995; 'Ten Soldiers Refuse Reserve Duty Because of PLO–Israeli Agreement', *BBC-SWB*, ME/2431 MED/4–5, 11 October 1995; Christopher Walker, 'Diehard Settlers Threaten to Wreck West Bank Deal', *Times*, 25 September 1995.
31. Serge Schmemann, 'The Political Finger-Pointing Begins', *New York Times*, 10 November 1995.

32. Michael Lerner, 'The Civil War Has Begun', *Tikkun*, Vol.11, No.1 (1996), p.35.
33. *New York Times*, 10 November 1995.
34. Peter Shaw-Smith, 'The Israeli Settler Movement Post-Oslo', *Journal of Palestine Studies*, Vol.XXIII, No.3 (1994), p.103.
35. This point is made forcefully in an editorial profile of Goldstein. See the article 'Ha-zva'a' (The Atrocity), *Ma'ariv*, 27 February 1994.
36. Yossi Klein Ha-levi, *Jerusalem Report*, 24 March 1994, pp.17–18.
37. Ehud Sprinzak, *New Outlook*, Vol.31, No.9 (1988), pp.14–15.
38. Yossi Klein Ha-levi, 'Torn Between God and Country', *Jerusalem Report*, 10 August 1995, p.16.
39. 'Minister Says Government Must Remove Gloves to Defeat Jewish Terrorism', *BBC-SWB*, ME/2457 MED/1–2.
40. 'Interior Ministry Bars Seven Militant American Jews from Entering Israel', *BBC-SWB*, ME/2492 MED/19–20; Editorial in *Ma'ariv*, 13 November 1995.
41. 'Minister on Threat to Israeli Democracy; Says Legal System Has Been Too Lenient', *BBC-SWB*, ME/2457 MED/2–3.
42. 'Peres Presents Cabinet to Knesset, Vows to Continue Rabin's Work on the Peace Process', *BBC-SWB*, ME/2468 MED/3, 23 November 1995.
43. Gerald Butt, 'God in the Palaces: the Growth of Religious Fundamentalism in Israel', *BBC Radio 4*, 17 January 1993. Benvenisti's comments were expressed during an interview for this programme.
44. Naftali Rothenberg, 'When Halacha Gets Used for Political Ends', *Jerusalem Post*, 14 July 1995.
45. This interpretation of *pikuach nefesh* was the subject of much vilification by West Bank Rabbis. See Michael Berenbaum, 'Who, What, When', *New Outlook*, Vol.30, No.1 (1991), pp.16–17.
46. Ian S. Lustick, *For the Land and the Lord*, New York, 1988, pp.109–10. Lustick makes the point that the impact of Lebanon saw the emergence of a dovish wing within Gush Emunim which embraced limited forms of territorial compromise under the scope of *pikuach nefesh*.
47. *Book of Genesis*, Chapter 15, Verse 18.
48. Hall-Cathala, *Peace Movement*, pp.149–50.
49. Ibid., p.148.
50. Thomas Friedman, 'Land or Life?', *New York Times*, 19 November 1995.
51. Chief Rabbi Jonathan Sacks, 'Sermon Notes for Shabbat Parshat Parah 5756', *Office of the Chief Rabbi*, Shushan Purim 5756.
52. Allan E. Shapiro, 'A Crossing of the Line', *Jerusalem Post*, 27 October 1995.
53. Bruce Brill, 'Now More Than Ever: What We Must Do To Get Muslims and Jews to Trust Each Other?', *Peace News*, International Centre For Peace in the Middle East, No.29 (1996), p.9.
54. See the poll carried out by the Tami Steinmetz Centre for Peace Studies at Tel-Aviv University during the course of January 1996. The results were published in *Ha-aretz*, 5 February 1995.
55. 'Ministers Condemn Religious Judgement as "Sedition Against Israeli Democracy"', *BBC-SWB*, ME/2488 MED/3, 16 December 1995.
56. Thomas Friedman, *New York Times*, 19 November 1995.

Israeli Identity in Transition

LILLY WEISSBROD

The signing of the Israel–PLO Declaration of Principles (DOP) in September 1993 reawakened a dormant ambivalence regarding Israeli identity. Awareness of this dilemma, initially confined mainly to intellectuals, has spread as the peace process proceeded. With the assassination of Prime Minister Yitzhak Rabin on 4 November 1995, it has become a malaise of the public at large. Due to the killing of nearly 200 Israelis in a string of suicide bombings following the signing of the DOP, by the time of his assassination Rabin had lost much of the popular support which had brought him to power in 1992;[1] yet the peace process has not been seriously jeopardized by the assassination. It would seem that the shock and general mourning exhibited by most Israelis expressed not merely grief over the loss of a statesman, or fear of a renewed confrontation with the Palestinians. It also revealed the realization that the social consensus had been disrupted and that this could no longer be ignored.

In contrast to the view that collective identities are being obliterated in post-modern societies, recent citizenship theory as well as communitarianists reassert the need in democratic societies for a basic consensus of citizens regarding their distinct identity.[2] This is so for two main reasons. First, Western democracies are pluralistic and would easily disintegrate unless some basic common values overrode the different views and values held by their multiple groups. Second, since democracies depend more on consent and less on coercion than other forms of government, compliance with laws and norms depends more on a consensus regarding the values from which the laws and norms are derived. As Anthony Smith has noted, such values cannot be freely invented but must rather rely on the culture of the society, namely, they are a reinterpretation of its past values and symbols to fit present circumstances and needs.[3]

The link between core values, a consensus regarding them and an articulation of identity was broken by the previous Israeli government when it engaged in a policy which contradicted the values on which the majority of Israeli citizens based their identity without offering a clearly defined new ideational underpinning. The present Israeli social polarization, accompanied by a debate and an active quest for a new

Lilly Weissbrod is a Tel-Aviv-based writer and commentator.

articulation of identity, serves to illustrate the hypothesized link
between these three factors. It also highlights society's need of a distinct
identity, a need which becomes particularly salient when that society
undergoes a radical change. Moreover, Israelis themselves have claimed
that universal values are inadequate as the sole basis of a societal
identity, which makes this case pertinent for the thesis of consensus
based on particularist values. The values on which a collective identity
rests are necessarily particular to that society, for identity is, by
definition, a boundary formation. To know who it is, a group must
distinguish itself from others, and specific values are basic ingredients of
such a boundary.[4] Even modernist theory, which bases ethics on abstract
universal values, concedes that the latter are merely rules according to
which consensus is achieved, while the content of the debate is the mark
of society's identity.[5]

This article will confine itself to the effects of the peace process on
the secular Jewish majority in Israel. The crisis of Gush Emunim and its
supporters, the national religious camp, have been analyzed elsewhere,[6]
and the dilemma of the Israeli Arabs requires separate treatment which
is beyond the scope of this article. Israeli identity is more complex than
that of other Western democratic societies. In addition to differentiating
themselves from other nation-states, the Israeli definition of who they
are must also contain an assertion of their moral right to be where they
are. That is so because the Palestinians have been claiming a right to the
same territory since the early days of the Zionist movement. Yet it
would seem that this does not disqualify Israel from being a test case for
the above thesis. It merely makes the explanation lengthier and
somewhat more difficult.

THE 'RIGHT TO THE LAND' DILEMMA

Though Jews have been singular in retaining their distinct identity
despite 2000 years of dispersal, Israeli identity has always been
equivocal. For lack of space here, a brief discussion of this ambivalence
will have to suffice. Emphatically secular, Labour Zionism clearly
defined Israelis as Jews returning to their historical homeland to be
nationally restored, as individuals by physical contact with its soil
(agriculture) and as a community by instituting an egalitarian society of
perfect justice. The protests of a native Arab population could be
countered only by quoting the Bible as the more ancient title deed to
the land.[7] The inconsistency between a very secular persuasion and its
grounding on a religious text par excellence was only partially resolved
inasmuch as the Bible was reinterpreted as a historical document. The
UN Partition Plan of 1947 ostensibly resolved the dilemma. The Plan
constituted international recognition of the Jewish/Israeli title to part of
the land and, by agreeing to it, Israelis accepted the secular principle of

distributive justice as settlement of their dispute with the Arabs and were ethically absolved, though *post facto*.

Yet some Israelis have never really renounced their right to the entire land. This became obvious soon after the occupation of the West Bank, the Gaza Strip and the Golan Heights in 1967. This was evidenced by the euphoria of Israelis visiting the 'liberated' sites most closely associated with Biblical events, such as Hebron, ancient Jerusalem and Jericho; by the decision to hold on to this territory despite international objections; and by the relatively quick acceptance of 'New Zionism' as the new Israeli identity. A new justification for the Israeli presence in the entire land thus became necessary, since Israelis obviously no longer practiced distributive justice. 'New Zionism' is a partially secularized version of the modern religious fundamentalist doctrine of Gush Emunim which reasserts the absolute right of Jews to the entire land, based on the Bible and later Jewish religious texts. 'New Zionism' was articulated and implemented by the hawkish Likud government, which came into power in 1977. It demarcates Israelis clearly vis-à-vis others as Jews taking rightful possession of their religious/historical heritage, where they are instituting a modern technological society based on Jewish community values of mutual responsibility and aid, in place of Western consumerism and competitiveness. In consequence of the Jewish emphasis contained in 'New Zionism', some Israelis have re-adopted some Jewish customs, but they have done so primarily as an expression of Jewish *culture* rather than religion, with the majority of Israelis remaining secular. Yet they have emphatically denied the right of Palestinians to any part of the land, claiming their right to be the ultimate right because it is based on the Bible. To cover up the inherent dilemma of secular people basing the justification for their territorial rights on Divine Will, this Israeli identity was heavily augmented by security arguments and by Israeli magnanimity in conceding residential rights to Palestinians. This ethical foundation is shaky and out of step with a time when self-determination and human rights have become the leading values in the West. It is therefore hardly surprising that, while Labour Zionism was adopted by the majority of Israelis, 'New Zionism' has never become as dominant and has mustered the support of no more than just over half of the population. Compared with the pre-1967 era, the national consensus has weakened (giving rise, for example, to the protest over the 1982 Lebanon War) but has remained basically intact.

So long as the Palestinians in the territories remained acquiescent, they seemed to confirm Israeli protestations that the occupation was benevolent, that it had enhanced Palestinian living standards, and that it had infringed not on human rights, but merely on political ones. But the Palestinian uprising which broke out at the end of 1987 (*intifada*) refuted all these claims. It made manifest the Palestinian rejection of the

Israeli proprietorial claim to the entire land, and also demonstrated that no foreign occupation could be benevolent. As Palestinian violence escalated, Israel employed increasingly repressive measures until its claim to exercise fairness and justice became untenable. The situation on the ground was lending support to advocates of Israeli withdrawal from the occupied territories, first voiced in the 1970s by a few of those secular Israelis who had never accepted 'New Zionism' as their articulation of identity.

DISPUTERS OF 'NEW ZIONISM'

The pioneers of the peace movement in the early 1970s reinterpreted the original Labour Zionist formulation of Israeli identity in New Leftist terms current at the time. They compounded its ambivalence by an additional equivocation. It was necessary for the country to be partitioned not merely because both peoples had equal historical rights to it, but in order to ensure the Jewish nature of Israel. Jews, the People of the Book, had the mission of establishing a perfectly just society of participatory democracy and social equity, a mission which Palestinians could not – or would not – share. Unless Israel withdrew to its previous borders, Palestinians would either be deprived of their political rights, an offence against democracy, or turn Israel into a binational state, in which case it could not fulfil its mission.[8]

Moreover, the contradiction between the Jewish nature of Israel and its democratic structure has existed since the inception of the state, which has a considerable Arab minority. Both principles are contained in the Israeli Declaration of Independence; the clash between them comes to light most clearly in the Law of Return, which discriminates against the Arab citizens of Israel in granting entry and extending automatic citizenship to any Jew arriving in Israel, and to none other but a Jew. Yet the incompatibility of the two principles was ignored, especially after restrictions on Israeli Arabs had been lifted in 1966. Once Israeli Arabs enjoyed all formal citizenship rights, the principle of democracy was seen to be observed, in view of the Israeli conception that democracy was the rule of the majority.[9]

The tension between the Jewish and the democratic nature of Israel has grown as New Left ideas gave way to modernist ones in the West and as the latter have influenced the mindset of secular Israeli intellectuals. Uncontestable majority rule is untenable when individual rights and self-realization attain prime importance. In Israel, this shift to individualism has been gradually promoted by the judiciary and is far from complete. Since the late 1970s, the High Court of Justice has adjudicated increasingly in defence of citizen rights against the state and in defence of freedom of expression and action of dissenting groups – that is, in defence of pluralism. The change in the concept of democracy has been cautious. Furthermore, until recently it was never extended to the Palestinian inhabitants of the occupied territories.[10] Indeed, the principles of individualism, pluralism and the concomitant one of self-determination have not been widely accepted by the general public, as research on democracy in Israel indicates. In research commissioned by the Ministry of Education, only 11 per cent of pupils aged 16–18 regarded the safeguarding of individual rights and the right of dissent as essential to a democratic system; 48 per cent preferred a Jewish State over a democratic one; only 49 per cent supported the right of public criticism of the regime, and 41 per cent favoured the censorship of views which offended against core Israeli values.[11] Similarly, in 1987, 34.6 per cent of adult respondents considered Israel to be too democratic (because it did not outlaw a party advocating Palestinian independence), growing to 44 per cent in 1990; only 51 per cent would grant Israeli Arabs the right to demonstrate.[12]

Peace Now, the most activist among the small peace movements, was formed in 1978. It advocated withdrawal in return for peace, initially for security reasons alone.[13] Since these were easily matched by equally convincing security arguments supporting occupation, by 1985 Peace Now began to underpin its practical reasoning by an ethical one. Yet it was careful to remain within the Israeli consensus, as its leader Zali Reshef underlined in an interview.[14] Peace Now chose to emphasize the corruptive influence of occupation on the occupier, rather than the injustice to the occupied.[15] This argument gradually convinced even some of the most ardent adherents of the Jewish Right to the entire Land of Israel: by 1994, some Gush Emunim members admitted that the rule over an unwilling alien population might blemish Israelis morally.[16]

The linkage between withdrawal and modernist values of human rights and self-determination began in 1981, when some Peace Now activists joined RATZ, a party which until then had been promoting civil rights inside Israel.[17] The implications of this link were not fully realized until the Palestinians, by means of their uprising, articulated their right to political self-determination and increasingly publicized Israeli infringements of human rights in the occupied territories. The *intifada* also induced some Israeli academics to question the assertion of Labour Zionists that distributive justice had indeed been practiced until 1967 and had exonerated Israelis from any alleged injustice to the Palestinians: instances were emphasized in which Palestinians had been expelled in 1948–49[18] and the emphatically defensive nature of all Israeli military operations was questioned.[19] Others have challenged the very premise that the unilateral exercise of distributive justice absolved Israelis from their 'original sin', namely settling in an area inhabited by others against the wishes of the latter.[20]

'Post-Zionists', the radical minority within the peace camp, admonish Israelis to atone for their moral self-righteousness by adopting and exercising the truly universal modernist values of human rights, the rule of laws which also protects the rights of minorities, and the right of self-determination applied to Palestinians and not merely to Israelis. They assert that the narrow 'tribalism' of an ethnic/religious collective is incompatible with the pluralism and individualism of modern democracy. Because it is pluralistic, no modern society can have any common values except those which are universal. The historical rights to a territory of an ethnie are as irrational as are religious ones. A society has a just claim to its existence in its territory only if it adheres to universal norms. Since Israel is not applying such norms to the Palestinians, it must relinquish its rule over them.[21]

CONTRADICTORY LEADERSHIP MESSAGES

The *intifada* sensitized Israelis to the corruptive effects of occupation on the occupier. The signing of the DOP then pushed into the limelight the 'Post-Zionist' narrative, which had been confined to debates among a small number of academics, journalists and writers. It seemed reasonable to infer that if the government voluntarily relinquished Israeli rule over the West Bank and the Gaza Strip, it did so because it recognized the Palestinian right of self-determination, though the latter is not mentioned in the DOP, nor in any official Israeli statement. Furthermore, if the government voluntarily agreed to release Palestinian prisoners, it thereby implicitly admitted Israeli infringement of Palestinian human rights. Yet, the Israeli government has not committed itself to either principle unequivocally. In the 1992 elections, Labour did not win a majority. To come to power, it formed a coalition with the small Leftist MERETZ Party.[22] MERETZ and a circle of younger Labour leaders were the driving force behind the government recognition of the PLO as a partner for negotiations, resulting in the DOP. The majority of decision-makers accepted the need for peace with the Palestinians, in order to put an end to terrorism, or in order to facilitate peace negotiations with neighbouring Arab states, or again in order to reinstate the moral rectitude of Israel. None accepted the 'Post-Zionist' arguments, though ostensibly acting on them at times, but not consistently.

The two chief Labour leaders, Yitzhak Rabin and Shimon Peres, made completely different appeals in support of the peace process,[23] neither of which provides a satisfactory formulation for the new Israeli identity required by such a policy watershed. Consequently, the public has remained confused. Rabin asserted that the continued longing for their homeland gave Jews the right to the entire land they had possessed and claimed that Israel's Jewishness was his main concern.[24] Hence, the peace process with the Palestinians was a reluctant agreement to partition. Since over two million Palestinian citizens would preclude a

Jewish State, a complete separation between the two peoples was required, though without granting the Palestinians full sovereignty, nor the entire West Bank.[25] Israel would eventually annex areas near its pre-1967 borders which contained large blocs of Jewish settlements, as well as a strip along the Jordan river.[26] Rabin reiterated these arguments in a Knesset speech on 5 October 1995, a month before his assassination. Clearly, his view was far removed from 'Post-Zionist' moralist admonitions, nor was it guided by the early Zionist principle of distributive justice. It based itself on history, largely ignoring Palestinian counter-claims. The ancient longing of the Jewish people to return to their homeland is a poor justification for settling a land whose inhabitants also had a long history of residence; demographic factors are a poor excuse for withdrawing from part of this land, unless democracy and the rights of minorities are a major concern. Yet they were not: instead, the safety of Israelis was Rabin's top priority, secured by separation and a somewhat mollified Palestinian population in an autonomous region.[27] This articulation of Israeli identity can convince neither 'New Zionists', who object to the withdrawal from parts of the Land of Israel, nor Labour Zionists who find themselves amoral occupants of an ancient heritage which they are to share with others very reluctantly.

The message of Shimon Peres, Foreign Minister and subsequently Prime Minister of Israel, has been of a different nature. It can be summarized in the slogan 'peace for the sake of a prosperous Israel in a prosperous Middle East'. Israel is withdrawing from the occupied territories in order to reconcile the Palestinians and, thereby, the entire Arab world, to its presence in the region.[28] Israel's presence is justified by Jewish brain-power, namely the ability to help its Arab neighbours attain Western affluence and progress by creating an economically cooperating Middle Eastern bloc.[29] Since reconciliation with the Palestinians is merely a means to the end of a New Middle East, Peres envisions a functional solution in which the Palestinian entity will have jurisdiction over civil matters (excluding water and soil resources) and will eventually join a federation with Jordan.[30] This articulation of Israeli identity assumes that Israel's intellectual superiority and future service to the region will justify its presence there, but it is far removed from Jewish core values. It evokes principally individual hedonism (affluence) and the wish to emulate a Western lifestyle. It cannot distinguish Israelis from citizens of other Western democracies, nor will it distinguish them from their Arab neighbours once the promised New Middle East is established.

A third message was being conveyed by MERETZ leaders and the young Labour politicians who had been the pioneers of the peace process with the Palestinians. Without addressing the 'right to the land' issue at all, they speak mainly of the Israeli ethical corruption caused by rule over aliens. The violation of Palestinian human rights is also mentioned. In contrast to the main Labour leaders, they propose a sovereign Palestinian State, above all as a means to Israeli moral recovery and as compensation for the annexation of some territory densely populated by Jewish settlements.[31]

Nor did the opposition until the May 1996 elections, led by the Likud Party, offer any viable alternative formulation of Israeli identity. Benjamin Netanyahu, leader of Likud, has been unable to incorporate the seemingly irreversible peace process into a reformulation of 'New Zionism' (the identity articulation which his party espouses). At first, he simply reiterated 'New Zionism' and proposed to preserve its relevance by reversing the peace process, at least to some extent.[32] Likud then realized the unrealistic nature of this view, and by the end of January 1996 the party had reformulated its political programme to recognize as a *fait accompli* the steps taken by Israel so far, though without abandoning its commitment to 'New Zionism'.

Netanyahu won the direct elections for the premiership by a narrow margin and thus returned Likud to power. Dissatisfaction with the justifications for the peace process put forward by Labour leaders probably played a part in bringing about this victory, as did the realization of many voters that the two parts of the Likud message were incompatible and that the latter half ('New Zionism') would prevail. In fact, the Netanyahu platform was even more equivocal than the original Likud programme, justifying the continuation of the peace process for security reasons and calling this policy 'a secure peace'. 'New Zionism' had stressed the security advantage of retaining the West Bank as a strategic depth, yet its supporters were now called upon to relinquish this strategic depth. In a recent interview, the new prime minister clarified this point. He stated that enhanced Israeli security was a precondition for a continuing peace process. If that was so, why should Israelis support the latter if peace really constituted a danger? That question was left unanswered in the interview.[33]

So the Israeli public has been faced with conflicting justifications of a new policy which negates many of the values on which Israeli consensus has been built. While Rabin tried to justify this policy by early Zionist slogans stripped of their moral underpinning, Peres offered affluence and technological excellence as the new parameters of Israeli identity, while Netanyahu has been offering enhanced security. Even when coupled with the ethical compunctions of MERETZ, this is hardly a satisfactory articulation of an identity. Affluence and technological progress do not distinguish Israelis from other modern Western societies, while the moral qualms imply a previous state of virtue whose equivocality has meanwhile been exposed. None of these articulations of Israeli identity contain a convincing justification for Israelis living in Israel rather than elsewhere. The same holds true for 'Post-Zionist' arguments which reject the Jewish nature of Israel altogether.[34] Democracy and respect for human rights are laudable universal values. Yet deprived of any core values specific to Israelis, they cannot serve as a basis for identity which, by definition, distinguishes one person/group from another. In the above interview, the new premier was aware of this dilemma and tried to solve it by proposing an amalgam of unspecified Jewish and universal values which would reconstitute the shaken Israeli identity.

The confusion of the public, due to the divergent messages of the political leaders, has been exacerbated by the inconsistency of government actions related to the peace process. The stated intention of the DOP was to end the long-standing conflict and to establish peace between Israel and the Palestinians. Peaceful relations imply an eventual reconciliation, as was overtly symbolized by the famous handshake of Prime Minister Rabin and Chairman Arafat on the White House lawn. Yet many government actions contradicted this intention and implied an unabated hostility or ambivalence towards the Palestinians with whom peace was to be established. A few examples of this inconsistency will illustrate the many instances, which are too numerous to list in full.

First, the Jewish settlements on the West Bank constitute a major obstacle to a redrawing of final borders, the ultimate step in the peaceful resolution of the conflict. Israel undertook to stop the establishment of any further settlements, while the fate of existing ones would be agreed upon in the final stage of the negotiations. Prime Minister Rabin frequently antagonized the settlers publicly by pointing out the obstruction which they posed to the peace process. Building in many settlements went on unhindered, though, or was even initiated by the government: during 1994–95, schools and clinics were set up for the growing population of settlers; land near Nablus and Tul-Karem was confiscated, presumably to serve the expansion of nearby settlements. At the end of September 1995, the government went ahead with the second stage of the DOP, extending Palestinian self-rule to all population centres on the West Bank. Yet only a month later, it approved the appropriation of land near Ramalla from which settlers had been forcibly evicted earlier when they had staked a claim to it.

Second, according to the DOP, the status of Jerusalem would be determined in the final stage of negotiations. Yet building in 'Greater Jerusalem' and in East Jerusalem continued as government leaders repeatedly stated that undivided Jerusalem would remain the capital of Israel. At the same time, the Israeli government objected vehemently to the US Congress decision to move the US embassy to Jerusalem in official US recognition of this Israeli claim.

Third, the light sentences passed on Israelis who committed violent acts against Palestinians imply tacit official condonation of such acts and contrast sharply with official protestations of reconciliation. According to a report published in 1994 by *Be-tzelem*, an Israeli human rights organization, the cases of 48 Israelis accused of causing death to Palestinians during 1988–92 were still being processed in 1994. Of these, only one person has been convicted of murder and given a life sentence. Another six were convicted of lesser offences: three were given prison sentences of three years, 18 months and five months respectively, while the other three were sentenced to several months of community service. The remaining files were closed altogether.[35]

The contradiction between statements and actions has not lessened since the change of government; it has merely reversed direction, so to speak. The rhetoric is now more belligerent and the actions appeasing. Despite reiterated commitment to 'New Zionist' ideals, the Likud government negotiated the withdrawal of the Israel Defence Forces (IDF) from most parts of Hebron; it has not unfrozen building in the settlements in Judea and Samaria, and it has not made good its threat to discontinue the peace process unless the Palestinian Authority honoured all its obligations as laid down in the Oslo Accords.

The diverse messages and self-contradictory actions of the government regarding the peace process have had two complementary results. First, they have not tempered the long-standing polarization in Israeli society. The percentage of respondents recognizing the PLO as a partner for negotiations (one of the most dramatic changes in official Israeli policy) has not risen much since the signing of the DOP, amounting to 53 per cent in 1991, to 60 per cent in 1994 and back again to 53 per cent in 1995.[36] Forty-five per cent of respondents supported continued expansion of settlements beyond the pre-1967 borders in 1986, 46 per cent in 1993, 47 per cent in 1995, and 47.8 per cent in 1996.[37] Secondly, and paradoxically enough, while the public is clearly split on some issues, some people are of two minds. In a survey conducted in 1995, 73 per cent of respondents supported the continuation of negotiations with the Palestinians, though 53 per cent considered Arafat a terrorist, that is, totally untrustworthy.[38] Conversely, in 1994, 41 per cent of another sample supported expanding Palestinian self-rule beyond Gaza and Jericho, though 73 per cent did not trust the PLO to honour its agreements with Israel.[39] Clearly, part of these sample populations held self-contradictory views. The unwillingness to face the consequences of the 'altruistic' support of peace is another indicator of confusion: 45.9 per cent of respondents supported the peace process, but only 22.2 per cent supported evacuation of any settlements on the West Bank.[40]

Furthermore, the percentage of undecided respondents on major issues related to the peace process and, thus, to the future of Israel, demonstrates the failure of the leadership to convey a clear and convincing message. In the last quoted survey, 44 per cent of respondents were undecided regarding the evacuation of settlements on the West Bank; 27.4 per cent of respondents were undecided regarding the DOP, and 33 per cent could not decide whether the PLO was a partner for peace negotiations;[41] 31.5 per cent had no clear opinion regarding settlers on the West Bank.[42] In recent surveys, 29 per cent of respondents were undecided concerning the peace process in general and 41.3 per cent could not decide whether settlements in the West Bank were an obstacle to peace.[43]

Ambivalence also prevails regarding the very concept of peace. During August 1994–November 1996, support for peace in general averaged 60.35 per cent, but support for peace with the Palestinians averaged only 49.7 per cent and that with Syria 36.1 per cent.[44] It seems that at least for some of those 60 per cent who consider peace an attractive option, the meaning of peace in real terms is less than clear. The strong support for peace in general ostensibly indicates an acceptance of Peres's vision of a regional peace in the New Middle East. Yet support of integration in that Middle East is surprisingly low: according to the Tami Steinmetz Centre at Tel-Aviv University, only 29 per cent of respondents wanted Israel to integrate in the Middle East politically, only 23 per cent wanted it to integrate economically and a low 14 per cent wanted cultural integration.[45]

The large percentage of objectors to peace with Syria is a further indication of this uncertainty. Rabin's message has not been very persuasive either if half of the respondents still reject the PLO as a partner for negotiations. Though his desire for a Jewish State seems to be shared by the majority – 75 per cent of respondents supported separation from the Palestinian entity – its implications are not, since only 22.2 per cent supported evacuation of any settlements without which separation is an unrealistic aim.

THE IDENTITY QUEST

The confusion and uncertainty described above are but symptoms of the general malaise which Israelis have been experiencing since the signing of the DOP, because the latter has seriously undermined both aspects of Israeli identity. The voluntary relinquishment of part of the historical homeland is tantamount to an admission that a territorial claim based on ancient history may not be a valid title, as asserted, if it infringes on an equal claim made by another people and based on more recent history. If the DOP concedes the rights of Palestinians to part of Palestine, why not to all of Palestine, including the territory of the State of Israel? Partition merely redresses the injustice of coercive rule over another people, but it does not justify the Jewish return to Palestine. By conceding the Palestinian right of self-determination, Israel ostensibly deprives itself of that part of its identity which provides its moral basis for being in Israel. If Israelis were intruders in 1967, they were as much intruders at the turn of the century. An unethical origin is an unacceptable constituent of identity; no group asserts distinctiveness by dint of a trait or action to which it itself ascribes a negative connotation. At the same time, if the universal values of democracy, human rights, self-determination and individualism which have guided the peace process are accepted as the only valid ones, as their advocates demand, Israelis are also deprived of their uniqueness. The intellectual leaders of the peace camp deny any validity to group specificity, which they denigrate as tribal and obsolete. Yet universal values cannot be a substitute identity since they do not differentiate Israelis from others but, rather, underline the similarity of Israeli society with enlightened Western ones.

These issues have been raised since the DOP was signed, at first tentatively and primarily by intellectuals. A new movement was founded in December 1993, calling itself *Ha-tikava* (Hope), which wants to protect the Jewish identity of Israelis from the onslaught of 'Post-Zionists'. At the end of 1993, the editors of *Shdemot*, a periodical of the Kibbutz, held a dialogue with the editors of *Nekuda*, the monthly of the West Bank settlers. They sought to shore up their Jewish identity with arguments provided by Gush Emunim.[46] In October 1994, Yad Tabenkin, a research centre of the Kibbutz Movement, held a symposium on the incompatibility of democratic 'Post-Zionist' identity with the Jewish identity of Israel. Another symposium on 'Who Is an Israeli' was held at the Journalists House in Tel-Aviv in December 1994. Articles on the need for a new Israeli identity appeared, at first primarily in periodicals rather than the daily press. Titles such as 'New Israeliness', '[A Jewish state is] Not Normal', 'The New Jew as an Anomaly', or 'We Must Change Course'[47] bear witness to the recognition of the problem posed by 'Post-Zionist' assumptions and by the peace process. The authors express dissatisfaction with 'New Zionism', based on secularized Judaism, but provide no satisfactory alternative.

Realizing the implications of the peace process, some prominent spokesmen of the peace camp felt obliged to sustain the ethical justification of the Israeli presence in Israel. They suggested that the need of a persecuted people for a safe haven was a viable alternative to the historical claim.[48] This answer evades the issue and is inaccurate. Zionists chose the Land of Israel as their destination long before the Holocaust, at a time when the overwhelming majority of Jews could and did emigrate to the United States. Therefore, a safe haven is merely a *post facto* excuse. Furthermore, it implies that Israel must necessarily be Jewish, which contradicts the demand of that very same peace camp for a universalist Israel.

The dilemma which the peace process uncovered was vividly demonstrated at a conference on 'Jews and Arabs in Israel in an Era of

Peace', held at Tel-Aviv University in October 1994. In his keynote address, Anton Shammas, an Israeli–Arab writer, formulated the issue succinctly, as did two other prominent Israeli Arabs on the Panel, Shaykh Abdallah Nimr Darwish, a leader of the Islamic Movement in Israel, and Dr. Ahmad Tibi, special adviser to Yasser Arafat. They challenged Israel to face up to its equivocal identity and to reformulate it in light of the universal values which were guiding the peace process. The latter were allegedly incompatible with a Jewish Israel which could not accord equal rights to its Arab minority. Israel must renounce its Jewish character and become a truly democratic state. After all, Israeli Arabs, with ancient tenure, had national rights to the country at least equal to those of Israeli Jews, many of whom were recently arrived immigrants. All Jewish Israeli participants objected, particularly in view of the latter observation: once Israelis denied that Israel was a Jewish State, they automatically denied their historical entitlement to it. Since the historical argument was no longer as convincing as it had been prior to the peace process, it was not raised, but neither was any other which could provide ethical grounds for the insistence that Israel must remain a Jewish State. The principal argument was practical: Jews were the dominant majority which would never agree to such a change; the Arab demand was counter-productive and would lead to a self-defeating confrontation. Only Aluf Hareven, director of Sikui, an association for equal rights to Arabs, tentatively admitted the inherent justice of the Arab demand. He offered a compromise solution on the symbolic level which would not replace Jewish symbols, but supplement them with joint civic ones. This suggestion, later raised in the Knesset, was condemned outright. Even Minister of Economics Yossi Beilin, one of the young Labour leaders who had been instrumental in bringing about the DOP, reiterated in an interview that Israel would remain a Jewish State forever. It would neither change its name nor its anthem. Any majority had the right to define itself as it wished.[49]

A temporary lull in the debate, occasioned by a spate of terrorist attacks and fears/hopes that the peace process might collapse, ended with the withdrawal of Israeli troops from Palestinian population centres at the end of September 1995 and, particularly, with the assassination of Prime Minister Rabin. The withdrawal of troops ostensibly made the peace process a *fait accompli*, so that its consequences for Israeli consensus had to be thrashed out. Reactions to the assassination demonstrated the deep schism in Israeli society regarding these issues and the consequent difficulty, if not impossibility, of reaching a new consensus. The subject of Israeli identity has not disappeared from the public agenda since. Specifically, it has become an issue for those who endorse the peace process rather than primarily for its opponents, as had been the case before. Following are some examples. A conference was held at Tel-Aviv

University in December 1995, entitled 'The Last Nationality Question: Social Democracy, National Identity and Jewish Emancipation'; another conference, held in the same month, was entitled 'The Future of Israeli Society and Economy'; in a large announcement in *Ha-aretz* of 30 November 1995, contributions were invited for a volume entitled 'Cosmo-ethism: Israel, Zionism and Judaism'. Articles have proliferated, with titles such as 'Unifying Power', 'The Second Revolution', 'The Religion of Nationality Versus the Religion of Citizens', 'The Zionism of Tomorrow', 'Ideological Bankruptcy', 'Icons and Identity', 'A Farewell Party to Zionism', 'Israel Against Herself', 'A State of All Its Citizens', 'Hi-tech Zionism' and 'On Zionism, Post-Zionism and Anti-Zionism'.[50]

The Rabin assassination has brought home to all Israelis, except for outright protagonists of 'Post-Zionism', the need for a consensus based on society-specific values, which can only be Jewish in the case of Israel. At the above mentioned conference on the future of Israeli society and economy, Leftist intellectuals were agreed that, denuded of its unique identity, Israelis would opt for the lowest denominator of Westernism, namely a mindless consumerism and egoistical competitiveness. A leading Israeli Leftist author predicted that without a unique identity, which creates solidarity, conflicting interests would tear Israeli society apart. Jewish values were the only ones common to all Israelis; it was imperative to find some association between Israeli liberal democracy and its Jewish cultural heritage. The religious camp was best suited to re-imbue secular Israelis with the Jewish values abandoned under the influence of 'Post-Zionism'. A Jewish State, based on a symbiosis of Jewish and universal values, would underline Israeli distinctiveness vis-à-vis the world and preserve the moral integrity of Israelis as returnees to their homeland.[51]

This line of thought was apparently taken up by Prime Minister Peres, who co-opted Rabbi Meital into the government as representative of the moderate religious camp. Furthermore Peres, though the initiator of the DOP, became more reluctant than ever to accord eventual sovereignty to the Palestinians, possibly because a sovereign Palestinian state would constitute an ultimate renunciation of the Israeli right, as Jews, to the entire land. Once this is renounced, the Israeli right to their part of the land becomes doubtful, if not impossible to maintain. As already stated, the realization of this dilemma has spread to the population at large, especially to young secular Israelis who were so prominent in their grief and shock following the Rabin assassination. Since then, dialogue groups of secular and religious youngsters have multiplied, initiated largely by the secular who are seeking a set of Jewish values on which a renewed consensus can rest. Numerous Kibbutz groups have been meeting Yeshiva students; several hundred military officers and several scores of police officers have attended seminars with religious young people at Elul, a religious studies centre; a group of secular secondary school pupils has founded Hala, for dialogue with their religious counterparts; Gesher, an association of secular-religious rapprochement, has organized scores of dialogue groups upon request.

As noted earlier, the Netanyahu Government has not resolved the dilemma either, though it is more aware of it. Consequently, a programme of Jewish culture has been introduced by the Ministry of Education in the secular school system, which is to supply secular young Israelis with the Jewish values needed to mend their eroded collective identity. Furthermore, a number of religious institutes and colleges for secular Israelis have been established by Rabbi Menachem Froman, with the active support of prominent secular intellectuals; the former Minister of Immigration (a leader of MERETZ, the party most associated with promulgating universal values) is setting up a 'college of pluralistic Judaism'; at the inauguration of Bina, the Centre for Jewish Identity and Israeli Culture, in December 1996, the keynote addresses were held by Shulamit Aloni, former leader of MERETZ, and by Rabbi Yoel Ben-Nun, a moderate West Bank settler.

To date, the dilemma remains unresolved. Nobody has made clear which Jewish values should be re-adopted, or how they should be integrated in a secular modernist perception which can provide moral justification for the Israelis' presence in their country. One tentative suggestion by a MERETZ activist evokes a modern version of the 'light upon the nations' vision: Israel should re-define itself as the model synthesis of hi-tech affluence, ecological awareness and fair distribution of economic resources, combining, as it were, the best in modernity with the best in its ancient prophetic ethics.[52]

CONCLUSION

Israeli identity was shaken once before, after the 1967 War, but the present crisis is more severe. In 1967, the self-image of Israelis as Jews pioneering to re-establish national sovereignty was not questioned and, as Jews, they remained uniquely distinct vis-à-vis the world. The new political reality, in contrast, requires a novel justification for their right to be in a land also inhabited by others. At present, modernist values are contesting this fact, as well as any ethnic or religious uniqueness as a basis for collective identity. Consequently, the crisis is deeper and the quest for a renewed identity more intense. The dual nature of Judaism, which is both a religion and a nation, complicates matters still further. To re-define themselves successfully, secular Israelis will have to extract from the reservoir of Judaism those values which meet two requirements. First, in order to offset the challenge of modernism, these values must be sufficiently universal to satisfy modern ethical imperatives, that is, they must not run counter to the fundamentals of liberal democracy. Second, they must also be sufficiently specific to make Jewish Israelis distinct from others and morally entitled to their part of what once was the 'Land of Israel', or 'The Holy Land'. That is no easy feat.

The present Israeli predicament demonstrates and supplements the citizen theories mentioned above. The Israeli active quest for a renewed identity in the wake of great polarization supports the thesis that social stability is linked to consensus based on a society-specific identity, while the general recognition that only Jewish values can underpin this new identity supports the contention that the identity of a society rests on core values unique to its culture. Above all, the ongoing identity search in Israel shows the importance people attribute to having a unique collective identity and the impossibility of basing it on universal values alone. Some values are universal just because they are sufficiently vague to be acceptable to all. Their substance is given to them by each society in light of what it deems to be its particular virtues. The variety of interpretations given to democracy are just one example. Whereas American democracy is guided by the principle of human equality and equal opportunity, English democracy by the principle of fair opportunity to the talented, and German democracy by that of formalistic equality before the law.

The link between identity and consensus applies to societies in general, even when they are not undergoing such far-reaching changes as Israel is at present. When Margaret Thatcher wanted to mobilize support for her economic policy, she evoked past English greatness as merchants acting in a *laissez-faire* economy. American presidential candidates invariably recall specific American virtues such as self-sufficiency and human dignity to underpin their proposed policies. The above link is merely more obvious when a new policy changes reality to the point where the syndrome of values on which identity has been based no longer applies. Here again, Israel is not the only contemporary example. The reunification of Germany has produced similar uncertainties in each of the uniting societies. Though both had continued to insist on a vaguely defined common Germanness, their respective societies had actually grown completely apart due to their vastly different social-economic-political systems. When the two Germanies reunited, the two populations discovered their mutual estrangement and the need for a totally new collective identity, because the majority would not revert to the Nazi era, their most immediate common past. The leaders of reunified Germany have yet to articulate values acceptable to the two populations and drawing on a common cultural past.[53]

The Israeli case also augments citizen theories in pointing out the crucial role played by the political leadership in creating a fit between new policies and the requisite changes in identity based on core values. Unless leaders do so, consensus regarding their new policy is likely to be absent, or confined to a small part of the population, resulting in rifts, instability and a loss of leadership legitimacy. Possible reactions to an uncertain identity are political apathy or outright alienation, as was noted in both Israel and Germany even prior to the watershed in their policies.[54] The worst-case scenario is the development by some group of what Conversi terms an antagonistic identity which often results in political violence.[55] For lack of a viable syndrome of positive unique values, hostility towards an out-group becomes the major demarcator of the in-group. German Neo-Nazis are a case in point, as are Israeli fanatical religious nationalists, such as Rabin's assassin. Yet the probability of an antagonistic identity becoming widely accepted in Israel seems remote in view of the general condemnation of the assassination by the vast majority, including the national religious camp. The active search for a positive re-definition of identity, compounded by the wealth of Jewish values on which to draw, also decreases the likelihood that an antagonistic identity will be adopted by default.

Even should the peace process break down, awareness of the identity dilemma it has elicited has become too widespread in Israel to be ignored yet again. Though the exact formulation of a new Israeli identity is impossible to predict, it is unlikely to be devoid of Jewish values, however these may be interpreted.

NOTES

1. According to surveys, his rating as Prime Minister had been consistently lower than that of the Likud leader, Benjamin Netanyahu. In one poll, it reached a low of 32% against 45% for Netanyahu (Gallup, *Jerusalem Post*, 28 April 1995) and never rose above 42% against 46% for Netanyahu (Dahaf, *Jerusalem Post*, 23 October 1993).
2 For discussion of citizenship theorists and references see Will Kymlicka and Wayne Norman, 'Return of the Citizen: A Survey of Recent Work on Citizenship Theory', *Ethics*, Vol.104, No.2 (January 1994), pp.352–81. For the communitarian view, see Amitai Etzioni, 'The Responsive Community: A Communitarian Perspective', *American Sociological Review*, Vol.61, No.1 (1996), pp.1–11. A prominent exposition of the thesis on the post-modern levelling of societal variety is Francis Fukuyama 'The End of History', *The National Interest*, No.16 (Summer 1989), pp.3–19.
3. Anthony Smith, *National Identity*, Harmondsworth, 1991, p.11.
4. Daniele Conversi, 'Reassessing Current Theories of Nationalism: Nationalism as Boundary Maintenance and Creation', *Nationalism and Ethnic Politics*,Vol.1, No.1 (Spring 1995), pp.73–85.
5. See, for example, Juergen Habermas, *Moralbewusstsein und kommunikatives Handeln*, Frankfurt, 1983, pp.54–97.
6. Lilly Weissbrod, 'Gush Emunim and the Peace Process – Modern Religious Fundamentalists in Crisis', *Israel Affairs*,Vol.3, No.1 (Autumn 1996), pp.96–113.
7. For such Arab protests, see Lilly Weissbrod, *Arab Relations with Jewish Immigrants and Israel 1891–1991: The Hundred Years' Conflict*, Lewiston, 1992, pp.11–29.
8. Arie Eliav, *Eretz Ha-zvi* (Glory in the Land of the Living), Tel-Aviv, 1972, pp.46–57, 61–9, 159–61.
9. Yonathan Shapira, *Ha-demokratia Be-israel* (Democracy in Israel), Ramat-Gan, 1977, pp.25–46.

10. Ronen Shamir, 'Discretion as a Judiciary Power: the Politics of Reasonableness', *Teoria U-vikoret*,Vol.5 (1994). In fact, critics, such as Edy Kaufman and Alon Pinkas, have cast doubt on the viability of introducing liberal democracy in Israel when its principles are not applied to the Palestinians: see Edy Kaufman *et al.*, eds, *Democracy, Peace and the Israeli–Palestinian Conflict*, Boulder, 1993.

11. Zeev Ben-Sira, *Tzionut Mul Demokratia* (Zionism Versus Democracy), Jerusalem, 1995, pp.37–51.

12. Efraim Yuchtman-Yaar and Yochanan Peres, 'Public Opinion and Democracy After Three Years of Intifada', 'Israeli Democracy', Special supplement to the *Jerusalem Post International Edition*, Spring 1991, pp.21–9.

13. Mordechai Bar-On, 'The Winter Years 1974–77', *Politika*, No.51 (1993), pp.38–41. Bar-On is one of the founders of Peace Now.

14. Meir Levin, 'A Jewish Peace, a Zionist Peace', *Davar*, 19 August 1988.

15. Zali Reshef, 'The Ability to Influence', *Al Ha-mishmar*, 20 December 1985; Raoul Teitelboim, 'Another Such Occupation', *Politika*, No.2 (1985), pp.17–20.

16. Yehuda Kopel in 'Dialogue of Shdemot and Nekuda', *Shdemot*, No.126/2 (1994), pp.7–14; Azriel Ariel, 'Was the Aguda Method Right?', *Nekuda*, No.175 (1994), pp.16–19; Uri Elizur, 'On the Sin We did not Commit', *Nekuda*, No.180 (1994), p.25.

17. David Hall-Cathala, *The Peace Movement in Israel 1967–1987*, Houndsmills, 1990, pp.145–6.

18. Benny Morris, *The Birth of the Palestinian Refugee Problem 1947–1949*, Cambridge, 1987.

19. Anita Shapira, *Herev Ha-yona* (Land and Power), Tel-Aviv, 1992; Nurit Gertz, 'The Few Against the Many', *Jerusalem Quarterly*,Vol.30 (Winter 1984), pp.94–104; Lilly Weissbrod, 'Protest and Dissidence in Israel', *Political Anthropology*, Vol.4 (1984), pp.51–68.

20. Interview of Ilan Pappé and Tom Segev in 'On Zionism, Post-Zionism and Anti-Zionism', *Ha-aretz*, 15 October 1995; Baruch Kimmerling, 'Merchants of Anxiety', *Ha-aretz*, 24 June 1994.

21. Ilan Pappé, 'A Lesson in New History', *Ha-aretz*, 24 June 1994; Uri Ram, 'The Post-Zionist Debate: Five Clarifications', *Davar*, 8 July 1994; Zeev Sternhell, 'The Zionism of Tomorrow', *Ha-aretz*, 15 September 1995.

22. MERETZ is a merger of RATZ, advocating peace and civil rights, of Shinui which promoted public rectitude, and of MAPAM which supported social justice.

23. References will be mainly from TV and newspaper interviews because they reach a much wider public than the books written by political leaders.

24. David Makovsky, 'We Have Passed the Point of No Return', *Jerusalem Post*, 24 September 1995.

25. Aluf Ben, 'Separation as a Political Conception', *Ha-aretz*, 14 April 1995.

26. *Israel TV*, interview on 8 July 1995.

27. Ben, 'Separation'.

28. Baruch Kimmerling, 'The Non-Peace Process', *Ha-aretz*, 3 January 1996.

29. Yoram Beck, 'The Other Vision', *Ha-aretz*, 28 December 1995; Steve Rodan, 'Peres Spars with Arab Media', *Jerusalem Post*, 31 October 1995.

30. Orit Galili, 'Beilin Seeks Allies, Peres Retreats to Past Positions', *Ha-aretz*, 29 November 1995.

31. Uzi Benziman, 'Where Does This Lead To?', *Ha-aretz*, 1 October 1995; Israel TV interview of Yossi Sarid on 19 March 1995.

32. *Political Programme of the Likud*, February 1995; Israel TV interview on 3 February 1995; lecture held at Bar-Ilan University on 8 June 1995.

33. Ari Shavit, 'A New Middle East?', *Ha-aretz*, 22 November 1996.

34. See, for example, Aluf Hareven at a panel discussion on Jews and Arabs in an Era of Peace, held at Tel-Aviv University on 31 October 1994; Yosef Barnea, 'Not Only Jews', *Ha-aretz*, 12 September 1995; Avishai Margalit and Menachem Brinker interviewed in Netty B.Gross, 'Are We Still All Zionists?', *Jerusalem Post*, 29 September 1995.

35. Ran Kislev, 'Our Men in the Territories', *Ha-aretz*, 28 April 1995.

36. Gutman Institute of Applied Social Research, *Jerusalem Post*, 5 December 1991; Jaffe Center for Strategic Studies, *Jerusalem Post*, 27 March 1995.

37. Smith, *Davar*, 2 October 1986; Gutman, *Jerusalem Post*, 13 September 1993; Dahaf, *Yedi'ot Aharonot*, 6 January 1995; The Peace Index Project of the Tami Steinmetz Centre

of Peace Research, *Ha-aretz*, 5 August 1996.
38. Survey of Haifa University, reported in *Ha-aretz*, 12 September 1995.
39. Gutman, *Nativ*,Vol.39, No.4 (July 1994), pp.29–33.
40. The Peace Index Project, *Ha-aretz*, 6 August 1995.
41. BESA Centre for Strategic Studies, *Ma'ariv*, 3 January 1994.
42. Peace Index Project, *Ha-aretz*, 5 December 1995.
43. Ibid., 5 August, 2 October 1996.
44. Computed from the Peace Index Project published monthly in *Ha-aretz*.
45. Dan Leon, 'Part of the Mideast', *Jerusalem Post*, 24 March 1995.
46. *Shdemot*, No.126/1 (1993), pp.38–43; No.126/2 (1994), pp.7–14.
47. Uri Bar-Ner, 'New Israeliness', *Shdemot*, No.126/1 (1993), pp.55–6; Yosef Agassi, 'Not Normal', *Politika*, No.49 (1993), pp.2–3; Yosef Barnea, 'The New Jew as an Immanent Contradiction', *Shdemot*, No.126/1 (1993), pp.24–5; Yaakov Ariel, 'We Must Change Course', *Nekuda*, No.174 (1994), pp.14–17.
48. Zeev Sternhell, 'Farewell to Ancestral Tombs', *Ha-aretz*, 25 March 1994; Interview with A.B. Yehoshua, *Davar*, 5 September 1994.
49. Yosef Algazi, 'Woe to Us If We Don't Have an Arab Minister', *Ha-aretz*, 13 February 1996.
50. Shlomo Avineri, 'Unifying Power', *Jerusalem Post*, 5 February 1995; Zeev Sternhell, 'The Second Revolution', *Ha-aretz*, 17 November 1995; Baruch Kimmerling, 'The Religion of Nationality Versus the Religion of Citizens', *Ha-aretz*, 29 September 1995; Zeev Sternhell, 'The Zionism of Tomorrow', *Ha-aretz*, 15 September 1995; Yoel Markus, 'Ideological Bankruptcy', *Ha-aretz*, 2 February 1996; Jay Shapiro, 'Icons of Identity', *Jerusalem Post*, 13 December 1995; Dan Margalit, 'A Farewell to Zionism', *Ha-aretz*, 2 October 1995; Michal Widlanski, 'Israel Against Herself', *Jerusalem Post*, 24 September 1995; Yitzhak David, 'A State of All Its Citizens', *Ha-aretz*, 12 February 1996; Ilan Gilon, 'Hi-tech Zionism', *Ha-aretz*, 13 February 1996; Dan Margalit, 'On Zionism, Post-Zionism and Anti-Zionism', *Ha-aretz*, 15 October 1995.
51. A.B. Yehoshua, 'The People of Israel', *Ha-aretz*, 29 December 1995.
52. Gilon, 'High-tech Zionism'.
53. For a detailed discussion, see Lilly Weissbrod, 'Nationalism in Reunified Germany', *German Politics*,Vol.32, No.2 (August 1994), pp.222–32.
54. In the FRG, 66% of young respondents had no party affiliation, according to a Shell survey reported in *Die Zeit*, 6 November 1992; 45% of respondents had no interest in politics and 60% were dissatisfied with the government on which they had no influence, according to *Jugendliche + Erwachsene 85*,Vol.1, Opladen, Leske+Budrich, 1985, pp.21, 124. In Israel, only 11.6% of respondents trusted political parties and only 36% trusted the government, according to Ephraim Yuchtman-Yaar, 'Public Trust in Social Institutions', *Israeli Democracy*,Vol.1, No.1 (May 1987), pp.31–4.
55. Conversi, 'Reassessing Current Theories of Nationalism'.

Elections 1996:
The De-Zionization of
Israeli Politics

DANNY BEN-MOSHE

'Jabotinsky would not have been elected had he run'

Likud MK and Israel's Ambassador to Washington, Eliyahu Ben-Elisar, commenting on the Americanization of the Israeli elections campaign.

'Judgement Day' was how the Hebrew daily *Ma'ariv* editorial described Israel's 1996 elections,[1] but for all that was at stake the campaign itself was uncharacteristically subdued. 'Perhaps the most interesting thing about the current elections campaign', observed respected columnist Yosef Lapid, 'is that the public is not interested in it... Never have so many shown such little interest in so important an election.'[2] In his sardonic fashion, Labour leader Shimon Peres on the eve of the vote quipped that the campaign was 'most disappointing. Not one call of derision, not a curse or a boo wherever I went. I thought, what's happened to this country.'

This unprecedented disinterest and apathy at perhaps the most fateful moment in Israel's 48-year history, on the occasion when the Israeli public had been conferred with more electoral strength than at any time before, can be explained by four main factors. First, tempers and rhetoric were restrained by contestants in the aftermath of the November 1995 assassination of Prime Minister Yitzhak Rabin from which Israel was still reeling. Second, four suicide attacks which left over 60 people dead in Jerusalem and Tel-Aviv at the end of February and the beginning of March 1996, following over ten similar attacks since the Oslo process began, clearly sapped the energies of the Israeli public. Third, the new Presidential-style system of direct election of the prime minister led both candidates to adopt putatively centrist positions – peace with security for Likud's Benjamin Netanyahu and a strong Israel with peace for Labour's Peres – leaving little to argue about. Fourth, the de-centralization of ideology in Israeli society meant that

Danny Ben-Moshe is doing doctoral research in post-Zionism at Melbourne University.

impassioned ideological debate did not feature in the campaign. This fourth factor has ramifications extending way beyond the election itself, and requires careful consideration.

THE CAMPAIGN

The first question Peres was asked at an election rally at Ben-Gurion University concerned neither the peace process nor the fate of the Jewish People. Instead, a young student sought his views on the ecological problems of waste management in the Negev. The nature of this question is indicative of an election campaign which laid bare the increasingly peripheral role of Zionist ideology in Israel.

The absence of ideology is the result of de-Zionization which is facilitated through a process of de-Judaization, under which factors that determine Jewish particularism are negated, thus allowing normalization as a form of national assimilation. Ignorance of Judaism by Israeli youth was noted by the Ministry-of-Education-appointed Shenhar Commission, whose findings are supported by other research, such as a 1993 survey by Yair Oron of the Kibbutz Movement Teachers' College which found that, for over 30 per cent of secular students, being Jewish was not an important part of their life.

Concern over the level of Judaism in the Jewish State was a major tactic in the campaign strategy of the religious parties. With a Hebrew play on words a United Torah Judaism advertisement read 'we are God fearing, but you are fearful', challenging the secular public that they have a life without value, purpose or meaning. Similarly, the National Religious Party (MAFDAL, or NRP) used a secular spokesman to ask secular voters if they wanted a Jewish State and society or spiritual assimilation.

Americanization is the phenomena which is replacing Judaism and Zionism, and the campaign took on an American character consistent with the wider Americanization of Israeli society. This began with the pre-election party primaries – which although in Hebrew are known as *bechirot mukdamot* (literally early elections) were ubiquitously described as 'primaries' – and extended through to the Presidential-style campaign, including the television debate between the two candidates. Labour criticized Netanyahu's American-style campaign, but this clearly failed to have an adverse effect on an increasingly Americanized public, not least since Labour's own TV commercials featured McDonalds and Pizza Hut.

Consumerism is a major manifestation of Americanization, and the moderate political position the prime ministerial candidates espoused was directed at an electorate increasingly concerned more with itself than with issues of national concern. As Lapid aptly observed, 'The favourable economic situation breeds indifference... The public does not expect either an improvement if one party wins or a deterioration if one party loses. That breeds indifference...' There are inherent dangers in this, for in an era of absolute individualism, of 'me' rather than 'us', Israel could embark on a historical course without due consideration that could endanger the future of the Jewish People and the very existence of the Jewish State.

Detachment from Judaism combined with Americanization, with its concomitant consumerism, has resulted in a lack of Zionist ideology. This was evident by these elections being the first since 1967 in which The Land of Israel was not an election issue, despite the fact that its fate would be determined by the election's outcome. Neither of the prime ministerial candidates offered a Socialist Zionist, Revisionist Zionist or any form of ideological Zionist perspective on this previously fundamental matter in Zionist thought and identity. When asked if the ideological struggle for Judea and Samaria was over, Netanyahu – the heir of the Revisionist Movement established by Ze'ev Jabotinsky – conceded that 'we cannot always fulfil our dreams'. A lot has changed in Israel since the previous elections in 1992, when the then Prime Minister Yitzhak Shamir, in reply to the question of why he opposed leaving Gaza, simply stated: 'It is *Eretz Israel*' (The Land of Israel).

THE VOTE

The effect of this de-Zionization process was that together Labour and Likud polled just over half the popular vote, at 51.9 per cent, dropping from 76 to 66 Knesset seats. The two main ideological forces that have built and governed the country for the last 50 years now barely hold the support of half the population, including the all-important 400,000 first-time teenage voters. What has started with a decline in membership at socialist Kibbutzim, and in the Revisionist youth movement Betar, has ended in a major shift away from the two schools of thought which have dominated Zionism since the 1930s.

Although only 14 per cent of the Israeli population define themselves as strictly orthodox, according to an authoritative 1993 survey by the Guttman Institute of Applied Social Research, over 20 per cent of Jewish voters cast ballots for Orthodox parties. The NRP claims to have raised at least one but possibly two seats from secular votes, and the ultra-Orthodox Shas won up to six seats from secular voters, replacing Ultra-secular MERETZ as the country's third largest party! Incoming Labour MK Professor Shlomo Ben-Ami observed of this scenario, 'Jerusalem has defeated Tel Aviv'.[3] In a related development Likud, who are viewed as more affiliated to Jewish tradition than Labour, received 11 per cent more of the Jewish vote than their left-wing rival in the race for the Prime Ministership. These results can be explained by three factors:

- There is still a wide-ranging positive sentiment towards Jewish tradition amongst the non-Orthodox population, especially in the Sephardi community. For these people it is just as important that the environment their children grow up in is Jewish as that it is an environment of peace, and there was a perception during the Rabin-Peres administration that the former was being sacrificed for the latter.

- The new electoral system gave the electorate greater voting flexibility by providing two votes, one for the Prime Ministerial candidate and another for the Knesset. One NRP MK explained that this allowed the public 'to vote one ballot from the head, and one from the heart'.[4]

- Labour's close ties with the militantly secular MERETZ in government alienated many traditional-leaning centrist Israeli voters as a result of MERETZ's hostile attitude towards Jewish tradition. This was compounded by MERETZ's negative portrayal of Orthodox Jews in the elections campaign, which many Israelis, both Orthodox and Secular, felt bordered on anti-Semitism. *Ma'ariv* editorialized: 'Those who lost the election for Shimon Peres were MERETZ members whose smugness, which mocked the national values of the Jews, but related with holy trepidation to the national aspirations of the Palestinians, sent tens of thousands of voters, whose votes would have been enough to decide the vote, fleeing from Peres.'[5] Similarly, the *Jerusalem Post* editorialized: 'That Labour officials such as Deputy Education Minister Micha Goldman have suggested changing the national anthem and even the flag to accommodate the country's non-Jewish citizens may have had something to do with the repudiation of the Labour government.'[6]

Importantly, on presenting his government to the Knesset Netanyahu declared, 'The new government will nurture the values of the Jewish heritage in education, culture and the media.' Policy guidelines of the new government stipulate, 'Education will be grounded in the eternal values of the Jewish tradition, Zionist and Jewish consciousness, and universal values. The Book of Books, the Bible, the Hebrew language, and the history of the Jewish People are the foundation stones of our national identity, and will take their rightful place in the education of the young generation. The Government will strengthen the youth movements and promote youth participation in such movements, in an effort to strengthen their connection to the country and the State.'

However, with budget cuts hitting the education ministry, and with commitment to initiatives addressing the problem of secularization such as those outlined in the Shenhar report in doubt, it remains to be seen how Netanyahu will strengthen Jewish-Zionist education. Moreover, if the interest of Israeli youth is to be re-ignited in Judaism and Zionism there will have to be structural changes to the Israeli educational system coupled with an emphasis on new Zionist ideas, rather than old youth movement formulas which have become outdated.

Of the secular parties, only Israel Be-aliya addressed this issue with any degree of detail, stating that 'the educational system must help students realize their full potential, while instilling Jewish values into their lives'. This would be done by providing 'more hours to in-depth study of Jewish history and tradition, in all schools – religious and secular alike. Introducing a "History of Jewish Civilization" course which will acquaint students with the different aspects of life, tradition and history of Jewish communities around the world' and by expanding 'the network of open universities, educational radio, and television programmes, to teach the history, culture, literature and traditions of the Jewish People in Israel and in the Diaspora'.

That neither of the two prime ministerial candidates addressed the issue of secularization, which strikes at the heart of the future direction of the Jewish People in the campaign, is another sign of the ideological nadir in Israel.

THE DIASPORA

Consistent with the increasingly inward-looking approach of Israeli society, where broad Zionist visions for World Jewry have little place, the Diaspora was a non-issue in the election campaign. Harry Wall, Director of the Jerusalem office of the Anti-Defamation League, commented: 'Ignored is any consideration of the profound changes affecting Israel and its ties with Diaspora Jews.'[7] A World Jewish Congress briefing paper on the elections similarly noted that 'the question of Israel's relations with world Jewry are non-issues. Likud's Netanyahu has spoken of these problems, but clearly does not see them as a matter of high importance. Prime Minister Peres and the Labour leadership have chosen not to deal with them at all.'[8]

This state of affairs should be of particular concern to world Jewish leaders, because it comes at a time when plagued by assimilation they are calling with increased frequency on Israel to serve as a spiritual centre. Yet if Zionist ideology has little place at home, it will have even less of a place overseas. Relations between Israel and the Diaspora may be adversely affected by the rise of the religious parties and Government guidelines providing that 'the law of Conversion shall be changed so that conversions to Judaism in Israel will be recognized only if approved by the Chief Rabbinate'. This immediately rekindled the old flame of 'Who Is a Jew?' with the concomitant rupture in relations between a Government with a strong Orthodox component, and American Jewry which is dominated by the Reform and Conservative movements. As *Ha-aretz* editorialized, any move to disqualify Reform or Conservative converts from obtaining citizenship under the Law of Return would antagonize the Reform and Conservative Jewish communities in the US.[9]

Following the formation of the new Government, three key American Jewish fund-raising groups, the United Jewish Appeal, United Israel Appeal and the Council of Jewish Federations, introduced a resolution in the Jewish Agency assembly calling on the government to abstain from legislation that 'would re-define conversions, or other issues, in a way which may estrange major parts of the Jewish People from their linkage to the nation, to their culture and the Jewish State'. Elsewhere, when officials of the UJA and Jewish Federations presented a statement of support for Israel's new government, the heads of the Reform Conservative movements refused to sign. Rabbi Amiel Hirsch, executive director of ARZA, the American Reform movement's Zionist organization, warned that the campaign of the religious parties against the non-Orthodox would 'disenfranchise' the very Diaspora Jews who are active in synagogues, Jewish federations, and other Jewish organizations.

Contributing to this passionate debate, the National Religious Party daily, *Ha-tzofeh*, accused the Reform and Conservative Jews in the United States of interfering in Israel's internal affairs by threatening to end their support of Israel if religious legislation is passed. According to the editors, such measures constitute an attempt to impose their will on Israelis, advising Prime Minister-elect Netanyahu not to fear these threats just 'to appease marginal elements that want to bring the split within the American Jewish community to the State of Israel'.[10]

Netanyahu does not wish to become embroiled in a debate over the Law of Return with American Jewry. He will seek to rebuild some of the bridges burnt during differences of opinion over the peace process while he was in opposition, and he will want maximum support for diplomatic and military moves that may be unpopular in Washington. Hence, when speaking to the opening session of the Jewish Agency assembly Netanyahu explicitly mentioned Reform and Conservative Jews. Declaring 'we are one', he called for tolerance between secular and religious Jews, a move that the ARZA leadership found 'encouraging'. In resisting any change to the Law of Return, Netanyahu will find an unlikely ally in the Labour Party's Jewish Agency Chairman Avraham Burg, whose attempts to raise $200 million more than last year would be undermined in American Jewish philanthropic organizations whose membership is drawn largely from the Reform and Conservative movements.

Although neither the Reform nor Conservative movement has called on its members to withhold funding, a Rubicon has been crossed since attempts were last made to amend the Law of Return during the late

1980s 'Who is a Jew?' debate, which makes such a move more likely. Since the late 1980s Israel has experienced an economic boom while the Diaspora has been shocked into realizing the magnitude of the scale of assimilation. The Diaspora is under increased pressure to spend Diaspora dollars on local Jewish education, while the economic boom has led to an increasing number of Israelis, such as Yossi Beilin, calling for an end to traditional Diaspora fund-raising. Against this background, a new attempt to alter the Law of Return could lead to a cut in Diaspora fund-raising, although as *Yediot Aharonot* editorialized, any attempt by the Diaspora to impose 'economic sanctions' is 'economically meaningless'.[11]

Instead of severing funding for Israel entirely, Diaspora groups would be more likely to re-direct their funding to groups in Israel with which they identify, such as American Reform congregations supporting Reform institutions in Israel. This is ill-advised, for it carries two dangers. First, it would undermine the collective identification with Israel as a whole, a process which provides a basis for unity both within the divided Diaspora communities themselves and between Israel and the Diaspora. Second, such a move could set a precedent which would be followed by other Diaspora groups when Israeli governments adopt a policy they disagree with. According to this scenario, for example, under a Labour government Orthodox groups could direct their funds to disputed settlements (a pattern which was developing under the Rabin-Peres government).

A further danger for Israel–Diaspora relations which did not exist to the same degree in the late 1980s is the propensity for divisions within Israel to spill over into the Diaspora, as the debate on the peace process has clearly demonstrated. What could evolve is a Jewish World split along Orthodox-Pluralistic lines. It was in this vein that immediately following the elections, Zamira Segev, executive director of Hemdat, the Council for Freedom of Science, Religion and Culture, declared that she was planning a massive appeal to Jews around the world to defend religious freedom in Israel. However, if Diaspora communities are going to win the battle of Jewish continuity they can ill-afford to be beset by internal Secular–Orthodox division in their own communities and in their ties with Israel. Additionally, if the Reform and Conservative movements wish to offer a religious alternative to the Israeli public, they must remember that there is a difference between pluralism and secularism.

Once again, Israel Be-aliya was the only party contesting the elections to address the issue of Israel–Diaspora relations with any degree of seriousness. The party platform advocated that 'the ingathering of the exiles constitutes an essential component of Zionism', and stressed that 'Support for Jewish communities around the world must be a priority'. Israel Be-aliya uniquely raised practical considerations for the Israel–Diaspora relationship in a number of ways. These included proposals 'to involve Diaspora Jewry as an active partner in the development of the State of Israel', calling for re-organization of the Jewish Agency and the introduction of 'a special corps of teachers to be trained to teach both in Israel and the Diaspora, and that teacher and student exchange programmes be encouraged, in order to bridge the gaps between Jews in the Diaspora and Israelis'.

These ideas merit serious consideration by both the Israeli and Diaspora establishments as a means of bringing closer together Israel and the Diaspora, which are drifting apart. Only when mainstream political parties put their minds to the philosophical and practical aspects of the Israel–Diaspora relationship, as Israel Be-aliya has done, will a way be found to strengthen and develop the relationship at this time of tremendous transition in the Jewish World. If they do not do so, they will be abrogating the responsibility to the Jewish World that the Zionist movement conferred upon the Jewish State.

REBUILDING ZIONISM

Overall, Israel is clearly divided on the two fundamental inter-related issues which confront the state: the peace process and the country's cultural identity. Ultimately, division from the former could prevent the unity which is a necessary ingredient in any attempt to successfully establish a broadly based Jewish-Zionist identity which is necessary if post-Zionism is to be avoided. As President Ezer Weizman remarked in his address opening the 14th Knesset, 'since democratic regimes, by nature, cannot achieve total unity, and not everyone can be satisfied, I call on the chosen of the people to do everything possible in order to rise above the internal disputes and to reach the broadest possible consensus, without which it will be difficult to confront our external enemies.' Only by successfully resolving secular–religious differences can the establishment of a modern Jewish culture for Israel and World Jewry be achieved.

Commenting on the divisions with which Israeli society is beset, *Ma'ariv* editorialized that 'the 1996 elections will be seen as a crossroad, in which different population groups went their separate ways', and suggested that the success of Israel Be-aliya underscores the fact that Israel

will never be one homogeneous society, but at least four societies: the religious-traditional world, which today is producing enough energy to be an autonomous unit, independent of the secular population; the world of 'the round eyeglasses', which draws its inspiration from a certain measure of cosmopolitan criteria… which relate to Israeli identity as a kind of extra value; the central stream, which aspires to combine Zionist values with a bourgeoisie lifestyle, based on the

principles of western civilization; and the Arab public, which is trying
to settle the conflict between its life experience in the democratic
society which the Jews have established and their belonging to the
Palestinian people and the Islamic faith.[12]

Furthermore, the success of Shas demonstrates that old ethnic divisions
are far from over. This too must be addressed, for if left to fester it will
compound the divisiveness of the debate on the future Jewish direction
of the state, adding a highly charged Sephardi–Ashkenazi dimension
which could cripple any attempts at reconciliation and unity.

Importantly, in his first speech as Prime Minister-elect Netanyahu
declared before supporters in Jerusalem, 'The State of Israel is going forth
on a new path, a path of hope, a path of unity, a path of security, a path
of peace. The first and foremost peace that must be reached is peace at
home, peace between us, peace among us.' He continued, 'I turn to the
whole population of Israel, those who voted for me and those who did
not vote for me, I say to you that I intend to be the Prime Minister of
everyone.' For the future of Israel and World Jewry it is vital that this is
so. Only if the issues that sharply divide the Israeli nation are addressed –
sensibly, calmly, and candidly – can real unity, healing and progress occur.

If the trends towards secularization and normalization are to be
reversed, all Israeli political parties will have to devote time, thought
and resources to this issue. If Labour and Likud do not do so Judaism
will become the exclusive domain of the strictly Orthodox, which will
decrease the chances of establishing a broadly-based Jewish society in
which Judaism is not only the religion, but also the civic culture for the
majority. For this to arise the debate about the nature of Judaism and
Zionism in Israel must be addressed with the degree of urgency and
importance that is attached to the peace process.

While Labour may be seen to be the party to have distanced itself
from Judaism, both Labour and Likud must do their soul-searching
about the general alienation from Zionism and Judaism. Likud cannot
just lament the development of post-Zionism on the left, but must ask
itself how it let this trend develop by not offering a satisfactory
cultural or ideological alternative. Labour must find a synthesis
between its search for peace and the maintenance of Jewish-Zionist
identity rather than creating the conditions where the two become
mutually exclusive.

If the ultra-Orthodox parties take their new-found power to strictly
enforce the status quo or return to the pre-1992 status quo without
thinking progressively and creatively about the Jewish needs of the non-
Orthodox public, then perhaps this fading opportunity to instil
widespread affiliation, identification, and participation in Judaism will
be missed. An Ultra-Orthodox hardline would unleash a vicious cycle
with MERETZ responding with a secular hardline, so that polarization
and religious secular extremes become the permanent norm. The Ultra-

Orthodox demonstrations in mid-1996 over Sabbath road travel in Jerusalem's Bar-Ilan Street, which were met by MERETZ counter demonstrations, are a sign of such a phenomenon.

For its part, the national religious camp believes it is a post-Zionist mindset which enables secularism and a national detachment from the Land of Israel. Yet, they themselves have contributed to the distancing of Judaism and Zionism through their devotion to the Land of Israel at the exclusion of many aspects of Judaism. As a result, the Modern Orthodox community has become increasingly irrelevant in pre-1967 Israel, yet it has a pivotal role in building a bridge between Israel's religious and secular communities. If they want to counter post-Zionism they will have to consider this factor in the ongoing soul-searching that followed the Rabin assassination.

If the Diaspora wishes to see a revival and evolution of Zionism, which it has vested interest in doing, it will have to offer an ideological contribution to this debate. The Diaspora's traditional participation in Zionism through fund-raising is now largely irrelevant to this process. If Zionism is to be revived it may, under the propitious conditions of a prosperous Israel and a free Soviet Jewry, have to give serious consideration to Western *aliya*.

In the process of dealing with the Jewishness of the state it is vital that care is taken not to alienate the Arab population, for this would only strengthen the post-Zionist cause. The kinds of activity that will certainly not help address this highly sensitive area are Chabad's contribution to the last days of the elections campaign with advertisements that Netanyahu was 'good for the Jews', and a proposal for coalition guidelines by the religious parties that 'Issues that determine the fate, future and security of the Jewish People will be decided by a special majority (that is, a Jewish majority)'.

The Oslo Process has clearly had profound ideological ramifications beyond the re-adjustment of borders, but neither Labour nor Likud have adequately evolved their ideologies to the new circumstance. Unless and until they do so the ideological void in Israeli society will deepen, and Israel's direction will be shaped by non-Zionist perspectives from both the secular left and religious right.

CONCLUSION

The voting pattern towards Netanyahu and the religious parties reflects growing concern at the decreasing level of Jewishness in the state and demonstrates that a basic affiliation to Judaism still exists in Israel despite the growing prognosis of post-Zionism. This allows for the development of a centrist approach to Judaism entailing the establishment of a core system of Judaism in Israeli education and public life with which the majority can identify and unify.

There is clearly a nexus between the decline of Zionism and Judaism, and in seeking to revive both, the Zionist and religious communities must compromise. Balance is necessary if as many people as possible are to remain affiliated to Judaism and Zionism. For this to occur Israel's diverse groups must find common ground which will provide a framework for them to live with each other and with the non-Jewish minority. This can only be done by drawing on common experience which is Judaism, even if Jewish history and religiosity is interpreted and practised differently.

In a 1952 parliamentary speech, secular Prime Minister and founding father David Ben-Gurion declared, 'If the Jewish People want to have a Jewish State there must be Jewish life in it. Without Jewish life there can be no Jewish State.' The search for maintaining a Jewish life-style and preserving and developing a Jewish-Zionist identity in a global village where secularism and post-modernism are the norm is the challenge that now lies before the State of Israel and the entire Jewish People. In this process Israel does not have to follow the extremes of either America or Iran but can be somewhere in between. Its challenge is to strike a balance between the two, one that has not been achieved elsewhere.

Thus, once again a unique challenge stands before the Jewish People; but only by rising to this challenge can Israeli society cohesively resolve the issue of cultural identity and in the process secure the Jewish future through renewed Zionist vision. That ideology will be needed both in an era of peace when Jewish-Zionist character is not forced upon Israel by a state of war or if the peace process collapses, so that Israel has the inner conviction and wherewithal to overcome any military and economic hardships that may arise.

In his first Knesset speech as Prime Minister, Netanyahu declared 'Zionism is not dead'. The onus is now on him to make it a living reality.

NOTES

1. *Ma'ariv*, 28 May 1996.
2. *Jerusalem Post International Edition*, 25 May 1996.
3. *Ma'ariv*, 2 June 1996.
4. *Jerusalem Post*, 1 June 1996.
5. *Ma'ariv*, 2 June 1996.
6. *Jerusalem Post*, 2 June 1996.
7. Anti-Defamation League *Jerusalem Journal*, 7 May 1996.
8. World Jewish Congress, *Policy Dispatch* No.14.
9. *Ha-aretz*, 16 June 1996.
10. *Ha-tzofeh*, 10 June 1996.
11. *Yediot Aharonot*, 1 July 1996.
12. *Ma'ariv*, 18 June 1996.

Towards a New Portrait of the (New) Israeli Soldier

STUART A. COHEN

'Si vis pacem para bellum' (If you want peace, prepare for war). Quite apart from constituting sound strategic advice, this ancient Roman prescription also provides an appropriate normative description of the policies pursued by several states moving towards accommodation with their former enemies. Especially is this so in Israel, where sensitivity to the possible risks inherent in the current peace process is still high and where security concerns retain their virtually axiomatic priority on the formal national agenda. In this respect, as in many others, the tone was set by the late Yitzhak Rabin, and was emphasized in the open letter he addressed to all personnel in the Israel Defence Force (IDF) as early as June 1992:

> We, for our part, shall leave no stone unturned on the road to peace... As far as you are concerned, the possibility of peace can mean only one thing: the strengthening of the security framework... Soldiers and commanders! It is the task of statesmen to bring peace. Your task is to prepare for war. The peace talks must not be allowed to distract our attention.[1]

In attempting to assess the extent to which Rabin's exhortation might have been taken to heart, observers conventionally focus their attention on the mechanical nuts and bolts of Israel's military structure. As a result, the various available analyses of 'the military balance' tend to measure force ratios in terms of hardware (tanks, fighter planes). Manpower too is often reduced to a matter of statistics. Although undoubtedly relevant indices of Israel's military preparedness, these cannot constitute the entire picture. As strategic theory has long appreciated, and as recent research has emphasized, just as important a gauge of potential power is the quality and character of the individual troops entrusted with the maintenance and operation of whatever armour is placed at their disposal.[2] Such is the perspective adopted in the following essay. Concentrating principally on the human component of Israel's force structure, it seeks to provide a synoptic

Stuart A. Cohen is Professor of Political Studies at Bar-Ilan University and Senior Research Fellow at the BESA Center.

portrait of the individual Israeli soldier at a crucial watershed in the country's strategic history.

Existing studies of this particular subject are now beginning to show signs of age. Over a quarter of a century has passed since the appearance of Samuel Rolbant's pioneering *The Israeli Soldier: Profile of an Army* (New York: Thomas Yoseloff, 1970). It is also a decade since Reuven Gal published his more detailed *A Portrait of the Israeli Soldier* (Westport CT: Greenwood Press, 1986). Much of the information in both works remains valid. Nevertheless, the need for an updated analysis of the IDF's human profile is now acute, especially in the light of current changes in the society from which Israel's force complement is drawn. The peace process, particularly as signified by the interim accords with the Palestinians and the Peace Treaty with Jordan, certainly contributed to that atmosphere of change, but they do not constitute its sole cause. Further significant developments include the massive waves of immigration from Ethiopia and the former USSR; successive parliamentary upheavals (in 1992 and 1996), and the traumas of both the *intifada* (1987–93) and the Iraqi Scud missile attacks of 1991. In their own way, each of these developments has also generated radical re-alignments in national perspectives on security and other affairs. Equally profound, albeit even less amenable to itemization, has been the effect exerted by a simultaneous cultural movement away from traditional Zionist values, a movement fuelled by a more liberal press, increased exposure to values associated with post-modernism, and the flowering of a free market economy.

Elsewhere in the western world, the sociological profiles of armed forces have been revolutionized by similar pressures. 'Post-modern militaries' are smaller than their mass-based predecessors of the Cold War era; they also attract a different type of personnel, because they reflect a modified attitude towards the ethos of military service. Few of the men (and, increasingly, women) who now enlist do so out of a sense of patriotism, or in the prospect of symbolic rewards and societal status. Instead, most seek a degree of career satisfaction and material reimbursement, commensurate with the image they project of 'professionals in military employ', an image with which society largely accords. Contemporary military organizations, it has been argued, have been compelled to adapt to that circumstance.[3]

Such is not entirely the case in Israel, where conscription and reserve duty remain compulsory for most females as well as males, and where only a minority of whose military personnel are professionals. Even so, IDF servicemen and women are far from impervious to shifting currents of societal change. If anything, and precisely because they serve in what is still a militia force, they seem to be especially sensitive to the societal transformations that have occurred within the country over the past decade, and hence they differ in many essentials from their predecessors. The purpose of this article is to analyze that discrepancy and assess its extent.

The materials required for such an exercise are far more accessible than was once the case. In itself a token of the IDF's changing societal environment, this development owes much to the greater license with which all matters of relevance to the IDF are now openly reported and discussed, especially by Israel's increasingly intrusive media. Broadly-defined 'security affairs', although still enveloped in a general aura of secrecy (and subject to censorship), are no longer deemed beyond the bounds of public scrutiny. Instead, they have become prominent subjects of everyday discourse, feeding upon, and generating, a growing number of parliamentary enquiries, judicial reviews and press investigations.[4]

The IDF does not always welcome that degree of exposure.[5] Significantly, however, it has not altogether sought to retreat behind a wall of silence. Rather, and in response to the increasing public demand, the Israeli military has itself become a major source of primary data. Especially informative are both the annual reports published by the IDF Ombudsman and the more frequent press announcements which periodically summarize audits released by the military office of social and psychological research, the IDF judge advocate, the Manpower Branch and other sectors of the service. Even individually, the latter sources constitute a windfall for military sociologists. Read together over an extended period of time, they offer a mine of statistical riches, supplying what must be assumed to be reliable and up-to-date data on topics as diverse as charges involving drug offenses (which doubled in the period 1994–95), fatalities resulting from training accidents (20 in 1995, a drop from 25 in 1994, 46 in 1990, 49 in 1984 and 89 in 1978), deaths attributable to traffic collisions (5 in 1995 as opposed to 52 in 1988 and 46 in 1978); and losses from 'friendly fire' during the course of operations (16 in the period 1990–95).[6]

Although invariably enlightening, not all of the available data deserves to be considered equally salient to present purposes. Much, therefore, can be pigeon-holed for analysis on future occasions. Three questions, however, do deserve immediate attention, and will therefore be addressed sequentially in the pages that follow:

- To what extent has the *occupational* profile of the Israeli soldier altered over the past decade?

- How much has the *sociological* composition of the force changed, especially in terms of ethnic background, gender and religious affiliation?

- Finally, in what ways have the *cultural* norms espoused by servicemen been affected by modifications in the values to which non-military society attaches most importance?

CHANGES IN OCCUPATIONAL PROFILE

Notwithstanding the progressive changes which have taken place in the range of Israel's military commitments since the early 1980s,[7] the IDF's formal mission definitions have not been revised. The basic formula remains: 'Protecting the borders of the State of Israel and preventing war activities taking place within Israel's territory'.[8] What has changed, however, is the professional quality of the individual servicemen and servicewoman upon whom the fulfillment of those duties must ultimately depend. These can best be analyzed by examining various components in their 'occupational' profile.

Qualifications for Military Service

In terms of both education and health-care, Israel has always been an 'advanced' society. As a result, and as was reported by both Rolbant (p.210) and Gal (pp.76–96), an impressively large proportion of the males and females summoned to recruitment centres at the age of 18 have consistently attained high scores on the IDF's screening tests. That still remains the case. Nevertheless, figures released in the autumn of 1996 by the IDF Manpower Branch necessitate some revision in the traditional picture of the Israeli soldier as an essentially robust individual. According to senior sources interviewed in the autumn of 1996, only 64 per cent of the most recent conscript cohort was assessed to be physically fit for combat service – a decline from 76 per cent just a decade previously. Over the same period, the proportion of new recruits categorized to be suffering from psychological problems likely to impede their adjustment to military service had more than tripled, to 10 per cent. Much of the discrepancy in the figures can be attributed to the greater stringency of current IDF medical examinations, which have certainly become much stiffer than was once the case. As a result, the IDF has been able to identify those servicemen and women most likely to suffer a mental or physical collapse at a much earlier stage than was previously possible, and thereby to reduce the organizational costs and dislocations associated with a high attrition rate during basic training.[9] But that vindication cannot entirely suffice. Indeed, it is to a large extent negated by the finding that, even of the male recruits eventually drafted, fully one third thereafter exhibit physical and/or psychological difficulties likely to impair their performance. One fifth of the male draft complement are discharged from service prior to the completion of their full three-year terms of compulsory duty.[10]

Only in terms of educational qualifications does the profile of the current IDF soldier show a substantive improvement on previous standards. Gal reported that in 1981 60 per cent of all conscripts had completed 12 years of formal schooling. By 1995, that figure had jumped to 85 percent. Moreover, a growing number of recruits now also bring to the IDF the benefit of prolonged exposure to an expanding range of technological devices, such as computers.[11] The high standards thus set are often enhanced at successive stages of the individual soldier's subsequent military career. In 1995 alone, over 6,500 conscripts enrolled for courses in Israel's Open University during or immediately after their periods of active service (almost one third of that institution's total student complement).[12] In the regular complement, the thrust towards higher education is still more pronounced. Once the exception, the attainment of a university degree is now fast becoming the norm. As of 1994, 90 per cent of the IDF's battalion commanders were university graduates; a majority of personnel holding the rank of colonel and above also possessed a second degree.[13]

Training

In part, the rising educational profile of the Israeli soldier – and especially of the officer corps – mirrors the overall expansion in the number of Israelis attending institutions of higher education, which jumped by almost 60 per cent between 1990 and 1996.[14] It also reflects, however, a deliberate effort on the part of the IDF General Staff to upgrade personnel at all levels. Within the conscript segment, this policy finds expression in the proliferation of pre-draft military courses (*kadatzim*), which have become mandatory for male and female recruits selected for assignment to an expanding range of duties, especially the fields of intelligence and electronic warfare. At the professional level, the tendency is still more obtrusive. Since 1992, for instance, the Manpower Branch has initiated several development programmes which together offer a limited number of talented personnel (NCOs and officers) in field and technical positions the prospect of 'fast track' promotions, in return for contracting for additional terms of professional duty. Significantly, none of these programmes (code-named, individually, *mashav*, *ofek*, *shavit* and *marom*), focuses solely on the attainment of narrowly-defined military expertise. *Ofek*, for instance, also provides opportunities for studies towards a university degree, on IDF time and at IDF expense. Therein, presumably, lies one of their principal attractions, especially since current IDF policy is to make the attainment of a university degree a condition for promotion to the rank of lieutenant-colonel.[15]

Popular Israeli parlance categorizes all such initiatives as symptoms of military 'professionalization'. Although loosely employed – and, indeed, regarded as entirely inappropriate by some of the commanders best placed to judge[16] – the term nevertheless remains instructive. Essentially, it reflects a sense that the IDF has of late attempted to divest itself of many of the quasi-amateur attributes associated with its traditional posture as a 'people's army', and thereby tailor its structure to the more specialized requirements of contemporary warfare. Signs of that development, although already evident by the mid 1980s (and hence duly noted by Gal),[17] have since become far more pronounced. At the end of the decade, Lieutenant-General Dan Shomron, IDF Chief of Staff 1987–91, publicly called for the creation of a 'smaller and smarter' force. His successor, Ehud Barak (COS 1991–95) was even more insistent on the need to adapt the IDF to what he called 'the future battlefield'. The state-of-the-art weapons to which Israeli troops now have access (and which they must expect to meet in war) cannot easily be absorbed into the existing framework, but require a fundamental overhaul of force doctrines and structures.[18]

The IDF from which Barak retired in 1995 differed markedly from that in which he had enlisted as a conscript in 1959, and even from that which he had inherited in 1991. Most obviously is this so in terms of its arsenal. On land, sea and in the air, Israel's primary and secondary battle platforms have been vastly upgraded during the past decade; its entire logistic and communications infrastructure has similarly been transformed, with computerized command and control systems and accessories penetrating every branch of service. Attempts have also been made to trim manpower. True, in absolute figures the total number of Israelis liable for one form or another of service did not decline during Barak's tenure of office. Nevertheless, the size of the IDF certainly lagged behind Israel's overall demographic growth during the same period. In part, that process resulted from the instigation of a more selective system of conscription, especially for women (see below, pp.92–93). More effective, however, was the progressive reduction in summonses to reserve duty, which declined from a total of 9.8 million man-days in 1988 to under 6 million in 1995.[19] Although both measures owed much to budgetary pressures, they also articulated a fundamental shift in the IDF's entire manpower strategy. Gone, apparently, are the days when IDF force planners might seek to reduce Israel's inherent demographic inferiority by simply conscripting every man and woman available for service. Instead, the dominant ethos is on quality rather than quantity and on the utilization of the Israeli soldier's technological literacy to exploit the 'force multipliers' with which the IDF's arsenal is now equipped. Although by no means complete,[20] the acceleration of that trend now seems assured.

As Barak himself never ceased to point out, an improvement in training programmes constitutes an essential corollary to the modernization of the IDF's hardware. From the perspective of the individual soldier, this is indeed the area in which recent change is probably most pronounced. Progress became especially marked after the conclusion of the first Oslo Accord between Israel and the PLO in September 1993. Thereto, and as Barak himself conceded shortly before retiring from office, since December 1987 much of the IDF's attention had been distracted from long-term preparations for the 'future battlefield' by the pressing need to meet the very different challenges unexpectedly presented by the Palestinian *intifada*. Conscripts and reservists from all arms were deployed in large numbers on what were essentially constabulary missions, for which only some units (notably, the 'Border Guard', *mishmar ha-gvul* and 'masqueraders', *mista'arvim*) in fact possessed the requisite skills and adequate preparation.[21] Notwithstanding attempts to rotate counter-insurgency duties in a manner which would reduce their aggregate influence on the battle-readiness of the units involved, ultimately the *intifada* came to hold the IDF virtually in thrall. In reserve infantry and armoured brigades, especially, training exercises (already cut back due to budgetary pressures) were further reduced in length and quantity, and even then frequently interrupted; command attention, especially at junior and middle-range levels, was likewise intermittently diverted. Above all, the challenge posed by what was essentially a 'primitive' form of warfare threatened to reduce the operational (and in some cases moral) standard of the force as a whole. As military historian Martin van Creveld acidly warned: 'What used to be one of the world's finest fighting forces is rapidly degenerating into a fourth-class police organization'.[22]

A review of IDF training programmes conducted in 1995 by the State Comptroller conveyed a far more heartening impression. In just three years, she reported, the force had managed to make up much of the ground previously lost. Inevitably, several deficiencies remain. Altogether, however, the report audits a marked improvement in standards across the entire board of IDF instruction. It also reveals a substantial increase in the time and expense devoted to the conduct of specialized combat-training exercises, especially in the conscript and regular complements. Not even the need to maintain fairly substantial garrisons of elite fighting formations in the south Lebanon 'security zone' seriously retards this development. Now that the Oslo accords with the Palestinians have substantially reduced the IDF's need to deploy large numbers of troops on riot-control missions, it can concentrate far more attention than was previously available to enhancing the quality of its personnel. As a result, new courses of instruction have been instigated (and older courses revised) in an impressively wide spectrum of fields, ranging from armoured warfare to air combat, and from signals intelligence to technical maintenance. Particular care has been lavished on improvements among the various strata of command echelons. NCO courses, for instance, have been upgraded; more emphasis is being placed on the standards and status of company sergeants; instruction in the IDF's Staff and Command College has been entirely overhauled; and the simulation exercises offered to senior officers entirely modernized.[23]

Experience

Underlying the occupational portrait presented by both Rolbant in 1970 and Gal in 1986 was the image of the Israeli soldier as a seasoned combatant, whose martial skills had been refined by personal participation in numerous armed encounters.[24] Such was indeed the case. In the 25 years between 1948 and 1973, the IDF had fought five 'high intensity' campaigns against large Arab armies; it had also conducted a large number of various 'low intensity' military operations against *fedayun* and *fatah* 'irregulars'. This record supplied the IDF with an enormous reservoir of continuous battlefield experience which, especially since active reserve duty remained mandatory for males until the age of 55, could easily be transmitted in an unbroken chain from one generation of servicemen to another. Just how valuable that asset could be was amply demonstrated by the course of the Yom Kippur War in October 1973, when reservists and conscripts combined in order to staunch – and ultimately turn back – the initial tide of military defeat.

Today, the situation is very different. Compared to their predecessors, the vast majority of contemporary Israeli soldiers possess relatively little personal experience of conventional and modern warfare, especially on a large scale. One reason lies in the accelerated rate at which successive cohorts of veteran reservists are now being retired from active duty. In combat units, the 'ceiling' for reserve duty has already been lowered to 45 years of age (elsewhere it is 51); largely in response to domestic pressure, further reductions can be expected to follow.[25] Manpower allocations necessarily reflect that development, and hence largely deflate one of the most persistent of popular myths regarding the force. Other than in times of war, reservists no longer constitute the bulk of Israeli soldiers in actual service. Indeed, according to the Manpower Branch, in 1996 they accounted for just 2 per cent of the total active complement.

Still more pertinent is the change which has taken place in the IDF's chronicle of operational activity. The Air Force, certainly, has embellished its tradition of service, undertaking a distinguished series of long-range strikes and acting as 'flying artillery' nearer to home. But the record of the ground forces displays no such linear development. Operation *Peace for the Galilee*, mounted in June 1982 against PLO and Syrian units stationed in southern Lebanon, constitutes the IDF's only sizable land campaign since 1973 – and even that hardly qualifies since it witnessed relatively few major clashes between mechanized formations. Otherwise, recent IDF ground operations have been confined to three more limited modes: counter-insurgency missions (in the Lebanon, and the occupied territories); company-size border encounters with bands of infiltrators; and stand-off artillery strikes against Hizbollah concentrations in southern Lebanon (such as Operations *Accountability* [1994] and *Grapes of Wrath* [1996]). Israel's deliberate non-participation in any of the land and air battles of the 1991 Gulf War further exacerbated this situation. Not only did it deny the second generation of IDF rank and file of an opportunity to experience large-scale combat, but more seriously, it also deprived the present generation of senior generals (many of whom were still making their way up the rungs of the military hierarchy in 1973)[26] of the chance to test at first-hand their own familiarity with the command and control conditions imposed by the technological 'revolution in military affairs'.

Whether or not a lack of personal combat experience might of itself impair the Israeli soldier's military performance is a question which generates considerable debate. In their public pronounce-ments, successive ministers of defence and chiefs of staff ritually insist that contemporary IDF troops are just as capable as were their predecessors of rising to whatever military challenges they might be called upon to meet. Most obviously is this true, they claim, in the case of the elite *sayarot* (reconnaissance units), which form integral components of every combat arm. Specifically trained to carry out 'surgical' combat operations and high-quality intelligence missions, the *sayarot* have increasingly come to be cast in the role of the 'cutting edge' of the IDF as a whole. In accordance with the model provided by the prototype of the genre, the General Staff *sayeret* (originally formed in 1957), *sayarot* in the infantry and armoured brigades, together with their equivalents in the Navy ('*shayetet* 13') and Air Force (*shaldag*), make particularly heavy demands on those conscripts who volunteer for service in their ranks. Candidates have to meet especially stiff entrance requirements and to undergo an exceptionally tough and lengthy schedule of training. The standards thus set, it is claimed, ultimately permeate the entire Force, whose overall quality of potential combat performance the *sayarot* thereby enhance.[27]

Critics posit a less sanguine view. In the last analysis, they argue, the predominance of *sayarot* owes much (too much) to recent changes in the composition of the General Staff. Once dominated by personnel who had risen through the ranks of the armoured corps, or thereafter of the parachute brigade, the current General Staff contains a high proportion (some 20 per cent) of graduates of *sayarot*, on whose behalf they serve as well-placed advocates. Although understandable, their attachment to their former units is not necessarily justified, since whatever operational benefits the recent growth of *sayarot* promises to confer might be outweighed by the dislocations in overall force structures to which they give rise. There exists no evidence to show that the *sayarot* serve as role-models which the vast majority of IDF combat personnel can hope to emulate. On the contrary, according to one school of thought, the deliberate concentration of scarce talent in a handful of crack units merely exposes, and perhaps exacerbates, the deficiencies in the battle-worthiness of regular combat formations.[28] To put matters another way, the *sayarot* have accentuated the differentials which must inevitably exist in any armed force between the highly proficient few and the relatively mediocre many.

Support for the latter contention would seem to be provided by the current operational record of the IDF as a whole. Since many of the operations mounted by the *sayarot* still remain classified, their own record cannot be easily assessed. Other units, however, are known to have performed less than satisfactorily under fire. Indeed, the recent public register of IDF operational failures is almost as lengthy as that of its operational successes. Since the early 1990s, even conscripts attached to the highly trained Golani and Givati infantry brigades have succumbed with embarrassing regularity to comparatively primitive ambushes in southern Lebanon. On occasion, reservists have performed still more discouragingly. One small but nevertheless telling example occurred in the early summer of 1996, when a patrol of reservists, none of whom possessed any previous combat experience, was mauled in broad daylight by a handful of infiltrators along the Jordanian border, an encounter which cost the IDF three fatalities and the local division commander his job.[29] In the aftermath of the recriminations generated by the IDF's enquiry into the incident, tactical failures were also uncovered in more elite reserve formations. A survey carried out by the IDF parachute school, for instance, uncovered an accident rate of 9.1 per cent amongst reserve formations during training drops.[30]

Structure

Fears that the majority of IDF combat personnel might be losing some of their battle edge are compounded by evidence of what appears to be a still more fundamental occupational malaise. Notwithstanding the General Staff's nominal commitment to a much 'leaner' Force (which the preference for *sayarot* itself seems to encapsulate), the IDF in fact now evinces signs of flabbiness. Particularly unsuccessful have been efforts to trim the ratio between 'teeth' and 'tail', whose disproportion – despite being forcefully censured a decade ago[31] – has since grown even more stark. Only in part does that development reflect a genuine need to expand the rear workshops and similar technical facilities upon which all modernizing armies necessarily depend. More often, it results from a proliferation of administrative and maintenance slots, to which increasing numbers of recruits are directed after basic training.

Recently senior IDF sources have provided various indications of the dimensions of that trend during the course of several interviews. They report, for instance, that only 20 per cent of the total complement currently serves in combat units. Most of the remainder fill the ranks of formations devoted to combat support (14 per cent), technical (18 per cent) and – especially – administrative (27 per cent) duties. As a result, the IDF suffers from a dearth of personnel in some fighting and combat-auxiliary units, whilst administrative posts are frequently over-staffed,[32] as the current Chief of Staff (Lieutenant-General Amnon Lipkin-Shahak) has publicly pointed out. According to the outgoing commander of the Planning Unit in the Manpower Branch, 'grey unemployment' is particularly rife amongst female conscripts, only a small proportion of whom perform combat-related military functions. But the phenomenon is also marked amongst males, a reduction of whose conscript terms (he argues) would in many cases considerably benefit the force, not least by improving its work ethic and reducing costs.[33] Precisely such a policy was indeed advocated late in 1993 by the 'Shafir Commission', specifically established at Barak's initiative with a mandate to study future IDF force requirements.[34] However, since most of its recommendations still await government approval, the movement continues apace towards a more sedentary posture in the occupational profile of the average Israeli soldier. Only a minority are assigned to protracted field assignments. For the majority, military service principally involves reporting for assorted clerical duties from 8am until 5pm, more often than not in air-conditioned facilities located in or near a major city – and even then (since 1992) on just five days a week.[35]

Similar occupational characteristics affect other segments of the IDF force structure. In the reserve sector, they result in stark discrepancies in summonses to duty between combat personnel and those posted to support or service formations. Indeed, one estimate calculates that only 30 per cent of all available reservists are now called to annual duty (some for only a single day per year), and that the entire burden of reserve service ultimately falls on roughly 20 per cent of the nominal complement.[36] Amongst professionals, structural distortions are similarly prominent. In adherence to Barak's calls for force reductions, some 5000 professionals were declared redundant during his period of office. Nevertheless, the total number of personnel on the military payroll obstinately rose. Part of the increase presumably reflects the success of the career programmes referred to above, which were indeed instigated with the purpose of preventing a seepage of talent from the military to the civilian sector. But much more must be attributed to the gradual relaxation of the rule which traditionally compelled most professional IDF officers to retire after only some 20 years of service. As a result, the average age of the General Staff, once remarkably young but already rising when Gal submitted his *Portrait*, has since 1986 crept up by another 4–5 years.[37]

This is not altogether a deleterious process. Indeed, it has been justified and encouraged by Shahak, principally on the grounds that it provides the IDF with access to a pool of experience hitherto often wasted.[38] Nevertheless, it also generates the picture of an inverted pyramid. Thanks in large part to its tradition of rapid promotion, the force still suffers from a dearth of *long-service* NCOs, cadres which in other forces are considered essential vertebrae.[39] Worse still, its total complement of captains and lieutenants has apparently declined over the past decade, in some formations by as much as a half. Senior officers,

however, during the same period came to constitute a far more
prominent part of the IDF's overall profile. Statistics released early in
1996 by Haggai Merom, the then chairman of the Knesset Foreign
Affairs and Defence Committee, suggest rampant job inflation in this
segment since 1985. Broken down by rank, the figures are 41 per cent in
the case of *aluf* (major-general); 30 per cent in that of *tat-aluf* (brigadier-
general); 17 per cent at the rank of *aluf mishneh* (colonel); 31 per cent
at that of *sgan aluf* (lieutenant-colonel); and almost 100 per cent in the
case of *rav-seren* (major).[40]

More significant than the quantity of personnel involved is their
uneven distribution. According to informed media reports, internal IDF
surveys show that in line-combat and combat-support units the
proportion of officers to other ranks has generally remained stable over
the past decade. In rear service and command echelons, however, the
growth in senior appointments considerably exceeds changes in the size
of the overall complement. In the manpower branch the discrepancy
amounts to 24 per cent; in the military police to 43 per cent and in
intelligence to 84 per cent. These trends threaten to make Israel's army
uncharacteristically top-heavy. Even as matters stand, many IDF division-
size formations (*ugdot*) seem to carry a far larger logistic tail than do their
approximate siblings in other western armed forces.[41]

CHANGES IN THE SOCIOLOGICAL PROFILE

Israel's original decision to construct the IDF on militia lines, and hence
to base its force structure on conscripts and reservists, rather than on
long-service professionals, reflected a variety of considerations.[42]
Budgetary calculations played a prominent part; as did more narrowly-
defined military estimates of the country's need to repel the threat of a
massive cross-border invasion. But undoubtedly the main stimulant was
a profound belief in the societal advantages which militia systems were
thought to bestow. These were stressed with particular vigour by David
Ben-Gurion, Israel's first Premier and Defence Minister (1948–53 and
1955–63), and the man principally responsible for creating the IDF and
defining its character. From the very first, Ben-Gurion intended the
military to become an instrument of new Jewish 'nation building' and a
symbolic focus of national sentiment. Above all, he envisioned the IDF
as a bonding institution within whose framework Israel's otherwise
fractured society could be welded into a homogenous whole. A system
of universal and mandatory military service was deemed essential to
that purpose. Only thus, too, could the IDF become, not a segregated
professional sector, but a true 'people's army', and as such
representative of the entire body of the nation's citizenry.[43]

Ben-Gurion's vision of the IDF as a national 'melting-pot' was only
partially fulfilled. True, military service in Israel does perform a

basically integrative societal function.[44] Nevertheless, adherence to the principle of universal conscription has never been entirely rigid. Consequently, although the draft undoubtedly helps to moderate some social inequalities and tensions, the manner in which it is enforced (and relaxed) has at the same time accentuated others. At no point in its history did the composition of the IDF ever precisely mirror the demographic profile of the country at large.

Long ago illustrated by Kimmerling,[45] only four of the most blatant deviations from the norm of equal service need be itemized here:

- The marginal status of Israeli non-Jews was exacerbated by the non-recruitment of all but Druze, Bedouin and Circassian males (and even they were usually conscripted into segregated 'minority units').[46]

- Gender equality was similarly prejudiced by the explicit ban on assigning female troops to combat roles and by their consequent over-representation in mundane clerical postings.[47]

- The anomalous position of the ultra-orthodox Jewish community was underscored by the provisions which existed for either discharges (granted to females claiming that military service conflicted with their religious life-styles) or extended draft deferments (granted to full-time students in a seminary of higher religious learning).[48]

- Finally – and, by the standards of Ben-Gurion's original vision, most ironically – military service also helped to perpetuate ethnic distinctions between Jews of 'Sephardi' (oriental) and 'Ashkenazi' (mainly European) extraction. Principally, this was because of the unequal distribution of respective members of these communities amongst the various branches and ranks. Far from being objective, many of the educational and psychometric tests employed in order to grade recruits and determine their assignments reflected areas of achievement in which Ashkenazim could score more highly than Sephardim. By and large, therefore, (inevitably, exceptions abound) troops drawn from the latter sector of the population were more likely to perform menial service tasks. Conversely, Ashkenazim comprised a disproportionate share of officers, especially in higher-grade support units and of elite fighting units (and figured more prominently amongst recipients of awards for bravery).[49] In this respect, youngsters brought up on kibbutzim, almost all of Ashkenazi extraction, constituted an especially noteworthy sub-category for a long time. Although never more than 5 per cent of Israel's entire Jewish population, they at one stage supplied almost 30 per cent of IDF NCOs, and according to Gal (p.83) a large share of its pilots and servicemen in other combat elites. Rolbant (p.187) calculated that kibbutz youngsters accounted for 40 per cent of casualties in the 1967 war.[50]

Altogether then, the IDF has always been a 'differentiated' force, in which separate segments of the population perform diverse categories of service. A survey of recent developments merely confirms that portrait, and adds to it several further layers of complexity. Whilst several of the older anomalies in the IDF's sociological profile have certainly dissipated in recent years, none have been entirely eradicated and some have become further pronounced. What is more, all are now supplemented by new categories of distinctive service patterns amongst additional population groups. The following sections seek to specify the most prominent areas of continuity and change.

National affiliation

Random reports suggest that the IDF is adopting an increasingly liberal attitude with regard to the military service of non-Jewish minorities. Although the overwhelming majority of Arab citizens, male and female, are still excused the draft, the proportion of Druze, Bedouin and Circassian troops steadily grows, especially in the professional segment. Indeed, in some Druze villages military salaries now rival agriculture as the single most important source of local income. Equally significant are the changes taking place in the status of the troops concerned. In comparison to the past, fewer of the soldiers drawn from Israel's various non-Jewish 'minorities' serve in their own segregated units; similarly, less are subjected to a discriminatory ceiling of promotions. In 1995 alone, the IDF publicized the appointment of a Druze officer to command of a Division (with the rank of brigadier-general) and the graduation of the IDF's first Arab Christian second lieutenant.[51]

It would be incorrect to exaggerate the influence of such developments on the present profile of the IDF. National affiliation remains the primary criterion for enlistment, with the result that members of non-Jewish minorities are still subject to several service disabilities. Most strikingly, the vast majority of Muslim Arab citizens continue to be automatically exempted from the draft (and therefore denied eligibility for some social security benefits to which only ex-servicemen and their families are entitled), principally on the grounds that they would be confronted with an impossible dilemma were they ever called upon to participate in a war against other Arabs. Such considerations carry far less weight in the cases of Druze and Bedouins, whose applications to enlist consequently receive much more positive consideration. Thereafter, however, discriminatory practices continue to be applied. As far as is known, no Druze or Arab troops are posted to computer units, to the Air Force or to the Intelligence Branch, entrance to all of which requires a high grade of security screening. Neither do they serve in many of the *sayarot* and their equivalents. Instead, they tend to be concentrated in two other branches of service. One is the 'Border Guard' (*Mishmar Ha-gvul*; nominally attached to the

Police Force), which relies heavily on Arabic-speaking troops for the conduct of constabulary operations vis-à-vis the Palestinian population in the occupied territories. The other is the regular combat formations on line-duty along Israel's borders, in which several Druze professionals have earned distinction as forward scouts.

This situation produces a lopsided effect. National minorities are under-represented in the elite combat and support units whose role in 'the future battlefield' the IDF considers to be so crucial. By contrast, Druze troops (especially) constitute a disproportionately high element in formations which shoulder much of Israel's 'current security' burden. It is in the latter that they have been most fully integrated into service and there that their officers have risen most prominently in rank. Perhaps inevitably, casualty figures reflect that development. In September 1996, the Druze village of Churpah in the western Galilee (total population just 5,000) suffered its 22nd fatality in combat since 1948 – a concentration of battlefield losses unmatched by any other single sector in the entire country.

Ethnic Discrimination

Discrepancies between troops from Ashkenazi and Sephardi extraction evince similar persistence. Undoubtedly, time has done much to narrow many of the socio-economic cleavages once so prevalent between these two communities within Israeli society at large. Concurrently, the proportion of Sephardi conscripts drafted into high-quality military formations has visibly grown, as has their representation at senior levels of command (illustrated, inter alia, by the appointment of Lieutenant-General Moshe Levi, the son of an Iraqi immigrant, as the twelfth COS in 1983). As a result of both processes, service in the IDF has undoubtedly contributed to the upward mobility which has been one of the most marked characteristics of Israel's Sephardi community as a whole. Nevertheless, the impression of progressive integration thus generated is qualified by evidence that other ethnic differentials within the force remain stark. Sephardim continue to outnumber Ashkenazim in the rosters of conscripts discharged from service because they do not meet basic educational requirements. Conversely, Ashkenazi servicemen continue to enjoy better chances of military advancement. A recent survey of the career patterns of over 2,000 male troops found, for instance, that the promotion prospects of Sephardi recruits decreased the higher they sought to climb within the IDF hierarchy. They were marginally more likely to become staff-sergeants and sergeant majors (29 vis-à-vis 25.4 per cent). At more senior ranks, however, the ratio was entirely different. Whereas some 12 per cent of Ashkenazi recruits became second and first lieutenants during their conscript terms, only 3.5 per cent of Sephardim did so.[52] An overhaul of military psychometric tests, designed to correct their inherent bias, might presumably alter that situation. Meanwhile, however, the ethnicity profile of the force continues to exhibit distortions. Ethnic integration has been successfully attained only at the base of the military pyramid. Its apex remains far more accessible to Ashkenazim than their demographic weight would justify. In 1996 over 70 per cent of the General Staff was still of Ashkenazi extraction.[53]

Gender

Over the past decade, the IDF has taken several steps towards breaking down many of the formal barriers which traditionally placed Israeli servicewomen at a military-professional disadvantage.[54] Female conscripts now possess access to a growing range of duties, with many technical and support units becoming almost entirely dependent on their services as radar monitors, air-traffic controllers and operators of computerized communications systems. Widespread gender integration similarly prevails in field postings, where females now comprise a significant proportion of tank instructors (a posting which demands graduation from the tank commanders' course), medical orderlies and staff officers. Their assignment to front-line roles in other combat units (such as the *Mishmar Ha-gvul*) has also become more pronounced. A particularly symbolic threshold was crossed in November 1995, when in a much publicized landmark decision Israel's Supreme Court upheld a female conscript's claim to be granted entry to the IAF's pilot training course.[55] Nevertheless, as has always been the case, the IDF – like all other armies – remains a distinctly male-orientated organization. In part, this is because of the comparative ease with which females are entitled to claim exemptions from conscript service – and frequently do so.[56] In statistical terms, still more salient is their virtual absence from the reserve segment. (Although the National Security Law of 1988 formally imposes reserve duty on females until the age of 34, this requirement is virtually negated by the blanket exemptions which it grants to married women and expectant mothers). But the IDF's predominantly male character also reflects the influence of a more specifically intra-institutional bias. Not only is the principle of gender segregation virtually enshrined in the continued maintenance of a distinctive Womens' Corps (*Chen*), a formation long dismantled by other western forces. It is also buttressed by adherence to the standing General Staff regulation which forbids the assignment of females to active combat roles, principally on the grounds that they might be exposed to sexual assault should they ever be taken captive in battle.

Equally insidious effects result from the sense that females, because unlikely to perform reserve duty, might also give the IDF a far shorter return on investment in training. Only the most talented of woman conscripts are accepted to the units for which their educational qualifications and psychometric ratings make them qualified. A large proportion continue to be employed in basic clerical functions, where – as already noted – the IDF in any case suffers from over-employment.[57] Political pressures, of which the most important emanate from Israel's increasingly articulate 'Women's Lobby' and its parliamentary supporters, prevent the IDF from responding to this situation by introducing a blatantly selective system of female conscription (which the Shafir committee considered to be the rational organizational solution). But they have not prevented the implementation of successive reductions in the terms of the female draft as a whole. Even formally, female conscripts serve shorter terms than do males (24 months as opposed to 36). In practice, the divergences are still greater. Only 15 per cent of the female conscript complement complete even 24 months of service; the remainder receive early discharges. By contrast, the overwhelming majority (80 per cent) of male recruits serve out their full three years of duty.[58]

The consequences of this situation reverberate throughout the life-span of the servicewoman's career. Exclusion from combat assignments, for instance, necessarily restricts the range of roles to which females might be posted. Equally significantly, it furthermore constitutes a barrier to advancement to the most senior of command postings, for which (even in the equivalent of G1 units) extensive combat experience is considered a *sine qua non*. This explains the persistence with which females continue to be severely under-represented in IDF command postings and why none has ever risen above the rank of brigadier-general. Indeed, a tally taken by the CO of the Manpower Branch in April 1995 revealed that the entire complement of females at lieutenant-colonel and above amounted to just seven (less than two per cent of the total).[59] Figures released to the author by the IDF Spokesman's Unit (relating to 1994) further revealed that, on average, female officers also have to wait progressively longer than their male equivalents for promotion. At the rank of colonel, the discrepancy amounted to 13.4 months.

New Immigrants

Although originally a predominantly immigrant society, most of Israel's population growth between the mid-1950s and mid-1980s resulted from natural increase. The sociological profile of the IDF portrayed by both Rolbant and Gal reflected that situation. Justifiably, both studies employed the past tense when referring to the military's absorption of new immigrants; neither found it necessary to treat this particular class of servicemen as a specific category of analysis.[60] That is no longer the case. Since the late 1980s, almost 750,000 immigrant Jews have been granted Israeli citizenship under the terms of the Law of Return. Of these, some 50,000 arrived from Ethiopia and over 600,000 from the former USSR. Since roughly ten per cent of the new immigrants are males formally eligible for conscript or reserve service, the military-organizational consequences of this sudden and unforseen influx promise to be profound.

On average, new immigrants (*olim*) score even higher on IDF physical and psychometric tests than do native-born Israelis (codified as *vatikim*). Data made available to the author in the summer of 1995 by the deputy commander of the IDF Manpower Branch reveals that recruits do so in every category of evaluation. Eighty-nine per cent of new immigrant conscripts possessed the requisite physical qualifications for combat duty (as opposed to 64 per cent of *vatikim*); proportionately more were graded as future officer material (65 vis-à-vis 53 per cent). Particularly marked was the ratio of *olim* who turned up to induction centres after completing some form of post-high school education (46 per cent, as opposed to a national average of 8.5 per cent). As the same source also shows, however, the IDF can exploit relatively little of the talent thus made available. In fact, almost half (43.6 per cent) of the new immigrant conscript complement labour under burdens generically categorized as 'placement handicaps' (the relevant figure in the case of *vatikim* is 30.2 per cent): in many cases they lack a command of the Hebrew language; they often come from families which have yet to become acclimatized to the country and find a place in its labour market (a circumstance which undoubtedly also impedes the enlistment of their fathers into the reserves); and a large minority (24 per cent, vis-à-vis just 2.4 per cent amongst *vatikim*) are the sole offspring of their parents, and hence excused assignment to combat functions.

One IDF response to this situation has been simply to forego the full enlistment of all new immigrants – and thereby cut back on the extra financial costs which accommodation to the special needs of so large a group would otherwise entail. That policy is now generally adopted with respect to males over the age of 29 on arrival in Israel, who are given absolute discharges from service after just one day of formal duty. Most of those aged 21–29 are immediately drafted into the reserves after only 3–4 months of basic training.[61] Immigrants of conscript age, who now amount to roughly 15 per cent of each annual conscript cohort, receive no such concessions. Hence, the difficulties of their integration into regular military service tend to be particularly severe. A survey conducted in June 1994 indicated that as many as 34 per cent of all new immigrant recruits suffered from what were termed 'severe adjustment problems' (compared to a national average of 9 per cent); moreover, ten of the 38 suicides reported by the IDF in 1993 involved immigrants (four of whom were from Ethiopia).[62]

Many such phenomena are undoubtedly temporary, and must be expected to disappear with the passage of time. In the interim, the IDF itself attempts to moderate their impact – most notably by the conduct of especially-tailored pre-conscription 'preparatory' courses for new immigrants and the maintenance of an extensive (and expensive) staff, specifically charged with responsibility for responding to the immigrant soldier's special requirements. Notwithstanding such efforts, however, new immigrants cannot yet be said to constitute a fully-integrated segment of the IDF's complement. Rather, their conscription has even further augmented sociological discrepancies within the force.

Comparisons between the service patterns of immigrants and native conscripts are in this respect particularly instructive. An analysis of the figures supplied by the deputy commander of the IDF Manpower Branch in 1995 shows that the proportion of new immigrants assigned to combat units (over 20 per cent) slightly exceeds that of *vatikim* (under 19 per cent). But this divergence seems likely to increase. As we shall see below, 'motivation to service' in many combat units is declining among many segments of the native sector; in the case of immigrants, it is reported to be rising (by some accounts by as much as 100 per cent per annum).[63] Even as matters stand, however, the service functions of the two classes of conscripts displays some sharp contrasts, reflecting discrepancies in their relative military status. The proportion of new immigrants assigned to what are categorized as 'quality' and 'technical' functions (less than 10 per cent in both instances) lags far behind the national average (13 and 19 per cent, respectively). By contrast, they are over-represented amongst the IDF's complement of drivers and similarly low-grade logistic troops.

These developments necessitate a further corrective to the overall portrait of progressive sociological homogeneity presented by both Rolbant and Gal. Undoubtedly, the IDF remains an overwhelmingly native force, comprised for the most part of personnel born and bred in Israel. For the first time since the 1950s, however, it is having to accommodate a substantial minority of new immigrant conscripts, few of whom have grown up with the consciousness that protracted military service might constitute an unavoidable stage in their passage to adulthood. The proportional concentration of many of these troops in particular service segments (together with their relative exclusion from others), although perhaps temporary and perhaps inevitable, amplifies their collective impact on the contemporary IDF's overall sociological profile. How long it will take the new differentials thus created to disappear, and how that process might be accelerated, now constitute a pressing concern.

'National Religious' Troops

Fissures between what are roughly designated 'secular' and 'religious' Jews have always constituted an integral feature of Israel's societal landscape. For reasons which need not concern us here, that particular divide has during the course of the past decade become still more salient. Indirectly and directly, it has contributed to various manifestations of political instability and change. Its influence on the profile of the IDF is now becoming equally marked.

The military service pattern of religious Israeli Jews displays a striking dichotomy which, with only slight deviations, generally parallels their affiliation to, respectively, the 'ultra-orthodox' (*haredi*) and 'national-religious' communities. *Haredim* tend to exercise their right to avoid the draft in increasingly higher proportions (in absolute terms, their number has also grown). Females seek exemptions on the grounds that military service would pose a threat to their religious life-styles (a claim which was originally conditional on verification by a religious tribunal, but which since 1978 has been dependent solely on a written declaration by the applicant). Males apply for lengthy deferments by adducing evidence that they have registered for full-time study in a religious seminary (*yeshiva*). Neither of these concessions is at all novel (see above n. 48). What has changed is the degree to which they have been applied. Altogether, *haredim* are estimated to comprise some 8 per cent of the total population. Their proportion in the IDF is very much lower – and declining. Indeed, according to recent estimates, *haredim* (an increasing proportion of whom are Sephardim) have since 1977 been requesting deferments at an annual rate which exceeds the overall population growth by a factor of seven. They now account for almost one third of all Jewish male non-enlistees.[64]

Whilst *haredi* religious Jews are thus of their own volition under-represented in the IDF, 'national religious' citizens (a category which encompasses both Ashkenazim and Sephardim, and which altogether now accounts for some 15 per cent of the overall population) are becoming an increasingly prominent part of the force, and indeed often a distinctive segment within it. That development represents a significant departure from the situation portrayed by both Rolbant and Gal, neither of whom discerned anything extraordinary in 'national religious' patterns of service – and neither of whom therefore addressed its possible implications. That approach can no longer be sustained. One reason lies in the proliferation of company sized fighting formations composed almost entirely of conscripts who combine a shortened period of military service with a five-year programme of study in national-religious seminaries.[65] Another is the growing tendency of 'religious' recruits to enlist in combat services, where they now assume the role previously assumed by members of kibbutzim (whose representation in fighting units has dramatically declined).[66]

The possible implications of that transformation arouse conflicting emotions. In broad terms, the affirmative attitude towards military service displayed by so many national religious troops is welcomed, since it provides the IDF with a pool of high-quality and highly-motivated manpower. At the same time, however, their concentration in combat units also gives rise to some anxiety, principally on the grounds that it might foster military insubordination for religious and ideological reasons. The roots of this particular fear will be reviewed below. What warrants notice at the present juncture is the manifestations of 'national religious' service by which it has been generated. These are easily observed. Once comparatively rare, the sight of a knitted skullcap (*kippa sruga*, the most obtrusive mark of male national-religious affiliation) on the head of an Israeli soldier on active front-line duty is now commonplace. Particularly is this so in those units to which enlistment is elective and selection especially rigorous. The rate of national religious recruits to the *sayarot*, for instance, now far exceeds their ratio in the conscript population (perhaps by a ratio of 3:1). Where available, statistics with respect to the sociological breakdown of NCOs and junior officers tell a similar tale. At a rough estimate,[67] some 30 per cent of all IDF fighting servicemen in these ranks now wear a *kippa sruga*; as many as 60 per cent of those passing out in the first class of NCO infantry courses between 1994 and 1995 graduated from the national religious high-school system; the relevant figure in the infantry officers' training school was 100 per cent. Similarly, between 1995 and 1996 alone, the percentage of national religious graduates of the pilot training programme almost doubled (from 6 to 10 per cent; whereas the proportion of kibbutz members dropped from 19 to 12 per cent).[68]

   Thus far, more senior ranks in the IDF hierarchy have remained largely immune to this development. Beneath the rank of *Rav-Aluf* (lieutenant-general, reserved exclusively for the Chief-of-Staff), the most senior notches in the IDF hierarchy are *aluf* (major-general, of which there are usually about 20) and *tat-aluf* (brigadier-general, of which there are currently 35). With the exception of IDF Chief Rabbis, no national religious Jew has ever been appointed *aluf*; and only four are currently listed as *tat-aluf* (of whom two hold field commands). Whether such might continue to be the case – and, if so, for how long – are questions which analysts continue to ponder. One school of thought posits an upper-limit to national religious military advancement, set (it is thought) by the comparatively early age of marriage of most national religious males and their consequent dedication to family life, which a military career might be thought to preclude. Other observers, however, project a very different outcome. In their view, the penetration of the national religious community to the very highest echelons of the military profession is only a matter of time and must ultimately affect the composition of the IDF General Staff too.[69] Whichever scenario eventually unfolds, the internal complexion of the force has already begun to alter, thereby necessitating yet another correction to previous portraits of its sociological profile.

CHANGES IN THE CULTURAL PROFILE

Even more significant than the recent changes in both the occupational and sociological profile of IDF soldiers are those which have simultaneously taken place in their general comportment. The latter are here designated 'cultural' transformations, a term intended to encompass the attitudes which troops bring to military service and the manner whereby behaviour in the ranks conforms to (or deviates from) norms once considered hallmarks of the force as a whole.

Both Rolbant and Gal devoted several chapters to the Israeli soldier's 'cultural' profile, as thus defined. Of the two portraits, Rolbant's is by far the more effusive. Written in the immediate aftermath of the Six Day War, it was self-confessedly affected by the evidence of affirmative purpose which suffuses the record of that campaign (and to which contemporary American troop behaviour in Vietnam presented a stark, if unstated, contrast). What distinguished the behaviour of IDF troops, Rolbant argued (pp.148–69, 244–47, 291–98), was their sense of mutual responsibility; their dedication to service; their humanity towards enemy prisoners; and their sense that they were performing a mission with which Israeli society as a whole unreservedly concurred.

Overall, Gal struck a similarly positive note. Although critical of the shortcomings exposed during the Lebanon War (especially in his perceptive concluding chapter), Gal was nevertheless confident that the traditional 'fighting spirit' of the force remained largely unimpaired. So too did its character as a 'people's army', in which the narrowly-defined career interests of the minority of salaried troops were subsumed within an ambience which projected military service as an essential rite of citizenship.Survey data, he reported, showed that in the mid-1980s the vast majority of conscripts still showed themselves remarkably eager to enlist for duty (and to volunteer for placement in front-line fighting units, pp.58–73). Once in uniform, moreover, their morale remained similarly high. In part this was thanks to their officers, all of whom are schooled to inspire confidence by 'leading from the front' and setting an example of tactical initiative (pp.143–65). Even more important, however, was the existence of a remarkably tight 'buddy syndrome' within the ranks, itself sustained by the experience of regular and equitable conscript and reserve duty. The bonds of affinity thus forged, Gal argued, not only contributed to the IDF's operational effectiveness. They also eased the transmission into the military domain of humanistic and democratic values basic to Israeli civilian life (pp.231–45).[70]

In many essentials, the portrait of an essentially liberal and idealistic Israeli civilian-soldier thus projected by both Rolbant and Gal remains valid. For most troops, military service remains (as it has always been) a civic right as well as a public obligation. Moreover, civil-military boundaries in Israel continue to be exceptionally permeable, and thus to permit a high degree of lateral interaction between the two domains of national life at all levels.[71] This situation helps to preserve the societal esteem of men in uniform and largely explains why the IDF retains its status as the most widely respected of all Israeli institutions.[72]

Beneath that surface of overall continuity, however, relations between Israeli society and the IDF have undergone substantial change during the past decade. So too, more specifically, has the cultural profile of a growing number of Israeli soldiers. Although many continue to display the cultural attributes listed by Rolbant and Gal, a growing number do not. As much is now candidly admitted by virtually all articulate members of the General Staff. One indication of their sensitivity to the shift is provided by *The Spirit of the IDF: Values and Basic Rules*, which was unveiled in June 1995 by the IDF Education Corps. Compiled on the basis of extensive consultations with both the academic community and senior military personnel, this document sets out to provide servicemen and women with what its authors term a 'code' of military ethics. To that end, it lists 11 basic IDF 'values' and 34 additional 'norms'. These are itemized in the course of 177 pages of original text, a supplementary volume of eight suggested 'readings' and a lengthy appendix of educational 'kits', intended to provide commanders with guidelines and to serve as a work of reference on individual themes.

As the authors emphasize in their introduction, *The Spirit of the IDF* makes no claim to originality. Rather, it purports merely to summarize principles of conduct to which the force has supposedly always adhered (such as 'responsibility', 'the purity of arms', 'collegiality', and 'professionalism'), and to identify the elements of the Jewish and humanist traditions from which those principles of conduct reportedly derive their inspiration. This assertion begs for qualification. Even if there is nothing novel about the content of the 'code', the very fact of its publication nevertheless represents a significant departure. After all, 'norms of conduct' only require official formulation when there exists a suspicion that they might not be self-evident. Such is presently the case. The principles contained in the 'code' no longer seem to evoke intuitive cords of recognition. Instead, they need to be justified by exegesis and inculcated through instruction. Only thus, is the implication, can contemporary Israeli soldiers be educated towards modes of behaviour with which, in an earlier age, their forbears of all ranks seem to have spontaneously identified.

No single circumstance accounts for the General Staff's decision to commission the IDF's 'code of ethics'. In immediate terms, the process owes its origins to revelations of deviant and/or criminal Israeli troop conduct vis-à-vis Palestinian civilians during the course of the *intifada*, which resulted in the instigation of over 200 judicial proceedings against individual soldiers and their immediate superiors.[73] Probably just as important a stimulant, however, was a less tangible (but even more profound) sense that instances of IDF misconduct during the *intifada* might constitute just an extreme expression of a fundamental change in values which had begun to affect numerous other areas of army life. Why such changes might be taking place remains a matter for considerable debate. Do they reflect the morally destructive influence of over a quarter of a century of military rule over the 'territories' and their Palestinian inhabitants, as left-wing critics of Israel's security policies since 1967 frequently claim? Are they the consequence, rather, of wider cultural changes in Israeli society, whose overall ambience seems to have lost much of the ideological purity (and innocence) by which it was once supposedly motivated, and to have become altogether more cynical and hedonistic?[74] The discussion which follows makes no attempt to adjudicate between these views and their various permutations. Its purpose, rather, is merely to identify those indications which deserve to be considered most indicative of cultural change within the IDF and to analyze their possible implications.

Three indicators of current modifications in the Israeli soldier's cultural profile warrant particular attention:

• IDF troops of the late 1990s appear to be far more susceptible than were their predecessors to the pressure of extra-military influences on operational conduct.

• They are also more prone to permit politically motivated considerations to intrude upon their behaviour in uniform.

• Finally, and perhaps most important of all, many are also displaying attitudes towards military service which differ in several significant respects from the altruistic enthusiasm which Rolbant and Gal considered so predominant.

Extra-Military Influences on Military Conduct

As the late Dan Horowitz noted, the militia forces maintained by 'nations in arms' can constitute double-edged swords. Because composed for the most part of conscripts and reservists, they are far less likely than entirely 'professional' forces to develop an ethos of conduct which might be distinctive from (if not at variance with) that of the society from which they are drawn. For precisely the same structural reasons, however, a 'people's army' also tends to be especially responsive to broad shifts in national cultural perceptions with respect to the uses of armed force in general and to the societal status of the military in particular.[75] That is precisely what now seems to be happening to the IDF. The conditions which once enveloped the force in an aura of protective custody no longer hold. Its claim to constitute an incorruptible custodian of national Israeli virtues has been dented by sporadic exposes of both lapses in discipline and financial mismanagement in high places. More generally, its virtually totemistic status as the embodiment of new Jewish statism has been undermined by a protracted erosion in many of the civic values and symbols once considered axiomatic features of Israel's political culture. Largely as a result of both processes, senior military personnel, who in the immediate aftermath of the Six Day War (especially) were considered virtually infallible, have since 1973 become progressively 'demythologized', and hence gradually dispossessed of the virtual immunity to censure which their rank once almost automatically ensured.

Relationships between the IDF and the families of its servicemen provide one index of the sort of extra-military pressures to which the new climate of opinion gives rise. Increasingly, commanders at all levels are finding it necessary to make special provisions to accommodate parental demands for a say in determining the conditions under which their children serve and even the units in which they do so. Almost as a matter of course, parents of new recruits now receive the personal telephone numbers of their childrens' commanding officers. They are also invited to periodic 'parents' days', at which they enjoy an opportunity to air whatever grievances they might have. Many go much further. In recent years, formally constituted parental 'lobbies' have voiced public opposition to individual military appointments (on the grounds that the candidate concerned had been disciplined for offenses committed in a previous command) and, on one notorious occasion, to appeal successfully against the sentences passed on servicemen found guilty of desertion from their postings.[76] Equally indicative of the trend is the finding that one in every five of the complaints now addressed to the IDF Ombudsman emanate from parents and contain allegations of the mistreatment of their offspring.[77]

Analysts have yet to ascertain how much such phenomena might owe to the fact that so large a proportion of the fathers and mothers of today's conscripts (unlike their grandparents) are themselves veterans of the force, in which many still serve as reservists.[78] Its consequences, however, require little speculation. In the terms frequently employed by senior IDF officers, the current generation of parents has clearly crossed the line demarcating 'involvement' from 'interference'. In so doing, the same sources claim, they have (unwittingly) embarked on a path which seriously undermines the IDF's efforts to socialize new recruits into the realities of their new environment and thereby transform 'children' into 'soldiers'.[79] Other observers are still more critical. How much confidence, they ask, can be vested in troops who (as press photographs show) require the active physical assistance of their parents in order to complete the route march which marks the conclusion of infantry training courses? How mature are recruits who report to induction bases equipped with mobile telephones, symbols of their continued dependence on constant contact with their homes? Can they be relied upon to maintain the traditions of personal initiative and resourcefulness from which (as Rolbant and Gal stressed) so much of the IDF's reputation for tactical excellence once derived?[80]

The pertinence of such questions is compounded as a result of the influence simultaneously being exerted on the IDF by the process of judicial review.[81] Israel's legal system, once extremely compliant in its virtual subservience to the Defence establishment's broad interpretation of 'state security', has during the past decade adopted an attitude of increasing encroachment with respect to military affairs (and many others). Quite apart from severely curtailing the autonomy of the IDF censor, the civil courts now also exercise their prerogative to review and pass judgement on military behaviour in numerous spheres. One prominent instance is provided by the controversy which erupted during the *intifada* over the legality of the IDF's rules of engagement vis-à-vis Palestinian civilians. But that instance of judicial encroachment, although particularly significant, was by no means singular. Arguing that 'nothing lies beyond the bounds of judicial evaluation', the Supreme Court has also responded to calls that it pass comment on a wide range of other military-related issues, including (as already noted) the congruity of specific postings with the principle of gender equality. Families of soldiers who lost their lives during training exercises or operational missions (by far the most effective of the parental 'lobbies' referred to above) have insisted that the process be extended still further.[82] The IDF, they claim, cannot be expected to conduct an impartial investigation into such instances, which must therefore be subjected to judicial review by a civilian tribunal empowered to assess liability and apportion responsibility.

Without necessarily harking back to days when military immunity to all but the most extreme cases of misconduct was virtually assured, some observers nevertheless feel that the process of judicial encroachment might prove intimidating. Already, they suggest, it creates a widespread feeling that every officer on duty requires the services of an attorney, with whom he must consult before exercising the attributes of command. Confronted with the spectre of highly-publicized investigation by a civilian court, some commanders (it is claimed) now fear to exercise the sort of independent initiatives for which middle-rank officers in the IDF were once famed. Considering discretion to be the better part of valour, they instead prefer to refer decisions to their superiors or to play safe by 'going by the book'. Their self-confidence can hardly be increased by evidence which indicates that senior staff, when subject to similar pressures, often prefer to pass the buck of culpability downwards to the lowest feasible level of command, rather than accept responsibility for outcomes which their own orders were perhaps not comprehensive enough to cover.[83]

Political Pressures

Though parental or judicial intrusions on military life might thus modify the traditional cultural profile of the Israeli soldier, neither place at risk the fundamental cohesion of the IDF as a whole. Such is not the case, however, with respect to the growing influence of political affiliations and values on the loyalties of servicemen and their behaviour in uniform. Usually expressed through the medium of conscientious objection, this particular brand of extra-military pressures threatens to undermine the unity of the force and thereby to impair its operational utility.

Other than in the case of orthodox women who claim exemption from conscription on the grounds that military service might contradict their religious life-styles, Israeli law makes no allowances whatsoever for conscientious objection. During the vast majority of the IDF's history, neither were any such concessions required, primarily because blanket refusals to perform any military duty whatsoever for specifically pacifist reasons have been altogether exceptional. Thanks in large part to the absence within the Jewish religious tradition of anything comparable to the pacifist strain which runs through much Christian teaching, that still remains the case. Nevertheless, within the past decade, a phenomenon best termed as 'selective conscientious objection' has become increasingly prevalent. This does not posit a contradiction between all military service and a sectoral vocation or way of life. Rather, it articulates opposition to a precise type of military duty or to service in a specified locality at a specific time. As such, it constitutes a form of political protest against the government's use of the armed forces on particular missions.

Even in that limited form, conscientious objection was before 1982 so rare as to be statistically irrelevant.[84] Accordingly, it received no mention in the 'profile' of the force which Rolbant published in 1970. However, by the mid-1980s, when Gal composed his *Portrait*, the phenomenon could no longer thus be ignored. The Lebanon campaign of 1982–85 had already generated deep fissures in the Israeli public's traditional consensus on security affairs. As a result, Gal reported (pp.158–59, 184–85, 248–89), signs of political dissent were permeating the ranks. In 1982–83 alone, 86 reservists registered their conscientious objection to what they castigated as an 'unnecessary' (hence unjust) campaign by refusing orders to report for active service in the Lebanon; as many as five times that number gave formal or informal notice of their intention to do so, thereby reportedly compelling the IDF to withdraw their call-up papers. One brigade commander went as far as to resign his commission in the midst of battle. Altogether, it appeared, the posture of non-partisan neutrality previously nurtured by personnel in IDF uniform (conscripts, reservists and regulars alike) was beginning to give way to forthright expressions of political opinion.

From one perspective, events since 1986 have merely confirmed that trend. It became particularly pronounced during the *intifada* of 1987–93. Against a background of increasingly intense public controversy over the rights and wrongs of IDF operations during the Palestinian uprising, the incidence of conscientious objection steadily rose. According to official IDF statistics, 181 conscripts and reservists were placed on trial prior to 1993 for refusing orders to serve in 'the territories'; many more (the numbers cannot be computed with any precision) opted to express 'grey' disobedience, usually by informing their commanding officers of their attitudes and requesting transfers to other duties.[85] Hence, although conscientious objection undoubtedly remained a marginal phenomenon in Israeli military life, still confined to the peripheries of the overall complement, it had clearly emerged from the closet of public discourse. By the late 1980s, the right to ideologically-motivated military disobedience was being openly advocated by such extra-parliamentary pressure groups and watch-dogs as *Yesh Gevul* ('There is a Limit') and *Be-tselem* (The Israel Information Centre for Human Rights in the Occupied Territories). It also appeared intermittently on the agendas of the more liberal knesset factions. Soon after Likud's return to power in May 1996, 30 reservists attached to elite combat units re-iterated these themes, proclaiming their intention to refuse orders to undertake duties which they considered incompatible with the cause of Israeli–Palestinian reconciliation.[86]

Meanwhile, however, the phenomenon of conscientious objection amongst IDF troops had taken an entirely new turn. Until the early 1990s, almost all the IDF citizen-soldiers who refused summonses to military duty professed left-wing political opinions. Between 1993 and the summer of 1996, however, just one conscientious objector tried by a military court could be thus categorized.[87] Instead, the main locus of conscientious objection had shifted to the right of the Israeli ideological spectrum. That change first became pronounced with the conclusion of the Oslo Accord, signed by the Rabin government and the PLO in September 1993. The prospect that the Palestinian Authority would eventually gain control over much (perhaps all) of Judea and Samaria aroused visceral emotions, surpassing all other issues as the single most definitive fault-line between Right and Left in Israeli life. Feelings ran particularly high in the national-religious community, much of which regards those regions as part of 'Greater Israel' and hence as an inalienable portion of the Holy Land. Thus seen, refusal to participate in military activities designed to relinquish the Divinely-endowed patrimony became a fulfillment of a Divine command.[88]

Such opinions have been regularly (indeed, often stridently) voiced in *Nekuda*, the monthly bulletin of Jewish settlers in Judea, Samaria and the Gaza Strip.More methodically, they have on several occasions also been condoned by some of the rabbinical authorities whom many 'national religious' troops regard as their spiritual guides. A particularly striking instance occurred in July 1995, when a self-styled 'Union of Rabbis on Behalf of the People of Israel and the Land of Israel' issued a widely-distributed manifesto entirely devoted to an elucidation of the dilemma which might arise were military orders ever to conflict with religious injunctions. Although re-affirming their commitment to educate their pupils to service in the IDF, the authors nevertheless clearly demarcated the boundaries of military authority.

> We determine that the *Torah* [Divine Law] forbids the dismantlement of IDF bases and [their] transfer to gentile authorities....it is clear and simple that every Jew is forbidden to take part in any action which might facilitate the evacuation of a settlement, [military] camp or installation.[89]

The wave of remorse which followed Rabin's assassination in November 1995 (not incidentally, the crime was committed by a religious reservist who claimed to follow the dictates of 'Greater Israel' teachings) has undoubtedly ameliorated the aggressive tone of public debate which such announcements fuelled. Nevertheless, right-wing advocacy of the sentiments which they conveyed remains pronounced. The Netanyahu government, too, has been accused of 'betraying the nation's patrimony' by continuing negotiations for further troop re-deployments on the West Bank, with the result that the spectre of religiously-motivated conscientious objection to participation in such missions remains a pronounced feature of Israel's military landscape. This situation does not necessarily imply that the IDF stands on the verge of possible disintegration, generated by clashes of opinion between troops holding divergent political opinions. It does, however, bear testimony to the extent of the erosion already taking place in the cultural profile of the force as a whole. Once a symbol and embodiment of the integrative ethos of 'Statism', the IDF is now regarded by many troops as the executive arm of a partisan point of view. Should that impression spread still further throughout the ranks, compliance with orders might become altogether conditional on their congruence with the sectional affiliations of those to whom they are addressed.

Changing Attitudes Towards Military Service

As recently as the mid-1980s, the received wisdom still maintained that the overwhelming majority of Israeli soldiers (conscripts, reservists and regulars alike) undertook military service out of a sense of national duty, and not because they were either compelled to do so or in the expectation of financial reward. Admittedly, towards the end of the decade, Gal did indicate portents of change. Some professionals, he then wrote, were exhibiting some incipient signs of what Moskos had termed an 'occupational' rather than an 'institutional' relationship to the force, most notably by viewing their military careers as a stepping-stone to subsequent advancement in the private sector or in other public agencies.[90] But these instances, he hastened to add, were untypical, and were vastly outnumbered by those for whom military service provided a symbolic – even ritualistic – way of communicating their citizenship and asserting their commitment to the nation's well-being. Where available, statistics seemed to confirm that perception. Notwithstanding the vagaries of public mood apparent during the Lebanon War and the *intifada*, 'motivation' to service seemed to remain consistently high. Surveys which Gal himself conducted in 1980, 1984 and 1988 indicated that some 90 per cent of Jewish Israeli 18-year-olds looked forward to their enlistment, and expressed a willingness to serve even were conscription voluntary.[91] Reservists and regulars seemed equally enthusiastic. By most accounts, the former were reporting for duty with their accustomed regularity and good cheer and the latter contracting for additional terms of service in unprecedentedly high numbers.[92]

For some years now, observers have suspected the validity of this rose-tinted picture. Random media reports indicating an erosion in the 'stigma' once attached to non-enlistment amongst some segments of youth sounded one warning bell; another could be heard in the complaints voiced by reservists (and their wives) of inequalities in the distribution of reserve duty.[93] Nevertheless, not until the mid-1990s did the IDF itself show any inclination to grasp these particular nettles. By then, however, matters had assumed a momentum of their own. A further survey revealed that expressions of an affirmative attitude to military service amongst high-school students had dipped to under 75 per cent.[94] After considerable pressure, senior sources in the Manpower Branch confirmed, in November 1996, that 'motivation to service' (measured by willingness to serve in combat units) had declined at an annual rate of 2 per cent since 1992. In a series of public announcements, the new Chief-of-Staff (Lieutenant-General Amnon Lipkin-Shahak) resorted to more colourful language. 'We are witnessing a preference for the individual over the collective', he claimed. As a result, 'droves' of conscripts now resist enlistment in combat units. The situation was still worse in reserve formations, where applications for exemption from service had assumed 'epidemic' proportions.[95]

Whether those trends might be reversed (and if so how) is now under investigation by multiple commissions of enquiry. Already recognized, however, is the need for a more discriminate analysis of the available data than many of the immediately catastrophist reviews allowed. For one thing, the decline in motivation does not affect all units in equal proportions. Elite fighting formations, for instance, suffer no dearth of volunteers. Indeed, applications for recruitment into the various *sayarot* still exceeds available places by a ratio of 8 to 1. In the Air Force Pilot Training Course, the figures are 20:1.[96] A similar situation prevails in specialized technical branches associated with electronic warfare and computer systems, where recruits can expect to acquire the skills and experience most sought by subsequent civilian employees. Where the decline in motivation makes itself felt, however, is in the less 'glamorous' (and much more labour-intensive) combat and support postings, such as field engineers, drivers and some infantry and artillery sections. In the questionnaire which (since August 1994) recruits receive prior to enlistment, a dwindling ratio express a preference for such units; once assigned to them, many now claim to suffer from a medical disability, and apply for transfer to clerical duties. Roughly 4 per cent prefer to go to prison rather than to their allotted postings; another 10 per cent have to be physically man-handled on to the transports waiting to take them to their courses of basic combat training.[97] Colloquially known as the 'sayeret or nayeret [paper]' syndrome, such tendencies do not necessarily express a mass aversion to all military duty. Rather, they reflect a more subtle shift in priorities. For a growing number of contemporary Israeli recruits, considerations of personal satisfaction (assessed in terms of either future job prospects or immediate ego gratification) now take precedence over a sense of patriotic pride.

A second noteworthy feature of the phenomenon is its uneven spread amongst different segments of the population. The decline in motivation to service seems to be most pronounced amongst native-born youth from a secular and middle-class background, who supply the majority of the IDF's annual intake (and amongst whom Kibbutz youngsters constitute a specific sub-category, numerically small but, in view of their past record, symbolically prominent).[98] To a lesser extent, it can also be discerned in some new immigrant circles, particularly where the concentration of Russian emigres (70 per cent of the new immigrant population) is high.[99] By comparison, however, the 'national religious' community has been affected to a much smaller extent. Moreover, according to survey published in 1996, the decline in intention to enlist for a full three years of service amongst secular high-school students amounted to 14 per cent over the period 1986–95 (from 82 to 68 per cent); in religious high schools, by comparison, the relevant figure was much lower (from 86 to 81 per cent). Similar differentials emerge at other levels of enquiry. In 1995, 34 per cent of the secular respondents announced an intention of volunteering for combat units (down from 48 per cent in 1986) and 22 per cent to do so as officers (down from 31 per cent in 1986). Amongst religious respondents, the comparable figures were 49 and 35 per cent respectively in 1995, and 55 and 36 per cent in 1985.[100]

Various hypotheses have been advanced to explain that discrepancy.[101] One view focusses on the different levels of parental encouragement given to secular and 'national religious' groups. Another, more specifically, directs attention to the more 'patriotic' values inculcated in the national-religious network of high schools, youth movements and pre-draft colleges (which specifically educate towards service in combat units and where enrolment has multiplied some four times over the past decade). Yet a third hypothesis cites the influence of peer pressure, exerted by the fact that some national-religious recruits serve in their own segregated *hesder* units. Probably more instructive than the variations in such analyses is their common denominator: all suggest that, as a group, national-religious conscripts constitute almost the last vestige of the traditional type of Israeli soldier. Many of their secular counterparts – who together make up the majority of the IDF's overall force complement – now project an entirely different cultural profile. Raised in a progressively iconoclast ('post-Zionist') atmosphere, they have begun to substitute a cluster of inner-directed values for the ethos of collective compliance, thereby imparting a novel meaning to the notion of military service and its purposes.

Willy-nilly, the IDF has been compelled to adjust to that change. For the most part, it does so by seeking to improve the material compensation which troops can now expect to receive in return for their investment of time and energy. That approach marks a radical departure from the traditional view of military duty as a civic obligation, for which no pecuniary return was either sought or given. Not surprisingly, it therefore encounters considerable resistance in some quarters. Nevertheless, the process now extends throughout the force. Conscripts attached to combat units, for instance, have since 1995 received almost double the pocket-money paid to rear echelons. Intermittently, successive Chiefs of Staff have suggested that similar differentials be applied to reservists, with those summoned for especially lengthy tours of duty being entitled to tax rebates.[102] Most noteworthy of all, however (and far more radical) has been the IDF's corporate insistence that its professional cadres receive material renumeration commensurate with the priority of the national service which they perform.

Claims that IDF professionals are entitled to a preferential salary scale, although not entirely novel, have certainly gained increasing momentum over the past decade. As recently as 1984, the then Chief-of-Staff (Refael Eitan) had sufficient confidence in the altruism of his personnel to announce that they would voluntarily forego the 6.9 per cent pay rise granted to all government employees. The climate presently pervading the force discourages any such flourish. In the interval, IDF professionals have been granted considerable wage increments, which have accustomed them to an entirely different standard and have enabled them to leap-frog their equivalents in other public-service sectors, often by a margin of 20 per cent. That gap becomes even wider when calculations are extended to include their various fringe benefits – prominent among which are housing, car and recreation allowances, tax rebates, retirement bonuses and, above all, a particularly generous pension scheme.[103]

Treasury officials calculate that the proportion of domestic defence expenditure devoted to these various entitlements has almost doubled over the past decade (from 27 to 48 per cent), a statistic whose import is magnified by the finding that expenditure on acquisitions and services has dropped by roughly the same amount and that the overall proportion of the domestic GNP devoted to defence has been halved, to roughly 11 per cent.[104] This intolerable burden on the national budget, they insist, must be cut. But spokesmen for IDF interests vigorously – and publicly – reject that suggestion, principally on the grounds that its implementation would be bound to exert a dangerously adverse influence on long-term professional recruitment. Appearing before the Knesset's Foreign Affairs and Defence Committee in July 1996, the Chief-of-Staff advised that the professional servicemen whom the IDF most requires (especially in areas of 'hi-tech' specialization) could only be attracted to service by the promise of salaries similar to those offered in the civilian sector. At the same time, the Commander of the Manpower Branch warned that even the hint of wage-cuts had already led 'numerous' officers to submit their resignations.[105] Subsequent protestations of devotion to duty (even at reduced incomes) by several commanders did little to alter the impression thus created. The 'cultural' profile of many IDF professional soldiers has begun to change in parallel with that of a growing number of conscripts and reservists – and largely for the same reasons. Influenced by the mores pervading the society of which they feel a part, few now express a willingness to subordinate personal considerations, as measured in terms dictated by the market-place, to the collective good. Instead, unprecedented numbers insist (sometimes vehemently so) on as much financial compensation for their military services as society can afford to pay. In the words of the commander of the IDF Staff and Command College:

> The plague of careerism has begun to spread amongst us. Fewer of us ask themselves what we might give to the army and country. Instead, we check to see what we have received, and what more we might get.[106]

By the standards of all previous portraits of the IDF soldier, that constitutes a shift of seismic proportions.

CONCLUSIONS

How the IDF might respond to the changes thus taking place in the occupational, sociological and cultural profile of its complement now constitutes a topic of major public concern. The polarity of the principal solutions currently being advocated testifies to the complexity of the task. Arguing that Israel still requires a 'people's army', one school of thought advocates investment in a series of educational programmes which might restore society's faith in the viability of a militia-based force, with all that is thereby implied in the concept of military service as an essential rite of passage to full citizenship.an alternative view, however, rejects all such attempts to turn the clock back. Instead, it suggests that the IDF follow the lead taken elsewhere in the western world, principally by accommodating itself to current alterations in the received portrait of the Israeli soldier and therefore re-constituting the entire force on more explicitly 'professional' lines. Given the place which the IDF continues to occupy in the national consciousness, debates over the respective rights and wrongs of these two proposals (and various intermediate variants) promise to be both emotionally-charged and protracted. Their ultimate resolution must be expected to affect not only the structure of Israel's military but – perhaps even more so – the very fabric of Israeli society at large.

NOTES

Research for this article was funded by the Israel Science Foundation, administered by the Israel Academy of Sciences and Humanities. The author also gratefully acknowledges the research assistance of Mr. Ya'akov Green.

1. Reprinted in *Davar* (Hebrew daily, Tel-Aviv), 27 September 1992.
2. C. Downes, 'Military Manpower: Strategic Asset, Liability, or non-Entity', *Defense Economics*, Vol.2 (1991), pp.353–63; S. Biddel, 'Victory Misunderstood: What the Gulf War Tells Us about the Future of Conflict', *International Security*, Vol.21 (1996), pp.139–79.
3. J. Burk, 'The Decline of Mass Armed Forces and Compulsory Conscription', *Defense Analysis*, Vol.8 (1992), pp.45–59; C. Dandeker, 'New Times for the Military: Some Sociological Remarks on the Changing Role and Structure of the Armed Forces of the Advanced Societies', *British Journal of Sociology*, Vol.45 (1994), pp.637–54; C.C. Moskos and J. Burk, 'The Postmodern Military', in J. Burk, ed., *The Military in New Times: Adapting Armed Forces to a Turbulent World*, Boulder, 1994, pp.141–62; G. Daniker, *The Guardian Soldier: On the Nature and Use of Future Armed Forces* Geneva, 1995, esp.pp.75–83.
4. Gad Barzilai, *War, Internal Conflicts and Political Order: a Jewish Democracy in the Middle East*, Albany, 1996.
5. General Ran Goren (former CO, IDF Manpower Branch), 'The IDF and the Media. Can the Clock be Turned Back?', *Ma'archot* (IDF journal), No.322 (1991), pp.20–23.
6. See, respectively: Report by the Judge Advocate, *Yedi'ot Aharonot* (Hebrew daily), 30 July, 1996; *Ha-Aretz* (Hebrew daily), 3 August 1995. See also *State Comptroller Report, Vol.46 (1995)* (Hebrew; Jerusalem, 1996), pp.753–9; report of CO Manpower Branch, *Ha-Aretz*, 18 January 1996; and 12 May 1995.
7. Stuart A. Cohen, 'Israel's Changing Military Commitments, 1981–1991: Causes and Consequences', *Journal of Strategic Studies*, Vol.15 (1992), pp.330–50.
8. Israel Tal, 'National and Collective Security' *Ma'archot*, No.314 (1989), pp.2–6.
9. Report by Dr. S. Koren (CO Mental Health Unit), *Ma'ariv*, 4 May 1994 and CO Combined Field Command Manpower Brigade, *Ba-Mahaneh* (IDF Hebrew weekly), 11 May 1994.
10. CO Manpower Branch, press conference; *Ha-Aretz*, 24 October 1996.
11. On the importance of experience with computer games for the handling of modern tanks, for instance, see interview with the commander of a tank brigade in *Davar*, 12 May 1995. One significant exception to the rising education standards must be noted. The Intelligence Branch complains that decreasing numbers of recruits now possess

Arabic language skills. *Ba-Mahaneh*, 6 July 1994.
12. *Davar*, 17 May 1995.
13. *Davar*, 8 February 1995, compare Gal, *Portrait*, pp.128, 167 and the criticisms long ago expressed in M. Pa'il, 'Israel Defense Forces: A Social Aspect', *New Outlook*, 18 (January 1975), pp.40–44.
14. *Bulletin of the Council for Higher Education*, 8 August 1996, p.1 (Hebrew).
15. *State Comptroller Report: Vol.46 (1995)*, Jerusalem, 1996, pp.866–73.
16. See, for example, interview with Major-General Yossi Ben-Hanan, outgoing CO National Defence College, *Ha-aretz*, 11 August 1994. 'I am not pleased with the situation in the IDF today. About 50 per cent of the colonels and 60 per cent of the brigadier generals did not graduate from the Staff and Command College or the National Defence College due to various circumstances'.
17. *Portrait*, p.134.
18. On the evolution of these notions: S.A. Cohen, 'The Peace Process and its Impact on the Development of a "Smaller and Smarter" IDF', *Israel Affairs*, Vol.1, No.4 (1995), pp.1–21.
19. *State Comptroller Report, Vol.46 (1995)*, Jerusalem, 1996, pp.845–56.
20. As is pointed out by, for example, E. Wald., *The Gordion Knot: Myths and Dilemmas of Israeli National Security*, Tel-Aviv, 1992, pp.167–71 (Hebrew); and Col. (Res.) S. Gordon, 'In Favour of Selective Conscription', *Ma'arachot*, No.328 (February 1993), pp.32–37.
21. Barak Interview in *Ba-Mahaneh*, 4 January 1994. On the *mista'arvim*, see: S.A. Cohen, '"Masqueraders" in the IDF', *Low Intensity Conflict and Law Enforcement*, Vol.2 (1993), pp.282–300.
22. *Jerusalem Post International Edition*, 18 February 1989. See also Z. Schiff, 'What Happened to the IDF in the Intifada?', *Ha-aretz*, 16 June 1989.
23. *State Comptroller Report, Vol.46 (1995)*, Jerusalem, 1996, pp.859–64 and 894–911. Detailed Reports on such improvements regularly appear in *Ba-mahaneh*. See also the particularly revealing interviews with Generals Shalom Haggai (CO Ordnance Branch), *idem*, 18 May 1995, and Chen Yitzhaki (CO Staff College), *Menahalim*, July 1995.
24. Rolbant, p.167; Gal, pp.166–7.
25. *Ha-aretz*, 9 September 1996.
26. The present Chief-of-Staff, for instance, was in 1973 a deputy brigade commander; his deputy (Matan Vilnai) was operations officer in the Central Command.
27. Interviews with Colonel (res.), Menachem Digli, a former commander of the GS *sayeret*, *Ha-aretz*, 21 June 1996, and with Lieutenant-General Amnon Lipkin-Shahak, ibid., 13 September 1996.
28. These views are collated in Ofer Shelah and Avihai Beker, 'An Unhappy Army', Part 1, *Ma'ariv*, 19 July 1996.
29. *Ha-Aretz*, 5 July 1996.
30. Ibid., 23 June 1996.
31. For a scathing indictment of this process during the period 1973–82, see: E. Wald, *The Curse of the Broken Vessels*, Tel-Aviv, 1987, pp.140–86 (Hebrew). The author was former head of the long-range planning unit in the IDF General Staff.
32. *Ha-Aretz*, 19 January 1996 and *Ma'ariv*, 16 February 1996.
33. Colonel Israel Einhoren in *Yedi'ot Aharonot*, 25 January 1996.
34. For a summary of the Report, *Ha-Aretz*, 29 November 1993.
35. Major-General Uzi Dayan (CO Planning Branch), cited in Aluf Ben, 'To Build the IDF Afresh', *Ha-Aretz*, 4 April 1995.
36. *Knesset* member Ra'anan Cohen in *Yedi'ot Aharonot*, 23 August 1996.
37. A. Oren, 'The Army Marches on its Age', *Davar*, 10 June 1994. Compare: Rolbant, *Profile*, p.92 and Gal, *Portrait*, pp.168–69.
38. Shahak's interview in *Yedi'ot Aharonot*, 24 May 1995.
39. R. Gal, 'In Favour of a Re-examination of the Existing Model of the Israeli Officer', *Ma'archot*, No.346 (1996), pp.18–25.
40. Report in *Ha-Aretz*, 7 Feb. 1996.
41. Alex Fishman, 'Too Many Generals', *Yedi'ot Aharonot*, 6 October 1995.
42. M. Nativ, 'IDF Manpower and Israeli Society', *Jerusalem Quarterly*, No.32 (1984), pp.140–44.
43. A. Kadish, 'A Professional or Popular Army? The IDF at the End of the 1948 War',

Ma'archot, No.349 (July 1996), pp.52–5; updating Rolbant, *Profile*, p.78.

44. O. Meisels, 'Military Service as a Central Feature of the Israeli Experience', *Sekirah Hodshit* (IDF monthly for officers), January 1993, pp.3–6.

45. B. Kimmerling, 'Determination of the Boundaries and Frameworks of Conscription: Two Dimensions of Civil–Military Relations in Israel', *Studies in Comparative International Development*, Vol.14 (1979), pp.22–40.

46. Compare Jack Katnell, 'Minorities in the IDF', *IDF Journal*, Vol.4 (1987), pp.40–45 and Gabriel Ben-Dor, 'The Military and the Politics of Integration and Innovation: The Case of the Druze Minority in Israel', *Asian & African Studies*, Vol.9 (1973), pp.339–70.

47. Anne R. Bloom, 'Women in the Defense Forces', in Barbara Swirski and Marilyn P. Safir, eds, *Calling the Equality Bluff: Women in Israel*, New York, 1991, pp.128–38. Compare: Rolbant, *Profile*, pp.136–45; Gal, *Portrait*, pp.46–57.

48. On the origins of both arrangements: M. Friedman, 'This is the Chronology of the *Status Quo*: Religion and State in Israel', in V. Pilovsky, ed., *The Shift from Yishuv to State, 1947–1949: Continuity and Change*, Haifa, 1990, pp.62–64 (Hebrew).

49. See table 10.5 in Gal, *Portrait*, p.200. In general: S. Smooha, 'Ethnicity and Army in Israel: Theses for Discussion and Research', in *State, Government and International Relations*, No.22 (winter 1983–84), pp.5–32 (Hebrew).

50. See also: Y. Amir, 'Effectiveness of the Kibbutz-Born Soldier in the Israeli Defense Forces', *Human Relations*, Vol.22 (1969), pp.333–44.

51. *Ma'ariv*, 10 February 1995 and *Ba-mahaneh*, 22 March 1995.

52. Y. Erez, Y. Shavit and D. Tsur, 'Are There Ethnic Inequalities in Promotion Prospects in the IDF?', *Megamot*, Vol.35 (1993), pp.23–37.

53. M. Zonder, 'White Soldier Beats Black Soldier', *Ma'ariv*, 21 June 1996. Compare, Aviad Bar-Haim, 'Patterns of Ethnic Integration Amongst Senior IDF Officers', *Megamot*, Vol.30 (1987), pp.276–86.

54. Interview with Colonel Israela Oren (CO Womens' Corps), *Davar*, 3 February 1995.

55. Supreme Court decision 4591/94; 8 November 1995; Alice Miller vs Minister of Defence, COS, CO Manpower Branch and CO Womens' Corps.

56. The CO Manpower Branch estimates that 32% of potential female draftees claim exemption; two-thirds of them on religious grounds. Interview, November 1996.

57. Einhoren, above note 33.

58. Interview, November 1996. For the effect on female motivation to service, see former head of research in IDF Unit of Sociological Analysis in *Ha-aretz*, 25 August 1996.

59. Ibid., 6 April 1995.

60. Compare, however, V. Azarya and B. Kimmerling, 'New Immigrants in the Israeli Armed Forces', *Armed Forces & Society*, Vol.6 (1980), pp.455–82.

61. On the budgetary rationale for this practices; Colonel Y. Fuchs to the *Knesset* Foreign Affairs and Defence Committee, *Ha-aretz*, 11 January 1995.

62. *Knesset* member Naomi Chazan in *Ha-aretz*, 30 June 1994. For later improvements see report by CO Manpower Branch, *idem*, 18 January 1996.

63. Major-General Yoram Yair (CO Manpower Branch), *Ba-mahaneh*, 6 Sept. 1995 and *Ha-aretz* 6 February 1996.

64. Manpower Branch interview, November 1996. For earlier estimates: Y. Cohen, *Enlistment In Accordance with the Halakhah*, Tel-Aviv, 1993, pp.30–40 (Hebrew).

65. The first such seminary was established in 1964. The number grew to 13 by 1980, and 24 by 1996. On this form of service: S.A. Cohen, 'The Hesder Yeshivot in Israel: A Church–State Military Arrangement', *Journal of Church and State*, Vol.35 (1993), pp.113–30.

66. M. Bar-Lev, 'Let them Join', *Meimad*, 1 (1994), pp.3–5; and Yair Sheleg, 'The New National Religious Character', *Yom Ha-shishi* (Hebrew weekly), 19 August 1994.

67. Avihai Beker, 'The March of the Skullcap', *Ma'ariv*, 8 March 1996; see also interview with Brigadier-General Yair Naveh (Chief Infantry and Parachute Officer), *Ha-zofeh* (Hebrew daily), 13 September 1996.

68. Compare *Bita'on Heil Ha-avir* (Israel Air Force journal), No.103, June 1995, p.8 and No.109, June 1996, p.12.

69. For a fuller discussion: S.A. Cohen, *The Scroll or the Sword? Dilemmas of Religion and Military Service in Israel*, London, 1997.

70. See also: D. Horowitz, 'The IDF: A Civilianized Military in a Partially Military Society', in R. Kolkowicz and A. Korbanski, eds, *Soldiers, Peasants and Bureaucrats*, London, pp.77–107.

71. R.L. Schiff, 'Israel as an "Uncivil" State: A Reconsideration of Civil–Military Relations', *Security Studies*, Vol.1 (1992), pp.636–58.
72. A survey which I conducted in July 1996 shows that 82.4% of the population expressed either 'confidence' or 'full confidence' in the IDF. Next in order of preference were the State Comptroller (76.1%); the Supreme Court (73.4); the government (31); the *kneset* (30.1); and the media (24.9). These findings confirm the 'indices' periodically published by E. Yuchtman-Ya'ar and Peres in *Israeli Democracy*, 1987–1991.
73. IDF Spokesman in *Ha-aretz*, 29 November 1994. Of the 300 troops charged (including 60 officers), three were exonerated.
74. See: B. Kimmerling, 'Ethics Enlists in the IDF', *Ha-aretz*, 14 April 1995.
75. D. Horowitz, 'Strategic Limitations of "A Nation in Arms"', *Armed Forces & Society*, Vol.13 (1987), pp.277–94.
76. See, respectively, *Ha-aretz*, 28 August 1995 and 25 December 1995.
77. *Ba-mahaneh*, 12 July 1995. The total number of parental complaints in 1994 amounted to over 2000.
78. Interview with Dr. Ya'akov Katz (School of Education, Bar-Ilan University), *Ha-aretz*, 12 September 1996.
79. Interviews with Chief-of-Staff Barak and General Yoram Ya'ir (CO Manpower Branch), *Ba-Mahaneh*, 28 December 1994 and 6 September 1995. For a sensitive study of this subject, see: A. Lieblich, *Transition to Adulthood During Military Service: The Israeli Case*, New York, 1989.
80. Major-General (res.), Ran Goren, 'Parents In Favour of Easy and Pleasant Service', *Ma'ariv*, 23 December 1994.
81. On which see, especially, Menachem Hoffnung, *Israel – State Security versus the Rule of Law, 1948–1991*, Jerusalem, 1991 (Hebrew).
82. E.g., the appeal of one group of families to the Supreme Court for a non-military investigation into the circumstances which resulted in the deaths of their sons. *Ha-aretz*, 6 September 1996.
83. Open letter to the Defence Minister from Colonel (res.), Ben-Zion Weiss, *Yedi'ot Aharonot*, 21 July 1996. Compare Gal's references to the 'small head' phenomenon (*Portrait*, pp.131–2).
84. For a review of the instances, see: Martin Blatt, ed., *Dissent and Ideology in Israel: Resistance to the Draft*, London, 1975.
85. These phenomena are fully explored in: Sara Helman, 'Conscientious Objection to Military Service as an Attempt to Redefine the Contents of Citizenship' (unpublished PhD dissertation; The Hebrew University of Jerusalem, 1993), and Ruth Linn, *Conscience at War. The Israeli Soldier as a Moral Critic*, Albany, 1996.
86. See text in *Ma'ariv*, 23 August 1996.
87. *Yedi'ot Aharonot*, 11 September 1996.
88. For a review of the materials: A. Naor, 'The National-Religious ("Credo") Argument against the Israel–PLO Accord: A World View Tested by Reality', *State and Religion Yearbook 1993*, pp.54–88 (Hebrew).
89. For the full text of this manifesto, see: *Ha-zofeh*, 13 July 1995.
90. R. Gal, 'Israel', in Charles Moskos and Frank Wood, eds, *The Military: More Than Just a Job?*, Washington, DC, 1988, pp.266–77. For the original thesis: C.S. Moskos, 'Institutional/Occupational Trends in Armed Forces: An Update', *Armed Forces & Society*, Vol.12 (1986), pp.377–82.
91. O. Mayseless, R. Gal, and E. Fishof, *General Perceptions and Attitudes of High-School Students Regarding Security and National Issues*, 2 vols Zikhron Ya'akov, 1989 (Hebrew).
92. Major-General Ilan Biran (CO Central Command), interview in *Davar*, 14 April 1995; and Major-General Yoram Yair (CO Manpower Branch), *Yedi'ot Aharonot*, 1 September 1995.
93. E.g. M. Ashlag, 'The Span of the Stigma', *Ha-ir* (Tel-Aviv weekly), 18 November 1992, pp.50–54.
94. Y. Ezrachi and R. Gal, *General Perceptions and Attitudes of [Israeli] High-School Students Regarding the Peace Process, Security and Social Issues*, Zikhron Ya'akov, 1995.
95. Lipkin-Shahak in *Ha-aretz*, 29 March 1995, 6 February 1996 and 9 September 1996.
96. Interview, November 1996. However, these figures themselves register some decline.
97. Interview, Manpower Branch, November 1996.

98. The general secretary of the National Kibbutz Movement claims that kibbutz youngsters still enlist in combat formations at a higher rate than the national average. However, he concedes that the percentage of volunteers for the officers' course has declined by some 18%. *Ha-aretz*, 28 August 1996.

99. Thus, in February 1996, the CO Manpower Branch reported that the rate of immigrant applications to combat units had doubled over the previous year, and amounted to some 33%. Compare: *Ba-mahaneh*, 1 February 1995 and *Ha-aretz*, 6 February 1996.

100. These results were kindly made available to the author by Dr. Ya'akov Katz of the Education Department at Bar-Ilan University.

101. For a fuller discussion: Cohen, *The Scroll or the Sword?* (above n.69).

102. E.g., Lipkin-Shahak in *Ha-aretz*, 2 September 1996.

103. Compare Gal, *Portrait*, p.37 with the far more detailed analyses provided by interview with N. Gilad (deputy head of budgeting in the Israeli Treasury), *Globus*, 23 August 1996, and N. Ze'evi, 'The IDF's Best-Kept Secrets', *Ha-aretz* weekend supplement, 8 November 1996, pp.18–25.

104. Although disputing the exact statistics, IDF sources do not deny the trend. Interview with Brigadier-General Michael Navon, head of General Staff Budgetary Branch, *Yedi'ot Aharonot*, 23 February 1996.

105. *Ha-aretz*, 7, 10 and 15 July 1996.

106. Brigadier-General Yitzchaki Chen, speech to graduates; *Yedi'ot Aharonot*, 31 August 1995.

THE PEACE PROCESS

Peace Despite Everything

EFRAIM KARSH

The signing of the 15 January 1997 Hebron Protocol providing for Israel's evacuation of some 80 per cent of the City of the Patriarchs, and for the full implementation of the (Oslo) Interim Agreement, including the completion of Israel's military redeployment in (that is, withdrawal from) the West Bank by mid-1988 seems to have removed, temporarily at least, the dark cloud hanging over the future of the nascent Arab–Israeli peace process since the election of Likud's leader Benjamin Netanyahu as Prime Minister of Israel in May 1996.

While the doomsday scenarios of legions of settlers swarming the West Bank following the elections have failed to materialize, the lip service paid by the new prime minister to the idea of Jewish settlement in Judea and Samaria (a theme which was conspicuously absent from his election campaign), his pronounced displeasure with the Oslo Accords (which he has nevertheless undertaken to observe), and his dismissive attitude to Palestinian Authority Chairman Yasser Arafat have been sufficiently alarming for many Arabs to try to cut Netanyahu down to size.

Speaking at a joint news conference with King Hussein of Jordan and President Husni Mubarak of Egypt on 5 June, before the formation of the new Israeli government, Arafat threatened that the Palestinians would declare their independent state in the not-too-distant future and that nobody would be able to stop them from doing this. While clearly violating the Oslo Accords which precluded unilateral decisions on the future of the occupied territories and provided for a *negotiated* Israeli–Palestinian settlement of their century-long dispute, this threat was whole-heartedly endorsed by Mubarak. 'History will prove that the Palestinians are going to establish a state now or thenceforth, whether we like it or not', he said. Even King Hussein, to whom the prospect of a Palestinian State has been anathema, felt obliged to state that 'the question is the right of the Palestinians on their soil, and we are for whatever they decide on. We will never under any conditions be a substitute for them'. Three weeks later, on 23 June, an emergency Arab League summit in Cairo defined the establishment of a Palestinian State, with East Jerusalem as its capital, as an essential ingredient of peace and warned the Israeli government against reneging on the peace process.

Efraim Karsh is Professor and Head of the Mediterranean Studies Programme at King's College, University of London.

Encouraged by this show of support Arafat escalated. When negotiations with the Netanyahu Government over Israel's redeployment in Hebron, due to be completed before the elections but postponed following the massacre of dozens of Israelis in a string of bombings by Islamic militants, seemed to be moving nowhere, in late September 1996 Arafat initiated armed clashes with the Israeli army in which 15 Israelis and four times as many Palestinians died. While this constituted yet another fundamental violation of the Oslo Accords, predicated on the exclusion of the use of force as a means to resolve Palestinian–Israeli differences, Arafat not only escaped international censure but succeeded in painting Netanyahu as the culprit of the escalation. This he did by presenting his move as a gallant attempt to defend the al-Aqsa Mosque, which he claimed was in a danger of physical collapse following the opening of an ancient Jewish tunnel under the Wailing Wall. Though a patently hollow pretext as some Palestinian spokesmen candidly admitted (the tunnel does not at all run under the al-Aqsa Mosque; it had been excavated for several years with the tacit approval of the Waqf authorities; and tens of thousands of tourists had already gone through it well before the Netanyahu Government opened its last exit),[1] Arafat's ability to sell his ploy to the international community reflected both the depth of the international isolation to which Israel had sunk following the elections and the ostensible fragility of the peace process.

Yet the instant predictions that the tunnel affair would derail the Israeli–Palestinian peace process were quickly disproved. Far from heralding its demise, the episode confirmed the process's vitality. Indeed, it will be argued in this essay that for all its uncertainties, the Arab–Israeli peace process is irreversible for the simple reason that it does not represent the whimsical act of the odd politician but rather the culminating point of a prolonged and tortuous process of disillusionment among Arabs and Israelis alike with the use of force as a political instrument.

This disillusionment began with the 1967 Six Day War, which dealt militant pan-Arabism a mortal blow and disabused many in the Arab World of their hopes to destroy the State of Israel. It continued with the 1973 October War, which shattered Israeli illusions that the Arabs could be forced into any solution. Although the impact of these wars sufficed to produce the Egyptian–Israeli peace treaty of 1979, another decade of intense violence was required to wear down the more intransigent players on both sides.

The eight year war between Iraq and Iran and the Iraqi occupation of Kuwait drove home to many Arabs that Israel was not the principal threat to their national security. Similarly, the disastrous Lebanese adventure convinced many Israelis that there was no military solution to the Arab–Israeli conflict. No less importantly, the war destroyed the

PLO's military infrastructure in Lebanon and sowed the seeds of the uprising in the occupied territories (*intifada*) which allowed the PLO to shed its commitment to Israel's destruction and to accept a two-state solution – Israel and a Palestinian state in the West Bank and the Gaza Strip. With this regional disillusionment reinforced by the collapse of communism and the end of the Cold War, the road to peace was opened.

1967: THE BEGINNING OF THE END

It is not a commonplace to view the 1967 War as a catalyst to Arab–Israeli reconciliation. Rather, it is normally regarded as 'the worst tragedy in the modern history of the Middle East... generating more hatred, violence, and bloodshed than at any time since the founding of the Jewish state'.[2]

However intriguing, this standard view is totally misconceived. If war can be inevitable, this is certainly the case with the June 1967 War. Given the intensity of Arab rejection of Israel at the time, only a major shock could catapult the Middle East from rejection and denial to acceptance and reconciliation. To Arabs, Israel has always been an artificial aggressive entity, implanted in their midst by Western imperialism, that had to be dislodged if the so-called 'Arab nation' were to regain its past glory. As candidly admitted by American-Palestinian academic, Edward Said, his 'was the generation raised in an Arab world, according the Jewish state no recognition at all ... Until 1967 it was almost impossible to use the word "Israel" in Arabic writing'.[3]

The magnitude of the 1967 defeat punctured this sterile bubble of denial and forced the Arabs to confront the reality of Jewish statehood in their midst. For the first time since the 1948 'catastrophe', a pan-Arab coalition was defeated by Israel, and in a far more humiliating manner. Then, only half of Palestine had been lost; now, the land was lost in its entirety, together with Egyptian and Syrian territories. In 1948 the relationship between victor and vanquished had been somewhat equivocal; while the Arabs had clearly failed to achieve their foremost war objective, destruction of the newly-established State of Israel, all belligerents tasted the sweetness of victory and the bitterness of defeat, as the war dragged on intermittently for nearly a year. In 1967, due to the swift and decisive nature of the war, there was absolutely no doubt as to who was the loser.

This, in turn, triggered a painful process of soul-searching, not only among intellectuals and political dissidents,[4] but also among some of the leaders responsible for the 1967 debacle. Even Gamal Abdel Nasser, the high priest of pan-Arabism and champion of the Arab campaign against Israel, seemed to be recoiling from the ideals he had been preaching for so long. The unification of the 'Arab nation', the removal of the

conservative Arab regimes, and even the destruction of the State of
Israel – all these fanciful objectives were suddenly expendable; they
were subordinated to the immediate goal of regaining those Egyptian
lands lost in the war, and to the daunting task of rehabilitating the
shattered Egyptian economy. The most vivid illustration of this
changing agenda was afforded by Nasser's grudging acceptance of UN
Security Council Resolution 242 of November 1967, which called for
Arab–Israeli peace in return for Israeli withdrawal from territories
occupied in the 1967 War, and his agreement to enter into indirect
negotiations with Israel on its implementation, under the auspices of the
UN special envoy, Gunnar Jarring. When accused by his Arab peers of
betraying the pan-Arab cause Nasser blustered:

> You issue statements, but we have to fight. If you want to liberate,
> then get in line in front of us... But we have learnt caution after the
> Yemenis dragged us into their affairs in 1962, and the Syrians into
> war in 1967.[5]

THE EGYPTIAN–ISRAELI PEACE

Whether Nasser was actually ready to make peace with Israel is difficult
to say. It is clear, however, that by the time of his premature demise on
28 September 1970 he had laid the ground for breaking with his own
pan-Arab legacy, something that his successor, Anwar Sadat, did with
great enthusiasm.

Already in December 1970 Sadat announced his readiness to make
peace with Israel in return for its complete withdrawal from Egyptian –
not Arab! – territories occupied in the 1967 War.[6] Two months later, in
a written response to Jarring, he reaffirmed this position by giving the
first-ever official Arab commitment 'to enter into a peace agreement
with Israel' in return for a complete Israeli withdrawal from Egyptian
territory, including the Gaza Strip. When his peace overtures failed to
produce the anticipated response, Sadat launched the October 1973
War which took Israel by complete surprise and broke the political
stalemate that had existed in the region since the 1967 War.

In many respects the October War was to Israel what 1967 had been
to the Arabs. The complacency that had gained hold over the Israeli
psyche following the astounding 1967 victory was irrevocably
shattered. The Bar-Lev line along the Suez Canal, the embodiment of
Israel's military prowess, collapsed like a house of cards. The Golan
Heights, supposedly the shield of the northern Galilee, proved no
barrier to a surprise Syrian attack. As the Arabs were consolidating their
early gains, the mood in Jerusalem was grim. Minister of Defence
Moshe Dayan was talking about the impending collapse of the 'Third
Temple'. A nuclear alert was reportedly called.

Consequently, the Israel that emerged from the 1973 trauma was a different nation: sober, mellowed, permanently scarred. It was still distrustful of its neighbours yet better tuned to signs of regional moderation; highly apprehensive of the security risks attending territorial concessions yet aware that land could not buy absolute security. Indeed, successive opinion polls in the wake of the October War showed a steady growth in public support for the 'territory for peace' formula. Israelis were most inclined to compromise over the Sinai Peninsula and least disposed to concessions over the Golan Heights. Yet if until the 1973 War the idea of withdrawal on the Golan had been a national anathema, in the spring of 1977 one in three Israelis was willing to consider such an option. On the future of the West Bank Israelis were almost evenly divided, with a slight edge for supporters of territorial compromise.[7]

Even at the time of the 1977 elections, when Labour lost power to Menachem Begin's right-wing Likud, three out of four Israelis were ready to trade part of the occupied territories, or all of them, in return for peace. This means that the elections were less of a victory for Likud, let alone for its territorial maximalism, than a vote of non-confidence in Labour's incompetence and corruption by a young and angry generation of Israelis. This would be vividly illustrated in future years when only 120,000 Israelis – 2.5 per cent of Israel's Jewish population – would make their home in the occupied territories, and would allow the Israeli leadership to reciprocate Sadat's drive towards peace with significant territorial concessions in Sinai.

Already in December 1973 an international peace conference on the Arab–Israeli conflict was convened in Geneva, for the first time since the late 1940s, with the participation of Israel and *some* of its Arab neighbours. A month later Egypt and Israel signed an agreement on the disengagement of forces along the eastern bank of the Suez Canal and the establishment of a buffer zone between the two armies, supervised by a United Nations Emergency Force (UNEF). This was followed up in September 1975 by yet another disengagement agreement, which involved substantial Israeli withdrawal in Sinai and which contained a mutual renunciation of 'the threat or use of force or military blockade against each other' and a commitment to the peaceful pursuit of a comprehensive peace on the basis of Security Council Resolution 338 of 22 October 1973 (in itself predicated on Resolution 242).

The significance of this agreement could not be overstated. By accepting peace on the basis of Resolution 338, Egypt effectively recognized Israel within its pre-June 1967 borders, something that was still anathema to most Arabs. In agreeing, in all but name, to end the state of belligerency with Israel, the largest Arab state distanced itself from the pan-Arab struggle against the Jewish State. What Sadat seemed to be telling his fellow Arabs was that there was no military solution to the Arab–Israeli conflict – only a political one – and the Arabs had better recognize this fact and follow the Egyptian lead. And if there remained any doubts about the Egyptian President's determination to sway the Arab World from war to peace with Israel, they were completely dispelled in November 1977, when Sadat made his historic visit to Jerusalem and, some 18 months later, concluded a fully fledged peace treaty with the Jewish State.

THE IMPACT OF THE IRAN–IRAQ WAR

The Egyptian–Israeli peace treaty was almost unanimously rejected by the Arab World. Egypt was expelled from the Arab League, Sadat excommunicated. A tough competition for leadership ensued between the two self-styled champions of the pan-Arab cause, Syria and Iraq. A radical Arab front was formed to nip the peace treaty in the bud, with the active encouragement and support of the Soviet Union.

Before long, however, the Arabs were to realize the limits of their power. Not only did they fail to subvert the Egyptian–Israeli peace treaty, but as the 1980s drew to a close Egypt had regained its focal role in the Arab World, with its moderate policy becoming the mainstream Arab line and its former detractors seeking its friendship and protection.

The most important single development contributing to this ocean change was the advent of the Islamic Republic in Iran in 1979 and the eruption of the Iran–Iraq War a year later. Tehran's relentless commitment to the substitution of its militant brand of Islamic order for the existing status quo, its reluctance to end the war before the overthrow of the Ba'th regime in Baghdad, and its subversive and terrorist campaign against the Arab monarchies of the Gulf – all this proved to the Gulf states that the Iranian threat exceeded by far the Israeli danger and that there was no adequate substitute to Egypt at the helm of the Arab World.

In March 1979 Saddam Hussein triumphantly hosted the Baghdad Summit which expelled Egypt from the Arab League. A year later he was pleading with the excommunicated Sadat for military support. As Egypt developed into an important military and economic provider – with more than 1 million Egyptians servicing the over-extended Iraqi economy – Saddam would tirelessly toil to pave the way for its reincorporation into the Arab fold, regardless of its peace treaty with Israel.

Furthermore, whenever his personal survival required Saddam had no qualms about 'supping with the devil'. In 1985 he sought to buy Israel's acquiescence in the laying of an Iraqi oil pipeline to the Jordanian port town of Aqaba by offering it $700 million over ten years. He even voiced public support for peace negotiations between the Arabs and Israel, emphasizing that 'no Arab leader looks forward to the destruction of Israel' and that any solution to the conflict would require 'the existence of a secure state for the Israelis'.[8]

Iraq's growing acquiescence in Israel's existence, which was sustained into the postwar period and manifested itself in support for the PLO's 1988 recognition of Israel as well as in tacit collaboration with Israel against Syria's military presence in Lebanon, was welcomed by the Gulf monarchies which, for their part, were making hesitant steps towards reconciliation.

In August 1981, much to Anwar Sadat's delight, Saudi Crown Prince Fahd put forward a peace plan which implicitly recognized Israel's right to secure existence. Thirteen months later this plan, in a somewhat revised version, was officially endorsed by an Arab League summit at the Moroccan town of Fez.

LEBANON: THE PRICE OF HUBRIS

A similar process of disillusionment took place in Israel as a result of a protracted and futile war. Instead of using the Iran–Iraq War, which pitted two of its enemies against each other, to try to pursue a negotiated settlement with its neighbours, Israel sought to impose its own solution on the Arab World by invading Lebanon with the declared aim of 'ensuring peace and security for the Galilee'.

As a preventive move designed to remove a military threat to the north, this was initially acceptable to many Israelis. However, it soon transpired that the Israeli cabinet, including Prime Minister Begin, had been manipulated by Minister of Defence Ariel Sharon and his Chief-of-Staff, Lieutenant-General Rafael Eitan, whose real plan had little to do with 'Peace for the Galilee'. This was to eliminate the PLO as an independent political actor, cut Syria down to size and neutralize it as a threat to Israel, install a sympathetic regime in Lebanon under the Christian leader Bashir Gumayel, strengthen cooperation with the United States while further undermining Soviet influence.[9] This combination of megalomaniacal war aims and their devious presentation to the cabinet and to the public at large, doomed Sharon's grandiose vision from the outset. The nation could be rallied behind the idea of 'Peace for the Galilee' but not behind Sharon's grand design. Finding themselves bogged down in the Lebanese quagmire fighting friend and foe alike, the Israeli Defence Forces (IDF) began to lose any sense of purpose, and the Israeli public lost its patience. 'I do not question, Mr. Begin, your legal right to use your majority (of sorts) in the Knesset to involve us in a war that you desire,' wrote novelist Amos Oz,

> But your lie will not be forgiven: You called upon our soldiers to sacrifice their lives for goals agreed upon (though in the manner in which agreement was arrived at is subject to debate), but in fact you led them to kill and to die for goals to which a great many of us are opposed. Please do not come to comfort our mourners: You have

caused a rift unlike any that has ever been before. Half the nation is turning its back on you in resentment, in fury, and in grief.[10]

When the folly led to the Sabra and Shatila tragedy – Lebanese militiamen were allowed into these refugee camps by the IDF to clear them of PLO guerrillas and massacred several hundred innocent civilians – the nation was swept by revulsion. Some 400,000 people, above 10 per cent of Israel's total population, took to the streets in the largest demonstration in the country's history. Recognizing the extent of public disgust the cabinet appointed an independent commission of enquiry and subsequently removed Sharon from his post and disassociated itself from his abortive design. This process was completed in 1985.

The Israeli public, divided as it had never been before, was gradually disabused of the perception of military force as a be-all and end-all. To most Israelis the Lebanese entanglement discredited the notion of 'war by choice' (as Begin so proudly called the war) and provided the ultimate proof that there was no military solution to the Arab–Israeli conflict.

PALESTINIAN PRAGMATIZATION

At the same time, the war had a sobering impact on the Arab states in general, and the Palestinians in particular. By destroying the PLO's military infrastructure in Lebanon and denying it a territorial base for attacks on Israel, the Lebanon War drove the Palestinians towards the political path. This culminated in the PLO's historic decisions in November and December 1988 to accept Security Council Resolutions 242 and 338 and to recognize Israel's right to exist.

A strong impetus to these decisions was provided by the eruption of the *intifada* in December 1987. This popular uprising did more to redeem Palestinian dignity and self-esteem than two and a half decades of PLO terrorism. Frustrated with the longstanding negligence and manipulation of their cause by Arabs and Israelis alike, the Palestinians in the territories proved capable of becoming self-reliant and rebuffing the Israeli occupation in a fashion they had never done before. This, in turn, brought the Palestinian problem to the fore of the Arab–Israeli conflict and enabled Arafat to overcome his hardline opponents within the PLO. With the Palestinians in the occupied territories anxious to see progress on the diplomatic front that would make their sacrifice worthwhile, the PLO could hardly afford to remain entrenched in its rejectionist posture which had led it to nowhere.

The more moderate stance adopted by the PLO led Washington to open official talks with the organization, for the first time in its history, and to put pressure on Israel to embark on a serious dialogue with authentic Palestinian representatives. Within Israel the reaction to the new Palestinian challenge was mixed. On the one hand, the *intifada* was met by a defiant mood by the right wing (including influential figures within the Likud Party), which viewed this development as the continuation by other means of the longstanding Arab desire to destroy Israel, and which advocated a tough policy in the territories. On the other hand, the uprising brought home the mounting costs of the continued occupation, thereby reinforcing the evolving general recognition of the need for a historic compromise between Arabs and Jews.

THE COLLAPSE OF COMMUNISM AND THE MIDDLE EAST

The evolution of regional moderation was further accelerated by the end of the Cold War and the unprecedented superpower collaboration attending it. Both Arabs and Israelis were naturally wary of these developments. In the past they had sensed a reverse correlation between the state of global detente and the room for manoeuvre of the smaller actors: the warmer great power relations, the narrower the lesser actors' freedom of action. For this reason they had traditionally viewed with much alarm any manifestations of superpower detente. Special dissatisfaction with the thaw in superpower relations was voiced in Damascus, which did not attempt to disguise its abhorrence of Mikhail Gorbachev's readiness to sacrifice Soviet regional interests – and allies – for the sake of superpower detente.

With this trend reinforced by the crumbling of the East European regimes, and all the more so – the disintegration of the Soviet Union, the radical regimes in the Middle East concluded that the region had been left to the mercy of the only remaining superpower, the United States, and its 'lackeys', first and foremost Israel.

This gloomy assessment led to the further weakening of the militant Arab camp, illustrated most vividly by the completion of Egypt's reincorporation into the Arab fold. Already in November 1987 an Arab League summit in Amman allowed the member states to re-establish diplomatic relations with Egypt. All Arab states quickly seized the opportunity, with the exception of Syria and Libya, as well as Lebanon which had increasingly come under the Syrian sway. Now that Arab radicalism was further afflicted by the momentous events in Eastern Europe, the Arab World made the decisive leap towards Egypt. In May 1989 Egypt took part in the all-Arab summit in Casablanca for the first time since its expulsion from the Arab League a decade earlier. Four months later Libya's radical ruler, Mu'amar Gaddafi, paid an official visit to Egypt, and in December 1989 President Hafiz Asad of Syria, who for more than a decade had spearheaded the Arab campaign against the separate Egyptian–Israeli peace, swallowed his pride and restored full diplomatic relations with Cairo.

THE GULF CONFLICT AND ARAB-ISRAELI PEACE

The final nail in the coffin of regional rejectionism was driven by the Iraqi invasion of Kuwait and the ensuing 1991 Gulf War. All of a sudden Israelis and Arabs found themselves in the same boat, as Saddam sought to legitimize his predatory move by portraying it as a noble attempt to promote the liberation of Palestine from 'Zionist occupation'. While the falsehood of this linkage was eminently transparent, the widespread emotional outburst it aroused, particularly when Saddam began firing his missiles at Israel, underscored the explosiveness of the Israeli–Palestinian conflict, if left unattended.

This exceptional convergence of destinies led to tacit collaboration between Israel and the Arab members of the anti-Iraq coalition during the conflict: the former kept the lowest possible profile, even refraining from retaliation for Iraq's missile attacks,[11] while the latter highlighted the hollowness of Saddam's Palestinian pretensions and participated in the war operations against Iraq. This, in turn, made it easier for US Secretary of State, James Baker, to kick off the Madrid peace process shortly after the war.

Indeed, more than America's newly-gained preeminence it was the trauma attending the Iraqi invasion of Kuwait and Saddam's survival of the Gulf War that brought Syrian President Hafiz Asad to Madrid. Contrary to conventional wisdom, Asad had never viewed the evolving New World Order as necessitating a fundamental revision of his longstanding rejection of Israel's existence, as illustrated by his acrimonious relations with Gorbachev and his venomous attacks on the PLO's 1988 recognition of Israel. Yet once his mortal enemy, Saddam Hussein, had swallowed Kuwait, Asad could not allow the Iraqi action to stand for fear that he would be Saddam's next victim. Hence his immediate joining of the anti-Iraq coalition; hence Syria's actual participation in the liberation of Kuwait and its outspoken opposition to ending the war before the physical elimination of Saddam Hussein.[12]

Paradoxically, the PLO's folly of siding with Saddam gave an important boost to Arab–Israeli reconciliation. Either in response to strong pro-Saddam sentiments among Palestinians in Jordan and the occupied territories, or due to frustration with Israel's indifference to its 1988 decisions, or because it was mesmerized by Saddam's hubris, the PLO leadership hedged its bets on by siding with Iraq. This was manifested by assiduous attempts to defuse the crisis on Saddam's terms – such as the dethronement of the Kuwaiti royal family and the complete satellization of Kuwait – something that was anathema to all Gulf regimes. When these efforts failed to produce results and the spectre of war loomed large, Arafat threw in his lot with Saddam. Should war break out, he told a cheering audience in Baghdad, a week before the actual outbreak of hostilities, the Palestinians would be 'in the same trench with the Iraqi people to confront the US-Zionist-

Atlantic build-up of invading forces, which are desecrating Arab lands'.[13] His deputy, Salah Khalaf (alias Abu Iyad), resorted to even more fiery rhetoric. 'The Palestinian and Jordanian people will stand by fraternal Iraq in any aggression against it,' he announced at a public rally in Amman. 'We shall not abandon Palestine. We renew the pledge to liberate Palestine inch by inch from the sea to the river'.[14] The PLO's 1988 recognition of Israel and its acceptance of a two-state solution seemed to have been expediently forgotten on the spur of this euphoric moment.

This folly cost the PLO dearly. The Gulf monarchies were neither forgiving nor forgetful. As the primary financiers of the Palestinian cause they felt betrayed by their beneficiaries; as hosts to a large population of Palestinian workers they felt threatened. This state of mind was illustrated not only by the harsh treatment of Palestinians in the newly-liberated Kuwait: within a month from the end of the war Saudi financial support for the PLO had been cut off, driving the organization to the verge of bankruptcy.

Starved of financial resources, marginalized at the Madrid peace process launched in October 1991, increasingly overpowered in the occupied territories by the HAMAS militant Islamic movement, and beset by growing internal infighting, the PLO was desperate for political rehabilitation – and Yasser Arafat, for a personal comeback.

For his part the newly-elected Israeli Prime Minister, Yitzhak Rabin, was becoming increasingly exasperated with the inconclusive peace process. Brought back to power in June 1992 on a straightforward peace platform, the 71-year-old former Chief-of-Staff, who had masterminded Israel's 1967 victory, was keenly aware that this was his last chance to go down in history as Israel's greatest peacemaker and was determined to seize the moment, come what may. And if this meant breaking the taboo, to which he had previously subscribed, and recognizing the PLO as the sole representative of the Palestinian people, so be it.

With the convergence of these Palestinian and Israeli undercurrents, against the backdrop of their long mutual disillusionment, the road to the 1993 Israeli–Palestinian accords and the subsequent Jordanian–Israeli peace treaty was short.

THE NETANYAHU GOVERNMENT AND THE FUTURE OF THE PEACE PROCESS

The main conclusion emanating from the preceding discussion is that the Middle East peace process is here to stay. The fundamental disillusionment with the use of force which gave birth to this process is very much alive, and neither Israelis nor Arabs have a better alternative for achieving their long-term national goals.

It is in this light that the results of the 1996 Israeli elections should be interpreted. More than anything else, Netanyahu's hair-breadth victory (receiving 50.4 per cent of the ballots compared to 49.5 per cent for incumbent prime minister Shimon Peres) reflects the agonized and convoluted state of mind of the Israeli public following the massacre of some 60 Israelis in a string of suicide bombings by Islamic militants in late February-early March 1996. As such, this victory was not a rejection of the Labour-led peace process but rather a vote of no-confidence in Peres, the man.[15] After all, Netanyahu was elected to bring 'peace with security' (within the Oslo framework), whatever this ambiguous promise of his meant, not to renege on the peace process. The overwhelming majority of Israelis, including most Likud supporters, have no desire to rule over the Palestinians and would readily disengage themselves from the tragic embrace that has locked the two peoples together since 1967. But, at the same time, many of them were deeply troubled by the way the Labour Government and Peres in particular had been implementing the Oslo Process. As they saw it, by feigning weakness Yasser Arafat had literally been allowed by his Israeli partners to get away with murder. He had consistently been speaking from both sides of his mouth – peace to Israeli and Western audiences, *jihad* to his Palestinian constituents. He had done nothing to curb the tidal wave of terrorist attacks by Islamic militants, let alone to disarm them as required by the Oslo Accords, before the latest spate of suicide bombings in February–March 1996 drove home to him that his policy might turn sour; and he evaded the abolition of those clauses in the Palestinian Covenant calling for the destruction of Israel for as long as was conceivably possible. Even when he grudgingly made this move on 24 April 1996, it was done in such a dubious fashion that it triggered a heated debate among Israel's 'Arabists' whether the Covenant had been changed at all.[16]

In this respect, Arafat is responsible for the results of the Israeli elections no less than the actions and inactions of the candidates themselves. Had he truthfully attempted to curb Palestinian terrorism from the outset, Shimon Peres might still be Israel's prime minister. For several months after Rabin's assassination he led the polls by a comfortable majority of 20 per cent; once HAMAS massacred dozens of Israelis within the span of a week, this majority evaporated like thin air. Why Arafat preferred to test the patience of the Rabin-Peres administration rather than tackle the problem of Palestinian terrorism is not difficult to understand. What he failed to grasp, however, is that the patience of the Israeli public might be far more quickly exhausted than that of its government.

As things were, Netanyahu's election turned out to be the best thing that had happened to Arafat since the beginning of the Oslo Process. The new prime minister's hard-line image, matched by his glaring lack of experience in government, allowed the Palestinian leader to project himself as the paragon of virtue to substantial Western audiences which had hitherto been critical both of his abidance by the Oslo Accords and of the corrupt and repressive nature of his regime. This enhanced manoeuvrability was vividly demonstrated by the September 1996 Palestinian-initiated armed confrontation which was widely blamed on Israel, and by the negotiations over the IDF's redeployment in Hebron, whose prolongation was shrewdly attributed to Israel.

Whether this improved bargaining position will be sustained during the final-status negotiations, due to start within two months after the implementation of the Hebron Protocol, will depend on a multitude of factors, notably Arafat's ability to continue to exploit Netanyahu's learning curve, on the one hand, and to prevent the resurgence of Islamic terrorism, on the other. What is eminently clear, however, is that while sporadic resort to force by the Palestinian Authority in pursuit of specific objectives cannot be ruled out, it is only through a true dialogue that the Palestinians will be able to achieve their ultimate goal: an independent sovereign state.

Likud's ascendancy has also been a blessing in disguise for Asad, though for wholly different reasons. Unlike the Palestinian mainstream body politic, which seems more or less resigned to peaceful coexistence with Israel, for Asad peace with Israel is the worst of all worlds, a price to be paid only as a means of last resort; and an exorbitant price indeed. This is not only because powerful circles in Syria on which Asad's personal rule hinges, notably the military/security establishment, benefit from the continuation of the Arab–Israeli conflict; not even because, as a member of the tiny Alawaite minority dominating a reluctant Sunni majority for three decades, Asad cannot afford to be seen as turning his back on the pan-Arab ideals which he has championed for so long. It is rather because he is probably the last genuine apostle of the pan-Arab gospel, which views Israel as an artificial entity, planted in the Middle East by devious Western imperialism as a means to weaken and divide the so-called 'Arab Nation'.

Throughout his entire political career, Asad has consistently argued that the Arab–Israeli conflict is a mortal struggle over 'existence' and 'destiny' that must eventually be settled in favour of one of the two protagonists; and since the Arabs enjoy a marked superiority over Israel in the most fundamental elements of national power they are bound to triumph at the end of the day, provided they adopt a long-term historical perspective, keep their nerve, and reject easy solutions and short-cuts. As he has never tired of articulating, the Israelis are no more than neo-Crusaders; and just as the 'Arab Nation' defeated this past enemy after a long-drawn struggle, so it would overcome the present 'Zionist invader'. When asked by *Newsweek* magazine, shortly before the convocation of the 1991 Madrid Peace Conference whether he was 'prepared to accept, as a permanent fact of political life, the existence of a Jewish state in the Mideast', Asad could not bring himself to say the Y word, not even in a qualified form.

'I can say Syria is in favour of what the U.N. resolutions stipulate,' he said.

'Do you accept the existence of a Jewish state in the Middle East?' the interviewer persisted.

'This has to be put forward in the conference', Asad replied. 'If everything is to be decided here in this interview, what will remain for the peace conference?'

'If you don't say that you accept the Jewish state, can you say that you have substantially changed your attitude toward Israel?'

'We have changed nothing. What is there that should be changed?'[17]

That the Syrian President has not abandoned this recalcitrant historical vision altogether, despite his grudging participation in the American-led peace process, has been evidenced by his negotiating style which has been geared more to placating 'the only remaining superpower', as the United States came to be called after the disintegration of the Soviet Union, than to convincing Israel of the sincerity of his intentions. Notwithstanding Rabin's and Peres's expressed readiness to withdraw from the Golan Heights in return for genuine peace, Asad acted as if he was in no hurry to regain his lost territories. He refused to accelerate the peace talks by elevating them from ambassadorial to ministerial level, let alone to meet his Israeli counterparts in person. He also continued to condition a Syrian–Israeli peace on the complete resolution of the Palestinian problem yet kept on raising the threshold of such a deal: as long as the Palestine Liberation Organization (PLO) openly called for the destruction of Israel, Asad pledged allegiance to any solution amenable to the organization; once the PLO recognized Israel in 1988, Syria immediately castigated this move; and when the PLO carried this recognition a step further by signing the September 1993 Declaration of Principles (DOP) with Israel, a chill wind blew from Damascus and the Syrian-based Palestinian terrorist, Ahmad Jibril, threatened PLO Chairman Yasser Arafat with death. An equally hostile reception was given to the Israel–PLO follow-up agreement of September 1995 on the withdrawal of Israeli forces from most of the West Bank. Last but not least, while maintaining the low-keyed diplomatic channel in Washington Asad has been conducting a nasty war by proxy against Israel in South Lebanon through the Hizbullah guerrilla organization and has sheltered the worst enemies of peace among the Palestinian organizations, some of which have been engaged in a brutal terrorist campaign aimed at derailing the very same process of which Syria is ostensibly a part. This recalcitrance played a significant role in Labour's defeat, not least by painting Prime Minister Peres, who went out of his way to strike a quick deal with Syria, as a hopeless optimist.

Hence, just as Netanyahu's election has improved the Palestinian bargaining position vis-à-vis Israel in the quest for peace, so it has improved Asad's ability to evade this quest altogether. Labour's determined drive to peace forced the Syrian President to play along, biting his lips in frustration over the rapid improvement in Israeli–Arab relations and trying to stall the Israeli–Syrian negotiations without incurring the American wrath. Now that the Netanyahu Government has slowed down the talks with the Palestinians in its strive for 'peace with security', has lost much of the political credit enjoyed by the Rabin-Peres Government in Washington and the world at large, and has antagonized a good many Arab leaders, Asad can relax his guard. Crying foul play, he has urged the Arab World to stop the normalization process with Israel and to restore the recently abandoned economic boycott of the Jewish State. So long as Netanyahu did not come forward with a bold initiative, Asad could entrench in his position in an effort to weaken the nascent peace process.

Yet in his heart of hearts Asad knows that there is no alternative to the peace process. Even a new Arab–Israeli conflagration, whose spectre has been looming larger than ever since 1982, would hardly prove a panacea. True, such an encounter might throw the peace process into a temporary disarray; but then it might not. Since Israel would not be destroyed by force of arms, a military confrontation is bound to result in the resumption of the peace talks, and not necessarily on terms favourable to the Arab side; which is precisely what Asad has sought to evade in the first place. Were he genuinely interested in peace, or even in regaining the Golan Heights, he could have seized Rabin's preparedness to such a move, reported to Asad by the US Administration. It makes no sense whatsoever to decline an Israeli offer of the entire Golan Heights only to initiate a military escalation, let alone an armed confrontation, aimed at reviving the peace process which could, in the best possible scenario, give Syria the same gains it has already been offered.

All this means that notwithstanding the predictable mutual posturing and brinkmanship, probably even the occasional stepping over the brink, the Arab World is bound to stick to the peace process. So is the Netanyahu Government, which has realized during its early months in power that it would be exceedingly difficult if not virtually impossible to disengage from the general line set by the Rabin-Peres Government. Netanyahu can slow down the Oslo Process, especially if the Palestinian Authority fails to curb the more militant elements in Palestinian society; but he cannot stop it altogether without running the risk of being swept from power at the end of his four-year term, if not much earlier. After all, the Israeli public has given Netanyahu a mandate to bring 'peace with security', and will settle for nothing short of this. To judge by Netanyahu's undertakings in the Hebron Protocol, and by the scarcely-veiled hints emanating from his inner circle of a possible acquiescence in an independent Palestinian State,[18] the new prime minister seems to have realized the simple truism that, in the final account, there is no alternative to peace. None whatsoever.

NOTES

1. See Andrea Levin, 'The Media's Tunnel Vision', *Middle East Quarterly*, Vol.III, No.4 (December 1996), pp.3–11.
2. Donald Neff, *Warriors for Jerusalem: The Six Days that Changed the Middle East*, New York, 1984, p.352.
3. Edward Said, 'Holy Land of My Fathers', *Observer*, 1 November 1992, p.49.
4. See, for example, Sadiq Jalal al-Azm, *al-Naqd al-Dhati Ba'd al-Hazima* (Self-Criticism after the Defeat), Beirut, 1969; Kamal al-Faramawi, *Yawmiyat Sajin fi-l-Sijn al-Harbi* (Military Prison Diary), Cairo, 1976, p.185; Ahmad Hamrush, *Qisat Thawrat 23 Yuliu, Vol.5: Kharif Abd al-Nasser* (Story of the July 23 Revolution, Vol.5: Abd al-Nasser's Autumn), Beirut, 1978, pp.145–71; Abdallah Laroui, *The Crisis of the Arab Intellectual*, translated from the French by Diarmid Cammell, Berkeley, 1976, pp.31, 176.
5. P.J. Vatikiotis, *Nasser and his Generation*, London, 1978, p.245.
6. *New York Times*, December 28, 1970.
7. Russell A. Stone, *Social Change in Israel: Attitudes and Events 1967–1979*, New York, 1982, p.41; Baruch Kimmerling, *Zionism and Territory: The Socio-Territorial Dimensions of Zionist Politics*, Berkeley, 1983, pp.175–78.
8. *International Herald Tribune*, 27 November, 5 December 1984.
9. Ze'ev Schiff and Ehud Ya'ari, *Israel's Lebanon War*, London, 1984, p.304.
10. Amoz Oz, *The Slopes of Lebanon*, translated from the Hebrew by Maurie Goldberg-Bartura, London, 1990, p.31.
11. It is still widely unknown that Israel's restraint was largely due to an explicit Jordanian–Israeli understanding, reached at a secret meeting in London between King Hussein and Prime Minister Yitzhak Shamir shortly before the outbreak of hostilities. See, Moshe Zak, 'Israel and Jordan: Strategically Bound', *Israel Affairs*, Vol.III, No.1 (Autumn 1996), pp.51–5.
12. See, for example, *Damascus Radio*, 4, 5, 10 March 1991.
13. *Baghdad Voice of the PLO*, 8 January 1991.
14. *Al-Ra'i* (Amman), 2 January 1991.
15. For elaboration of this issue see my 'Introduction: From Rabin to Netanyahu', *Israel Affairs*, Vol.3, No.3 & 4 (Spring–Summer 1997) pp.i–viii.
16. Indeed, in the 'Note for the Record' attached to the Hebron Protocol, the Palestinian side undertook to 'complete the process of revising the Palestinian National Charter'.
17. *Newsweek*, 5 August 1991, p.16 (emphasis added).
18. See, for example, interview with David Bar-Ilan, Netanyahu's senior policy adviser, *Jerusalem Post*, 20 December 1996.

From War to Peace: Obstacles, Prospects, and Implications of the Middle East Peace Process

MOHAMMED Z. YAKAN

During the past three decades the Middle East has witnessed some major existential developments, the effects of which will continue to influence its countries and its peoples for generations to come. These included the toppling of the monarchical regime in Iran and the rise of radical and militant religious movements in the region, the two Gulf wars, Anwar Sadat's visit to Jerusalem in November 1977, the Lebanese crisis and the dislodging of the Palestine Liberation Organization (PLO) from Lebanon, the end of the Middle East's role as a centre of Cold War tension and the subsequent change in the strategic significance of several of its countries to the former East–West protagonists, the reduced power of the oil-producing countries due to the drop in world oil prices, the increased burdens of military expenditure and the mounting international indebtedness of Middle Eastern countries, a relative drop in funds from international sources of finance, and finally the widening gap between the have and have not countries in the region. Of all these developments, Sadat's 1977 Jerusalem visit has probably exerted the greatest impact on the course of the Arab–Israeli conflict.

This visit sparked a series of dramatic events in the Middle East which subsequently led to a string of peace agreements and accords and the initiation of the ongoing Middle East peace process. For the first time since the start of the Arab–Israeli conflict, the official representatives of Israel, the Palestinians, and several Arab states have opted to cultivate the possibility of peace and to put an end to a conflict that continues to leave tragic marks on their respective peoples, societies, and economies. For a variety of reasons, including conflict fatigue, the parties to the Arab–Israeli conflict have expressed a desire for genuine peace. Each of them saw cooperation with the other parties

Mohammed Z. Yakan is Associate Professor of International Relations at the United States International University, San Diego.

as crucial to their respective strategic interests, as well as to meeting their respective national objectives.

Clearly, this desire on the one hand, and the agreements, accords, and ongoing negotiations on the other, are vital first steps towards comprehensive peace in the Middle East, but they are definitely not peace. If anything, they are essential steps which, on their own, are insufficient for achieving and maintaining peace. To borrow E.H. Carr's assessment of the consequences of the First World War, peace 'cannot be achieved by the signing of pacts or covenants "outlawing" war any more than revolutions are prevented by making them illegal'.[1]

In order to achieve a lasting peace in the Middle East, the conditions of peace would first have to be met and established. This in turn depends on the protagonists' satisfaction with the terms of the peace agreements, their fairness, and their positive and rewarding results for their respective societies. They would have to realize that it is in their mutual interest to seek peace. In the words of the late Israeli academic Yehoshafat Harkabi; '[Peace] agreements that endure do so not because the sides involved have made a commitment to abide by them forever... but rather because a mutual interest has been created in not reverting to a state of war'.[2]

Moreover, the great majority of people in the region, and not simply their governments, would have to embrace the cause of peace. They would have to feel that the peace envisaged in the concluded agreements is a positive peace and not a negative one – positive in the sense that all 'ordinary people' can feel its advantages. They would have to sense that it is not simply an end to the state of belligerency between their respective countries. Furthermore, the regional governments and nations would have to forego their obsession with security and narrow selfish national objectives, and instead look forward to the establishment and nourishment of the human, and not merely the political and military, conditions of peace. In other terms, they would have to normalize their relations, end all manifestations of hostility towards each other, and delve in joint productive ventures at both the public and private levels. In short, the Middle East peace process would have to be transformed from a formal governmental concern into a people's concern and, moreover, new conditions would have to be created to avert the possibility of the resumption of hostilities. By all indications, this is still a remote prospect. It will be a while before Jews, Christians and Muslims in the Middle East can bind themselves in a fraternity of peace.

That the conditions of an enduring peace are still lacking is exemplified in the formidable psychological, political, economic, social, and cultural problems in the area. If these problems are not rapidly and constructively addressed they may disrupt the Middle East peace process, if not reverse the progress that has already been made.

This essay seeks to address several aspects of these problems, so as to generate some general proposals the application of which may be helpful in giving a momentum to peace at the grass-roots level.

PSYCHOLOGICAL CHALLENGES

The psychological challenges are by far the most important. Since 1917 Arab–Jewish relations have been characterized by mistrust, hatred and, above all, fear. Nationalism, the phenomenon causing so many European and international conflicts and wars at least since the advent in 1648 of the Westphalian territorial nation-state system, has also bedeviled the modern Middle East. In favouring the establishment of a national home for the Jewish people in Palestine and pledging British facilitation of this objective, the Balfour Declaration of 2 November 1917 planted the seeds of ethnic conflict between the Arab and Jewish peoples. Though making plain 'that nothing shall be done which may prejudice the civil and religious rights of existing non-Jewish communities in Palestine, or the rights and political status enjoyed by Jews in any other country',[3] the declaration sparked the conflict which Arabs and Jews are still trying to resolve.

The establishment of a national home for one people cannot be attained without reverberations to the other people living there. There are bound to be drastic demographic transformations in the area where it is to be founded for the simple reason that no national home can be peacefully established anywhere on earth without ensuring one's preponderance within the respective territory. This, in turn, is certain to antagonize the other national group(s) in the area, which for their part can scarcely be expected to welcome, accept or condone any scheme that would inevitably come at their expense. This situation is further exacerbated when a third party determines the territory's future without prior consultation with the indigenous populations, not to speak of giving them a say in the matter.

In favouring the establishment of a national home for the Jews in Palestine without any prejudicial effects on the civil and religious rights of the Arab population which was then the predominant majority in the country, the Balfour Declaration embodied two contradictory and irreconcilable notions. As such it was the product of either great naivety or superb perfidy on the part of its author: naivety if the British failed to foresee the inevitability of a national conflict in the Promised Land; perfidy if the Declaration was merely a divide-and-rule tactic, aimed at obstructing future connection (and unity) between the eastern and western flanks of the Arab World and at the same time pitting Arabs and Jews against each other.

In my view, all evidence points to the latter option, namely, that the Declaration was a reflection of the perfidy of contemporary British foreign policy. Both Arabs and Jews fell for the scheme, though Britain acted only in its own self-serving interest; the Arabs and Jews were thus entrapped in a tragic conflict that was to continue to inflict great harm on their respective peoples for nearly a century.

British perfidy apart, both Arabs and Jews have been victims of their own ethno-centric ideologies. As a consequence, fear has emerged as the predominant factor colouring and shaping their policies and relations with each other. Manifested in lack of trust, and in mutual suspicion and animosity, fear emanated and became entrenched among the population as a result of extremists' violence on both sides, a long history of mutual war-oriented propaganda, Arab–Israeli wars and the uprooting and displacement of peoples as a result of these wars. To the present day fear continues to plague Arab–Israeli relations and, understandably, is unlikely to dissipate in the foreseeable future.

Overcoming fear appears to be the foremost challenge to permanent peace in the Middle East. In fact, the divisions between Arabs and Israelis regarding the peace process in general and the Oslo Accords in particular can best be understood in terms of fear. Partly it is a fear of the unknown, and certainly of an undefined and unclear future; partly it is a fear of the sacrifices that both parties would have to make in order to lead the peace process to its ultimate end.

On the part of Arabs in general, and the Palestinians in particular, there is the fear that their aspirations for a sovereign and an independent state, with East Jerusalem (which was united with West Jerusalem and proclaimed the 'eternal' capital of Israel following its occupation in the 1967 Six-Day War) as its capital will not be condoned by Israel. It is the fear of devolving into a small Bantustan on a portion of the West Bank and the Gaza Strip, territories without the means of even separate development or survival.[4] It is the fear that the peace process will not recognize their rights to self-determination, repatriation, land-property redemption, or compensation; that the Israeli government will drag out the talks with the Palestinians while changing the facts on the ground and expanding Jewish settlements in the occupied lands.[5] This fear stems from Arab/Palestinian distrust of Israel's non-committal pronouncements with regard to the future title of the West Bank and the Gaza Strip, and their uncertainty of whether Israel would be willing to recognize these areas as Palestinian territory. Hence it is a fear that Israel's role in the peace process is that of a Trojan Horse, whose ultimate aim is, through peaceful means, the subjugation of the Arab World to its influence, if not control.

On the part of Israelis it is the fear of the adverse consequences of giving up the occupied territories (the West Bank, the Gaza Strip, and the Golan Heights), considered important for reducing Israel's vulnerability to attacks from the east. It is the fear of becoming defenceless if the country shrinks to the pre-1967 War borders, squeezing its territory 'too close against the sea'.[6] It is the fear emanating from the fact that, for the first time since 1947, Israelis have to define the country's permanent borders, a decision that may not guarantee them the safe haven that they aspire to. It is the fear of what they see as an imminent process in the direction of a Palestinian State – a state which they view as detrimental to their national security and over which they may have no influence or control. Among settlers, it is a fear of losing the homes they established in the occupied territories after the 1967 War. Among Israeli religious groups, the loss of access to, and control over, the biblical Land of Israel is a cause of great anxiety. Israeli religious groups view the relinquishment to Palestinians of the West Bank, the Judea and Samaria of biblical Israel, as betrayal of the cause of 'Greater Israel', *Eretz Israel*, their biblical homeland. As the *Economist* observed,

> the bulk of Israelis who are suspicious of the peace process have something altogether more straightforward on their minds. It is called fear. They are afraid that if Israel gives up the West Bank [and the Golan Heights] and shrinks back behind the 1967 borders, the Arabs will eventually cut its throat.[7]

Fear is a common reality. It is not a feeling that is restricted to opponents of the Middle East process. It is also shared by Israel's Labour party which launched the present process. In fact, fear is one of the main factors which prompted this party to accept the principle of land for peace: the fear that the incorporation of the West Bank into Israel may eventually threaten the Jewish character of the State of Israel, thus leading to the establishment of a bi-national state. As put by the *Economist*,

> what Mr. Rabin's [Labour] government had been doing is simple... Since the original purpose of Israel was to create a country – the only country – in which Jews form a majority, it would be folly to incorporate within its borders millions of Arabs who would multiply until they outnumbered the Jews. So [Labour] has long promised to trade some of the land Israel captured in the six-day war of 1967 for peace. The most contested bit of land, the West Bank, is populated mainly by Palestinians: well over 1m of them, as against fewer than 120,000 Israelis who have settled there since 1967. When Mr. Rabin was [defence] minister, he tried in vain to squash the Palestinians' intifada uprising against the military occupation. In trying, he learnt that the Palestinians would no longer be subdued. All the more reason to withdraw. That, in a nutshell, is the case for peace.[8]

This fear was implicit in numerous statements by Yitzhak Rabin. Shortly before his assassination on the evening of 4 November 1995 he told the

New York Times: 'I don't believe that for 2,000 years Jews dreamed and prayed about the return to Zion to create a binational state'.[9] It was also implicit in his interview with columnists Rowland Evans and Robert Novak after the signing of the West Bank agreement (Oslo II) at the White House on 28 September 1995. In this interview, Rabin said:

> My goal is not the whole land of Israel. I believe that dreams of Jews for two thousand years to return to Zion were to build a Jewish State and not a binational state. Therefore I don't want to annex the 2.2 million Palestinians who are a different entity from us – politically, religiously, nationally – against their will to become Israelis. Therefore I see peaceful coexistence between Israel as a Jewish State – not all over the land of Israel, on most of it, its capital the United Jerusalem, its security border the Jordan river – next to it a Palestinian entity, less than a state, that runs the life of the Palestinians. It is not ruled by Israel. It is ruled by the Palestinians.[10]

Rabin concluded his interview by affirming:

> This is my goal – not to return to the pre-1967 lines but to create two entities. I want a separation between Israel and the Palestinians who reside in the West Bank and the Gaza Strip and they will be a different entity that rules itself.[11]

Fear is a complex reality in Arab–Israeli relations. It has governed these relations since 1917, and it cannot be expected to dissipate by the signing of an agreement or a series of agreements. It explains much of Arab and Israeli rational and irrational behaviour in the past and at present, and will probably continue to explain it for an indeterminate time in the future.

This challenge is not over. In order to transform the peace agreements into a lasting peace, this fear will have to be addressed through miscellaneous short-term and long-term confidence-building measures. This task will not be an easy one.

POLITICAL CHALLENGES

At the political level, the agreements between Israel and Egypt, on the one hand, and Israel and Jordan, on the other, have resolved a crucial problem in Arab–Israeli relations, namely that of mutual recognition and acceptance. As a result of the Camp David Accords that set the framework for peace in the Middle East, and the subsequent peace treaty of 26 March 1979, both Egypt and Israel ended the state of war, recognized each other, and agreed to establish full diplomatic relations with each other. Moreover, Israel agreed to withdraw from Sinai, allowing Egypt to reassert its sovereignty over the peninsula. The Taba enclave remained disputed until late 1988, at which time it was awarded to Egypt by international arbitration.

Unlike the armistice agreement of 1949, drawn in accordance with pure military considerations, the 1979 peace treaty provided for political and legal recognition between the two states on the basis of their current territories. In so doing, it dispelled one major element of tension between the two states.

Likewise, the Israeli–Jordanian peace treaty of 26 October 1994 ended the state of war between Israel and Jordan. Article 1 of the treaty stated: 'Peace is hereby established between the Hashemite Kingdom of Jordan and the state of Israel'.[12]

The Israeli–Jordanian agreement was also drawn up on the basis of political as well as military considerations. It delimited the boundary of the two states once and for all and provided for the establishment of full diplomatic relations and economic cooperation between them, starting with the termination of economic boycotts. Under the terms of this treaty, the British Mandatory line, with minor modifications, was recognized by both parties as their respective international boundary. Additionally, Israel ceded to Jordan sovereignty over a small territory which it occupied in the Arab–Israeli War of 1967. The treaty thus allayed Arab fears in general, and Jordanian fears in particular, regarding Israel's territorial ambitions beyond the east flank of the Jordan River.[13]

The Israel–PLO 1993 agreement provided for mutual recognition between the two parties and laid the principles of Palestinian interim self-government in the occupied territories starting with Jericho (West Bank) and the Gaza Strip. The agreement comprised three letters (dated 9 September 1993), and the Declaration of Principles on Interim Self-Government Arrangements of 13 September 1993 (DOP). The three letters covered the mutual recognition portion of the agreement, whereas the Declaration which was signed on the White House lawn covered the principles that would govern the Palestinian interim self-government in Jericho and Gaza.

The first letter was from PLO Chairman Yasser Arafat to Israeli Prime Minister Yitzhak Rabin. In this letter, Arafat related the PLO's recognition of the 'right of the State of Israel to exist in peace and security', its acceptance of United Nations Security Council Resolutions 242 and 338, and its commitment 'to the Middle East peace process and to a peaceful resolution of the conflict between the two sides', as well as to the settlement of all outstanding issues 'relating to permanent status' through negotiations. Moreover, he declared the PLO's renunciation of 'the use of terrorism and other acts of violence', and its commitment 'to assume the responsibility over all PLO elements and personnel in order to assure their compliance, prevent violations and discipline violators'. Furthermore, Arafat promised 'to submit to the Palestinian National Council for formal approval the necessary changes in regard to the National Covenant', namely to annul 'the provisions of the Palestinian Covenant which were inconsistent with the commitments' stipulated in the letter; in the meantime he defined these provisions as 'inoperative and no longer valid'.[14]

The second letter was from Arafat to Norwegian Foreign Minister Johan Jørgen Holst. In this letter, he embraced the PLO's declaration which encouraged and called upon 'the Palestinian people in the West Bank and the Gaza Strip to take part in the steps leading to the normalization of life, rejecting violence and terrorism, contributing to peace and stability and participating actively in shaping reconstruction, economic development and cooperation'.[15]

The third letter was from Prime Minister Rabin to Arafat. In this letter, Rabin maintained that in light of the PLO commitments [included in Arafat's letter of 9 September 1993] the Government of Israel has decided to recognize the PLO as the representative of the Palestinian people and commence negotiations with the PLO within the Middle East process.[16]

Finally, the Declaration of Principles defined the principles of Palestinian interim self-government in the West Bank and the Gaza Strip.[17]

Clearly, the three agreements in question were important turning points in the modern history of the Middle East. But all of them, especially the Israeli–PLO agreement, provide for further negotiations regarding the establishment of a lasting peace. In other words, these documents, especially the Israeli–Jordanian and Israeli–PLO agreements, were not all-inclusive peace packages. Many important issues were either not mentioned at all, or deferred, possibly for consideration in the future. Some of these issues are of a critical nature. If left unsolved, they may well disrupt the entire peace process and its achievements.

The omissions may have been intentional. It is highly probable that the agreements were concluded primarily to secure a commitment on the part of their parties to change conditions which were no longer acceptable to any one of them, to make the same parties aware of the opportunities and risks that are likely to face them in the course of changing these conditions, and finally but slowly, to develop relationships within the frameworks by which fundamental changes could be made through further negotiations. Simply, it may have been intentional to help erode psychological barriers to negotiations, and thereupon gradually narrow the differences in the positions of the parties of the conflict prior to reaching the final settlement. But irrespective of the reasons underlying the omissions, the issues whose consideration was deferred are very serious.

The Camp David Accords, for example, secured the return of all occupied Egyptian territories to Egypt, but did not get beyond an agreement on a general formula for dealing with Palestinian demands.

They left unresolved substantive Palestinian issues, such as claims to sovereignty over the West Bank and the Gaza Strip, demands for Israel's withdrawal from – and moratorium on new settlements in – the occupied territories, and demands for recognizing the Palestinians' right to self-determination. Reportedly, the then Israeli Premier Menachem Begin refused to prohibit the establishment of new Israeli settlements in the West Bank and Gaza, and moreover declined to commit his country to the principle of withdrawal from the West Bank and the Gaza Strip in exchange for peace. The only substantive commitment that he was willing to agree to, and that was incorporated in the Camp David Accords, was to respect the 'legitimate rights of the Palestinian people'. No more, no less.[18]

Hence, the general formula of the Camp David Accords with regard to Palestinian issues was general, vague, and indefinite in nature. It provided that 'Egypt, possibly with Jordan, would negotiate guidelines with Israel for a transitional period of no more than five years. At the outset of this period, the Palestinians in the occupied territories would be able to elect a 'self-governing authority' to manage local affairs. Israel, however, would continue to be responsible for 'internal and external security'. The agreement also stipulated that the 'Palestinians would not be able to participate on their own behalf in negotiations until talks began on the "final status" of the disputed territories'. The latter talks were to begin 'as soon as possible but not later than the third year after the beginning of the transitional period'.[19]

In short, the Camp David Accords ended the state of war between Egypt and Israel, but did not get far beyond this level to issues, including substantive Palestinian issues, that affect not only the implementation of these accords, but also their very existence. As put by Borthwick:

> Peace has been arrived at between Egypt and Israel, but the territorial claims of these two states were not sharply in conflict. The truly difficult negotiations are in respect to East Jerusalem, the West Bank, and Gaza, where both Jews and Palestinians have historic claims. With a background of [almost three fourths of a] century of conflict between Arabs and Israelis, deep hostility between Palestinians and Israelis, memories of the Holocaust ever present for Jews, and the humiliations of imperialism still fixed in the minds of Arabs, total peace is not going to be arrived at quickly or easily. All parties will have to agree to something each finds less than desirable.[20]

Regarding the Israeli–Jordanian agreement, such critical issues as the position of Palestinian refugees and displaced persons in Jordan and the final status of Jerusalem, were vaguely addressed. Questions relating to refugees and displaced persons were deferred and tabled for resolution 'through three committees: a quadripartite committee with Egypt and the Palestinians; the multilateral group on refugees; and a framework working in conjunction with the permanent status negotiations'.[21] Moreover, the treaty recognized Jordan's special role in the Muslim holy shrines in Jerusalem, but again noted that when the permanent-status negotiations take place, 'Israel would give high priority to the Jordanian historic role in these shrines'.[22] There is nothing conclusive in the treaty about the refugees, the displaced persons, and the status of Jerusalem.

Hence, these issues continue to be serious challenges to the peace process. Because of the grave nature of these issues, they are vulnerable to domestic developments within Israel, Jordan, the West Bank and the Gaza Strip, Egypt, and the Arab World at large. Because of their sensitive nature, their resolution in the future is not likely to please all parties concerned, or at least not all segments of the Israeli and Arab populations. To all appearances, their resolution does not seem feasible at this juncture, and at least not in the near future.

Regarding the first issue (refugees and displaced persons), Jordanians, for example, are already apprehensive of losing the Jordanian character of their state. Since Jordan is a poor and overpopulated country which cannot survive without foreign aid, some Jordanians feel that they would be better off without the large Palestinian population, currently estimated at more than half of Jordan's total population, which competes with them for the country's limited jobs and resources. This also explains why the relations between Jordanians and Palestinians have continued to be governed by various forms of overt and covert tension.

Moreover, Arab countries with Palestinian refugee populations are likely to resist any attempt that calls for resolving this problem by having Palestinian refugees settle in Jordan. These countries, especially Lebanon, fear that such a solution would set a precedent for the permanent settlement of Palestinian refugees in their respective territories, a factor that would disturb, if not destabilize, the demographic power balances within their societies. The Palestinian factor has already proved to be one of the primary causes of the Lebanese civil war, impacting on the country's sensitive confessional (sectarian) system. Solving the problem by settling Palestinian refugees in the host countries may lead to another civil war in Lebanon, tipping the demographic balance in favour of the Sunnite minority, a prospect that the other 17 religious minorities in Lebanon do not welcome. As put by Harkabi:

> The Arab states... recognize that as long as there is no Palestinian state they too will have no rest. Their commitment to the Palestinians stems not only from national sentiments but also, and most importantly, from calculations of their own self-interest. They

are apprehensive that the Palestinians, if they do not settle down, may destabilize their own countries.[23]

Conversely, many Palestinians in diaspora, especially those in Jordan, Syria, or Lebanon, may prefer to be repatriated to areas of their original habitats, some of which are currently located within Israel's internationally recognized territory.

What applies to the Israeli–Jordanian peace treaty applies also to the Israeli–PLO agreement. In fact, the issues that Israelis and Palestinians still have to address are highly problematic and controversial.

First, the Israel–PLO agreement was not between two states, and more importantly, it was not conclusive. It was between a state, the State of Israel, and a non-state organization (PLO), the representative of the Palestinian people. To judge by the terms of agreement, the former appeared as the party that outlined the Declaration of Principles while the latter appeared to have accepted the principles and agreed to comply with their provisions.

In other words, the PLO did not join the negotiations as a government representing a state, nor did it enter them with the full powers of a constituted government. Its delegation to the Madrid peace process (the members of which were approved by Israel) was part of the Jordanian team, and while Palestinians and Israelis indulged in secret direct talks in the Norwegian capital of Oslo, the Israel–PLO agreement lacked the attributes that are normally associated with formal government-to-government agreements.[24] The PLO, for example, was not pictured as a fully-fledged government but was rather regarded as a representative of the Palestinian population – not the entire Palestinian people but essentially those of the West Bank and the Gaza Strip. Hence the DOP could not be considered an agreement between two equal partners. As observed by Bannerman,

> The Israeli government insisted that no one from the PLO, the Palestinian diaspora, Jerusalem or members of the Palestine National Council (PNC) could represent the Palestinians. Furthermore the Israelis demanded that the Palestinians participate as part of a joint delegation with the Jordanians.[25]

Moreover, under the terms of the Israeli–PLO agreement, outstanding issues 'including the status of Jerusalem, refugees, security arrangements, borders, relations and cooperation with other neighbours, and other issues of common interests were deferred 'until after the election of a "Palestinian Interim Self-Government"'. This latter body, known as the Council, would enter into negotiations with the Government of Israel regarding these issues. Hence, the agreement deemed the election of the Council as an 'interim preparatory step toward "the realization of the legitimate rights of the Palestinian people [of the West Bank and the Gaza Strip] and their just requirements"' as well as towards reaching 'a permanent settlement based on Security Council Resolutions 242 and 338'.[26]

Clearly, the outstanding issues that the agreement has referred to, and other questions of common interest that were not specifically mentioned (such as the Israeli settlements in the occupied territories and the Palestinian quest for statehood) are critical issues which could be easily manipulated by dissatisfied elements among the Jewish and Palestinian peoples in order to wreck the entire peace process. True, the DOP affirmed that negotiations regarding the permanent status of the territories, as well as other outstanding issues, would commence as soon as possible 'but not later than the beginning of the third year of the interim period'.[27] Yet no one can predict precisely how long these negotiations would take, or whether or not they could lead to a successful conclusion, especially since the substantive issues still to be addressed are both critical and controversial. These centre on the Palestinian quest for independence; the status of Jerusalem in general and East Jerusalem in particular; delimitation of the borders of the Palestinian entity; the future of Israeli settlements; defence and security of the West Bank and the Gaza Strip; the future of the Israeli Arabs; and miscellaneous questions relating to Palestinians in diaspora, such as repatriation, compensation, and land redemption. So long as these issues are not resolved to the satisfaction of all parties concerned, they will continue to threaten the Middle East peace process and its achievements. Indeed, it is no exaggeration to say that the future of the Middle East depends on their resolution.

Most regrettably, these substantive issues are not wholly reconcilable. For example, while the Palestinians call for the establishment of an independent sovereign state in the West Bank and the Gaza Strip with East Jerusalem as its capital, the Israeli government seeks to grant them a self-rule of sorts that would not include Jerusalem or have the sovereign attributes of a fully-fledged state. The message from the Palestinian electorate on 20 January 1996 was clear in considering the elections as 'the foundation stone for a Palestinian state'.[28] Virtually, 'all the candidates who ran for the 88-seat council did so on a nation-building platform – promising voters an independent, democratic Palestinian state with Jerusalem as its capital'.[29]

The position of the Israeli public with regard to the aspirations of Palestinians for statehood is as equivocal as that of their government. A recent poll conducted by the daily *Ma'ariv* showed that '48 [per cent] of Israelis oppose statehood for the Palestinians, 38 [per cent] support the idea, and 13 [per cent] refused to answer the question or gave an ambiguous [response]'.[30]

Obviously, the issue of settlements is directly connected to that of independence. If Palestinians are granted an independent state, a far-fetched possibility, the news of the settlements and their inhabitants would occupy the headlines, and eventually, might be resolved by compensating and/or resettling their inhabitants. However, if Palestinians are granted an entity that is short of complete statehood, a more likely scenario, then it is highly probable that the settlements would remain intact, and be provided with the protection of Israel.

Since 1967, the population of Israeli settlements in the occupied territories has increased from about 27,500 in 1983, and 60,000 in 1987, to 205,000 in 1992 (including Jerusalem).[31] Many of these settlements were established by Amana, the settlement arm of the extremist Gush Emunim movement – a movement that has repeatedly expressed its resistance to any measure(s) that would lead to relinquishing the West Bank to Palestinians. The question is how one can peacefully reconcile the two quests – the exigencies of an independent Palestinian state (if granted) and those of the continued presence of Israeli settlements in this 'foreign country'? The solution would seem to lie in the principle of reciprocity. But is this possible? The answer is definitely no.

As regards the territory of the Palestinian entity, it is highly likely that this will occupy a smaller area than the internationally recognized areas of both the West Bank (5,860 square kilometres) and the Gaza Strip (360 square kilometres). Excepting the issue of East Jerusalem, it is highly probable that some areas on which Israeli settlements were established after 1967 will be excluded from the Palestinian entity. It is also likely that they will be recognized as Palestinian territory, but will be leased to Jewish settlers for long periods of time. A third possibility is that of placing them under a special Israeli–Palestinian regime. The first scenario is most serious, and if attempted, may provoke both Palestinian and other Arab opposition that may in turn derail the entire Middle East peace process.

The question of East Jerusalem is by far the most difficult. In fact, '[n]othing in the history of the Arab–Israeli conflict has been so contentious as the issue of Jerusalem.'[32] Since 1948, this issue has been covered by all United Nations resolutions about the Palestine question. Early United Nations resolutions affirmed the international character of this holy city and rejected its proclamation as Israel's capital. Later resolutions, especially those passed after the 1967 War, censured Israeli actions in the city, including its annexation of East Jerusalem. But all these resolutions were met by Israel's insistence on its claim to the city, including its eastern section.

In question is how to reconcile the Arab–Palestinian, Israeli, and international claims? Can Jerusalem become the capital of Israel, the capital of the Palestinian entity, and an international capital for the three monotheistic religions, Christianity, Judaism and Islam, at one and the same time?

Obviously, this is not an easy question to answer, especially if one takes into consideration the demographic and physical changes that have taken place in East Jerusalem since its occupation by Israeli forces in 1967. In the words of Palestinian activist Ghada Karmi, since its occupation,

> Israel has worked ceaselessly to create a permanent Jewish presence in Arab Jerusalem, and it is succeeding. In 1993, for the first time, Israelis outnumbered Palestinians there by 160,000 to 155,000, a figure which is set to rise if current settlement plans for the city go ahead. Since 1967, 31 [per cent] of Palestinian residents of Jerusalem have been displaced from their homes in various ways, and some 21,000 such families are currently homeless. Construction of Israeli settlements in and around the Arab half of Jerusalem has created the Israeli concept of 'Greater Jerusalem'. As the present mayor of the city, Ehud Olmert, recently said: 'I will expand Jerusalem to the east, not to the west... I can make things happen on the ground to ensure the city will remain united under Israeli control for eternity'.

Karmi also states that the Dutch cartographer, Jan de Jong, 'believes that Israel has a much more ambitious plan for the [city] than anything seen so far, the so-called "Metropolitan Jerusalem"'. In her view,

> [t]his is a vastly expanded area which will comprise about 1,250 sq.km, three quarters of which will be West Bank land. It will extend almost half way to Tel-Aviv in the west, to Halhul and Hebron in the south, beyond Ramallah in the north and up to Jericho in the east. Arab Jerusalem, which has already been transformed from a Palestinian city into what is effectively an Israeli settlement, will be wholly swallowed up, along with Bethlehem and other Palestinian towns and villages in the new Metropolitan Jerusalem.[33]

In light of Karmi's observations, the issue of East Jerusalem appears to be more complex than ever before. If the above plans are implemented, it is highly probable that by the time of the final status talks between Israel and Palestinians, which failed to start by the scheduled date of 1996, the evolving realities will have led to the situation where, in Karmi's words, 'there will be no Arab Jerusalem left to negotiate about'. In her assessment, the question of Jerusalem may be lost by default.[34]

What is debatable is the impact of these developments on the peace talks. Would they result in freezing the talks, stop the normalization process, and halt efforts aimed at broadening the coverage of the Middle East peace process? No one really knows or can predict this with certainty. To all appearances, conflict is likely to erupt not only if Palestinian statehood is not granted, but also if it is granted without recognizing East Jerusalem as the capital of the Palestinian state.

On the other hand, if the Palestinians are granted an entity short of a state, then ultimate sovereignty over the West Bank and the Gaza Strip will be in Israel's hands. Theoretically speaking the problem may be resolved by having Jerusalem serve as the capital of both Israel and the Palestinian self-governing entity. The latter scenario, however, does not comply with present Palestinian demands.

As regards international objections, they are likely to be neutralized with the help of the United States. Since 1968, the United States has vetoed five major UN Security Council resolutions regarding the international status of Jerusalem. More recently, on 9 May 1995, bills mandating the transfer of the US Embassy to Jerusalem were introduced into the Senate by Robert Dole, the then Republican US Senate majority leader and Republican presidential candidate, and into the House of Representatives by Republican Speaker Newt Gingrich. Though Secretary of State Warren Christopher quickly criticized this move as 'ill-advised and damaging to the success of the peace negotiations', it is highly likely that these bills will pass in due time. The PLO's immediate reaction was conveyed by Marwan Kanafani, an aide to PLO chairman Yasser Arafat, who reportedly said that if the US Embassy was moved to Jerusalem, '[the] [PLO]–Israel accord will be null and void'.[35]

In light of these considerations, the issue of Jerusalem is clearly the most critical. According to Amos Perlmutter, the

> [peace] process could collapse completely over [this issue], which is just what Oslo was designed to avert. Israelis will not accept a divided Jerusalem as their capital, nor will the Palestinians accept anything less than the establishment of East Jerusalem as their capital and Palestinian–not Jordanian–control over the city's Islamic shrines. Both sides continue to thrust Jerusalem onto the agenda, which could make the holy city the straw that breaks the camel's back.[36]

Finally, the issues that relate to diaspora Palestinians are most crucial. If their demands are not fairly met, their influence and power, especially in Lebanon, Syria and Jordan, are more than enough to affect the entire Middle East peace process, if not to abort it. Even if absorbed by the host Arab states, Palestinians in those countries have and will continue to bear a significant influence on regional developments. A solution that would be satisfactory to the Palestinians in the occupied territories may not be amenable to diaspora Palestinians; should they feel betrayed, or regard the peace agreements as unfair insofar as they are concerned, their alienation and grudge will continue to grow and may eventually erupt, causing all sorts of unpredictable instabilities in the area. Unless this challenge is fairly addressed, the challenge of Palestinians in the diaspora will continue to constitute a threat to any peaceful settlement in the area, hinder any meaningful entrenchment of peace, and in time may lead to another cycle of unrest in the Middle East. Hence it is arguable that granting the Palestinians statehood is tantamount to installing a safety valve for the Middle East process. Instead of aggravating their alienation and inflaming their anxieties, such a development would make them feel that they have not been forgotten, betrayed, or discarded. At least it would make them feel that the process has resulted in giving them a country with which they can identify.

The above-mentioned issues are critical ones, and by all indications are going to generate a great deal of contention when the final-status talks eventually start. It will be no exaggeration to say that this stage of the negotiations can make or break the entire peace process. To all appearances, it will be a clash of conflicting, if not irreconcilable, demands.

ECONOMIC CHALLENGES

Another major challenge to the peace process in the Middle East relates to the disparity in the economic conditions and standards of living between Israelis and the Palestinians of the West Bank, the Gaza Strip, and East Jerusalem.[37] This disparity is likely to become a thorn in any effort that aims to foster meaningful economic cooperation between Israelis, Palestinians, and Arabs. Economic conditions are deplorable among Palestinians of the West Bank, the Gaza Strip, and East Jerusalem. Their localities are pockets of poverty, and as such, they will continue to be natural breeding places for alienation, agitation, and violence. Under the prevailing conditions, the Palestinians of the occupied territories are easy prey to revisionist, revolutionary and extremist incitement, as are the Palestinians in refugee camps in some neighbouring Arab countries where they are economically restricted and disallowed to pursue gainful and productive occupations. No country can enjoy peace when pockets of poverty are within it, adjacent to it, or around it.

For example, the breakdown of the total Palestinian population in the Israeli occupied territories shows that 19–20 per cent of the 2,175,086-strong community (July 1994 estimate) live in 16 of the refugee camps run by UNRWA (United Nations Relief and Works Agency for Palestine Refugees in the Near East). In the West bank, about ten per cent of the 1,443,790 Palestinians (July 1994 estimate) live in eight refugee camps, 25 per cent in 25 towns, 13 per cent in East Jerusalem, and the rest in rural areas. In the Gaza Strip, two-thirds of the 731,296 Palestinians (July 1994 estimate) are registered with UNRWA as refugees, and half of these live in eight refugee camps.

Both areas have negligible natural resources, and both depend on remittances of workers employed in Israel and the Persian Gulf states for survival. In 1991, for example, Gaza's GNP was estimated at $380 million with -30 per cent real growth rate, and the West Bank's at $1.3 billion with

-10 per cent real growth rate, whereas Israel's GDP was estimated at $54.6 billion with 5 per cent real growth rate. During the same year, national product per capita in the Gaza Strip was $590 and in the West Bank $1,200, compared to $12,000 in Israel. In terms of unemployment, in 1991 the rate of unemployment in the Gaza Strip was estimated at 20 per cent, in the West Bank at 15 per cent, and in Israel at 11 per cent. These differences do, and probably will continue to impact on the attitudes and the behaviour of both the Palestinian and Israeli populations. Discrepancies in standards of living are not healthy conditions for the normalization or the promotion of natural peaceful relations among nations.[38]

Yes, the peace agreements that were concluded with Egypt, Jordan and the PLO tried to address this issue. They provided for economic cooperation, development banks, housing projects... But, regretfully, it seems that since the conclusion of the Oslo Accords the Palestinian poor have become even poorer. As Sara Roy correctly observes, the economic conditions in the Gaza Strip and the West Bank have never been worse in certain critical respects. The United States government and other sources indicate that 'at least 14 per cent of all Palestinians of the West Bank and the Gaza Strip, or what amounts to about 300,000 people, are now living

> at or below the absolute annual per capita poverty level of between $500 and $650. The Israeli absolute annual per capita poverty line, by contrast, is $2,500. ('Absolute' poverty is based on what it costs to sustain one person for a year.) In regional terms, the number of permanently poor breaks down to 20 per cent of Gaza's population and 10 per cent of the West Bank's. By some estimates, at least one-third of the Palestinian poor were forced into poverty after the Oslo accord was signed.[39]

In fact, however, 'the 14 per cent poverty figure is probably low; poverty [in the West Bank and the Gaza Strip] tends to be under-reported, given the social safety net provided by extended family and friends and poor statistical data gathering'.[40]

In light of Roy's observations, unemployment (which minimally stands at about 20 per cent in Gaza) is a major problem that will have to be addressed to avoid creating the conditions of have and have-not societies along ethnic and religious lines. If left unresolved, this problem will continue to plague Israeli–Palestinian relations, thus threatening the achievements made so far in the Middle East peace process. This in turn will ensure that the blame for the depressed economic conditions in the West Bank and the Gaza Strip is put on Israel, the Israelis, Arab parties, the United states, and most importantly on the Middle East peace process and whoever has been directly or indirectly involved in it.

An enduring peace in the Middle East, thus, cannot be achieved without focusing attention on whatever contributes to relative parity in the economic conditions of the parties to the peace. Without this condition, peace will devolve into a temporary and contrived arrangement. Clearly, no peace can be maintained if built on shaky grounds. Sooner or later, it will flounder.

CULTURAL CHALLENGES

Though Arabs and Jews share many similar traits emanating from their common Semitic heritage, their societies are linguistically, religiously, and socially different. The two peoples support different aspirations, outlooks, and ways of life.

Israelis in general, especially those of European extraction (Ashkenazi Jews, in contrast to those of Afro-Asian extraction, the Sephardic Jews) are Europeanized, urbanized and technologically oriented. This contrasts greatly with the orientation of great segments of the Palestinian people, in particular those of the West Bank and the Gaza Strip. The latter group is more rural, more sedentary, and less technologically oriented. Are the two cultures reconcilable, and can the peace process create conditions that would avert a clash between them? Is it possible for Jews, Palestinians and other Arabs to live in peace?

It is not easy to answer these questions. Notwithstanding the fact that Arab-Muslim treatment of Jews has historically been somewhat more benign than that meted on them in Christian Europe, and that Arabs and Jews are often described as 'cousins' (due to their semitic descent and their origin of a joint patriarch, Abraham), during the twentieth century Arab–Jewish relations have taken a confrontational course. This is due to a multitude of causes, including separate paths of development, ignorance, the abuse of religious beliefs for political ends, secularism, religious fanaticism, and most importantly – the subordination of the cultures of both peoples to chauvinistic nationalist ideologies.

According to E.H. Carr, nationalism was a blessing to some peoples and a curse to others.[41] As far as Arabs and Jews are concerned, nationalism seems to have been a mutual curse. Had it not been for this phenomenon, the Middle East could most probably have been spared many of its modern conflicts.

Currently, Arabs and Jews are culturally further apart than ever before. This is especially evident in the relations between Israeli Jews and Israeli Arabs. Broadly speaking, an amicable relationship is not plausible, especially with Israeli Muslims who are perceived as likely sympathizers with the Islamic movements in the region, including radical ones. But Israeli Arabs, whether Christian or Muslim, are looked upon as sharing a different 'generic ethnic and political identity with many common cultural symbols and institutions'.[42] The fact that they have lived together for almost 50 years if not more, has not contributed to a shift in attitudes on the part of both Israeli Arabs and Jews. Both communities are estranged constituents of one state. As aptly put by Israel Charney, 'The Jewish Israeli and Arab Israeli communities are for one another, to a large extent, "Us" and "Them". They are to one another "potential or likely enemies"'.[43] The members of these communities are mutually distrustful. They hardly mingle or socialize with each other; their children rarely encounter, mix, or meet with each other. Similar observations were made by Eliezer Ben-Rafael: 'Contacts between Jews and Arabs are infrequent outside work settings, and social images of each other are often derogatory.'[44]

Though increasing in the past decade or so, dialogues between Arabs and Jews in general, and Israeli Jews and Palestinians in particular, fall short of what is needed to bridge the gap between the two peoples. The dialogues rarely reach the masses of Israel's respective communities. This cultural estrangement is a dangerous hindrance to solid peace within Israel, peace between Israelis and Palestinians, and peace between the Jewish people and the Arab peoples at large. An Arabic proverb which some people attribute to Prophet Muhammad suggests the importance of communication in generating peace: *Al-insanu adduwun le-ma jahela* (human beings are enemies of what they do not know). It corresponds to UNESCO's concept of war, which describes it as a phenomenon that starts in the minds of people.

As long as this Arab–Israeli estrangement persists, the Middle East peace process will remain tenuous. Overcoming this cultural estrangement would require a joint Arab–Israeli programme, inspired by the universal principles of Judaism, Christianity, and Islam rather than the narrow chauvinistic, selfish, and interest-centric notions of nationalism. Arabs and Jews would have to reinterpret their modern histories along new lines. They would have to start thinking of their respective states not as states for the Arab or Jewish peoples but as territorial states much like many other states, providing full and equal rights for all their inhabitants.[45] Moreover, the programme would require the support and participation of the peoples of the region who in the final resort are the ones directly affected by war and peace and their consequences. The programme would have to transform the issues of war and peace in the Middle East into the concerns of the people.

No enduring peace in the Middle East can be achieved without the full support and participation of all the peoples of the region. Hence, it is imperative that the Middle East peace process be transformed from the current government-to-government peace to a *pax populi*. Can this transformation be achieved in the Holy Land and other areas of the Middle East? The answer is definitely yes. Only erstwhile pessimists would shun this possibility. Only pessimists would deny the human ability to find solutions to problems which appear to be of obdurate nature.

The success of the *Neve Shalom/Wahat al-Salam* village project in

Israel attests to the possibility of transforming the issues of war and peace to the grass roots levels of both Arabs and Jews. This village constitutes a community of Arabs and Jews who have chosen to live and work together with the ultimate goal of creating 'a microcosm of tranquility', as well as fostering peace education. Though still small, the project plays an indispensable role 'in forging the mutual trust vital to an enduring Mideast peace'.[46]

According to John Battersby, 'Since the village... was founded near Latrun in 1972, it has established a School for Peace to spread its influence through a series of peace workshops attended by some 15,000 Israeli Jews and Arabs and Palestinians from Gaza and the West Bank'.[47] The village has some 26 Israeli–Arab and Jewish families whose mission is supported by a conference centre, a kindergarten, a primary school (established in 1984), and the School of Peace. The importance of the project is evidenced by the fact that the kindergarten and primary school of *Neve Shalom/ Wahat al-Salam* 'are the only ones in Israel based on a binational and bilingual educational program for Jews and Israeli Arabs'. Unlike other Israeli schools, in the village's educational facilities '[children] are raised to respect one another's traditions and culture while maintaining their identities as Jews and Arab Muslims and Christians'.[48] More importantly, they are instructed in their own languages and exposed to their respective cultures, religions and traditions by both Arab and Jewish teachers.

Needless to say, the expansion of such a project or the introduction of comparable multiculturally-based projects would make both Arabs and Jews (Israeli and non-Israeli) aware of their differences, and would help in legitimizing these differences. Most importantly, through such projects tolerance, respect, and mutual cooperation would be generated between members of Arab and Jewish communities within Israel, in the West Bank and the Gaza Strip, and beyond these areas to the whole Middle East region, if not beyond.

CONDITIONS FOR PEACE

The previously discussed agreements, treaties and accords, though important breakthroughs in the peace process, signal only the start of a long journey towards establishing the conditions of a genuine and lasting peace in the Middle East. What they have accomplished is a weak and limited 'cool peace', which cannot be expected to evolve into a warm one before the following conditions are met:

• Justice must be rendered to all concerned, especially the Palestinian people.

• The peace process must broaden its scope to include most, if not all, parties to the Arab–Israeli conflict (or what amounts to regionalizing the peace).

- The peace process must be transformed from a state-to-state peace into a people-to-people peace.

- Arab–Israeli relations must have been normalized.

Justice for All Parties

These sequential and inter-related, if not inter-dependent, conditions are imperative for a genuine and lasting peace in the Middle East, and the first condition appears to be the most important. Without its resolution, success in moving to the other conditions may be virtually impossible.

Any contrary conclusion would be based on an underestimation of the impact of the following: the Palestinian factor on the region's politics; the centrality of the notion of justice in Arab culture and among the Arab peoples; the forces that underlie inter-Arab politics, and the workings of the Arab balance of power system; the impact of regional factors on the policies of individual Arab states; the core values of the Arab masses (which are not necessarily similar or identical to those of their governments), which if not given due respect, might induce all sorts of negative reactions; and, finally, the conditions of sound normalization politics.

All in all, it does not appear that genuine and permanent peace in the Middle East is possible if justice is not served. Any party or prospective party to the Arab–Israeli peace talks may jeopardize the entire peace process, if not destroy its achievements, if the concluded or prospective agreements do not lead to a fair conclusion, or are perceived not to be fair to all parties concerned.

That justice is an imperative condition for establishing a genuine and lasting peace is quite evident in past and present statements of Arab leaders. They all concur that the quest for peace must be based on justice. For example, in Anwar Sadat's statement before the Israeli Knesset on 20 November 1977, the notion of peace based on justice was mentioned not once or twice; rather, it was repeated 22 times in explicit and unequivocal terms. It was highlighted in the introductory notes, the core of his statement, and its conclusion. In the introduction, Sadat said:

> In all sincerity I tell you we welcome you among us, with full security and safety. This in itself is a tremendous turning point, one of the landmarks of a decisive historical change. We used to reject you. We had our reasons and our fears, yes... Yet today I tell you, and I declare it to the whole world, that we accept to live with you in permanent peace based on justice...[49]

In the core of his statement, he said:

> How can we achieve permanent peace based on justice? Well, I have

come to you carrying my clear and frank answer to this big
question... Before I proclaim my answer, I wish to assure you that
in my clear and frank answer I am availing myself of a number of
facts which no one can deny. The first fact is that no one can build
his happiness at the expense of the misery of others.[50]

He also said:

How can we achieve a durable peace based on justice? In my
opinion... the answer is neither difficult nor is it impossible despite
long years of feuds, blood, faction, strife, hatreds, and deep-rooted
animosity. The answer is not difficult, nor is it impossible, if we
sincerely and faithfully follow a straight line. You want to live with
us, in this part of the world. In all sincerity I tell you we welcome
you among us with full security and safety...[51]

Concluding his statement, Sadat said:

I have chosen to come to you with an open heart and an open mind.
I have chosen to give this great impetus to all international efforts
exerted for peace. I have chosen to present to you, in your own
home, the realities, devoid of any scheme or whim. Not to
maneuver, or win a round, but for us to win together, the most
dangerous rounds embattled in modern history, the battle of
permanent peace based on justice.[52]

Include All Parties

Similarly, permanent peace in the Middle East will not be achieved
without expanding the process to include all Arab states, or at least the
great majority of them. In fact, focusing on a handful of Arab states and
reaching agreements with them without the involvement of the rest of
the Arab states is a hazardous course which may result in the division of
the Arab World into two rival camps. True, concentration on a few
states at a time may seem tactically sound; but strategically speaking it
is a counter-productive course which flies in the face of the inter-
connectedness of Arab politics or the nature of power contests within
the Arab World. As Bannerman observes, in the past peace initiatives
have foundered 'in part because, with the notable exception of Egypt
under President Anwar al-Sadat, no Arab state was willing to proceed
without a consensus among Arab states... Egypt, however, suffered
subsequent years of isolation from the Arab world by signing a peace
treaty with Israel'.[53]

The Arab World comprises 22 independent states, but their politics
are, to varying degrees, strongly inter-connected and subject to shifting
alignments within the Arab balance-of-power system. The inter-
connectedness of Arab politics is especially exemplified in whatever
relates to the Palestine question. It must be understood that the

legitimacy of Arab governments is not a function of essentially domestic factors but rather of a combination of domestic and external Arab factors. In the words of Michael Hudson:

> Indeed, to approach the legitimacy problem of any particular Arab state without reference to conditions and issues common and salient to all Arabs, or to what most Arabs refer to as the Arab nation, would result in a monochromatic, two-dimensional analysis. To put the matter in a slightly different way, Arab politicians and Arab political behavior are evaluated not solely according to internal, intrastate criteria. It is impossible to make an adequate diagnosis of the legitimacy of a particular political system, regime, leader, or politician without reference to factors external to the Arab world. External factors... are of two types: The first is the influence, defined largely in terms of the classical instruments of power, such as threat, coercion, promise, and reward, from contiguous or neighboring regimes and movements.... The second type of external factor is more broadly identified as a set of evaluative standards that the noted Lebanese writer Clovis Maksoud has called all-Arab core concerns. The legitimacy of given leaders in a given state is determined to an important extent by their fidelity to these core concerns. At the present time... Palestine is the foremost all-Arab core concern, although not the only one.[54]

The importance of this point is quite evident in Sadat's statement before the Israeli Knesset, in which he warned against partial peace arrangements, the Israeli retention of the lands occupied during the 1967 War, overlooking or brushing aside the Palestinian question, and the failure to recognize the rights of the Palestinian people, including their right to establish their own state. In his view, all these factors were of unpredictable consequences, constituting hindrances to peace based on justice in the Middle East. Sadat concluded this section of his statement by stating that 'there can be no peace' in the Middle East 'without the Palestinians', or without entitling the Palestinians to have their own state.[55]

Why did Sadat refer to the Palestinians, the West Bank, the Gaza Strip, Jerusalem, the Golan Heights in his statement? Why did he warn against partial peace? Why did he not limit his concern to resolving the Egyptian–Israeli conflict? The answer is clear: the inter-connectedness of Arab politics and the centrality of the Palestinian factor in Arab politics. No Arab government can act with complete disregard to core Arab concerns. Hence a basic condition for a genuine and permanent peace in the Middle East is the broadening of its scope to include as many Arab states as possible, especially the leading ones. To all indications, this objective cannot be attained without a serious appreciation of the policy guidelines contained in Sadat's statement.

An Agreement between People

No less importantly, the peace agreements, treaties, and accords that were concluded between Israel on the one hand, and Egypt, Jordan, and the PLO on the other, are still government-to-government achievements. As long as they are not transformed into people-to-people agreements the whole Middle East peace process will continue to be based on shaky and unstable ground. Reviewing the Israel–PLO agreement, however, one cannot but feel that it enshrines separate development, hence inhibits the mixing of the two populations and indirectly obstructs natural communication between the two peoples.

For a settlement to work, it would have to be backed by the great majority of not only the Palestinian and Jewish peoples, but also the peoples of the neighbouring Arab states and world Jewry, the wishes of whom have a direct bearing on the Arab–Israeli conflict. Any settlement that fails to generate such support or is based on a simple majority vote of segments of both the Israeli and the Palestinian populations, is likely to stumble. It will be a shaky settlement lacking an important, if not vital precondition for a meaningful, genuine, and lasting peace in the Middle East. No settlement can endure without the support of all parties that directly or indirectly are affected by its terms.[56]

The factors underlying the assassination of Prime Minister Yitzhak Rabin in November 1995, and the ongoing opposition of some Palestinian factions, including the Islamic Resistance Movement (HAMAS) and the Popular Front for the Liberation of Palestine (PFLP), to the Israel–PLO accords exemplify the magnitude of the problems that are still to be addressed. Rabin's assassination, for example, brought into the open the hidden conflict between the exigencies of Israel as a state (and essentially a secular one) and those of Israel as a nation, expressing the religious aspirations of Jews from all around the world in what they perceive as Eretz Israel. Moreover, it exposed the deep divide in the Israeli body politic between proponents of the peace process and its opponents; and between those who are willing to reach a compromise with the Arabs and barter land for peace on the one hand, and those who are sceptical about peace with the Arabs and decline any trade-offs or territorial concessions to Arabs on the other. The Israeli withdrawal from the Sinai Peninsula, the West Bank, and Gaza, and the prospective Israeli withdrawal from the Golan Heights cannot but alarm proponents of the second view. Some of them regard withdrawal (and prospective withdrawal) from what they consider integral parts of Eretz Israel as a retraction from, if not betrayal of the biblical heritage – the religious-national foundation of Israel.[57]

Likewise, a settlement that renders self-rule, or even the right to separate development, to the Palestinians of the West Bank and the Gaza Strip will be viewed by some Arabs and Palestinians as serving the exigencies of the PLO and its leadership, but not necessarily those of the

Palestinian people (and their descendants) who are dispersed in the region (about 3 million in Arab countries) and around the world. Nor would these changes serve the postulates of both secular and religious movements in the Arab World which regard Palestine as an integral part of either the Arab, the Syrian, or the Islamic homeland.

Like rightist Jews, diaspora Palestinians will have several concerns about any future settlement. They will ask: what is in it for us or our descendants? Can we return to Yafa (Jaffa) and Haifa? Can we repossess our parents' or grandparents' homes and properties? Would we be regarded as citizens of equal status and have the same rights enjoyed by Israeli Jews? Can an Israeli State support our secular, national, or religious beliefs? Likewise, a member of HAMAS cannot but regard the recognition of Israel as a retraction from his declared belief that Palestine as a whole is rightfully his.

Israeli Palestinians

Even without these factors, the issue of the Israeli Palestinians is bound to surface sooner or later. Those Israeli Palestinians who remained in Israel after 1949 and opted for an Israeli citizenship are bound to pass through an identity crisis. Moreover, Israelis would have to address the issue of whether or not a demographically growing Palestinian minority vis-à-vis a slowing population growth among Israeli Jews would not endanger the country's Jewish character. Some Israeli Palestinians may feel better off by relocating to the West Bank or the Gaza Strip. On the other hand, some Jewish groups, especially the most extremist among them such as Kahane Hai (Kahane Lives), may feel that the preservation of Israel's identity as a Jewish state will be better served by encouraging Israeli Palestinians to resettle elsewhere. To some members of the Israeli right, '[all] the policies of this government [meaning Rabin's Labour government] are against the Torah'.[58] Moreover, to some members of the Jewish Right, the killing of 29 Arab worshippers in Hebron by Baruch Goldstein in February 1994 was justified on the ground that 'the people he killed were potential murderers'. Obviously proponents of such views would prefer not to see any Arab either within Israel proper or in the West Bank, the Gaza Strip, or the Golan Heights (which they regard as part of Eretz Israel, or 'the promised land'.[59]

Other Israeli groups, including members of the Likud party, had and continue to have reservations about the Oslo Accords. To use Bannerman's description, their policy favours 'creeping annexation' of the occupied territories, or what amounts to a rejection of whatever negotiations that lead to the exchange of land for peace.[60] They have doubts whether these agreements can bring peace, and, moreover, believe that 'the desire to destroy the Jewish state, is still a primary Arab goal'.[61]

According to David Bar-Ilan, former Editor-in-Chief of the

Jerusalem Post and currently Prime Minister Benjamin Netanyahu's political adviser,

> Those who oppose the Oslo agreements [in Israel] truly fear that giving up strategic areas will endanger the very existence of the country. Others are certain that in the absence of a peace agreement now, the country will be embroiled in a devastating war. The 'anti's' see in Oslo the end of the Zionist dream. The 'pro's' view the agreements as the first step to a thriving, peaceful and prosperous Middle East in which Israel will play a major role.[62]

Similarly, the January 1996 elections in the West Bank and the Gaza Strip for the 88-member Palestinian Council and the chairman of the Palestinian Authority exemplify the significance of some of the above-mentioned issues. These elections showed a split in the position of West Bank and Gazan Palestinians with regard to the whole Israeli–PLO agreement – a split that resulted in the decision of the HAMAS and the PFLP not to participate in the elections. More importantly, they confirmed the Palestinian aspiration for an independent, sovereign, and democratic state with East Jerusalem as its capital. The electoral campaigns on the one hand, and the results of the elections on the other, reflected a determination to realize these goals. On the whole, they were viewed, especially by Palestinians, as a crucial step towards their attainment. As Serge Schmemann has observed, voting in Jerusalem, for example, turned

> into a clash of competing claims and myths between Palestinians who declare their ultimate goal to be a state with East Jerusalem as its capital, and Israelis who proclaim Jerusalem their indivisible and eternal capital.[63]

The results of the elections constitute an endorsement for Arafat's and the PLO's approach to peace with Israel, leading to his overwhelming victory (85 per cent of votes cast) against his sole opponent, Samiha Khalil, a left-wing candidate. They also led to the victory of his Fatah faction of the PLO, whose members virtually won most of the legislature's 88 seats.[64] Clearly, this indicates that a great majority of the West Bankers and Gazans have accepted a gradual peace process. In question is whether Arafat can deliver the kind of peace which Palestinians, or the great majority of them, aspire to. Can he put a halt to the opposition of the HAMAS and the PFLP movements to the Israel–PLO peace process, or at least neutralize their ability to wreck the process? Can he reach an agreement with Israel and Jordan on the future status of Jerusalem? Can he resolve the problem of the 130,000 Jewish settlers in the West Bank, and of the 3 million Palestinian refugees in neighbouring Arab states in a way that is acceptable to all parties concerned? Nobody knows.

CONCLUSION

These issues exemplify some of the major challenges to peace in the Middle East. They are existential in nature and certainly cannot be addressed without a concerted Arab–Israel effort focusing on the causes of opposition among segments of Arab and Israeli populations, as well as on negative perceptions held by both populations. This calls for extensive confidence-building measures at all levels.

So far, however, no serious effort is being made to develop such measures. HAMAS's resumption of suicide bus-bombings on 25 February and 3–4 March 1996, for example, confirms this conclusion. These bombings, which resulted in the killing of nearly 70 people and the wounding of hundreds, placed the whole peace process at the mercy of Palestinian and Jewish extremists. As a consequence, the Israeli government declared an all-out war against Islamic militants, reimposed an indefinite closure of the border between Israel and the West Bank and Gaza, and threatened to reconsider the planned withdrawal of Israeli troops from Hebron and to erect fences between the West Bank and Israel. It followed these measures by imposing virtual siege on all Palestinian towns and villages, closing down a number of Islamic institutions, and ordering 'demolition of houses of families of suicide bombers, seeking to convince future bombers that their families will pay'.[65] Additionally, the Israeli government announced that it would import 16,000 additional foreign workers to replace 'Palestinian workers prevented from reaching their jobs by closings of their territories'.[66] Though the bombers appear to have originated from Hebron, which was still under Israeli control, Israel demanded that Arafat crush his main political foe, the HAMAS movement, and the latter responded immediately by arresting hundreds of people for suspected links with the militant organization, ordering all Palestinians in the self-rule areas to hand in unlicensed arms, and cracking down on Islamic institutions believed to have connections with HAMAS. Martin Indyk, the US Ambassador to Israel, reportedly stated: 'We want more stick and less carrot from Arafat. The process of co-opting has failed'.[67] Furthermore, an international conference on terrorism was held in the Egyptian resort of Sharm al-Sheikh, on 13 March 1996, with the participation of President Clinton and leaders from the Middle East and Europe. All these reactions took place at a time when Israel entered a bitter election campaign and witnessed mounting demands by Likud supporters and Jewish rightist groups to suspend the peace talks with the Palestinians and to re-assume full control over the security of both the West Bank and the Gaza strip.

Undoubtedly, some of these counter-terrorism measures may prove harmful to the peace process. They are spontaneous reactions and, in their nature and implications, do not address the issue in question. To use the words of *Ha-aretz* correspondent Ori Nir:

To a nervous nation, Mr. Peres's get-tough approach [had] enormous emotional appeal. But more damage than good may [have] come from pushing Mr. Arafat into this dangerous corner or from stalling the peace process.[68]

Nir's statement is well placed. The reactions did not provide an answer to why HAMAS decided to end a six-month lull and to resume its suicide-bombings. This move can be understood as a revenge for the killing of one of HAMAS's most prominent figures, Yahya Ayyash, nicknamed 'The Engineer' on 5 January 1996, presumably by Israeli intelligence agents. Also, it may be interpreted as an expression of HAMAS's growing isolation as a political force in the West Bank and the Gaza Strip. More importantly, it may be interpreted as an attempt to 'bomb its way' to the negotiating table, or to stop the persecution of its supporters and secure the release of its prisoners. Above all, the resumption of bombings may be a calculated move to provoke the Israeli authorities into tough measures which would hurt Palestinians and shake their commitment to the peace process, if not attract them to HAMAS's ranks. This is all the more so if HAMAS does indeed maintain a close relationship with Iran.

It seems that at the time HAMAS suffered from growing isolation and was keen on reaching a settlement that would acknowledge its role as a political actor, secure the release of its prisoners, and relate a message 'to Israel,... Arafat, and to [its] own political leaders... that any rapprochement or truce must include them'.[69] This was evidenced by the joint statement issued by its political and military wings on 29 February 1996, following the first two bus-bombings, in which they offered a conditional ceasefire in the campaign of suicide bombings, 'if Israel halted "organized terrorism" against HAMAS and other Palestinians and released all HAMAS prisoners'.[70] This offer was correctly interpreted by Nir as an indication that HAMAS was 'looking for a pretext to stop the violence', having realized (especially after the elections in the West Bank and Gaza) 'that most Palestinians do not support [it]'.[71]

In light of the above considerations, the reactions to the bus-bombings seem to have rested on poor understanding of the HAMAS phenomenon, hence proved harmful, if not detrimental, to the peace process. They dented Prime Minister Peres's image as a peacemaker, hurt many Palestinians who did not condone HAMAS's terrorist activities, possibly alienating them from the peace process, and weakened Arafat's legitimacy by turning the Palestinian Authority (PA) into a police-authority and enhancing a growing perception among his opponents that he was becoming a 'colonial stooge'.[72] Not least, the Israeli counter-measures seem to have won HAMAS more converts – precisely the opposite of their intended goal. As pointed out by the *Economist*,

HAMAS is much more than its military arm. It is a social and religious organization, running an array of civic institutions... Arafat has left these institutions intact – and initiated a quiet dialogue with HAMAS's civilian leaders, attempting to co-opt them into the political process. He did not convince all of them, but his efforts produced a more pragmatic HAMAS leadership, particularly in Gaza. These are men whose aim is less to scupper the peace process than to exist politically within it.[73]

This state of affairs probably explains Nir's warning against the employment of policies that are likely to hamper the politicization of extremist groups in the West Bank and the Gaza strip, and hence the peace process. In his view, 'Israel must not sacrifice the peace process in its efforts to fight the militants'.[74]

Whether Arab or Jewish, extremist groups ought to be won to the cause of peace. Obviously, this objective cannot be attained through all-out wars against such groups and/or their supporters. Such all-out wars are self-defeating – all the more so if employed indiscriminately. According to the *Economist*, Arafat was under great 'Israeli and American pressure to go after HAMAS, root and branch: to dismantle the Islamists' infrastructure of schools and charities which, [according to] the Israeli government, [camouflaged] their military operations'. In the view of the prestigious weekly,

Arafat's stick and carrot policy towards HAMAS... had been showing slow, incremental results. For nearly a year, [he had] been acting forcefully against Islamist activists. In Gaza, his security forces [had] arrested several hundreds of suspects, earning stern rebukes from Palestinian, international, even Israeli human-rights organizations in the process. In the West Bank, Palestinian police forces [had] worked with Israeli security services, a liaison that led to the destruction of Qassam cells in Jenin, Jerusalem and Hebron... But Israel and America [were] telling him to crush HAMAS, military and political wings alike. Polls [showed] that the overwhelming majority of local Palestinians [opposed] terrorist operations; HAMAS's own support among them [was] down to 10 per cent. But if... Arafat [acted] against the group in the way the Israelis [were] urging, the whole organization could [have] become an outlawed, and even more murderous, religious militia.[75]

The Israeli elections of 29 May 1996, which placed Benjamin Netanyahu, leader of the Likud party and a recognized opponent of the principle of land for peace, as the new prime minister of Israel, provide further proof of the challenges that continue to face the Middle East peace process. Netanyahu's election had an immediate adverse impact on this process. 'To mention the least, his election, has affected the momentum of the process, while in addition, putting many of its parties and supporters on alert. Such concerns were particularly clear in the reaction of the Arab League summit of 21–23 June to Netanyahu's election as prime minister, as well as to the policy guidelines he related to the Israeli Knesset on 18 June 1996'.[76]

Netanyahu's severe reservations about the Oslo Accords and his reluctance to honour Israeli commitments to Palestinians with regard to scheduled withdrawal of Israeli troops from most of Hebron, freezes on settlements, and resumption of 'final status' talks, as well as his earlier repeated refusals to meet with the PNA's Chair, Yasser Arafat, not only provoked negative Palestinian and Arab reactions, but also worried many Israelis, including President Ezer Weizman.[77] Indeed, the latter was prompted to announce, on 25 August 1996, that 'he would meet with Mr. Arafat if Mr. Netanyahu did not'. Reportedly, the President felt that the Middle East process 'was approaching a dangerous halt', and that 'a continued freeze could lead to a deterioration of the security situation in Israel'.[78]

During the press conference that followed his meeting with President Weizman on 25 August, Prime Minister Netanyahu stated that he 'was not elected to be the Prime Minister of the Palestinians'. Additionally, in an interview on the evening news of the same day, he said that 'he was holding off meeting with Mr. Arafat to insure that the meeting would be substantive'. Netanyahu moreover maintained: 'We have passed over the era of declarations... I would like a meeting that brings results.'[79]

Arab response was quick in coming. Egyptian President Husni Mubarak threatened to cancel a scheduled regional economic summit 'if Israel [did] not proceed with talks with the Palestinians', and subsequently refused to join the American-sponsored emergency summit in Washington, DC, on 7 October 1996. Similarly, Qatar decided to freeze the construction of a gas pipeline to Israel and to put on hold its plans to open a trade office there, while Jordan announced its intention to go ahead 'on building a joint dam with Syria that Israel strongly opposes'.[80] In a statement to the official Qatar News Agency, Qatar's Foreign Minister Sheikh Hamad Bin Jasim al-Thani said: 'Qatar supports the peace process and hopes Israel will change its attitude. It's in its interests to do so. If not, Qatar will take the necessary measures to deal with the situation, in coordination with other Arab countries.' In an interview for the BBC Arabic Service, he also said that his country 'had been in a state of shock since the Israeli elections, and it would have to reconsider its relationship with Israel if the peace process faltered, particularly on the Syrian and Lebanese tracks'.[81]

The Israeli response was probably best exemplified in the tone of several commentators who, according to American journalist Serge Schmemann, 'were becoming frustrated with the deterioration in Israeli–Palestinian relations'. In his view, Nahum Barnea, a popular columnist for the daily newspaper *Yediot Aharonot*, expressed this frustration by charging 'that the situation stemmed not from the Government's right-wing bias but from its "arrogance, its thick-headedness, its blindness"'. He cited Barnea as claiming that

> the Government's foot dragging on negotiations could be understood as policy, but that there was no reason to humiliate Mr. Arafat by refusing to let him fly his helicopter to the West Bank, or to create a 'provocation' by moving new mobile homes into Jewish settlements, or to destroy a Palestinian centre for the disabled in Old Jerusalem, or to continue keeping Palestinians from jobs in Israel.[82]

Israeli frustration with the deterioration in Israeli–Palestinian relations was also apparent in the reports of Ze'ev Schiff, the military correspondent of the daily newspaper *Ha-aretz*, who 'reported that all Israeli security and intelligence agencies had been warning Mr. Netanyahu of a dangerous deterioration in relations with the Palestinians. He said the coordinator of activities in the Palestinian territories, Major-General Oren Shahor, had recently written a harsh letter to Mr. Netanyahu warning of a possible blowup'. 'Not one promise made to the Palestinians has been fulfilled, including the promise of more meetings following Foreign Minister David Levy's meeting with Arafat,' Schiff added. 'But what undoubtedly caused the current turnaround is the humiliation and degradation of Palestinian Authority Chairman Arafat.'[83]

President Weizman's intervention and Arab, Israeli, and international pressure appear to have persuaded Netanyahu to change his mind – to adopt a less categorical view towards the Oslo Accords, declare his willingness to have 'a meeting [with Arafat] that brings results', and finally to meet with Arafat on 4 September 1996.[84] But whether or not this change will continue in the future, leading to resumption of peace talks on the basis of understandings and agreements that have already been achieved during the Rabin-Peres premiership remains unclear.

The violent confrontations in East Jerusalem, the West Bank and the Gaza Strip, which erupted on 24 September 1996 following the opening of an archaeological tunnel next to al-Aqsa mosque, the third-holiest Muslim shrine, cannot but be viewed with great concern. It violated an understanding with former Israeli governments, and more importantly, 'the tunnel opening breaches [the] Islamic Waqf's authority over the area'.[85] Coupled with the failure to resolve some of the critical issues which were not addressed by the Israel–PLO, and later the Israel–PNA agreements, and to honour earlier understandings and commitments between the former Israeli government and the Palestinians, this new crisis contains the seeds of either derailing the entire Middle East peace process, if not destroying its already secured achievements, or of enticing all parties to the process to seriously re-engage in a concerted effort to intensify the quest for peace.

Because of these and other challenges, some observers have already given up hope for the peace process. They consider the efforts at making peace in the Middle East futile. As early as 1995, for example, Amos Perlmutter declared that 'The Declaration of Principles signed by Israel and the Palestine Liberation Organization... at the White House on September 13, 1993, is for all intents and purposes dead'. In his view, the 'repeated atrocities by Palestinian suicide bombers... serve only as dramatic illustrations of just how ineffectual the so-called Oslo accord has become'. His conclusion was that

> Oslo will probably linger on like a comatose patient on life support. But as it stands today, this will be a long, tortuous, and unsatisfactory process, carried on amid the din of HAMAS terrorism and the building of additional Jewish Settlements. Ultimately, the demise of Oslo threatens to topple the [Rabin] government and render Arafat obsolete. The Middle East peace process may stagger on, but the Oslo accord will never yield its desired fruit.[86]

Perlmutter and other Arab and Jewish pessimists, however, should be reminded that the road to peace, any peace, is rarely smooth. Conflict management, conflict resolution, and peace building are cumbersome processes. The parties to the Arab–Israeli conflict in general and to the Israeli–Palestinian conflict in particular, cannot be led to peace without great sacrifices, and rarely is peace achieved without dissidents.

Irrespective of the current impasse and possible setbacks in the future, however, the seeds of an Arab–Israeli peace have already been sowed. To borrow Barry Rubin's words: 'The Arab–Israeli Conflict Is Over'.[87] 'It is only a matter of time before the seeds of conflict will erode and the fruits of peace will start to blossom. This blossoming is bound to show up in enhanced cooperation between Israel and its Palestinian and Arab neighbours.'[88]

NOTES

1. Edward Hallett Carr, *Conditions of Peace*, New York, 1943, p.xxiii.
2. Yehoshafat Harkabi, *Israel's Fateful Hour*, New York, 1989, p.5.
3. 'The Balfour Declaration', Document 7, in Walter Laqueur and Barry Rubin, eds, *The Israeli–Arab Reader: A Documentary History of the Middle East Conflict*, Harmondsworth, 1984, pp.17–18.
4. According to Donald Neff's estimates, now 'Israel is handing back four [per cent] of the West Bank – less than 100 square miles – or, depending on how you look at it, at most 25 [per cent] – less than 600 square miles'. Neff, 'Israel's Breathtaking Achievement', *Middle East International*, No.517, 19 January 1996, p.17.
5. In this regard, Prime Minister Yitzhak Shamir reportedly stated after the electoral defeat of the Likud bloc in June 1992 that 'his intention had been to drag out the talks with the

Palestinians while changing the facts on the ground'. Shamir stated frankly, 'I would have conducted the autonomy negotiations for ten years, and in the meantime we would have reached half a million souls in Judea and Samaria.' M. Graeme Bannerman, 'Arabs and Israelis: Slow Walk Toward Peace', *Foreign Affairs*, Vol.72, No.1 (1993), pp.148–50.

6. 'Israel After Rabin: The Impossible Mission', *Economist*, 11 November 1995, p.23.
7. Ibid.
8. Ibid.
9. Quoted in Neff's 'Israel's Breathtaking Achievement', p.17.
10. Ibid.
11. Ibid.
12. *Keesing's Record of World Events*, News Digest for October 1994, 40:10:40253.
13. Much of the territory ceded to Jordan, however, was to be leased to Israeli farmers under a 25-year lease agreement. For the main provisions of the Israel–Jordan agreement see: ibid., News Digest for October 1994, 40:10:40253.
14. For the full text of the letter see: 'Special Document File: The Peace Process', *Journal of Palestine Studies*, Vol.23, No.1 (Autumn 1993), p.115.
15. For the full text of the letter see: ibid., p.115.
16. Ibid., pp.115–16.
17. The Declaration of Principles on Interim Self-Government Arrangements consisted of 17 articles and four annexes. Article I considered the aims of the negotiations. It described the primary aim of the Declaration as that of establishing 'a Palestinian Interim Self-Government Authority, the elected Council, (the "Council") for the Palestinian people in the West Bank and the Gaza Strip, for a transitional period not exceeding five years, leading to a permanent settlement based on Security Council Resolutions 242 and 338'. Article II centred on the framework of the interim period. It declared that the framework was as set forth in the Declaration of Principles. Article III dealt with elections to the Council and their modalities. It described the Council's election as a vital 'interim preparatory step toward the realization of the legitimate rights of the Palestinian people [of the West Bank and the Gaza Strip] and their just requirements'. Article IV focused on the jurisdiction of the elected Council. It stipulated that its jurisdiction would 'cover West Bank and Gaza Strip territory, except for issues that [would] be negotiated in the permanent status negotiations'. Moreover, it noted the agreement of both sides to view the latter two areas as a single territorial unit, the integrity of which '[would] be preserved during the interim period'. Article V covered the transitional period and permanent status negotiations. It stipulated that the 'five-year transitional period [would] commence upon [Israel's military] withdrawal from the Gaza Strip and Jericho area', that the permanent status negotiations would 'commence as soon as possible, but not later than the beginning of the third year of the interim period', and that these would cover 'remaining issues, including: Jerusalem, refugees, settlements, security arrangements, borders, relations and cooperation with other neighbours, and other issues of common interest'. Article VI considered preparatory transfer of powers and responsibilities. In this regard, it covered the withdrawal from the Gaza Strip and the Jericho area, as well as the transfer of authority from the Israeli military government and its Civil Administration to the authorized Palestinians for this task. In this regard, it declared that the mentioned withdrawal and transfer would take place upon the entry into force of the Declaration, that the transfer of authority would cover the areas of education and culture, health, social welfare, direct taxation, and tourism, and that the Palestinian side would also 'commence in building the Palestinian police force, as agreed upon'. Article VI also provided that '[pending] the inauguration of the Council, the two parties may negotiate the transfer of additional powers and responsibilities, as agreed upon'. Article VII dealt with the 'Interim Agreement'. It maintained that the Israeli and Palestinian delegations would negotiate an agreement on the interim period (the 'Interim Agreement' that would 'specify, among other things, the structure of the Council, the number of its members, and the transfer of

Palestinian Electricity Authority, a Gaza Sea Port Authority, a Palestinian Development Bank, a Palestinian Export Promotion Board, a Palestinian Environmental Authority, a Palestinian Land Authority and a Palestinian Water Administration Authority, and any other authorities agreed upon, in accordance with the Interim Agreement that [would] specify their powers and responsibilities'. Finally, it declared that the Civil Administration and the Israeli military governments would be dissolved upon the inauguration of the Council. Article VIII dealt with public order and security issues. In this regard, it empowered the Council to establish a strong police force for the purpose of guaranteeing public order and internal security for the Palestinians of the West Bank and the Gaza Strip.Moreover, it affirmed that Israel would continue to exercise the responsibility for defence against external threats, as well as that for the overall security of Israelis (in the West Bank and the Gaza Strip). Article IX dealt with laws and military orders. It empowered the Council 'to legislate, in accordance with the Interim Agreement, within all authorities transferred to it'. Moreover, it stipulated that '[both] parties [would] review jointly laws and military orders presently in force in remaining spheres'. For the full text of the agreement see: ibid., pp.115–24.

18. William B. Quandt, ed., *The Middle East: Ten Years After Camp David*, Washington, DC, 1988, p.4.
19. Ibid., pp.3–4.
20. Bruce Maynard Borthwick, *Comparative Politics of the Middle East*, Englewood Cliffs, 1980, p.113.
21. *Keesing's Record of World Events*, News Digest for October 1994, 40:10:40253.
22. Ibid., p.40253.
23. Harkabi, *Israel's Fateful Hour*, p.13.
24. For the question of Palestinian representation see, for example: Shimon Peres, *The New Middle East*, New York, 1993, pp.3–7, and Bannerman, *Arabs and Israelis*, pp.148–9.
25. Bannerman, ibid.
26. 'Special Document File: The Peace Process', *Journal of Palestine Studies*, Vol.23, No.1 (Autumn 1993), p.116.
27. Ibid., p.117.
28. Graham Usher, 'The Message from the Palestinian Electorate', *Middle East International*, 2 February 1996, p.3.
29. Michael Jansen, 'East Jerusalem's Rising Confidence', *MEI*, p.5.
30. Haim Baram, *MEI*, 2 February 1996, p.6.
31. Colbert C. Held, *Middle East Patterns*, Boulder, 1994, p.269.
32. Ghada Karmi, 'Must the Palestinians also Lose Jerusalem?', *Middle East International*, 26 May 1995, p.16.
33. Ibid.
34. Ibid.
35. *Keesing's Record of World Events*, News Digest for May 1995, 41:5:40573.
36. Amos Perlmutter, 'The Israel–PLO Accord is Dead', *Foreign Affairs*, Vol.74, No.3 (1994), p.63.
37. For recent studies on the social and economic conditions of Palestinian society see: Marianne Heiberg and Gier 'Vensen, *Palestinian Society in Gaza, West Bank and Arab Jerusalem*, Oslo, 1993; Sara Roy, *The Gaza Strip, the Political Economy of De-Development*, Washington, DC, 1995; Simcha Bahiri, *Economic Consequences of the Israel–PLO Declaration of Principles*, Jerusalem, 1994; Serge Schmemann, 'Palestinians Stage a Strike and Israel Gets the Message', *International*, 30 August 1996, pp.1 and A4; and Sammy Smooha, *Arabs and Jews in Israel: Change and Continuity in Mutual Intolerance*, Boulder, 1992.
38. The figures were derived from: Central Intelligence Agency, *The World Factbook 1992*, Washington, DC, 1992, pp.123, 165–7, 372–3; Central Intelligence Agency. *The World Factbook 1995–96*, Washington, DC, 1996, pp.144–5, 195–6, 431–2; and Held, *Middle East Patterns*, pp.268–73. Palestinians within Israel are of two groups, refugees and non-refugees. In 1990–91, those falling within the former group were estimated at about 150,000, whereas those of the latter group, that is Israeli Arabs, at 580,000. See Smooha, *Arabs and Jews*, Vol.2, p.288.
39. Sara Roy, 'The Reason for Rage in Gaza', *Christian Science Monitor*, 12 January 1990, p.20.
40. Ibid.

41. E.H. Carr, *Nationalism and After*, London, 1945.
42. Israel Charney, 'One Very Simple Idea: a Possible Israeli Contribution to a Lasting Middle East Peace', in Elise Boulding, ed., *Building Peace in the Middle East*, Boulder, 1994, p.289.
43. Ibid., p.288.
44. Eliezer Ben-Rafael, 'Democratization in the Middle East: Democracy in Israel – Values, Conflict and Power', Paper prepared for the International Peace Research Association (IPRA) Commission on Peace Building in the Middle East, Kyoto, Japan, July 1992, p.12.
45. This is one of the central themes of Boas Evron's *Jewish State or Jewish Nation?*, Bloomington, 1995.
46. John Battersby, 'Oasis of Peace In a Desert of War: Experimental Arab–Jewish Community in Israel Strives to Foster Mutual Trust Between Cultures', *Christian Science Monitor*, 16 January 1996, pp.10–11.
47. Ibid., p.10.
48. Ibid.
49. Foreign Affairs and National Defense Division, Congressional Research Service, Library of Congress, Committee Print CP-957, *The Search for Peace in the Middle East: Documents and Statements, 1967–1979, Report for the Subcommittee on Europe and the Middle East of the Committee on Foreign Affairs, U.S. House of Representatives*, Washington, DC, 1979, p.224.
50. Ibid., p.225.
51. Ibid., p.226.
52. Ibid., p.227.
53. Bannerman, *Arabs and Israelis*, p.143.
54. Michael C. Hudson, *Arab Politics: The Search for Legitimacy*, New Haven, 1977, p.5.
55. In addressing the question of a permanent peace based on justice, Sadat affirmed the inter-connectedness of the politics of the Arab World and the importance of the Palestinian factor in these politics. In this regard, he said: 'Frankness makes it incumbent upon me to tell you the following: First, I have not come here for a separate agreement between Egypt and Israel. This is not part of the policy of Egypt. The problem is not that of Egypt and Israel. An interim peace between Egypt and Israel, or between any Arab confrontation state and Israel, will not bring permanent peace based on justice in the entire region. Rather, even if peace between all the confrontation states and Israel were achieved in the absence of a just solution of the Palestinian problem, never will there be that durable and just peace upon which the entire world insists. Second, I have not come to you to seek a partial peace, namely to terminate the state of belligerency at this stage and put off the entire problem to a subsequent stage. This is not the radical solution that would steer us to permanent peace.'
He also maintained: 'What is peace for Israel? It means that Israel lives in the region with her Arab neighbours in security and safety. Is that logical? I say yes. It means that Israel lives within its borders, secure against any aggression. Is that logical? And I say yes. It means that Israel obtains all kinds of guarantees that will ensure these two factors. To this demand, I say yes... In short then, when we ask what is peace for Israel, the answer would be that Israel lives within her borders, among her Arab neighbours in safety and security, within the framework of all the guarantees she accepts and that are offered to her. But, how can this be achieved? How can we reach this conclusion that would lead us to permanent peace based on justice? There are facts that should be faced with courage and clarity. There are Arab territories that Israel has occupied and still occupies by force. We insist on complete withdrawal from these territories, including Arab Jerusalem.'
He affirmed the above points by noting that '[any] talk about permanent peace and security' in the Middle East 'would become meaningless' if Israel continued to 'occupy Arab territories by force of arms'; that no peace 'could be built on the occupation of the land of others'; and that 'the Palestine cause ... is the crux of the entire problem'.
The Search for Peace, p.228.
56. For example, a settlement which does not have the support of Diaspora Jews and Palestinians, whose members constitute vital sources of support to both Israel and PLO, respectively, cannot but be of unpredictable adverse effects on both parties of the conflict.
57. Joel Greenberg, 'Rabin is Laid to Rest, Mourned by Israel and the World: Israelis Hold Assassin's Brother As Suspected Accomplice in Plot', *New York Times International*, 7 November 1995, pp.A1, A9.

58. Alan Cowell, 'The Israeli Right: Among Hard-Liners in Hebron, Ambivalence and Brooding but Little Grief', *New York Times International*, 7 November 1995, p.A 10.
59. Ibid.
60. Bannerman, *Arabs and Israelis*, p.150.
61. David Bar-Ilan, 'An Israeli View: Out of Tragedy and Trauma, a Slim Hope for Consensus', *Jerusalem Post*, 12 November 1995, reproduced by *San Diego Union-Tribune*, 12 November 1995, p.G 4.
62. Ibid.
63. Serge Schmemann, 'In Palestinian Vote, Message Lies in the Mandate', *New York Times*, 20 January 1996, p.Y3.
64. The elections have attracted about 75 per cent of 1,013,235 registered voters, 672 candidates to the legislative body, highlighted the issues of an independent, sovereign, and democratic state with Jerusalem as its capital. For details see John Battersby, 'Birth of a Nation. Almost', *Christian Science Monitor*, 19 January 1996, pp.10–11; and Battersby, 'Historic Vote Catapults Palestinians Closer to Peace and Nationhood', *CSM*, 22 January 1996, pp.1, 14.
65. 'Arafat's Dilemma', *Economist*, 2 March 1996, p.40.
66. Serge Schmemann, 'Arafat Men Seize 3 in HAMAS as Peres Says It Is Not Enough', *New York Times*, 11 March 1996, p.A4.
67. Ibid.
68. Ori Nir, 'Don't Corner Arafat', *New York Times*, 1 March 1996, p.A17.
69. 'Arafat's Dilemma'.
70. Nir, 'Don't Corner Arafat'. See also: 'HAMAS Offers a Halt to Attacks in Israel', *New York Times*, 29 February 1996, p.A6.
71. 'Arafat's Dilemma'; 'Don't Corner Arafat'.
72. 'Terrorism Forces Peres From Brink of Triumph', *New York Times*, 10 March 1996, pp.1, Y6; Perlmutter, 'The Israel–PLO Accord', p.66. According to Knight Ridder News Service, the measures have 'turned the West Bank into 465 virtual prisons – one for each sealed off village – keeping most Palestinian cars off the highways and preventing residents from leaving their villages, much less going to work'. As a consequence, stores turned empty with 'mostly bare shelves', gas stations closed because they could not replenish their resources. In Gaza, rice and flour and other basic food items, as well as supplies of medicines became rare or disappeared. 'Israel Moves Fast, Firmly to Crush Arab Terrorism', *San Diego Union*, 7 March 1996, A15; 'After the Bombs', *Economist*, 2 March 1996, p.39.
73. 'After the Bombs', p.39.
74. Nir, 'Don't Corner Arafat'.
75. 'After the Bombs'.
76. Mohamad Z. Yakan, 'Prospects of Economic Integration and Development in the Post-Arab–Israeli Conflict Era', paper presented at the 14th Annual Meeting of the Association of Third World Studies, Troy State University, Montgomery, Alabama, 3–5 October 1996, p.64.
    The Israeli government's guidelines included the following statements: 'The government would work to broaden the circle of peace with all its neighbours.' On the Syria track, the government agreed to conduct negotiations 'without preconditions'; yet it viewed 'the Golan Heights as essential to the security of the state and its water resources' and stipulated that 'retaining Israeli sovereignty over the Golan' would constitute 'the basis for an arrangement with Syria'. The government was committed to negotiating with the Palestinian National Authority 'with the intent of reaching a permanent arrangement'. However, it ruled out the prospect of Palestinian statehood and retained the right to send troops into Palestinian self-rule areas if it perceived the security situation to warrant such action. Settlements in the West Bank, Gaza, the Negev, Galilee, and the Golan Heights were deemed of 'national importance to Israel's defence and an expression of Zionist fulfillment'. The government would 'act to consolidate and develop the settlement enterprises in these areas, and allocate the resources necessary for this'. It also declared that 'Jerusalem, the capital of Israel, is one city, whole and undivided, and will remain forever under Israel's sovereignty'. *Keesing's Record of World Events*, News Digest for June 1996, 42:06:41167.
    Netanyahu's notable opposition to the principle of exchanging land for peace, in addition to his policy guidelines, was disquieting to many countries whose governments

continue to be involved in the Middle East peace process. They were especially alarming to the PNA and the Arab states which had already concluded peace treaties with Israel, as well as to those contemplating or negotiating with Israel in order to arrive at a peaceful resolution of the Arab–Israeli conflict once and for all. In fact, it provoked all Arab governments into holding a summit meeting at Cairo on 21–23 June 1996. This culminated in the communiqué of 23 June, which included the following points:

The establishment of a comprehensive and just peace in the Middle East requires a complete Israeli withdrawal from all occupied Palestinian territories, including Arab Jerusalem, to enable the Palestinian people to establish an independent state with Arab Jerusalem as its capital. The summit called for Israel's complete withdrawal from the Syrian Golan Heights to the 4 June 1967 line; for Israel's full and unconditional withdrawal from southern Lebanon and the Western Bekka [Biqqá] to the internationally recognized borders, in implementation of UN Security Council resolutions 242, 338 and 425 and the principle of 'land for peace'; and for the resumption of peace talks on all tracks.

The Arab countries' commitment to continue the peace process in order to achieve a just and comprehensive peace was a goal and a strategic option. This commitment required similar serious and unequivocal commitment on the part of Israel in accordance with the principles agreed upon at the 1991 Madrid Conference, especially the land-for-peace principles. Any violation by Israel of these principles on which the peace process was founded, any retraction on the commitments, pledges and agreements reached within the framework of the process, or any vacillation in implementing them would set back the peace process and would entail dangers and consequences which would plunge the region back into a spiral of tension and compel the Arab countries to reconsider the steps they had taken towards Israel within the framework of the peace process.

All settlement activity in the occupied Syrian Golan Heights and the occupied Palestinian territories, particularly Jerusalem, should halt. The summit emphasized that a comprehensive and just peace could not be achieved unless a solution was found for the issue of Jerusalem and for the problem of Palestinian refugees'. Ibid., pp.41166–7.
77. Yakan, 'Prospects', pp.65–6. On 2 August 1996, for example, the Likud government lifted a four-year-old freeze on building new settlements in the West Bank and Gaza. For reactions to this measure see: MacFarquhar, Neil, 'Israel Will Allow Settlers to Build', *New York Times*, 3 August 1996, p.Y4.
78. Serge Schememann, 'Israel President Prods Netanyahu to Meet With Arafat', *NYT*, 26 August 1996, p.A3.
79. Ibid.
80. Ibid.
81. Peter Feuiherade, 'Qatar & Israel: Frozen Plan', *Middle East International*, 2 August 1996, p.15.
82. Serge Schememann, 'Palestinians Stage a Strike And Israel Gets the Message', *New York Times International*, 30 August 1996, pp.1, A4.
83. Quoted in ibid., p.A4.
84. Schememann, 'Israel President'.
85. Ilene R. Prusher, 'Middle East Peace Rocked by Stones, Bullets, Mistrust', *Christian Science Monitor*, 27 September 1996, pp.1, 9. The opening of the tunnel was criticized by Israeli author David Grossman. Writing in *The Independent* (London), Grossman maintained that 'the opening of the tunnel in Jerusalem was symptomatic of the Israeli prime minister's contemptuous disregard for the feelings of the Palestinians, the very people whose trust and eventual goodwill he must win if he is ever to deliver on his promise to the Israeli electorate to provide "peace with security"'. Quoted in the editorial of *Middle East International*, No.535, 4 October 1996, p.2.
86. Perlmutter, 'The Israel–PLO Accord', pp.59, 61.
87. Barry Rubin, 'The Arab–Israeli Conflict Is Over', *Middle East Quarterly*, Vol.III, No.3 (September 1996), pp.3–12.
88. Yakan, 'Prospects'.

Peace-Making with the Palestinians: Change and Legitimacy

YAACOV BAR-SIMAN-TOV

Peace initiatives and peace agreements constitute drastic and often sudden breakpoints in states' relations with their neighbours. This is especially the case when the stakes are highest, are most central to core values and interests, and have the potential to spill over into the widest range of associated areas. This state of affairs is particularly applicable to protracted conflicts.

The shift from war to peace is generally perceived as a great opportunity, since peace is a most significant value and vital interest for both decision-makers and the public at large. Peace means not only the end of war, but greatly improved conditions for social and economic development. However, even when essentially favoured, the shift from war to peace is often difficult to contemplate and to carry out, especially in situations of protracted conflict. The numerous potential problems attending such a shift include not only the recognition and interpretation of a new situation but also the need to change attitudes and values and to deal with issues of value complexity, uncertainty, risk-taking, as well as of legitimacy and consensus-building.

In high-dissonance situations, perceptions of enemies will be intensely resistant to change. Yet value complexity, uncertainty, and risk-taking are even more difficult to contend with, since they emerge when both the political elites and the public are called upon either to choose which values and interests must be sacrificed for the sake of peace, or to sacrifice peace so as to prevent damage to other values and interests. Hence, legitimacy and consensus-building for the preferred policy are paramount needs.

The problems of attitudinal change, value complexity, uncertainty, and risk-taking play a major role in Israeli political life, in that peace policy is no less a domestic issue than an external one. Since the value of peace would seem to contradict other values such as territory, security, settlement, and ideology, the political leadership must acquire widespread legitimacy for shifting from war to peace.

Yaacov Bar-Siman-Tov holds the Giancarlo Elia Valori Chair for the study of Peace and Regional Cooperation at the Hebrew University of Jerusalem.

This essay will examine the complexity of Israel's peace-making with the Palestinians, focusing on two main issues: Yitzhak Rabin's and Shimon Peres's attitudinal change towards the PLO and the Israeli–Palestinian conflict, and their failure to acquire general legitimacy for peace-making with the Palestinians.

THE REASONS FOR ATTITUDINAL CHANGE

The process of attitudinal change is a pre-condition for shifting from war to peace. In order to make such a shift, Israeli decision-makers, political elites, and the public at large must be convinced that the other side has indeed changed its attitudes. After many years of a zero-sum conflict, changing Israeli perceptions of the PLO and the Israeli–Palestinian conflict was not simple. Any attitudinal change towards the PLO in particular entailed sharp personal and public cognitive dissonance, not least because it was widely perceived as betrayal of the Israeli national interest and national consensus. Indeed, to prevent the possibility of negotiations with the PLO, in 1986 the Knesset adopted a law making any meeting with PLO officials illegal. The attitudinal change, therefore, developed only gradually. In fact, it was the Likud Government of Yitzhak Shamir which initiated the process through its participation in the Madrid Peace Conference of October 1991.

This government, however, posed tough conditions: only a Jordanian–Palestinian delegation could present the Palestinian case at Madrid; the Palestinian delegates had to be residents of the West Bank and Gaza; and those delegates could not be representatives of the PLO or members of the Palestine National Council (PNC). Moreover, the delegates could not be individuals who had taken part in terrorist activities, and had to have consented to an interim agreement – which entailed the freezing of any claim for the establishment of a Palestinian state for at least five years. Essentially, the Palestinian delegates had to be independent of the PLO's dictates.[1]

It immediately transpired that the Palestinian delegation was not independent of the PLO, which both determined its composition and directed its negotiations. Gradually, a strange situation emerged: Israel refused to change its attitude towards the PLO, yet was negotiating in Washington with a Palestinian delegation which received its instructions from the PLO's headquarters in Tunis; hence, informally and indirectly, Israel was in effect negotiating with the PLO. Because of the Likud Government's ideology, however, the negotiations reached an impasse in terms of both procedure and substance.[2]

Labour's coming to power in June 1992, under the leadership of Rabin and Peres, enabled the Israeli attitude to change, which in turn facilitated direct negotiations with the PLO. In other words, for this attitudinal change to be possible a change of leadership was required (as in 1977 with Menachem Begin regarding peace with Egypt). Yet this shift was not immediate; it developed gradually, necessitated some learning, and involved difficult personal and public cognitive dissonance.

In its campaign for the June 1992 elections, the Labour Party, including Rabin, promised to do its best to resolve the Arab–Israeli conflict in general, and the Israeli–Palestinian feud in particular. Rabin was impelled by the recognition that there was no military solution to the *intifada*, hence a political solution was needed. Just before the elections, personal security had been undermined by a wave of fatal stabbings by Palestinians, and Rabin believed that the only remedy was a separation between Israel and the Palestinians. He therefore promised autonomous rule for the Palestinians within nine months after the establishment of his government. This indicated a certain readiness to change attitudes towards the conflict with the Palestinians, though Rabin did not suggest breaking new ground and negotiating with the PLO.[3]

Following the establishment of the Rabin Government, the freezing of the settlement policy and Rabin's declarations that Israel should relinquish the dream of Greater Israel contributed to some degree of change in policy and behaviour but not in attitudes *per se*. The new government inherited the situation of the Madrid Conference and the Washington talks, including Likud's demands for a Jordanian-Palestinian delegation; this government, too, refused to recognize the Palestinians as an independent partner and opposed the inclusion of the PLO in the negotiations; yet it considered the possibility of separate negotiations with the Palestinian delegation, believing that this would give it an independent status and free it from the stifling supervision of the PLO.[4]

However, it soon transpired how difficult and ineffective were the negotiations with the Palestinian delegation, which was still directly controlled by Tunis. Moreover, the escalation of *intifada* violence made a political solution all the more urgent. These developments seemed to have convinced the Rabin Government that not only was the Palestinian option the only viable one, but that Israel would have to negotiate directly with the PLO. Yet since such negotiations would constitute a dramatic departure from Israel's longstanding policy, and violation of Rabin's and Labour's electoral promises, a change in the Israeli attitude towards the PLO and the Palestinian question had to be effected.[5]

The need for such attitudinal change became pressing. The general perception was that without a courageous Israeli initiative the peace process would collapse, leading in turn to further escalation of violence. Foreign Minister Peres stressed that if the PLO, because of its weakness, were to collapse, the only alternative would be the militant HAMAS. Moreover, throughout the negotiations in Washington the Labour

Government realized that the conflict with the PLO was not necessarily zero-sum, and that there had been some changes in the organization. The PLO no longer seemed to base its actual policies on its Covenant calling for the destruction of Israel, and no longer seemed confident of its ability to achieve its national aims via terrorism. Furthermore, the continued presence of the Israel Defence Forces (IDF) in Gaza was increasingly viewed by many Israelis as too costly. It was believed, however, that withdrawal from Gaza could only be effectuated through an agreement with an authorized Palestinian body that could take responsibility for the area after its evacuation. This, again, could only be the PLO because the alternative was HAMAS.[6]

Other factors contributed to the nascent change in the Israeli attitude. The dramatic global developments culminating in the dissolution of the Soviet Union and its withdrawal from the region were perceived by both Peres and Rabin as a rare great opportunity for a shift in the Arab–Israeli conflict. Rabin preferred to begin the negotiation process with Syria; but the Syrian track turned out to be very difficult, as President Hafiz Asad demanded an immediate Israeli readiness for withdrawal from the entire Golan Heights, including the removal of the settlements there, without committing himself to complete and unequivocal peace. At this point the Palestinian option became more attractive. It was assumed that with the Palestinians, Israel could achieve an interim agreement that would not, at least in the initial stages, require any major withdrawal or removal of settlements.[7]

There was also a personal factor in the attitudinal change. Both Rabin and Peres were in their early seventies; both realized that this might be their last chance to advance the peace policy they believed in, and felt that they owed this peace-making to their constituency and to history.[8] Thus, global and regional developments complemented deep personal feelings of accountability.

Nevertheless, Peres and especially Rabin had serious ideological, psychological, and political problems in changing their own attitudes towards the PLO, and they did so only when they had been convinced that the latter was prepared to alter the Palestinian National Covenant, to recognize Israel, to cease and denounce terrorism, to prevent other Palestinian organizations from undertaking terrorist actions, and to accept the idea of resolving the conflict peacefully and in stages.

The PLO's readiness to comply with Israel's conditions somewhat facilitated Israeli decision-making, but did not necessarily make coping with cognitive dissonance easier. Rabin's personal difficulties were clearly manifest at the signing ceremony in Washington in September 1993. For him (and for Peres) the change negated pre-existing values and beliefs, and it was the basic conviction that their decision was the right one which enabled them to surmount this difficulty. Also crucial was the real partnership that emerged between Rabin and Peres and their sharing of responsibility for the change, together with their joint belief that they could mobilize sufficient public support for their new policy.

The Israeli attitudinal change was deepened by the negotiations with the Palestinians on the implementation of the Oslo Agreement (Oslo I), culminating in a new agreement in May 1994 known as the Cairo Agreement, and by the negotiations on the Oslo II Agreement which was signed in October 1995. From the continual meetings and intensive talks with Yasser Arafat and other Palestinians, Rabin and Peres concluded that their interlocutors were genuinely interested in resolving the conflict with Israel, though there remained many obstacles in the process such as the continuing terrorist activities of the HAMAS and Islamic Jihad. Overall, as far as Rabin and Peres were concerned, the negotiation process reinforced their conviction in the necessity of the attitudinal change and resolved their cognitive dissonance.

LEGITIMACY FAILURE

Given the deep disagreements in Israel regarding the value of peace in relation to the concessions required to attain it, mobilization of legitimacy is necessary not only for the effective formulation and implementation of peace policy but also for coping successfully with the traumatic impact of this policy. It is also necessary for enhancing decision-makers' self-confidence in pursuing the policy, maintaining their desired identity images, and improving their performance in the peace process.[9]

Decision-makers must achieve a fundamental, stable, and comprehensive national consensus, encompassing substantial portions of the ruling elites, competitive elites, interest groups, and public opinion. While the Israeli 'constitution' or 'basic laws' do not require the government to submit the peace policy or peace agreements to Knesset or public approval, a tradition has developed, and accepted almost as a norm, whereby the government is expected to bring peace agreements to the Knesset for approval. Clearly, peace-making is a crucial issue in Israeli domestic politics, and decision-makers must take this into account.

One may differentiate between a formal and an informal process of legitimation. The former involves the established constitutional and legal stipulations regarding the formulation and implementation of peace policy. This includes political consultations, debates, and votes in each requisite political forum or institution – the political party, the cabinet, or the parliament. Sometimes a referendum or even general elections can be part of this process. The informal process of legitimation, in contrast, involves informal meetings with different constituencies, political and non-political.

Rabin and Peres realized that the opposition parties, as well as the right-wing interest groups including the settlers in Judea, Samaria, and Gaza, would strongly oppose the peace process with the Palestinians. Nevertheless, they believed that so long as the PLO agreed to end the state of war, including the suppression of terrorist actions by other Palestinian groups, and amend the Palestinian Covenant, the general public would endorse the peace policy because of the desire to leave Gaza and to enhance personal security, which had further deteriorated in the first few months of the Labour Government.[10] It seems, however, that Rabin and Peres did not foresee the extent and intensity of opposition to their peace initiative, hence they failed to convince the opposition parties, the right-wing interest groups, and a major part of the public of the necessity and value of the attitudinal change, its costs and benefits, as well as the prudence of its timing. Nor did they manage to control effectively the risks involved in the peace policy, to prove that a genuine peace was emerging, or to clarify the final aims of the peace policy as well as the strategies and tactics of implementing it. A more effective policy implementation might well have secured a wider legitimacy for it and enabled better coping with the opposition.

The remainder of this essay will examine the extent of support and opposition to the peace policy in the Knesset and in the public, and then analyze the failure to harness widespread support for it.

Parliamentary Legitimacy

Rabin and Peres had great difficulty in legitimizing the peace policy in the Knesset. Only 61 Knesset members supported the Oslo I Agreement, while 50 opposed it, eight abstained, and one did not participate in the vote. The government won the support of the Arab party and the ex-Communist party, which were not part of the coalition. Similarly, the Cairo Agreement was supported by only 52 Knesset members from the coalition as well as by the Arab party and ex-communist party; the opposition boycotted the vote to show that there was no majority among the public in favour of the agreement. In the Oslo II Agreement, only 61 Knesset members from the coalition and outside of it voted in favour, whereas, 59 voted against, including two Labour MKs.

Neither the opposition parties, nor the interest groups led by the West Bank and Gaza settlers, recognized the Knesset's formal approval as legitimizing the peace policy. In their view:

- Since the agreements had been supported by only a minimal majority of the Knesset, and given their crucial political and territorial significance – including recognition of the PLO and negotiation with it, as well as territorial concessions in Judea, Samaria, and Gaza – the government was obliged to ask for the nation's approval through a national referendum or by elections.

- The government had not only received a minimal majority in the Knesset, but had to rely on two 'deserters' from a right-wing party (two Yihud MKs who had left the Tzomet Party) and on non-Jewish and non-Zionist support from the Arab parties, which the opposition parties regarded as the PLO's 'stooges' in the Knesset. On issues so vital to the Jewish people, the opposition claimed, there was a need for a special majority that would neutralize the Arab vote in the Knesset, and for a referendum that would truly reflect the will of the Jewish population.

- By negotiating with the PLO and signing agreements with it, the government and especially the prime minister had violated their commitments to the voters in the 1992 elections. Thus they had broken moral bounds, and were obligated to call new elections in order to obtain the people's approval for the peace policy.[11]

- The government was not allowed to transfer any parts of Eretz Israel to foreigners, even if this was approved by the Knesset. Nor could a national referendum or even elections legitimize the exchange of land for peace. This argument manifests an alternative, non-democratic, religious ideology that derives its ultimate legitimacy from God.

In addition to their parliamentary activities against the Oslo Accords, and probably because of their failure in the Knesset, the opposition parties cooperated with extra-parliamentary groups such as the Yesha Council (which represents the settlers in Judea, Samaria, and Gaza). This mainly involved organizing public protest against the peace policy, especially anti-government demonstrations. Mass demonstrations were held on 7 September 1993, 27 July 1994, and 5 October 1995 – the first and third demonstrations against the signing of the Oslo I and II agreements respectively; the second was aimed at preventing a possible visit by Arafat to Jerusalem. Though impressive in size, these demonstrations were not followed by other significant activities, probably due to public acquiescence in the Oslo Accords and the fatigue of the potential demonstrators.[12]

The opposition parties also sought to de-legitimize the government and its policy. Although Benjamin Netanyahu and other Likud leaders were opposed to calling Rabin and Peres 'traitors' and 'murderers', anti-government propaganda included such derisory terms as 'wicked', 'insane', 'muddled', 'diseased', 'treacherous', 'reckless', 'obsequious', 'mentally deranged', 'bewildered', 'assimilated', 'destroying the dream of the Jewish people', 'possessed with making concessions', 'disconnected from Jewish values and tradition', 'forfeiting the right to the land', 'abandoning Eretz Israel', 'a two-time collaborator – once with a terrorist organization, and once against Jews', 'misleading the people', 'not telling the truth to the people', 'lying', 'endangering the people', 'leading Israel to suicide', 'leading Israel to a crash', 'shrinking Israel into Auschwitz borders'.[13]

Extra-Parliamentary Legitimacy

The government gained somewhat greater support among the public, but this too was not very widespread. In a poll taken in late August 1993, 53 per cent supported the Oslo Agreement, 45 per cent opposed it, and 2 per cent had no position.[14] Oslo II was supported by only 51 per cent with 47 per cent opposed and 2 per cent undecided.[15] From October 1994 to October 1995 support for the Oslo process actually decreased to less than 50 per cent, and was even lower in the Israeli Jewish sector.[16]

Following Rabin's assassination, public support reached its zenith in late November 1995. Yet despite the trauma of the assassination, by January 1996 support had dropped again.[17]

The Yesha Council acted directly to de-legitimize the government by portraying it as surrendering Israeli interests and values. Its main activity was to organize anti-government demonstrations in cooperation with the opposition parties, some of which escalated to violence, especially that of 5 October 1995, against Oslo II. Other extra-parliamentary groups that strongly opposed the peace policy with the Palestinians included the Yesha of Rabbis Council, the Committee for Abolition of the Autonomy Plan, and small ultra-right groups such as Kach and Eyal. In the latter part of 1995, a new group called Zo Artzenu (This is Our Country) was established, consisting mainly of settlers from Judea and Samaria; it organized civil disobedience activities, mainly in the form of blocking of central roads in order to disrupt civilian life.[18]

The settlers' behaviour expressed despair, frustration and disappointment. They regarded the government's peace policy as aimed at returning Israel to the pre-June 1967 borders, total evacuation of the settlements, and the establishment of a Palestinian state. They also believed that they themselves were the target of an effective de-legitimization campaign by the government, which sought to present them as anti-peace elements. The settlers also felt that the government had sacrificed their security.[19]

Indeed, the Yesha Council of Rabbis and other groups warned of the possibility of a civil war if the government continued its peace policy. Some rabbis called on soldiers to disobey any order to evacuate settlements, or even advocated violent opposition to soldiers who did evacuate settlers.[20] Concern grew that individuals and even small groups among the settlers might resort to violence, including assassinations not only of prominent Palestinians but also of left-wing Israeli politicians.[21] The Hebron massacre and the assassination of Prime Minister Rabin showed that these concerns were warranted. Since the government had actually not yet decided anything about final arrangements and no settlement had yet been dismantled, the readiness to resort to violence, including the assassination of the country's prime minister, indicated that the formulation and implementation of the final agreement would trigger strong opposition.

WHY DID LEGITIMACY FAIL?

The difficulty in acquiring widespread legitimacy stemmed both from the lack of the basic elements required for such legitimacy and from the government's failure to effectively utilize the appropriate strategies and tactics. More specifically, the government lacked a clear-cut peace policy as well as normative and cognitive legitimacy; failed to effectively manipulate symbols, language, and ritual; made imprudent use of defensive mechanisms and incompetent employment of offensive ones; engaged in de-legitimization; was unwilling to consider compensatory efforts; and lacked religious legitimacy.

Lack of a Clear-cut Peace Policy

To obtain formal and informal political legitimacy for shifting from war to peace, decision-makers must introduce a structured peace policy with three inter-related components: the design-objective of the policy; the strategy to be employed in its pursuit; and the tactics to be used in implementing the strategy.[22] The peace policy with the Palestinians, formalized by the Oslo I and II Accords and by the Cairo Agreement, was only at an interim stage. While it was clear that the peace plan aimed at resolving the Israeli–Palestinian conflict, the government failed to clarify the objective of its peace policy, especially in terms of the final arrangement. In sharp contrast, the PLO presented the interim agreement as the first stage towards the establishment of an independent Palestinian state.[23]

The reasons for not presenting the ultimate objective may have involved bargaining calculations vis-à-vis the PLO or concern about provoking massive domestic opposition at an early stage of the negotiations; nevertheless, such avoidance made it difficult to acquire widespread support for the Oslo Accords. It is indeed difficult to support an agreement whose nature and ultimate aims are unclear. Such issues as the permanent borders between Israel and the Palestinian entity, or the final status of Jerusalem and of the settlements were left uncertain. Contradictory statements about the final arrangement only increased the confusion: whereas Rabin and Peres opposed the possibility of the autonomy turning into a Palestinian state, preferring a confederation of sorts between Jordan and the Palestinian entity, other ministers came out in favour of a Palestinian state.

In addition to this absence of a design-objective, there was also ambiguity about the strategies and tactics of carrying out the peace policy. The Oslo Accords can be seen as part of a gradual programme of making peace with the Palestinians; still, without a clear-cut peace plan, it is difficult to comprehend the relationship between the strategy and tactics for implementing the plan and the plan itself. For example, it was not clear what strategy the government would use to prevent the development of the autonomy into a state, if indeed such an eventuality were to be prevented. Nor was it clear what tactics would be used in the event of continuous terrorist actions from Gaza or from West Bank cities that were transferred to Palestinian Authority control. The extent of HAMAS terrorist activity subsequent to the signing of the Oslo Agreement indicated that the government's ability to cope with this problem was indeed limited.

Lack of Normative Legitimacy

Decision-makers seeking legitimacy for their peace policy must be capable of persuading constituents that this policy is desirable because it is consistent with basic national values and interests and contributes to their advancement, and that the gains of peace outweigh its costs.[24]

Among the Arab–Israeli numerous feuds, the Israeli–Palestinian conflict is the most problematic – not only politically and ideologically but also territorially. At the same time of the Oslo Accord it was still difficult for many Israelis to change attitudes towards the Palestinians and the PLO. The government failed to convince the opposition parties and interest groups that the agreement conformed to national values and interests; the opposition continued to perceive the accords as posing a dangerous political threat and as challenging their basic beliefs (indeed, the accords placed in question the ideology of Greater Eretz Israel that had developed since 1967).[25]

The opposition political parties and elites rejected the whole idea of recognizing and negotiating with the PLO, which for them remained a dangerous enemy, a terrorist organization seeking to destroy Israel. Israeli concessions, in their view, would only weaken Israel and make it easier for the PLO to accomplish its political and military objectives, especially since the change in the PLO's attitude was only tactical. Moreover, they regarded the timing of the agreement as totally unfortunate because the PLO had been in a dire political and economic situation, if not on the verge of collapse, and Israel, as they saw it, had simply revived the organization with the agreement. There were also those who claimed that if the cost of peace was the return of Judea, Samaria, and Gaza or even parts of them, then keeping these territories was preferable to peace.[26]

Lack of Cognitive Legitimacy

Decision-makers must also convince others that they have both the knowledge and competence to achieve the proposed peace policy. They must show that they have a correct and realistic view of the conflict environment, that they have accurately assessed the other side's interest in reaching peace, and that they have the ability to steer the peace process in the desired direction.[27]

The government, however, failed to convince the opposition parties, the right-wing interest groups, and a major part of the public that it had control over the developments attending its peace policy, and that a real peace was emerging. The continuation of terrorist actions, Arafat's militant declarations, such as those calling for the continuation of *jihad*, and the failure to abolish the offensive parts of the Palestinian National Covenant as stipulated in the Oslo Accord, all seemed to indicate that the government had incorrectly assessed the conflict environment or the other side's peaceable intentions. The escalation of terrorist activity, mainly the suicide bombing, was exploited by the opposition to buttress their claims about the wrong-headedness of the peace policy.[28] The Oslo Accords have failed to strengthen tactical and personal security; more than 200 Israelis, both soldiers and civilians, have been killed in terrorist attacks since the agreement was signed. This was the most important factor in influencing the public, which apparently brought about Labour's failure in the May 1996 elections, though there were signs of such an imminent failure more than a year before the elections.

Thus, in a comprehensive public opinion survey conducted in March 1995, 45.9 per cent of the Jewish respondents believed the Oslo process to entail more dangers than prospects for Israel, whereas only 22.5 per cent gave the opposite response. Some 62.4 per cent expressed dissatisfaction with the peace process, compared to a mere 10.9 per cent who felt satisfied. A total of 64.4 per cent of the Jews said that Israelis' personal security had deteriorated, compared with 8.9 per cent who felt it had improved. Finally, 67.8 per cent of the Jewish respondents still believed that most Arabs would be prepared to eliminate Israel if they could, with only 14.7 per cent rejecting this assessment.[29]

Failure to Use Symbols, Language, and Rituals

Though gaining legitimacy for a peace policy is contingent on the perceived rationality of the proposed peace plan, legitimacy can also be promoted by conscious manipulation of national symbols, language, and rituals. Indeed, leaders may place greater emphasis on such efforts than on reasoned arguments, as they may believe that symbolic appeals will be more readily understood by important constituencies.[30]

The Rabin-Peres Government failed to make effective use of national and public symbols, or of hortatory language, in seeking legitimacy for its peace policy. As for the peace ritual, which included the ceremonies of the signing of three agreements, two in Washington and one in Cairo, this did not inspire unification or evoke a sense of exaltation – in contrast to the peace process with Egypt, which had created a real sense of involvement and enthusiasm. Rabin's personal difficulties, clearly manifest in the Washington signing ceremony in September 1993, only indicated that the prime minister himself had to vie with the attitudinal change. Once the government had basically failed to convince the public that the peace policy was desirable and worth pursuing, the manipulation of symbols, language, or rituals no longer had any chance of succeeding.

Defensive and Offensive Mechanisms

A distinction is often made between defensive and offensive mechanisms of legitimation. The relevant defensive strategies are apologies, excuses, buck-passing (or shifting responsibility), and justifications. The offensive strategies are termed 'enhancement' and 'entitlement'. Defensive mechanisms are ineffective and counter-productive; decision-makers cannot legitimize peace by minimizing their own responsibility for its costs, or blaming circumstances for the sacrifice of values and interests.

Enhancement and entitlement, thus, are better strategies. Enhancement aims at magnifying both the attractiveness of peace and the costs and risks of not making peace; entitlement aims at maximizing the decision-makers' responsibility for event.[31]

Rabin and Peres used both defensive and offensive strategies, especially justifications and buck-passing which proved ineffective. Both tended to blame the late prime minister, Menachem Begin, for creating a precedent of total withdrawal and dismantlement of settlements in the peace treaty with Egypt; hence, they argued, even if the Labour Government did its best to avoid such concessions to the Palestinians or the Syrians, this effort might prove futile. Those who opposed the Oslo process were not impressed; they maintained that although the Sinai precedent had indeed been a mistake, Sinai was not the same as Judea, Samaria, Gaza and the Golan since these areas were much more important in security, historical, and religious terms, and were populated by far more Jewish settlers than the Sinai.[32]

True, Rabin and Peres did use an entitlement strategy of taking direct responsibility for initiating the peace policy; but this was rather insufficient. The fact that the peace policy was initiated by Israel, rather than imposed on it, had only limited influence. Rabin's assassination, which indicated more than anything his full responsibility for the peace-making, rallied mass public support behind the peace policy, but only temporarily. Rabin's and Peres's use of an enhancement strategy was equally ineffective: they failed to demonstrate the diplomatic and economic achievements of peace-making, including the dramatic improvement in Israel's international status, most strikingly evident in the massive attendance of prominent world leaders at Rabin's funeral.

Use of De-Legitimation Strategy

The government and especially Rabin adopted a de-legitimation strategy against opponents of the peace policy, mainly the Likud Party, its leader, and the settlers; to some extent this was probably in retaliation to the opposition's de-legitimation campaign against Rabin. Likud was thus portrayed as the party that had itself made the most drastic concessions in peace-making, especially by returning the entire Sinai Peninsula and removing the settlements there; it was also characterized as a 'rejectionist' party, unrealistic, opposed to any diplomatic initiative, and lacking any viable alternative. Moreover, following every terrorist attack, Likud was charged with 'aiding' HAMAS and Islamic Jihad by censuring the government. Netanyahu was presented as an inexperienced leader, especially in security and international matters, who should not be taken seriously.[33]

For their part the settlers were blamed for endangering the peace process out of personal and ideological concerns. For them, Rabin claimed, retaining their homes in the territories, as well as their ideology of Greater Israel, which could only lead to a binational state, was more important than peace. Thus they were in a *de facto* alliance with HAMAS, since both parties opposed peace. This argument, used also by Arafat, was the most clear-cut attempt at de-legitimation of those who opposed the peace policy. Rabin seemed to be insensitive to the settlers' alarm and anxiety about their fate as the process moved forward; rather, he regarded them as political enemies who sought to harm him personally.[34]

Rabin and Peres downplayed the importance of the value of settlement. Though initially differentiating between 'political' and 'security' settlements, Rabin later maintained that the settlements as a whole had no security value and were actually a security liability.[35] However, recognizing the importance of the settlement issue for legitimizing the peace policy, and in order to avoid a domestic schism or at least delay it until the final stage of the negotiations, Rabin and Peres insisted in the Oslo Accord that during the interim stage no settlement in Gaza or the West Bank would be removed, even if this created a security problem. This decision did indeed prevent even greater opposition to the peace policy, but failed to forestall such opposition altogether. In a poll of West Bank settlers taken in late December 1995, only 20.6 per cent of respondents were prepared to accept removal of settlements even if a governmental decision on the matter was approved by a regular majority in the Knesset. However, 15.1 per cent said they would accept such a decision if approved by a regular Jewish majority in the Knesset and another 22.7 per cent if approved by a special Jewish majority in the Knesset. Some 30.8 per cent stated that they would disobey any decision whatsoever on their removal. Nevertheless, only 7.8 per cent of the settlers would consider the use of force to resist their removal, whereas 82.6 per cent would not.[36]

Rabin and Peres seemed to be insensitive not only to the settlers' painful feelings but also to their conflict of values. For most settlers, the historical tradition that connects the people of Israel to the Land of Israel is a central value. Rabin and Peres, however, created the impression that they themselves had no real conflict of values in relinquishing the territories, and were actually happy to do so since these territories constituted a political and ideological obstacle to the goal of a Jewish State with a Jewish majority. After Rabin's assassination, Peres attempted to open a dialogue with the settlers and the Yesha Council that would reduce the mutual de-legitimation.

Lack of Compensatory Efforts

To legitimize the concessions made for the sake of peace, decision-makers may also find it necessary to compensate those who will be most damaged by these concessions. However, when some settlers asked to leave their homes in Judea, Samaria, and Gaza, Rabin and Peres refused to compensate them, though some Labour MKs tried to find a legal way to do so. Peres emphasized his opposition to the idea even after Rabin's assassination, suggesting that the government was not responsible for those who willingly left these areas, and acquiescing in the continued presence of settlers there even under Palestinian rule. Thus, while as many as one-third of the settlers expressed willingness to leave in return for compensation, the government failed to deal with them effectively.[37]

Lack of Religious Legitimacy

A less important reason for the absence of widespread legitimacy for the peace policy was that groups among the settlers, as well as among the right-wing parties and extra-parliamentary groups, believed that no government had the right to relinquish any part of the Land of Israel; hence, whether the government's peace policy had legitimacy in the Knesset, or even in the public at large was immaterial. In other words, for them, legitimacy for a peace policy was based not on a democratic system but on a theological one, so that no policy that entailed territorial concessions in the Judea, Samaria, and Gaza, and removal of settlements could be acceptable. This problem of legitimacy is not limited to the political question of exchanging territory for peace; it also manifests the deeper conflict in Israel 'between the idea of an essentially secular state, one based on the rule of law and endowed with a "legal-rational" legitimation by its citizens, and the idea of a Jewish religious state based on "traditional legitimation, derived ultimately from God"'.[38]

CONCLUSIONS

Peace-making with the Palestinians constitutes a great opportunity for Israel and its neighbours; however, it also poses a serious domestic problem for Israel. The need to change attitudes and to make significant territorial concessions has confronted Israel with a severe crisis, probably the most severe since the state's establishment. Indeed, with the nation so deeply divided, the crisis is nothing short of traumatic. Rabin's assassination has indicated how dangerous for Israel's internal harmony the peace process with the Palestinians could be.

The main domestic problem is how to legitimize the peace-policy when the regular constitutional and legal stipulations regarding the formulation and implementation of this policy, such as Knesset approval, a national referendum, and probably elections, are not regarded as sufficiently legitimate by many opponents of this policy. Extra-parliamentary groups, and probably some political parties, will not acquiesce in the peace policies even if they are legitimized by the legal forums and processes.

As we have seen, some of those right-wing parties and groups deny in principle the legitimacy of any government to make territorial concessions. When the government's peace policy is defined as 'an act of national treachery' and illegitimate, then the adoption of extreme means to foil the policy, including threats of disobedience, assassination, and civil war, becomes more and more widespread.

Rabin and Peres failed to find informal tracks for bridging the gap between themselves and the opposition parties and groups; rather, the de-legitimation strategies employed by both sides only widened the rift. The discussion of legitimacy should also include the actual and potential behaviour of the party with whom the agreement is signed. Undoubtedly, the escalation of Palestinian terrorist activity following the signing of the Oslo Accords created a severe problem for the Israeli government, and the failure to cope with it effectively diminished its legitimacy. The defeat in the May 1996 elections was a direct result.

The election of Benjamin Netanyahu as prime minister indicated that the Israeli public, and particularly the Jewish sector, favours an alternative way of implementing the Oslo Accords rather than their abandonment. The fact that 82 per cent of the public supported Netanyahu's first meeting with Arafat, and 80 per cent supported the continuation of negotiations with the Palestinians, indicates that Israelis have adjusted to the attitudinal change and the peace process and want the process to move forward.[39] Moreover, in a poll on 26 September 1996, 63 per cent of the respondents indicated that they were not satisfied with the Netanyahu Government's handling of the peace process, while only 26.6 per cent expressed satisfaction with it.[40]

These facts show that the peace process has been accepted as a reality by the majority of the Israeli people. It seems that the downfall of the party that initiated this process, Labour, did not eliminate the peace process itself, and that most Israelis, including the Netanyahu Government, have adjusted in one way or another to the change.

Netanyahu will have great difficulty in making the necessary concessions, especially because of domestic constraints. The more concessions he will be called on to make, the greater the risks that his legitimacy may be further reduced in the eyes of his constituencies. Netanyahu had better learn Begin's, Rabin's, and Peres's lessons in coping with legitimacy and value complexity problems if he is to further the peace process with the Palestinians and Syria.

NOTES

1. Yitzhak Shamir, *Summing Up*, Tel-Aviv, 1994, pp.273–91 (Hebrew); Moshe Arens, *Peace and War in the Middle East: 1988–1992*, Tel-Aviv, 1995, pp.263–80 (Hebrew).
2. Shimon Peres, *Battling for Peace*, London, 1995, pp.321–2.
3. Yitzhak Rabin, *Knesset Records*, 13 July 1993, pp.8–12; David Makovsky, *Making Peace with the PLO: The Rabin Government's Road to the Oslo Accord*, Boulder, 1996, pp.82–3.
4. Peres, *Battling for Peace*, pp.320–23.
5. Rabin, *Ha-aretz*, 31 August 1993.
6. Shimon Peres, *The New Middle East*, New York, 1993, pp.9–10; Makovsky, *Making Peace*, pp.31, 34.
7. Rabin and Peres, *Ha-aretz*, 31 August 1993; Makovsky, *Making Peace*, pp.114–20.
8. Makovsky, *Making Peace*, pp.111–13.
9. On the question of legitimacy for peace see, Yaacov Bar-Siman-Tov, *Israel and the Peace Process, 1977–1982: In Search of Legitimacy for Peace*, Albany, 1994, pp.1–17.
10. Makovsky, *Making Peace*, p.62.
11. Benjamin Netanyahu, *Knesset Records*, 21 September 1993, pp.7685–700; *Foreign Broadcasts Information Service* (FBIS): Daily Report, 15, 24 September 1993, pp.22, 26; 6 May 1994, p.44; *Knesset Records*, 5 October 1995, pp.30–101.
12. Ehud Sprinzak, *Political Violence in Israel*, Jerusalem, 1995, pp.116–24 (Hebrew); *Jerusalem Post*, 6 October 1995.
13. These statements were made by Benjamin Netanyahu, Ariel Sharon, Rehavam Zeevi, Rafael Eitan, and Zevulun Hammer at the demonstration on 5 October 1995 (*Ha-aretz*, 6 October 1995).
14. *Yediot Aharonot*, 30 August 1993.
15. Ibid., 28 September 1995.
16. Ephraim Yuchtman-Yaar, Tamar Hermann, and Arieh Nadler, *Peace Index Project: Findings and Analysis. June 1994–May 1996*, Tel Aviv, Tami Steinmatz Centre for Peace Research, 1996.
17. Ibid.
18. Sprinzak, *Political Violence*, pp.108–30.
19. Ibid., pp.116–17.
20. *Jerusalem Post*, 30 August 1993; FBIS, 30 September 1993, p.51; *Ha-aretz*, 27 July 1995.
21. *Ha-aretz*, 20 June 1994.
22. Bar-Siman-Tov, *Israel and the Peace Process*, pp.8–9; see also Alexander L. George, 'Domestic Constraints on Regime Change in U.S. Foreign Policy: The Need for Policy Legitimacy', in Ole R. Holsti, Randolph M. Siverson, and Alexander L. George, eds., *Change in International Systems*, Boulder, 1980, pp.233–38.
23. Rabin, FBIS, 13 September 1993, p.36; *Yediot Aharonot, Davar, Hadashot*, 24 September 1993; *Ha-aretz*, 29 December 1993; Peres, FBIS, 2, 7 September 1993, pp.32, 49; 20 May 1994, p.30. Shulamit Aloni and Yossi Sarid preferred the establishment of a Palestinian state, FBIS, 4, 27 January 1994, pp.23, 31.
24. Bar-Siman-Tov, *Israel and the Peace Process*, p.9; George, 'Domestic Constraints', p.235; Yehudit Auerbach, 'Legitimation for Turning-Point Decisions in Foreign Policy: Israel vis-à-vis Germany 1952 and Egypt 1977', *Review of International Studies*, Vol.15 (1989), pp.329–40.
25. *Yediot Aharonot*, 24 December 1995.
26. Netanyahu, *Knesset Records*, 21 September 1993, pp.7685–700, 5 October 1995,

pp.30–101.
27. Bar-Siman-Tov, *Israel and the Peace Process*, p.9; George, 'Domestic Constraints', p.235; Auerbach, 'Legitimation', pp.329–40.
28. Sprinzak, *Political Violence*, pp.118–19.
29. Tamar Hermann and Ephraim Yuchtman-Yaar, 'Two People Apart: Israeli Jews and Arabs' Attitudes Towards the Peace Process' (unpublished paper).
30. Bar-Siman-Tov, *Israel and the Peace Process*, pp.10–13.
31. Ibid., pp.13–16; Auerbach, 'Legitimation', pp.335–36.
32. Peres, *Knesset Records*, 30 August 1993, pp.7551–66, 9 September 1993, pp.7589–601; Rabin, *Ha-aretz*, 31 August 1993. In a meeting with the Golan's settlers, Sharon apologized about the Sinai withdrawal and the removal of the settlements there in 1982 (*Ha-aretz*, 24 July 1995).
33. Rabin, *Ha-aretz*, 31 August 1993; *Yediot Aharonot, Hadashot, Davar*, 24 September 1993; Peres, *Knesset Records*, 9 September 1993, p.7601, 11 October 1993, p.2, 17 November 1993, p.1057; Rabin, *Ha-aretz*, 26 March 1995.
34. Rabin, *FBIS*, 5, 26 July 1994, pp.31, 34; *Yediot Aharonot*, 26 July 1994; Sprinzak, *Political Violence*, p.121.
35. Rabin, *FBIS*, 14 August 1992, p.17; *Yediot Aharonot*, 20 August 1992; *Hadashot*, 23 August 1992; *Davar*, 1 April 1994; *FBIS*, 3 May 1994, p.47.
36. *Ha-aretz*, 8 January 1996.
37. Ibid.
38. Erik Cohen, 'The Removal of the Israeli Settlements in Sinai: An Ambiguous Resolution to an Existential Conflict', *Journal of Applied Behavioral Science*, Vol.23 (1987), pp.140–41.
39. *Yediot Aharonot*, 6 September 1996; *Ma'ariv*, 1 October 1996.
40. Poll taken by Tami Steinmatz Centre for Peace Research, Tel-Aviv University, 26 September 1996.

The Potential of Ambiguity: The Case of Jerusalem

IRA SHARKANSKY

Long identified as a source of religious inspiration, Jerusalem may now serve as a learning opportunity for political accommodation. On the surface, the noise of absolute and irreconcilable demands seems to assure yet another period of extreme rhetoric and perhaps violence. Yet with all the absolutism of political verbiage, there has been a willingness on the part of leaders to behave differently than they speak. In contrast to the strict monotheisms that compete in revering Jerusalem, and the reminders of the violence that is possible, the greatest contemporary lesson of the city may be in the utility of creative ambiguity. The lessons apply not only to Jerusalem but to other difficult conflicts.

Israeli officials speak ritually about a united city that will serve as the country's capital forever. Their repetition of the slogan suggests an insecurity about a reality where religious and ethnic communities maintain their separation. Palestinians and Jews live in their own neighbourhoods, read their own newspapers, send their children to their own schools, use their own bus lines and taxi companies. Palestinians in East Jerusalem academic high schools prepare for higher education in Arab countries, and few have the command of Hebrew that is typical of Arab students elsewhere in Israel. As a result, most of the Arabs who study at the Hebrew University are from outside Jerusalem. Inter-marriages are discouraged in both Jewish and Palestinian communities and are small in number. Israeli critics of the policies pursued by the national and municipal governments have asserted that the Palestinians of East Jerusalem are more integrated with the Palestinians of the West Bank than with the Jews of Jerusalem. They conclude that Jerusalem is divided *de facto*, and that its Palestinian sector might as well acquire formal status as the capital of Palestine.[1]

Additional divisions appear within the Jewish, Christian, and Muslim communities. Ultra-Orthodox and other Jews argue about religious law, individual freedom, and the possibilities for non-Orthodox Judaisms in the Jewish State. A score of Christian congregations compete with one another in demanding rights at holy places. Each community has support overseas as well as locally. The

Ira Sharkansky is Professor of Political Science at the Hebrew University of Jerusalem.

Vatican and Moscow have expressed historic concerns for the Latin and Orthodox churches in ways that recall the run-up to the Crimean War. The city's Muslims have rival chief muftis: one appointed by Jordan and another by the Palestinian Authority. A former deputy mayor counted 37 instances of bloody changes in regime over a history of 3000 to 4000 years. He tried to deal with contemporary tensions by dividing the city into ethnic and religious boroughs.[2] When he failed at local reform, he went off to Harvard and earned a PhD. The whole enterprise has been deemed fit only for an international regime.

The delicacy of Jerusalem's situation recalls the epigrams attributed to Carl Von Clausewitz and Mao Tse Tung: that war is a political instrument, a continuation of political commerce, a carrying out of the same by other means; or that politics is war without violence, while war is politics with violence.[3] The relevance is that violence stands ready to take over when politicians fail. The medium of politics is persuasion and voting, the pursuit of success over an opponent, and movement in one direction or another. Military campaigns pursue victory and the capacity to dictate to a defeated enemy. The closeness of politics and war appears in the politicians' use of military language. Since their 1993 accord, however, Israelis and Palestinians are more like adversaries than enemies. Therein lies the potential for politicians to use ambiguity in order to deal with some of the most intense issues that remain unresolved.

COPING AND AMBIGUITY

The concept of coping is more appropriate for Jerusalem than any effort to solve its complex problems once and for all times. Coping implies something less than solutions. It includes the acceptance and even manipulation of ambiguity. Words like adapting, managing, dealing with and satisfying appear in discussions of coping.[4] Coping appears to be a way that Jews over the ages have dealt with the ambiguities of their situation and awesome kinds of stress. Stereotypes of Jewish behaviour, including those associated with anti-Semitism, feature adjustment to circumstances, the manipulation and exploitation of opportunity.

Jerusalem manifests the historic problems of the Jews: too few and weak to be genuinely autonomous, and marginal with respect to powerful outsiders. The city has long been on a border between east and west. Under the Greeks, Romans, and Crusaders it was in the far east of western regimes. Under the Babylonians and Persians, it was on the western edge of eastern empires. Modern Jerusalem includes one of the world's major fault lines between west and east, separating the Jews from the Arabs. A minor fault line of this kind runs through the Jewish community, and sets off Jews who came from Asia and North Africa from those with roots in Europe. Two instances of Jewish tragedy occurred when the city's residents did not cope successfully with the tensions between cultures. The Books of Maccabees describe the violence between cosmopolitan Jews who had become Hellenized and zealous Jews during the period of the Greeks. Josephus describes a similar condition under the Romans.[5] Modern disputes between religious and secular Jews recall those ancient conflicts. Rabbis and secular politicians cite the civil wars to warn their followers against extreme acts that might weaken the entire community in the face of external enemies.

Jerusalem has proved difficult for its rulers, some of whom have displayed a willingness to sacrifice part of their sovereignty for an increased likelihood of peace. When the Muslims recaptured the city from the Crusaders, they turned back into mosques a number of the buildings that the Christians had made into churches. However, they left the especially sensitive Church of the Holy Sepulchre in Christian hands in order to avoid provoking another crusade.[6] During the late Ottoman period in the nineteenth century, the Turkish rulers of the city accepted the intervention of more powerful foreign governments. The United Kingdom, France, Germany, Russia, and the United States acquired concessions and provided protection to those residents of Jerusalem who claimed their citizenship.[7]

Jerusalem's history has shown the problems of implementing enlightened policies. There are stories of Roman soldiers who insulted Jews by baring their bottoms in the vicinity of the Temple when their commanding officers were seeking to accommodate Jewish sensitivities.[8] They illustrate a problem that has troubled rulers in other situations: policy is made not only by ranking officials, but by the lowest ranking functionaries who encounter the public and affect how policy is actually delivered. The riots and repression that followed the insulting behaviour of Roman soldiers complicated any efforts of the Roman or Jewish elites to accommodate one another.[9]

MANAGING AMBIGUITY

The Israeli record in Jerusalem since 1967 shows a willingness to govern by managing ambiguity. The regime has insisted that it controls a united city, but has accepted less than full sovereignty at sensitive points. Muslim and Christian religious authorities have been given *de facto* control over their holy places. Israeli authorities forbid Jewish prayers on what Jews call the Temple Mount in order to avoid offending Muslim sensitivities for what they call Haram al-Sharif and its Dome of the Rock and al-Aqsa Mosque. Israeli officials have allowed Palestinian businessmen and professionals to practice under Jordanian licenses and the supervision of Arab associations, rather than force them to accept Israeli licensing and the rules of an Israeli Chamber of

Commerce or professional societies. They have allowed Palestinians to deal in Jordanian dinars and other foreign currency, against the regulations of the Bank of Israel that applied to Israeli citizens and residents. Israel's tax authorities gradually imposed their own rates and standards of administration on East Jerusalem, which had been accustomed to much lower rates and the uneven quality of Jordanian enforcement. Municipal and national educational authorities have supported schools that teach according to Jordanian curricula and prepare their graduates for Arab universities. Israel offered, but did not impose citizenship on the Palestinian residents of Jerusalem. Israel allowed the Palestinians to keep their Jordanian papers, to renew them and register newborn children as Jordanians via the officials who operated an unobtrusive Jordanian consulate in the East Jerusalem Chamber of Commerce. In contrast with the Palestinian residents of Gaza and the West Bank, Palestinians in Jerusalem were provided with Israeli social benefits, including family payments, old-age and disability pensions, and subsidized health plans. Officials also allowed them access to Israeli employment opportunities without the curfews and border closings imposed from time to time elsewhere in the occupied territories.[10]

The Israeli regime's coping with the religious Jews of Jerusalem has included the postponement or modification of construction projects that threaten the sensitivities of ultra-Orthodox activists. As with several elements involving the Palestinians, the situation with religious Jews is one of managed ambiguity rather than formalized concessions. The city's Palestinians have had to accept a strong Israeli presence along with some compromises of Israeli sovereignty. Religious Jews, for their part, have been granted delays and modifications of activities they deemed offensive. Yet neither the municipal nor the national government has given in to the demands of religious activists to halt public sector construction projects that encounter ancient Jewish graves.[11]

Events in Jerusalem since the signing of the Israeli–Palestinian accord in 1993 provide additional illustrations of governance via ambiguity. Israeli insistence on control over Jerusalem has not kept the government from agreeing that Palestinian residents of the city could vote in elections for the Palestinian Authority. Israeli insistence that the Palestinians' Orient House not be used for political activities gradually gave way to an acceptance of ceremonial visits there by ranking officials from foreign governments. Municipal and national education authorities have funded schools in the Palestinian sector and formally appointed the teachers and administrators, but consulted with representatives of the Palestine Liberation Organization (PLO) on issues of importance to them. Israeli insistence that the Palestinian police not operate in Jerusalem is at odds with reports that Palestinian opponents of the PLO have been picked up in the city by Palestinian security operatives and transported elsewhere for detention and investigation. An article in a Jerusalem newspaper expressed the ambiguity of policing with headlines that described, 'Joint Patrols (almost) of the Border Police and the PLO in the Eastern Part of the City', and 'Full Coexistence Even if Not a Formal Coordination'.[12] Critics chastize the Israeli establishment for its failure to plan and formulate policy rationally, and to solve Jerusalem's problems. Another view is that an acceptance of ambiguity reflects an acquired cultural capacity of Israeli Jews to cope with vexing problems.[13]

THE PROBLEMS AND OPPORTUNITIES OF AMBIGUITY

Ambiguity is both a way of dealing with problems that otherwise might be insoluble, and a source of stress that adds to the problems of policy-making. Israeli and Palestinian authorities proclaim goals for Jerusalem that appear to be irreconcilable. Activists on either side accuse their leaders of compromising basic goals. Community leaders assert that they do not concede basic issues, but thereby seem to deny their success in managing Jerusalem.

The problems of ambiguity are well known: Participants do not know exactly where they stand. It is not clear what they or their antagonists may do. There are no fixed boundaries or guidelines to behaviour that can be described as legitimate, reasonable, or acceptable. At the very least, ambiguity produces the stress of not knowing one's own limits or those of one's adversaries.

There is ambiguity in all political settings. The most enlightened of democratic polities posit values of individual freedom against those of communal order. The exact boundaries between individual rights and community needs are not clear, and the boundaries shift in response to political determinations of which proposals to enact into law, and how to enforce each law.[14] The boundaries between formal policy and informal rules of the game offer opportunities for individuals to stretch their rights, but without knowing for certain when the authorities will intervene and enforce the rules as written. How much faster than the posted speed limit can we drive without encountering the highway police? How loud can we party without the police charging us for disturbing the peace? What claims can we make on a tax return without triggering an audit? Such cases present temptations and potential embarrassment that add a bit of spice to conventional citizenship. Flexibility is an attraction, but ambiguous limits to acceptable behaviour invite irresponsible exploitation of flexibility. The situation is especially problematic where there has been a history of violence. If good fences make good neighbours, a situation of undefined boundaries between hostile communities raises the possibility of bloodshed.

Ambiguity serves politicians who make numerous promises that are far-reaching in their implications, without specifying just what will be delivered. Voters choose on the basis of generalized affection for a campaign. The successful politician as office-holder can choose among the commitments that can be reconciled with circumstances. It is a well-practiced craft that reinforces chronic cynicism about politicians, but generally does not threaten a regime.

The appeal of ambiguity for a policy-maker is the opportunity to skip over especially contentious issues in the hope that an 'understanding' will facilitate accommodations. Adversaries can reach agreement on the main outline of a programme without getting bogged down in all the messy details. Legislators enact laws that describe general lines of action, and leave the rule-making and implementation to administrative bodies. Members of the legislature should understand that they will not see the implementation of all that might fit within the frameworks they endorse. They can return to the subject at a later time if they are not satisfied with what administrators actually deliver, or they may decide to rest with the accomplishments achieved.

Policy-makers' 'mandates' are never precise. The fog of ambiguity may cover a bit of the emperor's nakedness. Vagueness or 'fudging' is a lubricant of political agreement. If one or another constituency eventually loses something in the implementation, the loss may be acceptable in light of other gains achieved. Even where a written agreement appears to be comprehensive, fuzziness about which provisions will actually be enforced allows flexibility to deal with evolving reality, limited resources, and unexpected crises. The test of ambiguity is its workability. If a programme survives the charges that it is not exactly what all its architects intended, it is likely to be a case of reasonable deviation from expectation.

Jerusalem is not the only instance of sensitive politics on the verge of violence where ambiguity has served to limit bloodshed. By the nature of ambiguity, the results have not been universally applauded. Wars have ended with dramatic pronouncements that have not fulfilled all their implications. The benefits are that the fighting has stopped and the killing limited, leaving a stage set for future decisions to rely more on politics and less on violence. The American involvement in Vietnam ended with pledges for the South Vietnam regime, which allowed American and Vietnamese histories to evolve separately. The violence did not end in Vietnam, but a process began whereby the United States military could extract itself and end its own casualties and its killing of Vietnamese.

Ambiguity may be most useful in close-knit communities with extensive areas of implicit agreement. It can operate in families and small communities, or when the attitudes of two sides in a dispute are forthcoming, generous, understanding and accommodating, rather than suspicious. In recent Israel history, ambiguity may have been more appropriate to the period when Israel and the Palestinians were represented by Shimon Peres and Yasser Arafat, before suicide bombings by Palestinian extremists, the escalation of tension in southern Lebanon-northern Israel and the military operation *Grapes of Wrath* that displaced thousands of families and resulted in numerous civilian deaths.

One story of failed ambiguity appeared in the Israeli press shortly after the opening for tourists of an ancient tunnel alongside the Temple Mount/Haram al-Sharif. Israeli authorities thought they had offered a package deal to Muslim religious authorities: development of an area called Solomon's stables as a mosque, in exchange for acceptance of Israel's opening of the tunnel. Israelis who attended one meeting perceived that Muslim officials shook their heads in apparent agreement. The tunnel's opening in September 1996 was associated with an outbreak of violence and numerous deaths. Then Muslims denied that any agreement had been achieved.

A breakdown in understanding may have come as a result of competitive divisions of responsibility on the Muslim side between religious and political authorities, with different figures loyal to the PLO, the Palestine Authority, Jordan, and Saudi Arabia. On the Israeli side, once the crisis occurred, there were competing assertions of 'we told you so' and 'you did not consult with us' between officials of the municipality, the national government, the military, police, and other security services.[15] There were conflicting claims among present and former Israeli ministers, the mayor of Jerusalem, and police officials with respect to whether the 'package deal' was with or without the agreement of the Muslims, whether Muslim authorities had sent a letter rejecting the opening of the tunnel, and whether the former police minister had transmitted such a letter to the government.[16]

The very nature of ambiguity makes analysis as risky as governance. A challenge for any discussion about the benefits of ambiguity in a given context is how to illustrate the point without being so specific that the scenarios offered will be outmoded by events in the near future. These scenarios of Jerusalem proceed from the principle that the recent past is the best guide to the near future. An observer or participant can never be certain that an activist of one camp or another will not exceed the boundaries of reasonable flexibility in ways that will trigger a cycle of escalating responses until the whole enterprise collapses for being untenable.

JERUSALEM SCENARIOS

The dangers of Jerusalem begin with religion and ethnicity. The city is holy to three faiths, each of which has elements of monotheism and doctrinal exclusivity. It is also on a cultural divide. For other democracies the boundary between east and west may be across the ocean or over the mountains. In Jerusalem it is across the street, and may even separate one apartment from another in the same building. The history of the city cautions reasonable politicians against the use of terms like 'crusade' or 'holy war', yet some individuals continue to speak in those terms. In distant Iran, Iraq, or Libya such rhetoric may be employed by political leaders who use the symbol of Jerusalem to placate populations restive because of local issues, without dangerous implications. However, their words resonate among Israeli politicians, add to their own rhetoric, and may limit their flexibility with respect to Palestinian demands.

The prospect of religious violence is part of Jerusalem's past and present. Jews worry about enraged Muslims who kill individual Jews while shouting God is Great! or suicide bombers who explode themselves and others on crowded buses. When such an event does occur the police mobilize to protect Arabs (and Jews who look like Arabs) on main roads near working-class Jewish neighbourhoods. There the chant is Death to the Arabs, and some crowds have shown their willingness to implement the slogan. An episode that enrages both Jews and Muslims occurred during the Jewish holiday of Succoth in October 1990. Israeli police killed 21 Palestinians on the Temple Mount in violent clashes triggered by Palestinian stoning of Jews who were praying below at the Western Wall.

In what may seem to be ironic, the intensity of faith that complicates Jerusalem also works in favour of ambiguity being used as a policy tool. Religious doctrines include concepts of Jerusalem above and Jerusalem below. Jerusalem above refers to the Holy City, a synonym for paradise with connotations of the other-worldly and the afterlife. Jerusalem below refers to the earthly city, with its sounds of traffic, the scurry of cats around the garbage, and the tensions of political competition. The optimistic feature of this situation is that politicians might reach agreement about the management of Jerusalem below, while leaving the faithful of each community to stand steadfast about how Jerusalem above will be governed once the messiah or prophet arrives or returns.

While some religious leaders of Jerusalem seem like harridans more concerned with realizing their monopoly of truth in the holy city, others express the spiritualism associated with Jerusalem above, and seem willing to realize their aspirations in paradise. The veteran Jordanian Prime Minister, Dr. Abd al-Salam al-Majali, demonstrated a facility with language and political concepts that offer the ingredients of accommodation:

> ... human brains that create problems can create solutions, too... The word Jerusalem is derived from sanctity or places of worship... Political Jerusalem is different from the religious Jerusalem that is sacred to the three religions. Thus, a political solution is possible.[17]

Yasser Arafat spoke in a similar manner on the eve of negotiations about the permanent solution for the Palestinian–Israeli conflict. Against Israeli insistence that Jerusalem not be discussed, he said that Palestinians could not be stopped from dreaming of having Jerusalem as the capital of their state. Israeli Prime Minister Shimon Peres responded that he did not object to Palestinian dreams. The hope is that Jerusalem and its residents will enjoy the fruits of the peace process, rather than be the point of contention that causes the process to fail.

The city's recent history works in favour of the agility and suppleness associated with coping by means of ambiguity. The concessions made by Israeli officials after 1967 reflect their sensitivity to the feelings of Jerusalem's Palestinians. Likewise the relative quiescence of the city's Palestinians during the years of *intifada* suggests that they perceived limits to what could be achieved in Jerusalem. Palestinians have made no secret of their opposition to the Israeli regime, but they have indicated their appreciation of a relatively placid existence with social services and access to Israeli employment opportunities.

The elemental requirement of managed ambiguity is to avoid aspirations that are impossible, and to continue with the theme of accommodations that already show signs of evolving. It appears to be beyond the realm of possibility to define fixed boundaries between Israeli and Palestinian sectors within the present municipal borders of Jerusalem, or to make a neat assignment of people and functions to separate municipal authorities. The borders of ethnic and religious neighbourhoods (Palestinian and Israeli, Christian, Muslim, ultra-Orthodox Jewish, and secular Jewish) change direction from one block to another, skip over islands of other communities, and contain not a few instances of variation from one building to another within the same block, or from one apartment to another within the same building.

It is unrealistic to expect the Israeli regime to abandon the neighbourhoods built since 1967 and to return Jerusalem to a status quo ante, whenever that might be dated. It is no surprise that Israelis have exploited their opportunities in the period since 1967. By 1990, 132,000 Jews lived in new neighbourhoods constructed on land that had been in the Jordanian sector prior to the 1967 War.[18] In the eyes of some this reflects the Israelis' lack of concern for justice. To others it is the result of legitimate Israeli concerns in the face of Arab threats against Jerusalem, and Palestinian boycotts of the political opportunities offered them. Few Palestinian residents of the city availed themselves of the opportunity to vote in municipal elections, and even fewer accepted the Israeli citizenship required for voting in national elections. In their boycotts, the community leaders sacrificed the power of one-quarter of the city's electorate. In placing the emphasis on 'whose city is Jerusalem?' Palestinians abandoned the more conventional struggle about 'who gets what?' within the city.

Assertions about justice and blame tend to frustrate efforts to cope with present realities. Palestinian pragmatists will seek whatever potential there is for satisfying Palestinian concerns within the outline of what exists. One set of opportunities lies just outside the municipal boundaries defined by Israel. Neighbourhoods and villages to the north, east and south (from Ramallah around to Bethlehem) are within the area assigned to the Palestinians and contain a sizable Palestinian majority. Palestinians can say they are developing 'Jerusalem' without infringing on the Israeli city. A bi-national metropolitan area can share the magic of the name 'Jerusalem' between Palestinian and Israeli authorities. Metropolitan utility lines and sewage can be administered by authorities with representatives of both national entities, and a mandate to share development budgets, water allotments, revenues, and personnel appointments in a way to reward both communities. Within the Israeli municipality the following accommodations would represent slight if any extensions of what already exists:

• Control of Christian and Muslim holy places by the religious authorities of each community. The present *de facto* arrangement can be formalized, perhaps (as suggested by former Mayor Teddy Kollek) embellished with a United Nations resolution that is adopted as Israeli law by the Knesset;

• Recognition of Orient House as a governmental seat of the Palestinian State, with a full panoply of flags, armed guards and red carpets for visiting dignitaries;

• Devolution of sensitive local services in the Palestinian sector, such as education, to individuals vetted by Palestinian authorities;

• Choice by residents as to the authority(ies) in which they register, vote, pay taxes, and receive social welfare benefits. This provision can be sweetened by allowing Palestinians to vote in both Israeli and Palestinian local and even national elections, and to provide protection against double taxation. Their status would resemble that of Israelis who also hold citizenship in the United States and other countries that permit dual nationality.

It is in the nature of ambiguity that arrangements are not flawless or free of tension. The choice of which Muslim and Christian religious authorities will prevail on Haram al-Sharif-Temple Mount and the Church of the Holy Sepulchre will demand the same spirit of concession and delicacy as conflicts between ultra-Orthodox and other Jews.

None of these steps are likely to pass without severe criticism from communal leaders who proclaim that they are not receiving enough from their adversaries, or are conceding too much to them. Both Israelis and Palestinians include substantial numbers of leaders and followers with a limited tolerance for ambiguity. Prominent among those who are sensitive to concessions are individuals who have been injured by inter-communal violence, and the families of those killed. Yasser Arafat proclaims on a regular basis that Jerusalem must be the capital of his Palestinian state. His use of the term *jihad* has its own problems of ambiguity. Against his assertion that *jihad* can mean a non-violent campaign in quest of a spiritual goal are translations of holy war with the connotation of mass hysteria and violence. One can hope that Arafat will be satisfied with an administrative centre in greater Jerusalem (currently being built in the southern part of Ramallah, close to the border of what Israelis call the Jerusalem municipality), Muslim control of Haram al-Sharif, and free access to Orient House.

The campaign leading up to the 1996 Israeli national elections testified to the emotions associated with Jerusalem. The opposition Likud party began its campaign by accusing Prime Minister Peres of seeking to divide the city and permitting the Palestinians to take part of it as a national capital. The response of Labour was to deny any such intention, and to assert that it was committed to maintaining a united city under Israeli rule. The minister for internal security also announced that he would tighten control over Orient House and forbid the kinds of visits by foreign dignitaries that he had, in fact, permitted. What was missing from the Labour party response was an effort to educate the Israeli public as to the complexity of the issues concerned with Jerusalem, and the possibility of dealing with them by recognizing the multiple meanings of 'Jerusalem'.

Why the shrill and stubborn response from the Labour party? Perhaps its leadership wanted to maintain a strong posture on the city, in preparation for the bargaining with the Palestinians, whose own leadership staked out a demand for a national capital in the city. If this was the thinking of the Labour leadership, it seemed weakened by comments made by figures in the left wing of the Labour party and its coalition partner the MERETZ party. They cited reasons of equity and pragmatism as requiring compromise with the Palestinians on the issue of Jerusalem. More persuasive is another explanation for Labour's formal posture on Jerusalem: its fear of the Jewish electorate's concern for the city.

Did this mean the party was lying to the voters? Perhaps not, as long as it did not specify what it meant by Jerusalem, and what it meant by not dividing it. Eventually it may be possible to explain a Palestinian governmental site within the Israeli city, and measures of autonomy for the Palestinian population that differ little if at all from practices already in place. Even easier to explain will be Palestinian developments in the area of Greater Jerusalem, much of which has already be assigned to the Palestinian authority.

There is nothing unnatural or impossible about having a nation's capital that is not all in one place. Until post-war Germany was

reunited, the Federal Republic of Germany had its legislative chamber
and key executive offices in Bonn, but maintained its supreme court in
Karlsruhe, and its central bank and state audit office in Frankfurt. South
Africa has its legislative chamber in Capetown and executive offices in
Pretoria. Even Israel compromises its insistence that Jerusalem is its
capital by keeping the Defence Ministry in Tel-Aviv while moving other
ministries to Jerusalem. There is nothing inevitable about a city
containing only one capital or the territory of only one national entity.
Brussels is the seat of the European Union as well as the Belgian
monarchy. New York City houses the headquarters of the United
Nations. Like countless embassies in national capitals, the territory and
accredited personnel of the United Nations enjoy a form of sovereignty
in New York without challenging national sovereignty over the
remaining land. The implications for Palestinians are that they might
develop a ceremonial site in eastern Jerusalem at the Orient House,
emphasize their spiritual affinity for the holy site of Haram al-Sharif
controlled by Muslim clerics, and develop other governmental sites
elsewhere in Greater Jerusalem, Gaza, and the West Bank.

There may be no avoiding Palestinian charges that the arrangements
would be too close to an unfair Israeli status quo. Nor will Israeli
nationalists avoid the charge that their government has departed from
the Zionist ideal of a united Jerusalem under Israeli control. Pope John
Paul II has a point when he says that Jerusalem is the world's city. The
intensity of international identity with Jerusalem is greater than in the
case of other 'world cities' like New York, Paris, and London. On the
other hand, Jerusalem has had a Jewish majority since the latter half of
the nineteenth century, and has been predominantly Israeli since 1967.
The Israeli regime has already demonstrated that it can make
concessions on issues that are spiritual and symbolic. Palestinian leaders,
as well as Muslim and Christian clerics, have shown themselves to be
concerned with spiritual and symbolic accomplishments, if not entirely
satisfied with them.

CONCLUSION

According to one Jewish tradition, there has been no prophet who
spoke for the Lord since Malachi, who preached about 500 BCE.
According to another Jewish tradition, the prophets spoke to their
times, criticizing the political and economic elites, and the priests, at
least as much as they spoke about the future. The biblical Amos may
have been trying to distance himself from fortune-tellers, magicians,
and hired sycophants of the royal court when he proclaimed that he
'was no prophet, nor a prophet's son, but a herdsman and a tender of
sycamore trees'.[19]

Rather than falling afoul of these traditions and risking a prediction, it seems wiser to specify some dangers that derive from ambiguity. Ambiguity works best if it is not defined clearly. It will help in the arrangements suggested here if neither Israeli nor Palestinian leaders make a point about what they are conceding or accomplishing. The success of ambiguity also depends on good fortune. Anger seethes just below the surface in each community about the accomplishments or threats of other communities, waiting to be ignited. A murder of Jews by an Arab, even if the Arab comes from outside Jerusalem, may force a tightening of what Israeli authorities insist is within their prerogative. If Israeli officials signal that they are truly resolute about barring foreign dignitaries from Orient House, it may lead Palestinian authorities to question the merits of what they have achieved. A strong reaction by Israeli security personnel to Palestinian violence could fan the sleeping embers of the *intifada*. In 1994 the killing of Muslims praying in the Cave of the Patriarchs in Hebron by Baruch Goldstein strained Palestinians' tolerance of ambiguity in much the same way as suicide bombings by Muslim fundamentalists infuriate Jews and threaten Israeli support for the peace process.

The optimistic view is that such events have occurred since the onset of the Israeli–Palestinian accommodations and yet have failed to dissuade national leaders from their course. The ambiguity of a situation containing hope for peace with a residue of violence has proved at least for a while to be more attractive than the appeal of retaliation by the escalation of brutality.

NOTES

1. Michael Romann and Alex Weingrod, *Living Together Separately: Arabs and Jews in Contemporary Jerusalem*, Princeton, 1991; Moshe Amirav, 'Jerusalem: The Open-City Solution', *Jerusalem Post*, 4 February 1990; and Amirav, 'Toward Coexisting in the Capital', *JP*, 18 October 1990.
2. Meron Benvenisti, *Jerusalem: The Torn City*, Minneapolis, 1976, p.vii.
3. Carl Von Clausewitz, *On War* (1833), London, 1968; for the quotation attributed to Mao Tse Tung, see *Bartlett's Familiar Quotations*, Boston, 1980.
4. George V. Coelho, David A. Hamburg, and John E. Adams, eds, *Coping and Adaptation*, New York, 1974; Herbert Simon, *Administrative Behavior*, New York, 1976; Tiffany M. Field, Philip M. McCabe and Neil Schneiderman, eds, *Stress and Coping*, Hillsdale, 1985; and Rudolf H. Moos and Jeanne A. Schaefer, eds, *Coping with Life Crises: An Integrated Approach*, New York, 1986.
5. *I Maccabees*, 1–2; and Josephus, *The Jewish War*, translated by G.A. Williamson, New York, 1970.
6. Karl R. Schaefer, 'Jerusalem in the Ayyubid and Mamluk Eras', PhD Dissertation, Department of Near Eastern Languages and Literatures, New York University, 1985; and Amnon Cohen, *Jewish Life under Islam: Jerusalem in the Sixteenth Century*, Cambridge Mass., 1984.
7. Yehoshua Ben-Arieh, *Jerusalem in the 19th Century: The Old City*, New York, 1984; idem, *Jerusalem in the 19th Century: Emergence of the New City*, New York, 1986.
8. Gerd Theissen, *Sociology of Early Palestinian Christianity*, Philadelphia, 1978.
9. Michael Lipsky, *Street-Level Bureaucracy: Dilemmas of the Individual in Public Services*, New York, 1980.

Attitude Change and Policy Transformation: Yitzhak Rabin and the Palestinian Question, 1967–95

HEMDA BEN-YEHUDA

Behind us is the Declaration of Principles with the PLO that has put an end to a bloody conflict that has endured for over 100 years. Before us, there is still much work to do in settling the differences between us – and particularly in cultivating good neighbourly relations between the two peoples.

Rabin's speech during the visit of President Bill Clinton in Jerusalem[1]

As the Netanyahu Government and the Palestinian Authority are poised to negotiate the final stages of the Transfer of Power Agreements, the post-Oslo 1993 process of rapprochement is regarded by some as an irreversible change in the Israeli–Palestinian conflict, while others consider it a course of action that does not accord with Middle Eastern realities and is therefore doomed to fail.[2]

The prolonged Jewish–Palestinian strife involves multiple issues: survival, sovereignty and legitimacy; territory, boundaries and security; history, religion, and ethnicity; natural resources, economic development and political power; regime type, internal stability and regional order.

Considering the complexity of these issues, it would be unrealistic to expect a sudden and comprehensive transformation from total conflict to genuine peace. Rather, an incremental policy is more likely to occur, characterized by frequent and at times drastic shifts from conflict to rapprochement and vice versa. This essay argues that an analysis of leadership attitudes is an essential element in explaining the political dynamics taking place in the Middle East. Decision-makers' attitudes are considered a fundamental component that shapes politics: consistent attitudes shape a coherent policy while inconsistent attitudes result in an oscillating one.

Hemda Ben-Yehuda is Lecturer in Political Science at Bar-Ilan University.

By way of exploring the particulars of the Israel–Palestine conflict, a project on Israeli decision-makers' Attitudes to the Palestinian Issue (IAPI) was initiated. It presented a theoretical framework for the analysis of attitudes in an Existence Conflict and examined patterns of continuity and change during the 1967–87 period in the attitudes of six Israeli leaders: Yigal Allon, Menachem Begin, Moshe Dayan, Shimon Peres, Yitzhak Rabin and Ariel Sharon.[3]

The Attitudes in an Existence Conflict (AEC) framework specifies ideal-type attitudes expected to be found in the context of an existence conflict where each of its adversaries demands recognition as a distinct national entity and claims the same stretch of land as its legitimate and exclusive territory.[4]

The purpose of this essay is to describe Yitzhak Rabin's attitude to the Palestinian issue during the 1967–95 period by applying the AEC framework. More specifically, it will address the following three questions: What was Rabin's attitude to the Palestinian issue during the above period? To what extent did his attitude correspond to the AEC propositions? What was the sequence of change in attitude components and did inconsistency occur?

Throughout his military and political career, Rabin had been intensively involved with defining and safeguarding Israeli security as well as with shaping and implementing its foreign and defence policy. As early as 1 January 1964, he became the Israel Defence Forces' (IDF) Chief of Staff, leading this force during the June 1967 Six-Day War. On 1 January 1968, Rabin retired from the army to become Israel's Ambassador to the United States, where he served for five years. Since then he held several positions: a member of the Knesset (the Israeli Parliament), Minister of Labour, Minister of Defence and (twice) Prime Minister. The dual character of Rabin's career – defence and civil – shaped his worldview: security and peace for Israel were his prominent and constant goals, yet the means to achieve them, as well as the partners to an agreement, changed over time.

Rabin makes an especially interesting subject for research on attitudes and policy since he was not only involved in formulating policy over an extended period of time, in multiple roles of both a military and a political nature, but he also served in several governments, some of which were led by his own Labour party while others (such as the 1984 National Unity government) were dominated by the Likud party, which played the key role in formulating Israel's foreign policy. Hence, Rabin's attitude had an ongoing impact on policy formulation for almost three decades of the Israeli–Palestinian conflict.

A review of the AEC and its postulates as well as a short summary of Rabin's attitudes in the period before the outbreak of the 1987 Palestinian uprising (the *intifada*) will serve as the starting point of this essay.[5] Two additional periods will then be addressed and compared with the first one: December 1987–September 1993, and October 1993–95. The former period commenced with the violent events of the Palestinian uprising, but also marked the beginning of direct and semi-formal negotiations between Israel and the PLO, which led to the September 1993 Declaration of Principles (DOP). During the latter period, the abstract DOP principles were translated into practical measures for the transfer of powers to the Palestinian Authority. These political and economic topics were agreed upon and formalized in the May 1994 Gaza-Jericho Accords, the August 1994 Protocol on Further Transfer of Powers, and the September 1995 Interim Agreement.

IN SEARCH OF TERRITORIAL COMPROMISE (1967–87)

The specifics of the cognitive, affective and behavioural attitude components expected in a pure existence conflict have been summarized elsewhere in seven propositions, spelling out decision-makers' tendency to:

1. Deny the adversary's claim to national identity.
2. Deny the relationship between the adversary and the contested territory.
3. Evaluate the adversary as strong in the short run but bound to lose over the long term.
4. View the adversary as hostile, harbouring political and even genocidal aspirations, and make no distinction between the adversary's aspirations and goals.
5. Express hostility towards the adversary, and associate negative traits with it.
6. Forward a self-centred ideology predominated by fundamental principles.
7. Formulate a policy involving a zero-sum mode of conflict resolution and advocating the exclusive use of military means.[6]

Findings on Rabin's attitude to the PLO during the 1967–87 period support all seven propositions. His attitude towards the Palestinian population was found to have moderated only slightly. Yet it is precisely this early nuance of a non-AEC type attitude which was subsequently to provide a starting point for additional attitudinal change and policy transformation.

During this first period, Rabin's attitude to the Palestinian issue was consolidated and put to the test of coping with daily realities. From the beginning of his political career, Rabin was a sworn advocate of political realism: he viewed the world through a state-centric lens and placed great emphasis on the security needs of his country and on the military means to promote them. Accordingly, for Rabin, the Palestinian problem was but a minor issue in the protracted Arab–Israel conflict. With a long military experience, dating back to Israel's 1947–49 War of Independence, Rabin's positions were filtered through a security prism: his main concern was Israel's existence and defence. Reflecting this state-centric worldview, the Arab states and not the PLO were seen as the main threat to be confronted at war and encountered at the negotiation table. After the dramatic change in relations between Israel and Egypt in 1977, Rabin hoped that this diplomatic breakthrough would persist and eventually lead to a peace accord between Israel and Jordan. Hence it was only with great difficulty that he reconciled himself to the inclusion of the plan for Palestinian autonomy as part of the Camp David Accords. Rabin saw the autonomy as an interim arrangement in which Israel and Jordan would jointly administer the territories; but under Jordanian pressure he relented and agreed to accept some form of Palestinian participation in the peace dialogue. This post-1985 change was induced not because Rabin internalized the growing international status of the PLO and support for its call for Palestinian statehood, but rather as a means to persuade Jordan to join the negotiation table.

Based upon his state-centric worldview, Rabin was explicit on the relationship between people and territory. He attributed great significance to the historical ties between the Jewish people and Eretz Israel yet maintained that security needs alone, and not historical or political rights, should determine Israel's future borders.

Rabin also recognized the political distinctiveness of the Palestinians residing on both banks of the Jordan River and their right for a state of their own. But his conclusion on the link between national identity and sovereignty was clear: since the Palestinians were an integral part of the Jordanian entity, a solution to their political aspirations should be found within a Jordanian-Palestinian federation.

While Rabin's willingness to differentiate between Israel's historical links and its political rights in the contested territories, as well as his recognition of Palestinian political identity, deviate from AEC expectations spelled out in propositions 1 and 2, his envisioned territorial compromise with Jordan sidesteps the Palestinian problem and therefore his overall approach accords with AEC expectations stated above.

Turning to the decision-maker's evaluation of the adversary's power and intentions, Rabin drew a sharp distinction between the PLO and the Palestinian population. His attitude to the PLO accords with propositions 3 on power and 4 on intentions, while some moderation in attitude is evident towards the Palestinian population. Rabin considered the PLO a terrorist organization geared to the destruction of the State of Israel. All the organization's specific goals were part of a 'programme of stages' designed to establish a so-called 'democratic secular' Palestinian state that would replace Israel. As such, Rabin regarded the PLO as an implacable foe and attributed to it politicidal aspirations.

Moreover, Rabin viewed the PLO as a strong and threatening opponent, whose power was on the rise. Even after the 1982 Lebanon War, which destroyed the PLO's infrastructure in Lebanon forcing it to move its operations to Tunis, Rabin contended that the PLO had been weakened by the crisis but had by no means been fully destroyed. He viewed the most hostile states – Syria, Libya, Algeria, South Yemen, Iraq and Iran – as core supporters of the PLO, and also regarded the organization as a pawn in the global superpower confrontation, used by the Soviet Union to undermine American diplomatic efforts in the Middle East. Yet paradoxically, despite this recognition of PLO power, Rabin viewed the organization's growing strength as an irksome problem requiring patience and lasting determination on Israel's part. This assessment accords with the AEC postulate 3, on power, which anticipates a hard struggle with a powerful adversary in the short run, and a high likelihood of overcoming the enemy over the long term.

Alongside this AEC position on the PLO, Rabin was also aware of some moderation in the Palestinian camp, where he detected some readiness to peaceful coexistence with Israel. This assessment of the Palestinian population's approach to Israel deviates somewhat from the AEC posture described above.

Rabin's affective attitude towards his adversary remained unchanged throughout this period. With regard to the PLO, his affections conform with AEC postulate 5, while his approach to the Palestinians as a whole deviates from this model. In the PLO, Rabin saw a terrorist organization which did not represent the Palestinian people, hence his refusal to regard it as a partner for future agreements. When referring to actual terrorist acts committed by the PLO, Rabin departed from his usual restrained style, using such harsh terms as 'organization of murderers' and describing Arafat as 'an angel of death'.[7] At the same time, Rabin maintained a fundamentally different and more forthcoming attitude towards the Palestinian population of the West Bank and the Gaza Strip. He regarded them as a social community entitled to live in peace and prosperity, was prepared to grant them all the necessary means to promote their standard of living and well-being, but did not consider them a fully-fledged national group deserving of its own independent state.

To examine the behavioural disposition of attitude, the AEC focuses on two dimensions: ideology and policy. Rabin's policy towards the PLO and the Palestinians was based on ten core, self-centred precepts:

1. A united Jerusalem as Israel's capital.
2. No independent Palestinian State.
3. Preservation of Israel's Jewish-democratic character, hence no rule over another people.

4. No to the annexation of the territories.
5. Defensible borders as a prerequisite for peace.
6. Military force has limitations: peace will be achieved through compromise.
7. Israeli settlements in security areas only.
8. No uprooting of Israeli settlements.
9. Maintenance of law and order in the territories and provision of means for an adequate standard of living for the local inhabitants.
10. No negotiations between Israel and the PLO.

Rabin regarded the establishment of an independent Palestinian State as the most serious threat to the State of Israel. Hence, the PLO which was fully committed to the establishment of such a state was a totally unacceptable political partner for negotiations. This precept remained unchanged despite the PLO's enhanced international status and Jordan's insistence that the Palestinians must join the negotiating process.

Moreover, Rabin's formula of 'land for peace' originated in his deep concern for the Jewish and democratic character of the State of Israel which would be endangered if Israel had to rule over one and a half million Palestinians. He was therefore opposed to annexing the territories, and stated his commitment to the well-being of the Palestinian population, but also rejected the idea of uprooting Israeli settlers from their homes. Recognizing the impact of settlements on the prospects of reaching any territorial compromise, Rabin contended that the future map of Israel should determine the location and spread of settlement rather than the reverse. He therefore strongly opposed a settlement drive in densely populated Arab areas and indicated that new settlements should be founded in 'security areas', namely, the Jordan Valley and around Jerusalem. Rabin emphasized that Jerusalem was the symbol of the Jewish people's revival and renewed independence in the Land of Israel and reiterated his vow that the city would never be divided again.

Finally, Rabin who after the 1982 War was well aware of the limits of military power, advocated the idea of peace through compromise but insisted that some boundary modifications, as well as Arab recognition of Israel's need for defensible borders, constituted a prerequisite for any territorial compromise.

Together, Rabin's ten precepts project a closely integrated ideological scheme which accords with AEC postulate 6. Even those principles dealing with the Palestinians, such as Rabin's opposition to the annexation of the territories, his objection to the continuation of Israeli rule over the Palestinians, and his commitment to the daily welfare of the Palestinians, stemmed from his concern for the preservation of Israel's identity as a Jewish-democratic state.

As far as actual policy was concerned, Jordan was Rabin's one and only partner for territorial compromise and peace arrangements on Israel's eastern border. In his view, bilateral negotiations between Israel and the Hashemite regime were to lead to a comprehensive peace agreement. It was only under the pressure of unfolding events inside and outside the region that Rabin accepted other diplomatic options. The Camp David Accords introduced a plan for an interim stage of Palestinian autonomy. Though reluctant to depart from his state-centric beliefs, Rabin placed great hopes on the diplomatic breakthrough that would follow the Israel–Egypt precedent. He was therefore willing to support multilateral negotiations even under international auspices, and to include new partners in the process alongside Jordan.

The 1982 Lebanon War also had an impact on attitudes and policy. It confronted Rabin with a reality of severe PLO military resistance and resulted in his new recognition of PLO military power. Rabin gradually accepted that even Israel's significant military power had its limits. Hence, in conjunction with his support for a persistent military struggle against the PLO, Rabin opted for a political solution that would accommodate Israel's security needs.

His moderate attitude to the Palestinian population, detected throughout the period, enabled the change in Rabin's behavioural disposition. First, in April 1985 Rabin accepted the inclusion of Palestinians who were not PLO followers as part of the joint delegation with Jordan. Later in 1986 he even agreed to accept PLO supporters from the territories, but not from the diaspora. This position reflected his willingness to promote genuine and effective local Palestinian representation but at the same time to preclude the participation of official PLO leaders. Yet even this new outlook could not overcome Rabin's core belief that the only long-term diplomatic solution that justified compromise and promised stability and peace was an agreement with Jordan. AEC proposition 7 is therefore supported throughout the period as far as Rabin's policy to the PLO was concerned, and even his moderated stance to the Palestinian population was to be implemented in the economic and welfare domains but not in the political sphere.

In sum, Rabin's attitude to the Palestinian issue during the 1967–87 years reveals little change over time, and a high degree of correspondence between attitudes and policy. An AEC posture to the PLO was continuously maintained, while nuances of moderation were detected towards the Palestinian population. Yet Rabin's overall state-centric worldview led him to consistently adhere to his one and only solution: territorial compromise with Jordan.

FROM 'IRON FIST' TO HANDSHAKE (DEC. 1987–SEPT. 1993)

During the above period, the seeds of transformation became visible. Rabin was keenly aware of the momentous international developments of the late 1980s, to which he often referred as proof that Israel, too, should 'join the campaign of peace, reconciliation and international cooperation that is currently engulfing the entire globe, lest we miss the train and be left alone at the station'.[8]

While Rabin's AEC posture towards the PLO was preserved, he translated his earlier recognition of Palestinian political identity and their links to the contested territories, as well as his awareness that Israel was unable to overcome the PLO by military means, into a new policy: an iron-fist response towards the Palestinian revolt accompanied by political negotiations with moderate Palestinians. Yet Rabin still did not view the PLO as a genuine representative of the Palestinian people. He often noted Palestinian lack of authentic leadership as the foremost obstacle to the resolution of the Palestinian problem and expressed the hope that 'if Jordan and such a leadership [of local inhabitants] emerge, that would be wonderful'.[9] Rabin tried to locate a suitable Palestinian partner and approached figures of the various strands in the Palestinian public with the question: 'Are any of you, any group among you, prepared to say that you – the residents of the territories – are willing to be our partner in a political settlement?'[10]

As his personal attempts to identify authentic interlocutors who would sidestep the PLO as a partner for an interim agreement came to a nought, and as the several rounds of talks between Israelis and Palestinians in Washington ran into a dead alley, Rabin realized that only the Tunis-based PLO leadership had real decisional power. 'This may not be pleasant, but it is a fact,' he said in explaining his conclusion, subsequently adding that 'peace is not made with friends, peace is made with enemies'.[11] This realization resulted in his grudging approval to the opening of the Oslo back-channel. Cognitive change with respect to the PLO and its leaders slowly led to a behavioural shift. But many of Rabin's affective AEC elements remained intact.

During the entire second period, little reference was made to the ties between Israel and the Land of Israel. A rare exception was made in Rabin's interview with the German newspaper *Der Spiegel*: 'I believe in the Jewish people's right to the entire Land of Israel. But the actual problem is the 1.7 million Palestinians in the territories who are a community that is completely different from us – in religious, cultural, and political terms. Therefore, even though I recognize the Jews' claim to all of Israel I do not want to annex 1.7 million Palestinians against their will because this would make Israel a binational state'.[12] Jerusalem was a single exception, an issue on which Rabin demonstrated a consistent and determined posture: 'Jerusalem, whole and united, has been and will remain the capital of the Israeli people under Israeli sovereignty... Every Jew, both religious and secular vows: If I forget thee O Jerusalem, let my right hand wither! This vow unites all of us and certainly applies to me being a native of Jerusalem.'[13]

At the end of this period, a certain change in Rabin's attitude could be discerned when he admitted that both Israelis and Palestinians maintained links to the same territory: 'We have been destined to live together on the same piece of land in the same country.'[14] This position, together with his move towards semi-formal negotiations with the PLO are deviations from AEC propositions 1 on identity and 2 on links. Conversely, on power, Rabin's attitude conforms to AEC proposition 3. Following the collapse of the Soviet Union, Iran replaced the USSR as the major source of support for extreme terrorist organizations such as the PLO, HAMAS and Islamic Jihad.[15]

As before, when Rabin referred to the adversary's intentions, he still regarded the PLO, HAMAS and Islamic Jihad as terrorist organizations waging 'a total war over our existence', whose goal was to destroy the State of Israel and 'to foil all the chances for peace'.[16] During this period, Rabin insisted that one of the PLO's most dangerous goals was the 'right of return', which he regarded as one of the gravest dangers to the State of Israel: 'If we accept [this demand] it would be tantamount to committing national suicide'.[17] However, unlike the 1967–87 years, Rabin now included the Palestinian population in this antagonist camp. He elaborated at length on the new aspect in the struggle introduced by the *intifada*: 'For the first time since 15 May 1948 we witnessed a struggle waged by the Palestinian inhabitants,' adding that 'this is a clash between two national entities waged through violence by civilians wishing to attain the same goals they could not achieve through terrorism and war.'[18] While recognizing that there were different factions within the Palestinian population, Rabin concluded: 'They are all united in their opposition to us.'[19] This conviction accords with AEC proposition 4 on the hostility of the adversary.

Rabin's attitude towards the Palestinians during this period reflected his disillusionment. The Palestinian uprising, which he had initially (mis)perceived as frequent and large-scale riots, but eventually came to view it as a civil uprising of a politically-aware population, convinced him that the Palestinians had openly declared both their hostility to Israel and their readiness to carry out an uncompromising struggle. He distinguished between past PLO attacks against Israel and the current events: 'What is taking place in the territories is not terrorism because no one is shooting at us, but a civil war waged by women and children.'[20] Moreover, he also identified a trend of radicalization and growing support for Islamic fundamentalist organizations. In a detailed description of the *intifada* Rabin explained: 'This is a confrontation between two different entities – different religiously and politically – and one might say nationally... Let us be candid: the majority of the Palestinian public identify with these organizations and with their objectives'.[21] As such, Rabin's moderate approach to the Palestinian population detected earlier was replaced with a more extreme posture conforming to the AEC during the second period. Turning to the affective aspects of political attitudes, Rabin's hatred to the PLO was broadened to encompass the Islamic Fundamentalist groups. All were 'terrorists', 'blood-thirsty animals', 'murderous' and unworthy leaders who led their people from 'one disaster to another'.[22] Talking about terrorism, Rabin resorted to the most extreme terms: '... terrorism in all its vile manifestations. This is the enemy facing us, which is indiscriminate, which chooses every way, every target, just because it is Jewish and Israeli'.[23] This approach accords well with AEC proposition 5 in that no change is evident in the affective component over time. Yet Rabin's negative feelings towards the PLO, HAMAS and Islamic Jihad did not spill over to his position towards the Palestinian population. Even in the midst of the *intifada*, which reflected popular resentment to Israeli rule and brought about severe civil turmoil in Gaza and the West Bank, Rabin preserved his conciliatory affective stance detected in the pre-1987 years,[24] supporting talks with the Palestinians to 'dampen the flame of hatred between the Palestinians and the State of Israel'.[25] The maintenance of this positive affective posture enabled Rabin to relentlessly call for the emergence of an authentic leadership from within the local population, which could be a real partner for the political arrangements that would lead to peaceful coexistence between Israel and the Palestinians.[26]

Aware of the need to reach an agreement with the Palestinians on a functional compromise in the territories for an interim period before a comprehensive plan could be negotiated, Rabin preserved his ideological precepts but changed some of his policy-oriented positions. Most frequently, he repeated three of his precepts mentioned earlier: a united Jerusalem as Israel's eternal capital; no negotiations with the PLO; and a total taboo on the establishment of an independent Palestinian State.[27] In accordance with proposition 6, these ideological precepts portray an AEC posture that rules out compromise. But alongside these beliefs, a third and more conciliatory element emerged: the limits of military force dictate a need for reaching peace agreements through compromise. Rabin realized that power politics and war would not enable Israel to reach its political goals of security and peace. Viewing the *intifada* as 'a continuation of the Israeli–Arab conflict by other means', he argued that since 'it could last much longer than we like... a solution in the sense of pacification along our frontiers can be found only through a political process'.[28]

The Palestinian uprising also led to a gradual change in Rabin's conception of the Israel–Palestinian rivalry. Departing from his earlier view that the Arab–Israel conflict was an inter-state affair, he recognized that the situation had become more complex, involving many non-state actors. As he put it: 'I would like to dwell on the complexity of this confrontation... It does not resemble the wars that Israel waged against the armies of Arab countries. Those were wars between armies with clear boundaries, with weapons used in accordance with internationally acknowledged rules... the boundaries are unclear in this [present] case'.[29]

Though territorial compromise was still Rabin's preferred path to peace, he became increasingly frustrated with Jordanian hesitation: 'It is about time that it [Jordan] makes up its mind. If it wants to be a party to the process, let it move its ass a bit'.[30] Alas, Rabin was confronted with new realities: as early as 1987 Jordan had disassociated itself 'at least administratively and legally' from the West Bank and was not willing to negotiate on behalf of the Palestinians. A new partner had to be found.[31]

Hence, Rabin who had until now placed his emphasis on a state-centric military balance, slowly shifted his approach in favour of legitimate political agreements that would stabilize the region and enhance Israel's security. Moreover, since even the threat of terrorism could not be solved militarily, Rabin was willing to forsake his state-oriented approach and search for some acceptable political arrangements with the Palestinians that might bring more tranquility to the territories. In a public address in 1994, he looked back at that period and reminded his audience: 'the 15 May 1989 [Likud-led unity government] peace initiative... was a historic turning point in viewing the Palestinians as a partner, separate from Jordan'.[32] Accordingly, Rabin supported the Madrid framework as it was the main diplomatic option that could serve as an opening for some diplomatic achievements. He even accepted the idea of an international framework for the peace talks, placing his hopes on the Washington negotiations that were to lead to an Israeli–Palestinian interim agreement.[33]

The most significant change in Rabin's behavioural disposition was his acceptance of autonomy as the only viable short-term solution. While his earlier and reluctant support for the plan had been based on the hope that autonomy would pave the way for renewed Jordanian participation in the peace process, in January 1989 Rabin placed his own four-phase plan for Palestinian autonomy on the political agenda. Though the internal political realities of the Israeli Unity Government made the Shamir plan of May 1989 the only negotiable option, Rabin's plan could be regarded as an embryonic version of the post-Oslo arrangements for a transfer of powers to the Palestinians.

Rabin's plan comprised the following four stages – pacification of the territories, elections, a transitional period and a permanent settlement:

We are talking right now of calm. It is inconceivable that elections will be held while violence is raging. Second, representatives of the territories will be elected by the inhabitants of the territories. They will elect not a municipal council but a political representation to stand for the 1.5 million Palestinians residing in the territories, provided that its goals are to negotiate [with Israel]. Thus, this representation will ultimately serve as the nucleus for the self-rule authority once expanded autonomy is established or once any other interim agreement takes effect. That representation, together with Jordan, will constitute our partner to negotiations for peace along our eastern borders.[34]

Rabin placed his hopes on the dynamics that would develop during the transitional phase:

> to create through an interim agreement... a new reality which may bring about a change in positions. We hope this change occurs on their side, but they have the right to hope the change occurs on our side. This is the logic and I think also the wisdom of dividing progress towards peace into stages.[35]

Separation was an additional aspect which emerged in Rabin's policy-oriented approach to the Palestinian issue. It was initially a result of the repeated short term closures imposed by Israel on the territories in the wake of terrorist attacks. But with the passage of time Rabin came to regard the notion of separation as more than a tactical-temporary measure: 'A separation can be a closure – which would lead to an explosion... or a political separation... but autonomy would not create separation'.[36] Though Rabin never regarded terrorism as a threat to the very existence of the State of Israel, he never underestimated the impact it had on personal security and daily life.[37] Hence, Rabin had foreseen the dangers of Jewish-Israeli citizens and Arab-Palestinians intermingling even before the Oslo process took place and warned that 'without separation there will be no personal security'.[38]

On the whole, change rather than preservation of attitude is evident during this second phase, with a gap emerging between the cognitive and affective elements which had undergone a minor change and the behavioural aspects which had undergone a major transformation. The conflict was now viewed by Rabin as a complex process in which states and other organizations confronted one another in violence, while simultaneously involved in regional peace negotiations. Rabin also recognized that Jordan had ruled out the option of territorial compromise. Hence, in an effort to quell the Palestinian uprising by blending military and diplomatic means Rabin adopted his own four-phase autonomy plan. The most significant change that occurred at the close of this period was Rabin's disillusionment with finding a genuine, non-PLO Palestinian leadership. This led him to declare that the Tunis-based PLO leadership was the only Palestinian representative capable of reaching binding decisions and implementing them. This change was the pre-condition to the Oslo breakthrough and to the September 1993 Israeli–Palestinian Declaration of Principles (DOP).

FROM AUTONOMY TO SEPARATION (OCT. 1993–NOV. 1995)

As noted earlier, from the onset of the Oslo process Rabin departed from his earlier view that the Arab–Israel conflict was a pure inter-state affair, recognizing the existence of a far more complex situation involving many non-state elements. After the signing of the DOP, Rabin frequently referred to the spill-over effects between the inter-state and the sub-state elements which were in his eyes a core barrier to stable diplomatic arrangements. As an illustration of these spill-over effects, he mentioned the relationship between Israel and Jordan. Though *de-facto* peace had long characterized the situation along Israel's border with Jordan, it was only after the start of the Oslo process and the rapprochement with the PLO that the two states concluded a formal peace treaty.[39]

During the third and last period under study, Rabin changed his posture on the political identity he attributed to the PLO while preserving his non-AEC view on the attachment of both Israelis and Palestinians to the contested territories.[40] The DOP marked a turning point of mutual Israeli–Palestinian recognition. At first, Rabin differentiated between internal (that is, inside the territories) and external PLO leadership, emphasizing the control of the former. However, as the extent of the PLO's control and effectiveness in the territories gained momentum, this distinction disappeared.[41]

On the links between people and territory, the earlier noted posture recognizing that both Palestinians and Israelis were deeply related to the same land was maintained.[42] Upon presenting the Oslo Accords to the Knesset, Rabin stated his belief that Israelis and Palestinians 'are destined to live together, on the same soil in the same land'.[43] This cognitive element in Rabin's attitude explains his behavioural change: he was aware of the importance of the Palestinian issue, accepted the Palestinians as a political entity, comprehended that both Israelis and Palestinians were associated with the same contested territory, and accepted the PLO as the representative of the Palestinians. In short, a significant deviation from AEC proposition 1 on identity and a smaller deviation regarding proposition 2 on links.

Rabin's position on the issue of Jerusalem was not only unchanged but was additionally highlighted. On 10 December 1994, upon his acceptance of the Nobel Peace Prize, Rabin stated: 'I am here as the emissary of Jerusalem, at whose gates I fought in the days of siege; Jerusalem which has always been, and is today, the eternal capital of the state of Israel and the heart of the Jewish people, who pray toward Jerusalem three times a day'.[44] Jerusalem was for Rabin a separate issue to which he attributed core importance and emotional ties.[45] Moreover, using some of his most affective terms, Rabin declared that: 'Jerusalem... the focus of our yearning and the embodiment of our dreams for thousands of years... is not subject to negotiation. Jerusalem is not a subject for bargaining... [it is] the beating heart of the Jewish people'.[46] Rabin regarded his ability to remove Jerusalem from the agenda of negotiations on an interim agreement as a major Israeli achievement in its peace talks with the Palestinians.

Rabin recognized the rise in the power of militant Islamic organizations. These groups were the recipients of extensive support from radical countries in the region which opposed the peace process, first and foremost Iran.[47] However, due to Rabin's awareness that only Arafat could conclude an agreement and ensure its implementation, the PLO was accepted as a full partner.[48] Each additional agreement reached with the PLO in the wake of the DOP was seen by Rabin as an indicator of PLO power and ability to control the Palestinian street,[49] strengthening his belief that the organization's shortcomings were due to its lack of experience and that with the passage of time the PLO's effectiveness would increase. This view deviates from Rabin's earlier position which, as stated in AEC proposition 3, expected an eventual decrease in PLO power in the long run.

This change in Rabin's attitude involved a new element, since, in contradiction to the earlier period, the deviation from the AEC was related to both the Palestinians and the PLO. With the partial quelling of the *intifada*, Rabin reverted to his previous conviction that the majority of the Palestinians were peace-seekers.[50] The significant change that occurred in Rabin's attitude at this time was his willingness to accept the PLO as a member of the 'good guys camp'. The DOP marked, according to Rabin, a turning point in the PLO's goals and policy. Rabin regarded the former as a 'reformed' terrorist organization which had finally resigned itself to peaceful coexistence with Israel and to a negotiated resolution of the ongoing conflict. He claimed that a change in the PLO's policy was also evident and that, since the signing of the DOP, Arafat's supporters refrained from the use of terrorism in their political struggle.[51]

HAMAS and Islamic Jihad remained in the 'bad guys camp'. Rabin continued to view them as 'hate-filled fanatics' who were a vicious enemy geared to the destruction of the State of Israel and the nascent peace in the Middle East.[52] He often described their activities in the most extreme language: 'They murder and abduct. They shoot indiscriminately... terrorism knows no borders and is liable to cross seas and oceans in order to sow death'.[53] When juxtaposed with the AEC, Rabin differentiated between the Palestinians and the PLO on the one hand and HAMAS and Islamic Jihad on the other. Rabin viewed this split in the Palestinian camp as 'a process of polarization among the Palestinians – polarization between the PLO, or part of the PLO, and the rise of the radical Islamic element: HAMAS and the Islamic Jihad... It is part of the dark wave of Islamic fundamentalism which is sweeping the Arab World'. He warned: '[Some] indiscriminately link those

Palestinians who want to continue the peace process with HAMAS and the Islamic Jihad. They are not the same. True, they come from the same people... they do not represent the majority [of the Palestinian population]'.[54] Towards the population at large, there is a significant deviation from AEC proposition 4, while with regard to the Islamic groups, Rabin's views accord with the AEC.

Between September 1993 and November 1995, Rabin's hostility to the PLO was replaced by a sense of partnership in a joint venture towards rapprochement. At first, Rabin still viewed the PLO leaders as 'those who held knives... pulled the trigger'; yet he concluded that 'we cannot choose our neighbours, or our enemies, not even the cruelest among them... most sworn and bitter enemies...'[55] Moreover, Rabin testified that he did not trust 'Chairman Arafat', and was actually feeling sick when requested to shake hands with him at the DOP signing ceremony in Washington.[56] However, when asked at the end of the period if it were true that he disliked Arafat, Rabin replied in a very neutral mode: 'Personal feelings are irrelevant to diplomatic relations. Mr. Arafat is at the head of the Palestinian Authority. We agreed to consider him our partner in this strategic plan.'[57] Moreover, with the signing of the 1995 interim agreement, Rabin brought to the attention of the audience that hearts no longer quivered at the sight of partnership and cooperation and described the long road that he and Chairman Arafat strode till they had reached the present stage: 'We began to get used to each other, we are like old acquaintances.'[58]

Rabin's earlier positive approach to the Palestinian population was also maintained during this period. So too was his negative stance towards HAMAS and Islamic Jihad.[59] Consequently, a moderate deviation from AEC proposition 5 can be detected in the affective component; yet this change is rather limited, since the antagonist sentiment that Rabin once felt vis-à-vis the PLO was now transferred to the Islamic fundamentalists.

Once Rabin had conceded that the PLO was Israel's only available partner, some ideological modifications were necessary. Yet, surprisingly enough, despite the major transformations that were evident in cognitive and even affective elements, only one – but meaningful – ideological change was made regarding the PLO as a partner for negotiation. Although Rabin realized that the PLO was the spokesman of the Palestinian people, he still maintained all his other convictions, notably: peace should be coupled with security; Israel does not want to control another people; and annexation is ruled out since it would endanger the Jewish-democratic character of the State of Israel and would not solve the Israeli–Palestinian conflict.[60]

On the question of the establishment of an independent Palestinian State Rabin did not change his negative position, continuing to view this potential development as the most serious threat to the State of Israel.[61]

As noted earlier, separation between two entities – Israeli and Palestinian – was as far as Rabin was willing to go in his attitudinal adjustment to the new regional developments.[62]

On the whole, with the exception of removing the taboo from the PLO and legitimizing negotiations with the organization, the remaining eight principles which formed Rabin's core ideological framework remained intact throughout the entire period under survey. This self-centred ideology supports AEC postulate 6. Compromise was enabled due to a cognitive change, but little ideological adjustment was notable.

On policy, Rabin's state-centric worldview of the Arab–Israeli conflict was replaced by a multi-dimensional view in which the Palestinian conflict played a core part. He emphasized that in the interim period until a permanent solution to the protracted Arab–Israeli and Palestinian–Israeli conflicts was reached, Israel should provide the population in the territories with the conditions that would assure them a proper standard of living, while maintaining law and order and ensuring Israel's security needs.

The policy changes advocated by Rabin accorded with his embryonic January 1989 plan. The negotiations he supported between Israel and the Palestinians were based on a two-stage formula: a five-year interim self-government arrangement, to be followed by negotiations on the permanent status issues. During the signing ceremony of the DOP on 13 September 1993 Rabin stated that he was 'fully aware of the difficulties that face the Palestinians and Israel in the solution of our problems... it is still a long way to go, with obstacles on the road that we shall have to remove, and it is possible to remove them.' This agreement 'could create a new reality, which would enable solutions that may exist today and a peaceful coexistence between us and the Palestinians.'[63] At the end of the period, Rabin declared that the long-term goal of the negotiations and interim agreements was to 'reach peace with a Palestinian entity in Judea, Samaria and the Gaza Strip, but not based upon the 1967 borders.'[64]

The proposal for a separation between Israel and the Palestinians, developed in the second period, was further crystallized during this stage and acquired a territorial dimension for the long-term solution. While the early notion of separation resulted from Israel's placing a closure on the territories to curb the rising tide of Islamic terrorism, it gradually transpired as Rabin's plan for future coexistence between two distinct entities: Israel and the Palestinian Authority. In effect, this plan was a new version of Rabin's territorial compromise, but with a new partner: the PLO. Rabin reached the conclusion that there would neither be a solution to the conflict and an end to terrorism, nor would security, well-being and peace be reached 'without long-term separation between Israel – albeit not in the 1967 borders – and a Palestinian entity existing by its side'.[65] However, while separation had clear territorial

TABLE 1
ATTITUDE CHANGE – RABIN ON THE PALESTINIAN ISSUE 1967–1995

Attitude Component	1967 – 1987	Sept. 1988 – 1993	Oct. 1993 – 1995	Change Over Time	Distance vs. AEC
COGNITIVE					
Identity	AEC posture to PLO but not to Palestinians who are recognized as a distinct group with political identity	AEC posture to PLO as non-representative of the Palestinians alongside with awareness of increased political cohesiveness in Palestinian camp but lack of leadership	Deviation from AEC with respect to both PLO as repre-sentative of the Palestinians and of the Palestinians as a political entity	Change	Significant deviation from AEC
Links	• AEC posture on the issue of Jerusalem • AEC posture on Palestinian links to Jordan • Deviation from AEC on multi-faceted links between Jews and Eretz Yisrael with no political significance	• Maintenance of AEC posture on Jerusalem • Deviation from AEC by the recognition that both Israelis and Palestinians are linked to the same piece of land	• Maintenance of AEC posture on Jerualem • Some deviation from AEC on Israeli and Palestinian links to the contested territories	No Change: Jerusalem Change: Israeli Palestinian links	Deviation from AEC
Goals	AEC posture to PLO but not to Palestinians	AEC posture: PLO, Palestinian and Hamas/Islamic Jihad goals – destruction of the State of Israel & the peace process	• Deviation from AEC: both PLO and Palestinian goals – coexist-ence and peaceful means of conflict resolution • Maintenance of AEC posture regarding Hamas/Islamic Jihad goals	Change: PLO/ Palestinians No Change: Hamas/Islamic Jihad	Deviation from AEC
Power	AEC posture to PLO with no reference to Islamic Fundamentalists	AEC posture: PLO, Palestinians and Fundamenta-list Islamic groups receive support and cannot easily be overcome	Deviation from AEC: decline in power of Funda-mentalist Islamic groups and increase in Palestinian support to Self-governing Palestinian Authority.	Change	Deviation from AEC
AFFECTIVE	AEC posture to PLO but not to the Palestinians	AEC posture to PLO and Islamic Fundamentalists but not to Palestinians	Deviation from AEC to PLO and Palestinians but not to Islamic Fundamentalist	Change: PLO No Change: Palestinians Islamic Fundamentalists	Minor deviation from AEC
BEHAVIOURAL Ideology	Mix of AEC and non AEC ideological precepts	Maintenance of mixed precepts both AEC and non AEC	Increase in non-AEC precepts alongside with maintenance of AEC precepts	Change: PLO No Change: All other precepts	Deviation from AEC
Policy: Nature of Conflict	AEC posture: interstate conflict	Deviation from AEC: recogni-tion of centrality of Israeli-Palestinian conflict	Deviation from AEC spillover between Arab-Israel & Israeli-Palestinian conflict	Change	Significant deviation from AEC
Partner	Jordan	Long term: Jordan Short term: Palestinians	Short & long term: Jordan, PLO	Change:	Significant deviation from AEC
Territorial compromise	Support	Support	Support of de-facto territorial compromise with Palestinian entity	Change:	Significant deviation from AEC
Autonomy	Rejection	Support	Support	Change	Deviation from AEC
Separation	No Reference	Support	Support	Change	Deviation from AEC

implications which almost certainly meant the establishment of a Palestinian State, Rabin was not willing to go as far as endorsing such a state. Accordingly he limited himself to talk about peaceful coexistence between Israel and a Palestinian entity 'which is less than a state', explaining that: 'I am convinced that the path chosen by the government... is bound to bring about a separation, but not along the border lines which existed prior to 1967'.[66]

AEC Proposition 7 is not supported during these years. It was Rabin's policy of compromise and his willingness to accept autonomy as a form of functional compromise, combined with certain territorial-compromise elements embodied in the plan for separation, that made the post-Oslo rapprochement between Israel and the Palestinians possible.

WHITHER RAPPROCHEMENT? FROM EXISTENCE CONFLICT TO COEXISTENCE

Table 1 presents the main findings on Rabin's attitude to the Palestinian problem during the 1967–95 period. As shown by the table, as well as by the preceding analysis, the shift in political preferences and plans – from total conflict to gradual accommodation – was a result of a change in four major elements in Rabin's approach to the Palestinian issue: his motivation and perceived need to find a settlement to the ongoing rivalry; his overall view of the protracted Arab–Israel conflict and the role of the Palestinian feud within it; his definition of preferable and available partners; and his characterization of the desirable type of agreement.

Rabin's position underwent a dramatic change over the years: from moderately pursuing an arrangement with Jordan that would end the inter-state conflict on Israel's eastern border and lead to a comprehensive peace treaty, to persistent efforts to implement an interim agreement with the PLO over the transfer of powers that would create a more stable five-year transitional period during which negotiations over a plan for separation and a permanent solution with the Palestinians and Jordan would take place.

Evidently, an attitudinal change of such magnitude was affected by the major political events, both global and regional, in which Rabin participated. His approach to the conflict during the 1967–73 period was primarily shaped by the 1967 Six Day War, the subsequent War of Attrition with Egypt, and the 1970 PLO–Jordan crisis. With the new sense of enhanced security of that period, Rabin felt no need to hasten the diplomatic process and therefore sought no alternatives to comprehensive peace with Jordan.

The October 1973 War triggered a new power configuration among the parties to the conflict. A major blow was inflicted on Israel and a gradual regional shift ensued, with the PLO gaining legitimacy and the Hashemite Kingdom losing its status both inside and outside the region. Israel's 1974–75 disengagement agreements with Egypt and Syria emerged as a possible model that could be applied to the eastern front as well. Slowly, the notion of comprehensive peace was replaced by a step-by-step strategy. Rabin's motivation for an agreement was increased but his chosen partner was still Jordan.

A certain policy change was evident when Prime Minister Rabin reintroduced the idea of a comprehensive peace agreement with Jordan. This was commensurate with the shift in American foreign policy during the Carter Administration which sought a comprehensive solution to the Arab–Israeli conflict and recognized the Palestinians' rights to a 'homeland' of their own. An additional notable change in Rabin's views during the Carter era was his recognition of the salience of the Palestinian problem, though he still believed that this should be solved within the framework of a Jordanian-Palestinian state. Negotiations aimed at this goal, as noted earlier, were to be conducted with a Jordanian delegation which could also include Palestinian representatives from the occupied territories.

Egyptian President Anwar Sadat's historic visit to Jerusalem and the signing of the 1978 Camp David Accords between Israel and Egypt caused a thorough reconsideration of former positions. The Camp David Accords represented a significant breakthrough in Israel's relations with Egypt, the most important state in the Arab World. Rabin thought that peace with Egypt would lead to agreement with other Arab states starting with Jordan. He supported the Autonomy Plan as part of the overall Camp David framework without letting partisan considerations bias his stand. The 1982 Lebanon War made the Palestinian issue the focus of Israeli and world attention. Although the PLO suffered a severe blow and was forced out of Lebanon, political schemes such as the Reagan Plan and Fez Resolution transformed its military defeat into a political success. In both the Middle East and the international arena the PLO's legitimacy and the Palestinian people's right to an independent state of their own were gaining widespread approval. Since the 1982 War, Rabin repeatedly expressed his conviction that the Palestinian problem could not be solved by military means and that the Camp David process was the route to be followed.

When Rabin became Minister of Defence in the 1984 National Unity Government, the Palestinian issue fell yet again under his direct authority. His main objective then was to drive a wedge between the PLO and the local inhabitants through a 'carrot and stick' policy. The stick was applied to the PLO and its supporters whereas the carrot was offered to inhabitants who rejected PLO directives. Jordan remained Rabin's only address for a political solution and he directed all his efforts and concessions towards the Hashemite regime; yet he was increasingly resigned to accept some form of Palestinian representation in the negotiations team.

The breakup of the Soviet Union and the 1991 Gulf War reshaped the political order in the Middle East, inducing Israel and the Arab World to reassess their positions to their protracted conflict. Rabin often mentioned the need for leaders to acknowledge the global and regional changes taking place in their milieu and to adapt their attitudes to the new environment. In his own words: 'We are living in a time of changing circumstances, and we must be able to adapt ourselves to these changing circumstances in order to achieve what Israel needs most – peace and security – without messianic illusions on the one hand or defeatism on the other'.[67]

On 30 October 1991, a conference, co-sponsored by the United States and the Soviet Union, was convened in Madrid to begin direct peace talks between Israel and Syria, Lebanon, Jordan and the Palestinians. Rabin supported this scheme so as to pacify the Palestinian uprising and to lure King Hussein into the peace process. However, a real breakthrough was only possible after a drastic change took place in Rabin's preferences regarding his partners to the negotiations. Following intense behind-the-scenes contacts between Israeli and Palestinian negotiators in Oslo, an agreement was reached between Prime Minister Rabin and PLO Chairman Arafat, to be signed on 13 September 1993 in Washington.

Shortly after the signing of the DOP, negotiations commenced between Israeli and Palestinian delegations on the interim agreement which led to the Gaza-Jericho Agreement, signed in Cairo on 4 May 1994, and to the Israeli–Palestinian Interim Agreement on the West bank and the Gaza Strip, signed in Washington on 28 September 1995, and covering subjects such as security arrangements, elections, civil affairs, legal matters, economic relations, Israeli–Palestinian cooperation, and the release of Palestinian prisoners.

CONCLUSIONS

This essay sought to describe Yitzhak Rabin's attitude to the Palestinian problem during the 1967–95 period by applying the AEC conceptual framework. Findings on attitudes and policy were presented for three different periods: 1967–87: in search of territorial compromise; December 1987–93: from iron-fist policy to negotiations; and October 1993 – November 1995: from autonomy to separation.

During the first period, Rabin's attitude to the Palestinian problem resulted from his inter-state worldview. His posture was a convergence between the search for his much desired territorial compromise with Jordan and his commitment to the welfare of the Palestinian population under Israeli control. While highlighting the Jordanian option, Rabin maintained an AEC posture towards the Palestinian problem in general and the PLO in particular. Yet a slight deviation from the AEC was already apparent in his attitude to the Palestinian population.

During the second phase, the seeds of transition became visible. While his AEC posture vis-à-vis the PLO was preserved, Rabin's attitude underwent a significant change. He realized that power politics and military force would not enable Israel to reach its political goals of security and peace. Moreover, he conceded that side-stepping the Palestinian leadership in Tunis had led neither to a solution to the complex and enduring Israeli–Palestinian conflict nor to the pacification of the uprising. In addition, Rabin understood that the resolution of the Israeli–Palestinian conflict was to be the first step towards peace agreements with Jordan, Syria and Lebanon. Finally, he concluded that peace, which was the real guarantee of Israel's future security, could only be reached through compromise that would entail a painful price. In order to achieve peace, to bring an end to the Palestinian uprising, and to break the political stalemate with the Palestinians, Rabin gave his reluctant approval to the opening of the Oslo back-channel.

The findings for the 1993–95 period reveal significant changes in the cognitive and behavioural attitude components: recognition of the centrality of the Israeli–Palestinian conflict as part of the Arab–Israel feud; acceptance of the PLO as the partner for territorial compromise; support for the autonomy plan as part of an interim agreement; and implementation of three accords signed with the PLO, which could lead to future separation between two nations attached to the same piece of land.

The rapprochement process between Israel and the PLO necessitated a change in Yitzhak Rabin's perception of the desirable interlocutor. Accordingly, from September 1993 onwards, Chairman Arafat and the PLO were no longer regarded as adversaries but rather as partners to the realization of a common future in the Land of Israel.

While major changes were identified in the cognitive and behavioural elements, only a minor deviation from the AEC was found in the affective component. As a result, the cognitive, affective and behavioural components of attitude do not reflect a well-synchronized or consistent process of attitudinal change. Rabin's recognition of the PLO did not transcend his willingness to regard the organization as the representative of the Palestinian people. The newly constructed Palestinian Self-Governing Authority was never considered a sovereign entity by Rabin. Though only a handful of affective expressions to PLO terrorism and hostility were found, the AEC posture to terrorism did not disappear. The focus of Rabin's hostility shifted from the PLO to the Islamic militants who were considered a part of the Palestinian camp. It can be said that HAMAS and the Islamic Jihad had fully replaced the PLO, with Rabin's past hostility towards the latter now directed towards the former.

Inconsistency denotes the extent of correspondence among the
cognitive, affective and behavioural components of attitude. As noted in
this essay, during the 1967–93 period, Rabin made a clear distinction
between the Palestinian population and the PLO, thus leading to a high
degree of consistency and internal harmony. The PLO was entirely de-
legitimized and tabooed, and the idea of a Palestinian State was rejected.
By contrast, Rabin recognized the Palestinians as a distinct national group,
accepted their national distinctiveness and expressed conciliatory feelings
towards them. This posture led to his search for a just solution to the
Palestinian problem: the Jordanian option. The *intifada* cast a dark
shadow over Rabin's coherent view and shattered his internal harmony:
the uprising triggered a change in his sentiments to the Palestinian people
and resulted in an iron-fist policy towards them. However, Rabin's
support for this AEC-type behaviour did not last long. In 1992 he yet
again mentioned the need for a territorial compromise and in 1993 talks
began with the PLO which led to Israel's recognition of the organization
in September of the same year.

On the whole, though Rabin preserved his core self-centred
ideological precepts and fundamental goals concerning peace and
security for the State of Israel, other elements in his attitude changed
profoundly over time, and at the end of the period under review, his
views deviated significantly from the AEC postulates. These changes in
attitude, identified in this study, enabled the implementation of the
post-Oslo 1993 process of rapprochement between Israel and the
Palestinians.

ACKNOWLEDGEMENTS

The author would like to thank the Philip Slomowitz Fund of the Centre of International
Communications and Policy at Bar-Ilan University for supporting this research, and Iris
Margulies for her research assistance.

NOTES

1. *Divrei Ha-Knesset* (Knesset Records), 27 October 1994, pp.910–11.
2. Efraim Inbar and Shmuel Sandler, eds, *Middle Eastern Security: Prospects for an Arms
   Control Regime*, London, 1995; Efraim Karsh, 'Between War and Peace', *Israel Affairs*,
   Vol.2, No.1 (Autumn 1995), pp.1–10; Amos Perlmutter, 'The Israel–PLO Accord is Dead',
   Foreign Affairs, Vol.74, No.3 (1995), pp.59–6; William B. Quandt, 'The Middle East on
   the Brink: Prospects for Change in the 21st Century', *Middle East Journal*, Vol.50, No.1
   (1996), pp.9–17.
3. On the AIPI Project, its framework and findings, see Yehudit Auerbach and Hemda Ben-
   Yehuda, 'Attitudes to an Existence Conflict: Rabin and Sharon on the Palestinian Issue
   1967–87', in K.S. Larsen, ed., *Conflict and Social Psychology*, London, 1993; idem,
   'Attitudes towards an Existence Conflict: Begin and Dayan on The Palestinian Issue',
   International Interactions, Vol.13, pp.323–51; Ben-Yehuda and Auerbach, 'Attitudes to an
   Existence Conflict: Allon and Peres on the Palestinian Issue 1967–87', *Journal of Conflict
   Resolution*, Vol.35, No.3 (1991), pp.519–46.

4. Auerbach and Ben-Yehuda, 'Attitudes towards an Existence Conflict: Begin and Dayan', p.144.
5. The AEC Framework, its propositions, as well as an analysis of findings on Yitzhak Rabin's attitudes in the 1967–87 period was presented in Auerbach and Ben-Yehuda 1993.
6. Ibid., pp.145–47.
7. Ibid., p.154.
8. *Divrei Ha-Knesset*, 13 July 1992, pp.8,9.
9. Ibid., p.9, and 26 October 1992, p.4; JDTV (Jerusalem Daily Television), 14 January 1988; JDR (Jerusalem Domestic Radio), 28 April 1989, JDTV 20 June 1990, JDR 23 November 1992, IDF Radio, 22 June 1992, 15 September 1993, all in *Foreign Broadcasts Information Service – Daily Report* (hereinafter FBIS).
10. FBIS, 14 January 1988.
11. FBIS, 30 August 1993; IDF Radio, 3 September 1993.
12. FBIS, 20 April 1992, pp.173–82.
13. *Divrei Ha-Knesset*, 13 July 1992, p.9.
14. Ibid.
15. FBIS: JDR, 6 March 1988; *Davar*, 12 March 1993, p.15; JDTV, Channel 2, 28 July 1993.
16. FBIS: JDR, 25 October 1993 and IDF Radio 7 March 1988, respectively. See also JDTV, 14 December 1992; JDR 22 February 1992; *Divrei Ha-Knesset*, 26 October 1992, p.4, 20 January 1993, p.2724, 3 February 1993, p.3078, 28 July 1993, p.6948.
17. FBIS: JDTV, 8 December 1988.
18. *Davar*, 12 February 1988, p.16, 24 February 1988, p.1,2.
19. FBIS: JDTV 8 December 1988.
20. FBIS: JDR, 22 February 1988.
21. FBIS: JDTV Channel 2, 22 March 1993.
22. FBIS: *Le Monde*, 21 October 1992, p.1, 6; JDR, 29 November, 15 December 1992, 22 February 1993.
23. FBIS: IDF Radio 8 March 1988 (from the Knesset).
24. *Divrei Ha-Knesset*, 26 October 1992, p.4.
25. *Divrei Ha-Knesset*, 13 July 1992, p.9.
26. FBIS: JDTV, 14 January 1988, 20 June 1990; JDR, 2 May 1988.
27. On Jerusalem see FBIS: JDTV, 16 March 1988, 10 September 1993, JDR 27 April 1989; on the PLO/Palestinian State, see FBIS: JDR 22 December 1987, 31 January 1989, 8 April 1993; JDTV 16 March 1988, 20 June 1990; IDF Radio 22 June 1992.
28. In an interview to *Der Spiegel*, in FBIS, 21 March 1988, pp.176–81; see also *Ha-aretz*, 29 December 1978, pp.1, 6; JDR 27 February 1988; *Divrei Ha-Knesset*, 26 October 1992, p.3, 20 January 1993, p.2723, 3 February 1993, p.3078
29. FBIS: JDTV, Channel 2, 22 March 1993 (from the Knesset).
30. Ibid., JDTV, 14 January 1988.
31. Ibid., 20 January 1989.
32. *Israeli Foreign Office Website*, 10 November 1994.
33. *Divrei Ha-Knesset*, 13 July 1992, p.8.
34. FBIS: JDTV, 20 January 1989; JDR 31 January 1989; BBC, 28 February 1989.
35. Ibid., IDF Radio, 18 May 1989.
36. Ibid. *Davar*, 12 March 1993.
37. Ibid. *Jerusalem Post*, 20 February 1989, p.10; JDTV, 4 September 1992.
38. Ibid. JDR, 8 April 1993.
39. *Divrei Ha-Knesset*, 15 May 1995, p.53 (unpublished stenographic protocol).
40. *Divrei Ha-Knesset*, 21 September 1993, p.7679, 28 February 1994, p.4906, 18 April 1994, p.6238, 11 May 1994, p.6880, 29 May 1995, p.21 (unpublished stenographic protocol).
41. FBIS: JDTV, 10 September 1993; IDF Radio, 15 September 1993.
42. *Divrei Ha-Knesset*, 28 February 1994, p.4906.
43. *Divrei Ha-Knesset*, 21 September 1993, p.7680.
44. *Israeli Foreign Office Website*.
45. *Divrei Ha-Knesset*, 21 September 1993, pp.7678–9, 7681, 11 May 1994, p.6880, 3 August 1994, p.10261, as well as the unpublished stenographic protocols of 15 May 1995, p.31 and 29 May 1995, p.14.
46. Ibid., 27 October 1994, p.14.
47. Ibid., 28 July 1993, p.6945, 27 October 1994, p.911, 15 May 1995, pp.52, 57

(unpublished stenographic protocol).

48. Ibid., 21 September 1993, p.7679.
49. Ibid., p.7681, 30 October 1994, p.4, 15 May 1995, p.46 (unpublished stenographic protocol).
50. Ibid., 18 April 1994, p.6238.
51. Ibid., 21 September 1993, p.7680, 3 October 1994, p.4, 15 May 1995, p.46 (unpublished stenographic protocol).
52. FBIS: JDTV, Channel 2, 23 January 1995.
53. *Divrei Ha-Knesset*, 27 October 1994, p.911. See also 18 April 1994, p.6242, 3 October 1994, p.4, 25 October 1994, p.754, 15 May 1995, p.46 (unpublished stenographic protocol).
54. 'Address at the Dayan Centre for Middle Eastern and African Studies, Tel-Aviv University, 10 November 1994', *Israeli Foreign Office Website*.
55. *Divrei Ha-Knesset*, 21 September 1993, pp.7679, 7680,7682.
56. Robert Slater, *Rabin of Israel*, London, 1996, pp.583, 586.
57. FBIS: *al-Watan al-Arabi* (Paris), 6 January 1995, pp.15–19.
58. At the signing ceremony of the Israeli Palestinian Interim Agreement, 28 September 1995, *Israeli Foreign Office Website*.
59. *Divrei Ha-Knesset*, 28 February 1994, p.4906, 18 April 1994, p.6238, 3 October 1994, p.4.
60. Ibid., 18 April 1994, pp.6240, 6242, 11 May 1994, p.6879.
61. Ibid., 20 January 1993, pp.2701, 2705.
62. Ibid., 18 April 1994, p.6243.
63. *Israeli Foreign Office Website*.
64. *Divrei Ha-Knesset*, 15 May 1995, p.45 (unpublished stenographic protocol).
65. FBIS: JDTV, Channel 3 from the Knesset, 28 February 1995.
66. FBIS: *Davar*, 29 September 1995, p.13; IDF Radio, 24 January 1995; JDTV, 23 January 1995.
67. *Israeli Foreign Office Website*, Address at the Dayan Centre.

The Golan Heights:
A Vital Strategic Asset
for Israel

DAVID ESHEL

GEOPOLITICAL BACKGROUND

Above the Sea of Galilee (also known as Lake Kinneret or Lake Tiberias) rises an escarpment, its height ranging from 800 to 1000 metres. Known as the Golan Heights, it covers a total area of some 900 square kms, rising gradually from south to north, its peaks towering over the Rift Valley to the west and south. These ancient hills were created by volcanic activity: lava pouring out from craters covered the high plateau with a layer of basalt. The highest point is Mount Hermon, a multi-peaked mountain rising to 2814 metres at its peak, which completely dominates the entire region; on a clear day its snow-covered summit can be seen from Mount Carmel at Haifa, more than 100 kms away. More importantly, the observation post high on its peak affords a view right up to Damascus – a considerable asset from a military point of view.

Once, when it was rich in pasturage, nomadic herdsmen roamed it with their flocks; hence its Arabic name – Jaulan, related to the word *jawal*, meaning 'nomad'. Little of this fertile heritage is now to be seen in the windswept, rocky area, almost completely devoid of vegetation, except on the southeastern slopes of Mount Hermon, where lavish fruit groves still grow.

As an integral part of that geographical area which borders with the Syrian desert, since Biblical times the Golan has been involved in many military conflicts. The Old Testament speaks of a place called Golan which was allotted to the tribe of Menasseh, one of the 12 Hebrew tribes which entered the Land of Canaan after the Exodus from Egypt during the thirteenth century BCE, over 3000 years ago. Great fortifications existed even then on the Golan; perhaps the best known was Gamla – the northernmost fortress of the Jewish rebels in the first century CE, no less crucial than Massada in the war against the Roman Empire. Although it fell to Roman legions after heavy fighting, in the

---

David Eshel is writer and commentator on military and strategic affairs.

year 68 CE, its ruins still tower high above the Sea of Galilee, a monument to Jewish fortitude.

Many more battles and campaigns were fought over the Golan Heights, due to their strategic importance as a communication line between the Fertile Crescent in the north, via Palestine to Egypt, North Africa and the Mediterranean Sea. In more recent times, September 1918 saw General Sir Edmund Allenby's army advancing in force over the Bnot-Yaacov Bridge, crossing the Jordan River, and capturing Quneitra and Damascus from the Turks who had ruled the area for centuries.

Since 1967, when the Heights were captured from Syria during the Six Day War, some 33 Israeli settlements have been established in that barren landscape. Today, looking up from Israel's richly vegetated Hula Valley (see Map 1), one cannot but be impressed by how the Golan Heights dominate the whole area. Rising at a sharp, steep angle, the slope to the northeast reaches a watershed at Tel Abu Nida, some 1000 metres high, and a few kilometres northwest of Quneitra. From here the area ascends northwards towards Mount Hermon and slopes downwards to the south until it reaches the Rukkad, a canyon-like stream falling steeply to the Jordan River below. A maze of ridges and wall-like lava patterns, completely impassable even to the most modern cross-country vehicle, covers most of the northeast from the slopes of Mount Hermon to the Quneitra–Damascus road. Further south the area becomes more open, allowing better movement, but scores of extinct volcanoes rising to a height of 200 metres cover the area, making excellent observation points and defensive positions. Seen from the northeast the ground slopes westwards until it reaches the sharp ravine towering over the Sea of Galilee, Israel's main natural water reserve.

Damascus, Syria's capital, lies only some 60 kms from Israeli-held territory. It is located, strategically speaking, in an extremely good position, being surrounded by high mountains to the north, a line of low hills to the west and a large salt marsh to the south and east. All the rest is a seemingly endless, barren desert. Five main roads run out of Damascus, while on the Golan itself there have been, since 1967, several important roads, some built wide enough to allow multi-convoy movement in two directions.

The Purple Line, established after the ceasefire of 10 June 1967, provided an excellent line of defence, located mostly along the watershed and enabling long-range observation. Integrated into the Israeli defence system are some of the volcanic hills of the area, among them the dominating 1200-metre Hermonit, north of Quneitra, and the 1250-metre Tel-Fares, south of the town. This hill commands a very dangerous sector east of Rafid, one of the likely invasion routes into Israel. Both of these sites proved vital in stemming the Syrian and later the joint Iraqi-Jordanian onslaughts during the 1973 Yom Kippur War.

MAP 1

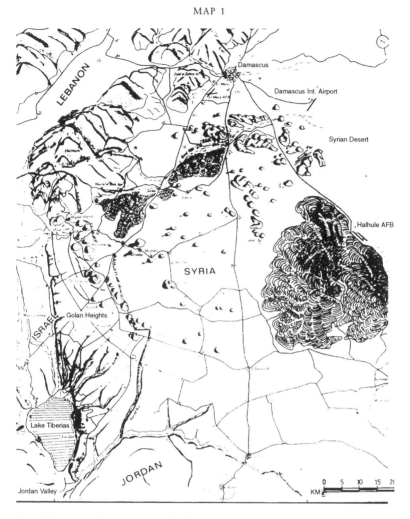

Israel currently commands about 1000 square kms of the Golan. Despite its considerable strategic importance, the Golan represents a very small fraction of Syrian territory. In fact, it is only 62 kms in length and is 25 kms at its widest, quite insignificant as buffer zones go, compared to, for example, the 300-km-long Sinai desert which separates Israel and Egypt.

In order to understand the geopolitics of the entire region, Lebanon must also be taken into account. The borders of northern Israel were drawn by the victors of the First World War, after much haggling. From a geostrategic point of view, however, the entire region seems one entity, divided by natural obstacles which we shall now examine in order to draw some conclusions as to possible operational options of both a defensive and an offensive nature.

MILITARY TOPOGRAPHY OF SOUTH LEBANON

Due to its topography, Israel's northern border lies on relatively good defensible ground. But what is known as the 'Galilee Panhandle', an area which pokes out like a finger from the Hula Valley northwards to Metulla, on the border with Lebanon, is a curious geographical phenomenon – the result of hasty, shortsighted decisions made by the French and British nearly 70 years ago. The outcome of these borders was years of tension and violence, since serious political and ethnic problems remained unsolved.

The facts are apparent to the most impartial observer: on its west the Panhandle leans on a mountain range, only partially under Israeli control, the rest belonging to Lebanon. While the northern border with Lebanon is situated on hilly ground, with at least some observation points and with a sophisticated barrier assuring substantial security against hostile infiltrators, the Panhandle has neither. Only 5000–7000 metres in width, it is dominated in the east by the Golan Heights which tower some 500 metres over the Jordan Rift Valley while, further north, the steep slopes of Mount Hermon command the entire scene. As if that were not enough, the Panhandle leans on the northern edge of the Ramim ridge on its western side, leaving it wide open to attack from the Marjayun valley, only a handful of kilometres from Israel's international border. Thus, it is obvious that the Galilee Panhandle is a defender's nightmare, with its open access to anyone coming from the north or east.

Indeed, one need not be an expert strategist to realize that from a military standpoint it is categorically impossible to defend the Galilee Panhandle or the eastern shores of the Sea of Galilee without some control over the dominating high ground on the Golan. History confirms this statement: on 15 May 1948, the newly-established State of Israel was invaded by three Syrian brigades on three separate fronts – the northern Panhandle, the Bnot-Yaacov Bridge and the eastern banks of the Sea of Galilee. The newborn Israeli Army, almost untrained, ill-equipped, but determined to fight, managed to hold up outflanking attacks on Zemach and Degania, where they withstood several armour-infantry attacks. But in the centre, Syrian tanks raced over the Jordan bridges, captured Mishmar Ha-yarden and continued to advance towards the main road at Rosh-Pina, threatening the cities of Safed and Tiberias. At this point the Syrians, on the way to linking up with a Lebanese force invading from the west, had nearly cut northern Israel in half. Only a last-minute effort succeeded in halting the advance, but Mishmar Ha-yarden and the area surrounding it remained in Syrian hands until the armistice in 1949. Near Kibbutz Dan, the Syrians attacked and captured the Banias region, with its important road junction and the source waters of the River Jordan, a coup which was to have far-reaching consequences later, when Israel and Syria were vainly searching for a workable solution under United Nations auspices.

The international borders between Israel and Syria, established way back in 1923,[1] still haunt Israeli military planners today, as they confront Hafez Asad's Syria in the peace process. One glance at the map drawn before 1967 (see Map 2) suffices for understanding the delicate problems that any strategic or tactical commander faces when attempting to plan a workable defence of northern Israel. Here one has to cope with topography, totally ignored by the makers of the international borders of 1923. The Panhandle was a political and military disaster from its inception – the result of an unfortunate compromise between two colonial powers haggling over trivialities. Making an enclave which thrusts deep into hostile territory was an idiocy: an absolute invitation to border disputes, which came about soon enough and have continued to this day. Another sore point for the Israelis was the cliffs rising above the eastern shore of the Sea of Galilee – an acute danger for a country whose sole source of water this was – since Syrian soldiers could, and did, fire at will upon the Israelis below.

MILITARY ASPECTS OF THE GOLAN

Before discussing the strategic problems facing both Israel and Syria, one should touch upon some of the military aspects in this region.

Four major campaigns have been fought over these windswept highlands in this century alone, three of them between the Syrian and Israeli armies. However, virtually nothing has changed to resolve the difficult issues which have remained unsolved since the unfortunate 1923 line was established. Any hopes for a future settlement, mainly stemming from over-optimistic politicians, disregard those hard realities.

After the 1948 War, a series of compromises by the UN Armistice Commission resulted in yet more serious problems, including three de-militarized zones and many undefined areas, the subject of more disputes. Time after time incidents escalated into serious fire-fights, as both parties tried to settle their territorial disputes by force. Life in the civilian Israeli settlements gradually became increasingly unbearable. The topography was clearly in favour of the Syrians, snug in their concrete bunkers high on the ridges, which the Israeli fire could hardly reach, if at all.

Matters came to a head when the Syrians attempted to divert the waters of the Jordan inside their territory, thus denying Israel the water it desperately needed. A conflict, known as 'the war over the waters' broke out and continued for several years. Israeli tanks finally decided the issue by firing point blank at long range, destroying the Syrian earth-moving equipment. The Syrian threat, however, continued until Israel occupied the Golan Heights in a lightning attack during the last days of the Six Day War. In October 1973 the Syrians tried to recapture the

Golan by force of arms; but by the early 1990s, with their Soviet patron no longer around, they had come to realize that their chances of regaining the area by military means are virtually nil, so they have resorted to peaceful means to achieve their aspirations.

By way of understanding the intricate problems faced by the current negotiators, this essay will examine the comparative strength and operational options of both parties against the backdrop of the strategic value of the Golan Heights and its surrounding area from the purely military point of view. Underlying this examination is the assumption that military planners have to adopt the 'worst case scenario', however politically unlikely it might seem. While there is no need to overestimate the enemy's potential, to underestimate it could spell disaster.

The Syrian Forces

The Syrian Army at present is formed around 12 divisions, 11 of which are armoured or mechanized. On the eve of the October 1973 War, Syria could field only two armoured divisions, the rest being partly mechanized infantry formations. Surprisingly, the latest addition, a new armoured division, was added in 1994 when the peace process was already in train. But this is not all that Syria has gained recently in its quest for strategic parity with Israel.

During the 1991 Gulf War, when Syria's 9th mechanized division took a purely token part in the American-led coalition against Saddam Hussein, the Syrian officers were able to get a glimpse of the making of modern warfare, Western style, and the result was devastating to their operational concepts, based on Soviet materiel and tactics. Modern tanks, such as the hitherto much-admired T-72M, which made up the backbone of the Syrian Armoured Corps, proved totally ineffective against Western tank guns which blew them to pieces at long range without the Iraqi crews being able to retaliate.

Since 1991, therefore, Syria has increased its arsenal of high quality tanks by nearly 50 per cent, using Saudi funds advanced after the Gulf War to purchase T-72 models from East European countries for cash. While this enabled the Syrian high command to improve the mobility and firepower of the greater part of their armoured divisions, the total number of high quality tanks is still below requirements if reserves and replacements are needed for an emergency. Moreover, these 1500 T-72s, not all upgraded models, will lose their operational serviceability within a few years if Syria does not devote sufficient funds for spares and upgrading to compete with the new technological developments taking place in Western arsenals. One thousand five hundred seems like a lot of tanks but once in battle, against modern firepower, this number will dwindle fast and, without substantial logistical backup – meaning not only funds but a national technological infrastructure – the army will lose its teeth fast once battle is joined. There are also 3000 older tanks in the Syrian order of battle, but they are unfit to combat modern armour and, apart from their nuisance value, will be fit only for the scrapheap if a serious effort to upgrade them is not undertaken soon.[2]

No one in Syria is better equipped to assess this situation than General Hikmat Shihabi, the veteran Syrian Chief-of-Staff, and President Asad's close confidant. These two men must realize on sober assessment that they have no viable military option in an all-out war with Israel in the foreseeable future and with the present strategic deployment by Israel on the Golan Heights. That is what really brought Asad to the negotiating table at Madrid, certainly not his ardent desire to make peace with the Jewish State. His long-term strategic goals remain unaltered; only his tactics have changed. To think otherwise would just be wishful thinking.

With all their logistical and technological weaknesses, however, the Syrian forces do present an acute threat by their very presence in highly strategic jump-off positions and, especially, because of the fact that their army is based on high alert, fully mobilized, mobile formations, ready to strike on the orders of a single man. Moreover, the eight armoured divisions with their almost 2500 tanks pack some formidable firepower. The Syrian army is one of the best trained and motivated in the Arab World and their troops have put up a tough fight whenever they encountered Israeli forces. One would therefore be taking a dangerous gamble in underestimating the fighting qualities of the Syrian soldier and his professional expertise and skill.

Another aspect which must be considered when assessing Syria's operational potential is the incorporation of its vast ground-to-ground missile arsenal into the overall strategic plan. A very dangerous situation could develop if the Syrians were to open a future conflict with a surprise attack by massive missile salvoes directed against strategic targets inside Israel, thus disrupting, or at least hampering, mobilization and deployment of reserves during the most critical phase of an opening campaign. Though Israel is well prepared for such a contingency and certainly far from helpless to retaliate, serious problems could certainly arise. This is perhaps the main reason why, even in an age of missiles and unconventional warfare, strategic ground and sufficient depth in territory is still a crucial factor, now perhaps more than ever.

Some experts dispute this claim, but they can only substantiate their point of view by proposing that in the nuclear age, in a strategic MAD stand-off, all conventional weapons and ground will have lost their meaning anyhow, as total mutual destruction would result. Such an assumption is naive and irresponsible, since, for nearly half a century, some of the bloodiest local wars have been fought despite or perhaps under the umbrella of nuclear weapons, and the absence or possession of ground has proved decisive on more than one occasion.

The Israeli Forces

The Israeli Army still rates among the most formidable, well-trained and motivated armed forces in the world today, but this situation could change rapidly if it were to lose some of its major assets as a result of a false sense of security created by irresponsible political delusions. Although better organized, equipped and trained since 1973, budgetary constraints are becoming evident which could seriously affect future deployment of regular forces on high alert status. Weapons are getting more and more expensive and becoming obsolete faster, a costly process which even a very security-conscious country will not be able to afford for long. However, in spite of current ideas about re-organizing the IDF into a professional-volunteer army, it seems realistic to assume that, for the next decade or so, the Israeli armed forces will remain unchanged and still be based on a main body of reserves, a method which has successfully survived several major emergencies.

Such a 'people's army' is geared into a finely tuned combination. Notwithstanding recent reports on a significant drop in motivation among conscripts and reservists alike,[3] the hard core of combat troops combines the highest personal motivation and professional skill with a great deal of combat experience, and can readily outfight and outgun any regional adversary. But, in order to keep this skill up to acceptable standards, time and space, as well as money, are needed. Time for mobilization and deployment; space to allow such deployment to roll off in order and with sufficient logistical backing for the duration of hostilities. To enter into battle unprepared or insufficiently equipped invites disaster, so time and space are crucial against surprise attack.

The Israel Air Force claims that it can provide both time and space on its own and, with their well attested boldness and courage, this could be true.[4] But not under all circumstances and, once again, to take a worst case scenario, one has to assume that the enemy will also take some precautions, aimed at blunting the edge of the Israeli armed forces in general, and its air force in particular. The Arab armies prepared for precisely such an eventuality when they made their surprise attack on 6 October 1973. They attacked under a dense umbrella of sophisticated Soviet air defence missiles, as well as hundreds of anti-tank missiles, both of which overcame the weaknesses their armies had shown during the 1967 Six Day War. The Egyptian and Syrian commanders, wisely learning from their painful experiences in battle, exercised surprising aptitude in finding workable solutions and creating severe headaches for the Israeli commanders, who were confident that their operational superiority still existed. They were wrong, and the price was a heavy one.

There is no reason why, if they choose to strike again, Arab commanders should not use their imagination and professional skill to overcome their operational and technological weaknesses at that future date. One must remember that in an open society like Israel there are few secrets left unpublished by the ever vigilant media, so most of the assets which could be fielded in a future war would be known to the enemy. On the other hand, the opponents, acting under the veil of strict totalitarian security and disinformation, will in this matter have the edge over the democratic state.

THE GOLAN HEIGHTS: A STRATEGIC BULWARK

Both Israel and Syria regard the Golan Heights and South Lebanon as important strategic assets, but to varying degrees. The Israeli presence so close to the Syrian capital, Damascus, is a constant reminder to Asad that his operational, if not political, flexibility is limited. This, and nothing else, explains the total quiet on the Golan front for over 20 years. Asad simply cannot afford a serious confrontation with the Israel Defence Forces (IDF) under the present conditions without endangering his capital. There are those, especially in some Israeli circles, who postulate that Asad has reached a strategic decision to make peace with Israel. This may or may not be true – nobody really knows what goes on in the mind of this skilful politician; but there are hard reasons for Israel to continue being suspicious, even if some sort of agreement does result from the present or future talks. First and foremost, the main issue is not resolved: the fact remains that Israel's strong strategic position will erode should it withdraw from the Golan Heights. The very reason for Syria's restraint would disappear the moment the direct threat to their capital is eliminated, which may in turn lead to a reassessment (whether by Asad or one of his successors) of the Syrian option.

True, it is arguable that the post-cold war world has changed so radically after the demise of the Soviet Empire that no Arab ruler can now afford to go to war. But this argument is only partly acceptable for the simple reason that Middle Eastern politics have never been, and are not now, ruled by great-power rivalry but rather by the interests of the local players themselves. Hence, just as Anwar Sadat launched the 1973 War against the wishes of Egypt's Soviet patron, Hafiz Asad sent his troops into Lebanon in the summer of 1976 in defiance of Moscow's warnings against such a move, and Saddam Hussein invaded Iran in September 1980 to the deep dismay of his Soviet ally, so Arab rulers may readily resort to the military option in the future, should they deem the gains of such a move to exceed its potential costs.

What, then, are the military-strategic dangers attending a future war· in the event of an Israeli withdrawal from the Golan? Signs of Syria's overall strategy were already evident in its intervention in the 1948 War, namely, to cut northern Israel in half and reach out for the Haifa Harbour, the ultimate Syrian goal. Important light on the Syrian strategic thinking was shed following the 1967 War, when documents captured at the Syrian headquarters at Quneitra revealed the strategic plan in all its detail. Codenamed 'Amaliyat Nasser', the Syrian plan envisaged a two-divisional sized attack. One prong would cross the Bnot-Yaacov bridge, cut the Galilee Panhandle at Rosh-Pina, climb up the mountain to Safed and drive armoured spearheads towards Acre, probably linking up with Lebanese forces coming south from Rosh Ha-niqra. The other division would drive around the Sea of Galilee, capture Tiberias and then drive on to Nazareth and Mount Carmel. The result: all northern Israel would be in Syrian hands. The 'Nasser Plan' was not just some imaginative operational study, but a well planned scheme, which might have succeeded if the IDF had been severely mauled in the battle of Sinai, and by Jordan. What saved the Galilee was the early destruction of the Arab air forces and the lightning strike by Israel's armour, which in a few days made all Syrian plans obsolete.[5]

Syria's second chance came in October 1973. Yet again, the Syrians went to great pains to plan an attack which they thought could succeed this time and achieve their strategic goals. Their concept was to mount an opening strike to regain the captured Golan Heights; then, if successful, they would exploit their success by a combined air-ground offensive to secure the Jordan bridges, feed several armoured spearheads through and then drive westwards to the coast, while a strike to the south would link up with the Jordanian armour in Samaria, probably with an Iraqi force joining in, thus threatening Israel's centre. To mount such an ambitious plan, Syria alone massed nearly 2000 tanks with over half of that number deployed in the breakthrough phase. According to their projection, the Jordan bridges would be captured by coup de main by airborne commandos; long before, so the Syrians estimated, Israeli armoured reserves could be expected in the theatre of war.

This plan was very dangerous for Israel, and it only failed due to two depleted Israeli regular armoured brigades, which virtually sacrificed themselves to stem the Syrian onslaught, mainly in what came to be known as the 'Valley of Tears', in a joint effort with the air force. It was touch and go until the reserves were able to mobilize, rush to the scene and stop the Syrian armour from descending down the slopes of the Golan to the Jordan valley. It does not take much imagination to conclude that had such a Syrian juggernaut faced the front on the Heights, nothing could have stopped it from achieving its objectives in the opening strike. What saved northern Israel in 1973 was the anti-tank obstacle north and south of Quneitra, which provided the defenders, outnumbered nearly 15:1 during the critical phase, with superior fire positions, plus the time and space available to roll on the reserves in the nick of time. Nothing has changed since then, from the military-strategic point of view, to prevent a similar attack if Israel were to withdraw from the Golan. The demilitarization of this narrow area will scarcely be an obstacle to such an offensive, not least in light of the far greater size, mobility and mechanization of the Syrian army in comparison with its 1973 precursor.

This is not to say that there will be an automatic Syrian attack on Israel once the latter had vacated the Golan Heights; only to argue that no peace agreement will survive unless predicated on solid military-strategic foundations.

CONCLUSION

The Golan Heights represent a vital strategic asset for Israel until a full and total change of heart takes place in this region. Its position on the Golan is defensive in nature and is part of the overall infrastructure, based on physical presence as well as intelligence monitoring assets. This overall defence posture safeguards the north of Israel and deters offensive Syrian options, either from Syrian territory or from Lebanon's Beka Valley. From the Syrian military point of view, the Golan is a purely offensive asset, a jumping-off position which, due to its topographical superiority to Israeli territory, gives them an excellent means of implementing their strategic aims.

Let me conclude this article by taking issue with the main arguments used by proponents of an Israeli withdrawal from the Golan Heights:

- *In the era of long-range missiles, territory can no longer be of vital strategic importance.* The truth is, of course, precisely the opposite. Missiles and non-conventional weapons have been in world arsenals for over fifty years, which did not prevent some of the most costly major conflicts from being fought under a nuclear umbrella. Moreover, although missiles can cause considerable damage and suffering (as London experienced during the Second World War), they are mainly weapons of terror with more psychological than military value in war. In achieving a military decision on the modern battlefield, ground forces have not lost their importance; hence topography and territory are still vital for safeguarding national security in the missile age. The more space to manoeuvre a small nation has under its control, the better are its chances of sustaining surprise attacks, especially where time and space are crucial factors, such as during mobilization and deployment of forces to endangered areas held by small forces of regular soldiers. Using natural and artificial obstacles combined in a well defined defensive infrastructure, a threatened country is better equipped to withstand any threat of surprise attack. In times of insecurity such factors can make the difference between victory and defeat.

- *There is no need for physical presence on the Golan since it can be compensated for by early-warning installations.* This claim, too, is largely misconceived. While the value of real-time intelligence monitoring cannot be over-estimated in times of tension, the problem is usually not lack of information but rather its (mis)interpretation by the intelligence community, and, moreover, the ability of the politicians to act upon this intelligence under international constrains. A fast, strong military reaction to a hostile action can be decisive; but in a democratic society this is easier said than done. Decision-making is even more difficult when facing an authoritarian regime which can afford to take fateful decisions on the spur of the moment with no fear of political feedback from its electorate. Repeated false alarms can be devastating to countries which depend on mobilization of large reserve forces, as their economies can grind to a halt following national emergency measures.

- *Syria's weapons arsenal is rapidly becoming obsolete, hence its bite is less harsh than before.* So long as the present international constellation prevails, this argument is valid, as there are only a few producers available to resupply large quantities of weapons with a short lifespan. However, as in the case of Egypt, where peace with Israel brought with it free access to hitherto untapped Western technologies and an influx of modern arms which had until then been denied, it is highly conceivable that a similar process would start once Syria signs an agreement sanctioned by the United States. This will give it access to new technologies, thus not only bridging the gap between the obsolete Soviet weapons at its disposal and the Israeli arsenal, but actually modernizing its armed forces and making them much more combat effective.

    Moreover, as the Syrian regime is based on strong internal military control, no sound leader would jeopardize his political hold by voluntarily reducing the size of his armed forces. A well equipped army will in turn increase the temptation to try and solve by force what negotiations have failed to achieve, or to take advantage of new opportunities as they arise.

- *President Asad has changed his strategy in the face of the fundamentalist threat.* The Islamic fundamentalist threat is real enough; however, Syria under the leadership of Asad is one of the few states which has so far been quite capable of stemming hostile activities by such radical elements. Moreover, the present regime has managed to establish and to sustain the Tehran-Damascus axis, in the face of a joint enemy – Saddam Hussein – and despite Syria's participation in the peace process since 1991. This development should be viewed with alarm by Israel, since a militarily strong Iran, especially one that is armed with nuclear weapons, could well provide Syria with the umbrella lost with the crumbling of the Soviet

Union, at least with regard to a ground attack against the Jewish State.

• *Demilitarized zones can prevent a surprise attack and become a confidence-building measure in the normalization process.* Israel has, unfortunately, had considerable experience of demilitarized zones, especially with Syria, of which there were three following the 1949 Armistice Agreement under UN auspices. They failed, not only in confidence building but in preventing further fighting. This time the results could be even more dangerous, since military capabilities have decisively grown on both sides. There are those who even propose not only demilitarization, but clearing the entire area of its (mainly Israeli) inhabitants so that, in the event of war, battles would be fought in a region clear of civilians. Such a view seems ridiculous: should the parties really opt for a peaceful solution, then surely the Heights will be populated by someone, and there will be no killing ground for troops to fight unhampered.

Above all, any comparison with the buffer zone in Sinai is irrelevant, due to the differences in size and topography. While Sinai provides a large-scale, barren buffer zone, perfectly suited to mobile warfare, at which Israel excels, the Golan does not. Its dominant features are all in the eastern sector of the Heights. Thus it would be imperative to maintain control over the access routes leading up to the western ridge, and to continue to deploy some troops on the tactically important ground features leaning on natural or man-made obstacles. To state that Israel would have sufficient leeway to active defensive measures in case of emergency might well prove mistaken, in the sense that political constrains might prohibit any timely moves to recapture the Golan in the event that the Syrians do not abide by the peace treaty. There are no perfect answers in military planning, but many uncertainties and contingencies can be foreseen, which must be provided for in order to reduce the risk.

• *Stationing of American troops on the Golan as part of the security arrangement will reduce the risk of confrontation.* Involving US troops as peacekeepers on the Golan could prove counter-productive for both parties, Israel and Syria. Based on past experience, the only workable way of preventing war is to maintain direct contact between the parties concerned. Any kind of mediation might only complicate matters and make them worse. Israel is a staunch ally of the United States, but this did not prevent (at times strong) disagreements between the two allies over key issues. Nor has the American support shielded Israel from serious Arab encroachments on its security (such as the Egyptian-Syrian attack in 1973, the Iraqi missile attack during the 1991 Gulf War etc.), or even been forthcoming in dire circumstances (such as the delayed American airlift during the 1973 War, or refusal to give Israel access to real-time intelligence during the Gulf War). How then can any reasonable nation accept a solution which denies it full access to vital information in an emergency and makes it dependent on a foreign country to provide or deny this information as it sees fit. More specifically, monitoring stations manned by foreign crews on the Golan have no practical value as, for a variety of reasons, their crews could be ordered to withhold information to one or both of the parties. Both Israel and Syria have too much at stake to gamble on the goodwill of others to safeguard their own national security.

A Final Word

At the end, the real issue is not how to persuade President Asad into an acceptable peace agreement with Israel. It is to ensure that Israel's future and territorial integrity are preserved by its own resources and without relinquishing, at least for the time being, the vital strategic assets at its disposal.

As long as the Middle East remains the unstable place that it is, rife with military arsenals which continue to grow at an unprecedented rate, and so long as regional imbalances continue to exist in the demographic, ethnic, religious and economic spheres, Israel would do better to be forearmed than forewarned. Peace in our time, in this area at least, seems still far from reality. Until the Muslim majority truthfully and irrevocably reconciles itself to the existence of their Jewish neighbour, Israel, for all its deep yearning for peace, will have to continue to rely on its own armed forces and strategic assets.

NOTES

1. Adam Garfinkel, *War, Water and Negotiation in the Middle East*, Tel-Aviv University, 1994; Arieh Shalev, *Israel and Syria – Peace and Security on the Golan*, Boulder, 1993; Moshe Brawer, 'The Boundaries of Peace', *Israel Affairs*, Vol.1, No.1 (Autumn, 1994), pp.41–64
2. Jaffee Center for Strategic Studies, *The Middle East Military Balance 1993–94*, Tel-Aviv, 1994; *World Defence Almanac 1994–95*; *Military Technology* (Bonn), 1995.
3. For the recent fundamental changes undergone by the Israeli army see Stuart Cohen's essay in this volume.
4. Israel TV, interview with Major-General Herzl Bodinger, Commander of the Israel Air Force (IAF), June 1995; W. Seth Carus, 'Threat to Israel's Air Bases', AIPAC Papers on US–Israel Relations, 1995.
5. *Atlas Carta, Israel – The Second Decade*, Map 104, Jerusalem, 1980.

Labour, Likud, the 'Special Relationship' and the Peace Process, 1988–96

JONATHAN RYNHOLD

Israel and the United States are often said to be participants in a 'Special Relationship'. Like other states that have a close relationship with the United States, Israel has maintained strong ties with various US administrations and the military industrial complex. Still, one of the key factors distinguishing the relationship from normal state-to-state relations are the strong and politically fruitful relations which the government of Israel maintains beyond these governmental bounds. The core of this relationship is with the organized American Jewish community, but it also incorporates Gentile groups and Congressmen who come together to make up a pro-Israel community. It is in regard to these groups that this essay will refer to a Special Relationship between Israel and the United States.

Traditionally, the pro-Israel community in the US has raised money for Israel and lobbied Congress to support Israel both politically and economically. Generally, this community accepted that when it came to existential issues such as Israeli national security, it was Israel's prerogative to determine its own fate; concerned outsiders should either be supportive of the Israeli government or keep silent. Similarly, Israelis generally accepted that their domestic political disagreements should not be aired in the US, where a united Israeli front should be presented. Until the mid-1980s this arrangement ran relatively smoothly and there was a consensus as to the respective roles of Israel and the pro-Israel community in the US. However, with the coming to power of a National Unity government in Israel in 1984, this consensus was challenged. Labour and Likud, the senior partners in the coalition, were divided over the peace process. As a result the Israeli government effectively pursued two foreign policies and this helped to undermine the presentation of a solid united Israeli front in the United States. Moreover, in the wake of the *intifada,* with the Reagan administration beginning to take stands opposed to Israeli government policy, in

Jonathan Rynhold is Tutorial Fellow in International Relations at the London School of Economics and Political Science.

particular by opening a US–PLO dialogue in December 1988, Labour and Likud also became divided over the role the pro-Israel community in the US should play in Israel's policy strategy on the peace process. Within the pro-Israel community in America, too, the outbreak of the *intifada* exacerbated divisions. Subsequently, the consensus underpinning the political operation of the Special Relationship came under great strain. Indeed since 1988, the 'golden rules' of the relationship – not criticizing Israel in public and not lobbying against the democratically elected government of Israel – have been severely eroded, if not completely destroyed.

What, then, were the reasons behind the conflicting approaches of Labour and Likud towards the Special Relationship's role in the peace process? Why did these respective approaches bring them into serious conflict with Israel's supporters in the United States? Why did Israel's supporters in the US become increasingly critical of Israeli government policies and even begin to lobby in Congress against the Israeli government? And what does all this mean for the future of the Special Relationship?

In order to answer these questions it is necessary to examine the interaction between the politics and political culture of this Special Relationship with regard to the peace process 1988–96. This essay will argue that between 1988 and 1992, when Likud was the dominant power in Israel, the conflict between Israel and its American supporters over issues related to the peace process was underpinned by a conflict over the meaning of Zionism and its implications as to the correct locus for the political loyalties of American Jews. In contrast, between 1992 and 1996 when Labour was in power, the conflict was not so much one that divided Israel from its American supporters as a conflict that cut across both the Israeli and US pro-Israel body politiques. It was a conflict between, on the one hand, an Israeli government with a basically optimistic and progressive worldview – a government that did not believe that non-Jews are intrinsically hostile and which tended to value the idea of Israel becoming a 'normal' country – against, on the other hand, those in the Likud and among Israel's supporters in the US with a pessimistic, Conservative worldview, that tended to have a more particularistic sense of Jewish identity, a strong perception of the Gentile world as basically antagonistic, and a sense of Israel as a 'special' state.

THE CORE TENSIONS WITHIN THE SPECIAL RELATIONSHIP

Following the creation of the State of Israel, and the realization that peace between Israel and her neighbours was not on the political agenda, Prime Minister David Ben-Gurion turned to world Jewry as Israel's only reliable ally. Subsequently, the Israeli government sought to institutionalize its relationship with American Jewry, the largest, richest and most powerful diaspora community, which was not only a source of financial support in and of itself, but was also the key to increasing the level of economic and political support from the US government. In this regard, two initiatives were taken. First, the American Israel Public Affairs Committee – AIPAC – was founded to lobby Congress and to help maintain public sympathy for Israel. On the advice of certain American Jewish leaders, AIPAC was formed as an independent American organization and not an agent for the government of Israel; this enabled it to utilize the American electorate's popular support for Israel as a tool in gaining Congressional support for the Jewish State. Second, in order to maximize support for Israel, Ben-Gurion sought to create a partnership with mainstream American Jewry which had traditionally been unenthusiastic about Zionism. In fact, he made what amounted to a 'concordat' with the largest Jewish organization in the US, the non-Zionist American Jewish Committee. In this agreement, in return for broad American Jewish support, the government of Israel agreed not to interfere in American Jewish politics and also recognized and accepted, as Ben-Gurion put it, that 'American Jews have only one political attachment and that is to the United States of America. They owe no political allegiance to Israel'.[1] This statement was demanded by American Jewry, to protect their position and status in America, which could be threatened if their support for Israel was construed as 'dual loyalty'.

For the vast majority of American Jews 'Zionism' meant political and philanthropic support for Israel and was certainly not a commitment to make *Aliya* (immigration to Israel) or an assertion of primary political loyalty to the state of Israel. Rather, support for Israel was seen by American Jews as an expression of their Americanness as much as their Jewishness. This outlook was articulated clearly by one of the founders of American Zionism Supreme Court, Justice Louis Brandeis. He declared that just as, 'Every Irish American who contributed towards advancing Home Rule was a better man and a better American for the sacrifice he made. Every American Jew who supported Jewish settlement in Palestine, though he feels that neither he nor his descendants will ever live there, will be a better man and a better American for doing so'.[2] Indeed, as Arthur Herzberg pointed out following the Six Day War, it was precisely, 'because Jews are now so very much at home in America... (that) it was possible for them in this crisis to be boldly Jewish in very angular ways'.[3]

In contrast, for Israelis, Zionism came wrapped up with the idea of *'Shlilat Ha-galut'*– the negation of the diaspora.[4] This concept involved both getting the Jews out of the diaspora and getting the diaspora (mentality) out of the Jews. The Zionist image of the diaspora Jew was of a weak and pliant soul, reliant for security and wellbeing on the good will of a host society, unwilling to proudly fight to protect Jewish rights, and hence living out an undignified existence. One of the key elements of the diaspora mentality that the Zionists sought to change was the style of Jewish politics. In place of what they perceived as the weak and cowardly quietistic diplomatic tradition of diaspora Jewry, with its reliance on the intercession of 'Court Jews' on behalf of the community, a process known as *Shtadlanut*, the Zionists advocated self-reliance, political independence and military power. Consequently, despite their recognition of the need for American Jewish support, the Israelis remained uncomfortable with this reliance.

'Getting the Jews out of the diaspora' meant simply that Zionists believed that all Jews should abandon the diaspora and immigrate to Israel. In other words, far from accepting the permanence of American Jewish political affiliation, by seeking to dissolve the diaspora, Zionism sought to make all Jews citizens of the state of Israel. Nonetheless, as Israel came to accept the limited potential for *Aliya* among American Jewry, successive governments of Israel continued take positions that put them at odds with the mainstream American 'Zionism'. Ben-Gurion had argued that 'it was always my view that we have to consider the interests of diaspora Jewry... But there is one crucial distinction – not what they think their best interests are but what *we* regard as their interests'.[5] Indeed, Israeli leaders generally understood this as implicitly meaning that the interests of world Jewry were equivalent to the interests of the state of Israel as interpreted by its government. In practice this meant that in pursuit of its primary interest in American Jewry – financial and political advantage – Israel tended to bypass concerns about 'dual loyalty' with the attendant threat of a rise in anti-Semitism. The most extreme example of this reaching fruition was the Pollard scandal,[6] which fully exposed Israeli disregard for threatening the 'Americanness' of American Jewish identity.

While the Israelis recognized that US Jewry represented a political asset, they had little respect for their Jewishness, let alone their Zionism, and remained generally disinterested in Jewish cultural exchange. Despite the size and importance of American Jewry, little time in the Israel school curriculum was devoted to studying the community.[7] Moreover, the Shamir government's inability to understand why the plan to amend the Law of Return to recognize only Orthodox conversion sparked a major crisis threatening to undermine American Jewish support for Israel, demonstrated the difficulty Israelis had in taking seriously non-Orthodox religious affiliation in America. Indeed, during the 'Who is a Jew' crisis which followed the 1988 Israel general election, Shamir appears to have been not unduly concerned by the fact that he was threatening the legitimacy of the Jewishness of American Jewish identity. Rather, he seems to have been prepared to face down a crisis with US Jewry and even face a drop in the amount of money they raised for Israel. This changed only when it was made clear to him that the passing of the law would weaken Israel's political power in the US and thus weaken both its ability to stand up to a pressure from an administration that had just opened a dialogue with the PLO, and its ability to guarantee the maintenance of aid through Congress.[8]

THE SPECIAL RELATIONSHIP AND THE PEACE PROCESS

The consistent position of the United States since 1967 has been in favour of a 'Land for Peace' formula to resolve the Arab–Israeli Conflict. During the Carter years, there were clashes between the administration and the Likud government over settlement activity by Israel in the West Bank and Gaza and even the very pro-Israel Reagan administration thought Israeli settlements were 'unhelpful'. In addition, from the mid-1970s onwards a number of important figures in the State Department were inclined to try and bring the Palestinians and even the PLO into the peace process, a policy which both major parties in Israel opposed throughout the 1980s. This was a potentially great problem for both parties in light of Israel's increasing reliance on American military aid and political support since 1967. But it was particularly a problem for the Likud which is ideologically committed to maintaining Israel's right to the whole land of Israel and which recognized the imperative of avoiding a choice between American support and possession of land.

The key to resolving this dilemma was the use of the Special Relationship to ensure the maintenance of American aid irrespective of the compatibility of Israeli policy on settlements or on the peace process to the demands of the administration. For the majority of the Reagan Presidency, Israel had no call to use the Special Relationship in this regard as Reagan was not interested in pressurizing Israel over the peace process. In this situation the Likud concentrated on maintaining the $3 billion worth of annual government aid and on developing its strategic relationship with the United States. The Special Relationship's role in Israeli policy regarding the peace process was confined largely to *hasbara* – spin doctoring – which consisted primarily of explaining to the American public and Congress why Israel opposed the PLO and territorial compromise.

For the Likud the aim of *hasbara* was limited. It was not designed to garner support for its whole land of Israel philosophy but to counteract the Arab spin on events, maintain a political atmosphere in Washington conducive to understanding Likud policies and thus prevent American pressure for a peace settlement along the lines consistently favoured by the State Department since 1967. Labour too had used *hasbara* and the Special Relationship to great effect between 1948–77. However, it was Likud which promoted *hasbara* to a high rank in its foreign policy and not just because the Executive was opposed to its ideological position on the Territories. The Likud tradition itself was more inclined to value *hasbara* as a tool of foreign policy.[9] Zeev Jabotinsky, the founder of Revisionism had emphasized the political significance of public opinion in liberal democracies for Zionism and in general; the Revisionist movement (the forerunner of the Likud) tended to believe that political rhetoric was more significant in politics than Labour.

The cosy relationship between Shamir and the American administration began to break down with the outbreak of the *intifada* in December 1987. Following this, Secretary of State George Shultz pushed the Palestinian question up America's diplomatic agenda, symbolized in the promotion of his own peace plan. Shamir's opposition to the Plan, increasingly irritated Shultz, who threw Likud into turmoil by opening a dialogue with the PLO in December 1988, just before he left office. The new Bush administration, unlike its predecessor, lacked a special emotional or ideological affinity with Israel. Furthermore, with the end of the Cold War in sight, the idea of Israel's usefulness as a 'strategic asset' was not popular in the new administration, especially after the Gulf War in which Israel appeared as more of a strategic liability than an asset to US interests. Shamir's relations with the administration were further undermined by President Bush's continual criticism of Israeli settlement activity and the fact that Bush was extremely angry with Shamir whom he felt had gone back on a pledge not to expand on settlement activity. For Bush, settlements had become the litmus test of whether the Israeli leader was taking him and the United States seriously. Subsequently, Bush refused to grant Israel $10 billion worth of loan guarantees to help absorb recent immigrants to Israel from the Soviet Union unless Shamir agreed to a complete settlement freeze in the occupied territories. Confronted by an antagonistic administration pursuing two major policies at odds with the Likud strategy to retain control of the territories, the Likud, and indeed key figures within the pro-Israel lobby, looked to the Special Relationship to redress the balance and defeat the administration without damaging America's long term political, economic and strategic support for Israel.

LIKUD, THE SPECIAL RELATIONSHIP AND THE PEACE PROCESS, 1989-92

Likud's strategy to reverse the administration's position promoted heightened activism by the pro-Israel community in the US, channelled through Congress in an attempt to challenge the administration. This was complimented by a widespread *hasbara* offensive designed to mobilize political support for the Israeli government position. As soon as the US–PLO dialogue opened in December 1988, Likud began to look for ways to end it. Subsequently, the Prime Minister's Solidarity Conference[10] for diaspora leaders was held in an effort to try to bolster opposition among Israel's supporters in the United States against the dialogue and simultaneously marginalize the doves who favoured talks with the PLO. As a result of the Conference, the Anti Defamation League (ADL) and the Conference of Presidents of Major American Jewish Organizations (Presidents Conference) began to monitor the PLO's role in terrorism, thereby complementing the efforts of Shamir's Advisor on Terrorism Yigal Carmon.

Likud also attempted to curtail the administration's dialogue with the PLO through legislation in Congress. They worked with their supporters in the US to lobby sympathetic members of Congress. Subsequently, a bill sponsored by Republican senator Jesse Helms, who had his own contacts direct with Likud party operatives, sought to prevent the administration speaking to any PLO official who had been previously involved either directly or indirectly, in terror. The Helms bill was defeated, but Congress did pass the Lieberman-Mack legislation which required the administration to report to Congress every 120 days on whether the PLO was complying with the terms of the dialogue, and also required that the President inform Congress in the event that the administration spoke directly with known terrorists. Indeed, reports compiled by Carmon and American Jewish organizations were presented by Carmon to the pro-Israel senators involved in monitoring PLO compliance.[11] However, according to a senior official then in the Israeli embassy in Washington, these efforts were not important in the actual termination of the dialogue, which occurred after PLO Chairman Yasser Arafat refused to condemn a terrorist attack by one of the Fatah factions of the PLO on a Tel-Aviv beach.

After the collapse of the National Unity government in March 1990, Likud faced an even greater clash with the administration when they attempted to get $10 billion dollars worth of loan guarantees to help absorb Russian immigrants, without agreeing to a settlement freeze requested by the administration. It was generally felt that the Special Relationship would be able to defeat the administration through their powerful support in Congress. Yoram Ettinger, a Likud loyalist who reported directly to the Prime Minister's Office from the Washington Embassy, informed Shamir in a cable on 4 September that the administration had only a very limited ability to control the agenda.[12] Indeed, the Shamir government was so confident of success that it included the first instalment of $2 billion dollars in the budget for the coming year ahead. Thus, the Israeli government formally submitted its request for the $10 billion in loan guarantees on 6 September, despite an appeal by Bush that they at least delay the request for 120 days until after the Madrid Conference had opened.

The Israeli-AIPAC strategy was to drum up grass-roots support among Israel supporters in the US public and in Congress. They did this by using media-friendly figures such as Deputy Foreign Minister

Benjamin Netanyahu, and Health Minister Ehud Olmert, to sell the message that this was 'humanitarian assistance'. Meanwhile, AIPAC and the Israeli Embassy worked Capitol Hill to drum up legislative support behind the Israeli demand. All the activity was set to culminate in Washington on 12 September when thousands of pro-Israel lobbyists were set to descend on the Capitol in support of loan guarantees. However, President Bush surprised the lobby by appealing straight to the American people on Television. As a result, Israel's position in Congress crumbled, Bush's request for a 120-day delay before considering granting the guarantees was granted. Even when negotiations recommenced in January 1992, the Israeli government was unable to drum up the necessary support within the Special Relationship to obtain the loan guarantees on its own terms.

AMERICAN JEWISH OPPOSITION AND THE LIKUD

The failure get sufficient support to confront the Bush administration on the loan guarantees issues was symptomatic of deeper rifts within Israel's relationship with its supporters in the US. The standard operating procedure of American Jewry allowed criticism of Israeli policy in private but not in public. Ultimately, it was generally accepted that when it came to existential issues such as National Security, it was Israel's prerogative to determine its own fate; concerned outsiders should either be supportive or keep silent. As Abe Foxman, the head of the ADL, put it, 'Israeli democracy should decide; American Jews should support'.[13]

It was during the Lebanon War that the Community consensus on not criticizing Israel in public had first been called into question, but it was the *intifada* which placed intolerable strains on that position. The pro-Israel community in the US had come to be as polarized as the Israeli public over the future of the territories and the Palestinian Question and despite public pronouncements of support for Likud's hawkish policies a majority of the American Jewish public and more importantly a majority of American Jewish leaders privately favoured the 'Land for Peace' formula.[14] This was a view which gradually began to seep into the open, in the form of public criticism of Likud policy and a refusal to unquestioningly follow the preferred Likud line on the question of the US–PLO dialogue and the loan guarantees.

The more marginal and most progressive elements of American Jewry were even beginning to meet with the PLO. In March 1989 the Israeli English language magazine 'New Outlook' sponsored a Conference at Columbia University where Israeli peace activists and MKs shared a platform with Palestinians and PLO figures. American Jewish academic Jerome Segal, who had met PLO leaders including Arafat, formed the Jewish Peace lobby which lobbied against the Israeli government and in favour of linkage of loan guarantees and a settlement freeze. He was backed by a number of Israel Peace Activists who broke the powerful taboo that Israeli public figures should not criticize the Israeli government while abroad.[15]

More worrying for Likud was the breakdown in support for their position among mainstream US groups. These splits weakened the image of a solid pro-Israel front, on which the Special Relationship relies to be really effective. On one visit to the US, Shamir was greeted by an open letter signed by 41 American Jewish leaders which informed him 'not to mistake courtesy for consensus or applause as endorsement for the policies you pursue'.[16] One member of the Presidents Conference had helped clear the way for the dialogue by meeting Arafat in Stockholm with five other prominent American Jews. The situation was such that when the US–PLO dialogue started one Shamir aide noted that 'Israeli officials were aghast that our friends in the United States did not rise in unison to criticize this step... our friends are either critical, passive or paralyzed'.[17] Subsequently, Foreign Minister Moshe Arens tried to get the Presidents Conference to strongly condemn the dialogue but the Conference refused to confront Bush over the opening of a dialogue with the PLO.[18] Meanwhile, a leading American Jewish Congress figure strongly criticized Israel's settlement policy,[19] while outgoing Chairman of the Presidents Conference, Seymour Reich, publicly criticized Ariel Sharon's public announcement to build 2500 homes in the territories.[20]

Worst of all for the Likud was the equivocal response of American Jewry to Tom Dine's call to those in his AIPAC constituency who disliked Israeli settlements in the territories to 'swallow hard, roll up your sleeves and get to work to fight linkage'.[21] Following President Bush's dramatic news conference the Prime Minister's Office still wanted American Jewry to fight the administration for the guarantees, but the community was divided over the issue and turned decisively against Shamir's confrontational approach.[22] American Jewish leaders publicly declared that they would not act as the lackey of the Israeli government, they had not raised the settlements issue and they were not prepared to fight it. Thus Shoshana Cardin of the Presidents Conference (the most important American Jewish organization) criticized the Israeli Finance Minister for stating that settlements were more important than loan guarantees and stated that the organization would take a low profile on the question of linkage and let a direct deal be worked out between the administration and the Israeli government.[23]

The pro-Israel community did not wish to confront Bush after his speech. In pragmatic political terms, following Bush's successful appeal to the American people, most of them genuinely believed that they could not defeat the President on the issue in Congress. However, American Jewry also sought to avoid a confrontation because they had been implicitly charged by Bush with dual loyalty, while AIPAC had been equated with a 'foreign interest'. President Bush told a press conference, 'We're up against very strong, and effective sometimes, groups that go up to the Hill. I heard today there were something like a thousand lobbyists on the Hill working the other side of the question. We've got one lonely little guy down here doing it... I'm going to fight for what I believe... And I don't care if I get one vote, I'm going to stand for what I believe here, and I believe the American people will be with me'.[24] This implicit charge of dual loyalty threatened, in the eyes of many American Jews, to raise the level of anti-Semitism in the US.[25] Indeed, one of the first things the Presidents Conference did following the speech was to obtain an apology from President Bush precisely on this point.[26] Even staunch supporters of the government such as Abe Foxman of the Anti Defamation League criticized the Likud for its lack of realism and its insensitivity to embarrassing American Jews.[27]

To the Shamir administration, the response of American Jewry appeared to fit the paradigm of typical diaspora Jewish behaviour. Netanyahu considered American Jewish reluctance to confront the Bush administration on the PLO dialogue a result of diaspora cowardice, in line with the Zionist myth of the weak diaspora Jew.[28] Similarly, all the advice given to Shamir by American Jewry telling him that his demands were unrealistic were dismissed by the Prime Minister's Office as just the pathetic attempts of American Jews to protect their own skin, by ingratiating themselves with the *Goyim* in a manner unbecoming a free people. Rather than support the cause of their own people, namely the State of Israel, they were cowering in front of President Bush. Even AIPAC's professional advice that a compromise was necessary was dismissed by key Likud figures Yossi Ben-Aharon, Yoram Ettinger and Moshe Katsav, as emanating from a sense of defeatism and a '*Galut* (diaspora) mentality'.[29]

Indeed, Likud's general response to increasing diaspora criticism was based on its perception that diaspora opposition stemmed from a '*Galut* mentality'. Yossi Ben-Aharon, Shamir's right hand man in the Prime Minister's office, argued that this diaspora mentality could be countered by pressurizing American Jewry – 'pulling a bit tighter'. This, he argued, would make American Jewry lobby forcefully on Israel's behalf. Ultimately, despite Israeli declarations of loyalty to the terms of 'the concordat', the Israeli government was not inhibited from interfering in American Jewish politics to weaken critics of its policies, nor was it overly concerned that the demands it was making on American Jewish support threatened the Jewish community with the charge of dual loyalty. As Shamir argued to the Presidents Conference back in 1988, 'Jews abroad have a moral duty to support the Israeli government, never a foreign government against Israel'.[30] American Jews who publicly opposed the Israeli government were viewed by

Sharon as 'informers' a reference Shamir found to be factually correct.[31] Moreover, Likud *hasbara* tried to re-energize support for its policies by underlining the past costs and potential future costs of American Jewish passivity in the face of their own government. Shamir asked American Jewry to 'learn the lesson' of the Holocaust and confront their sense of guilt; they had been strong but had done nothing because they had not wanted to endanger their own position in America by confronting the President in the name of European Jewry.[32] Overall then, Likud activities between 1989 and 1992 raised opposition within the Special Relationship primarily because they threatened the 'Americanness' of American Jewish identity by raising the opportunity for anti-Semites to charge that American Jews carried dual loyalties.

LABOUR, THE SPECIAL RELATIONSHIP AND THE PEACE PROCESS, 1992-96

Labour saw the Special Relationship through the prism of *Shlilat Ha-galut* as well. Prime Minister Yitzhak Rabin had an obvious disdain for *Shtadlanut* which was one of the reasons that, in contrast to Likud, the Special Relationship was almost peripheral to Labour peace process strategy. As Rabin wrote in his memoirs, 'Some of the leaders of the American Jewish community exercise their influence by means of a Shtadlan [Court Jew] the traditional intermediary who sought the favour of the ruling powers in Europe... I believe that the Israeli Embassy should assume the principal role of handling Israel's affairs at the political level'.[33] This attitude towards the role of American Jewry in the conduct of Israeli foreign policy was echoed by Collette Avital, Israel's Consul-General in New York 1993-96. She too objected to American Jewish organizations acting as self-appointed intermediaries in Israel's relations with America.[34] Disdain for *Shtadlanut* reinforced two strong political reasons for the minimal role assigned to the Special Relationship in Labour's peace strategy.

First, Rabin sought to limit the role of the Special Relationship because he believed that aggressive lobbying undermined the most important element in US–Israeli relations, namely the inter-governmental strategic basis of the relationship. Rabin's experience as Ambassador to Washington had led him to view Israel's relationship with the administration as the key to the deepening of strategic ties that he considered vital to the long-term survival of the State of Israel. Accordingly, the key factor was that Israel had to demonstrate to the US that it fitted in with, and was useful to America's strategic objectives in the Middle East and beyond. Thus, as Ambassador, Rabin had been cool about supporting the Jackson-Vanik legislation in Congress, which linked Détente to freedom for Soviet Jewish Refuseniks, for fear of alienating the administration. For the same reason Rabin opposed

AIPAC's efforts to prevent the sale of F-15 jets to Saudi Arabia in 1982, preferring instead that Israel be compensated.[35] But for Rabin the loan-guarantees fiasco was the worst of all; by fighting a losing battle, AIPAC had been party to one of the most serious wedges between the US and Israel since Eisenhower threatened Ben-Gurion over Israel's refusal to withdraw from the Sinai in 1957. Hence, on his first visit to the US as Prime Minister in August 1992, Rabin lambasted AIPAC for its role in the loan-guarantees affair and informed them that it was for him and the government of Israel to negotiate with the administration and not for them.[36]

Yet the most powerful reason for Labour's attitude towards the Special Relationship's role in the peace process was that in contrast to Likud, Labour preference for 'Land for Peace' enabled it to work closely with the State Department and the administration. The Foreign Ministry, under Shimon Peres, decided it no longer needed to engage in *hasbara*. Peres argued that good policies did not need *hasbara* and that the raison d'etre of *hasbara* had been the need to explain the lack of a peace policy; now that Israel was pursuing peace with the PLO, policy spoke for itself. Consequently, the Foreign Ministry tried to shift the emphasis of their work away from *hasbara* towards the promotion of economic relations.[37] Without an emphasis on *hasbara*, there was no political urgency in maintaining the link with American Jewry. After all, this relationship had been primarily built up as an antidote to 'the siege' which the Israeli government appeared to sense was virtually over. Just prior to Oslo, Rabin declared, 'It is no longer true that we are necessarily a people that dwells alone. And it is no longer true that the whole world is against us.'[38] One consequence of this sense of 'normalization' was that the Special Relationship with American Jewry seemed of little future political importance to Israel and consequently the Jewish State had less interest in maintaining close ties with the pro-Israel community in the US. As Deputy Foreign Minister Yossi Beilin explained, 'Labour's coming to power pulls the rug from under AIPAC. We want US involvement in the peace process; their (AIPAC under Likud) agenda was to keep the Americans out. We want peace based on compromise, and their agenda was to explain why compromise was impossible'.[39]

Moreover, with Israel beginning to consider itself a reasonably well-off country, there was a growing acceptance that Israel should phase out the $1.4 billion in annual civilian aid granted by America. If Israel did not need the civilian aid, it would presumably have less need for a powerful pro-Israel lobby. When Beilin told a group of American Jews that Israel did not need their money, American Jewry felt betrayed.[40] Nor did Rabin's sharp criticism of Beilin ease relations with US Jewry, as Rabin was primarily concerned with the impact Beilin's statement would have on $3 billion worth of annual US government aid to

Israel.[41] Indeed, the weakening of relations was already apparent by virtue of the fact that Rabin left vacant the position of advisor to the Prime Minister on Diaspora Affairs until American Jewry began to challenge his peace policies through Congress.

In fact, the Special Relationship was actually somewhat of an irritant to Labour's peace policies. For in order to protect the peace process and close relations with the administration, Labour sometimes had to restrain the lobby. This was particularly in evidence on issues relating to Jerusalem. Following the Hebron massacre, the UN Resolution condemning the act referred to Jerusalem as occupied territory. The unity of Jerusalem being an emotive and unifying issue among American Jewry and Israel, AIPAC wanted to pressure the administration to veto the bill. However, the unofficial Israeli government line was that AIPAC should not do so because the implications of a US veto might prevent the PLO from returning to the peace negotiations. As Peres put it, 'Too big a victory for Israel is not in the interests of the peace process'.[42] Instead, the administration ended up just abstaining on the offending line referring to Jerusalem as occupied territory.

For American Jewry, the issue of Jerusalem as the undivided sovereign capital of Israel had always been a consensus issue of great symbolic importance and consequently what appeared to be Israeli non-chalance regarding the symbolism of the Jerusalem question caused friction between American Jewry and the Rabin government. In January 1995 after promotion of the issue among American Jewish groups 93 senators wrote to Secretary of State Warren Christopher regarding the moving of the American Embassy to Jerusalem, and subsequently Senator Robert Dole sponsored a bill in Congress to that effect. Both the administration and the Labour government were not keen on Dole's bill as they feared that bringing up the issue of Jerusalem at this stage could cause the peace process to collapse. In addition, Rabin was concerned not to embarrass the administration on this point.[43] For opponents of the Labour government the issue was a good one on which to attack, as it would be difficult for Rabin to publicly oppose the move without doing great damage to his standing in Israeli public opinion. Consequently, despite private reservations Rabin publicly supported the move when he met Dole in May.

LABOUR AND ITS AMERICAN JEWISH OPPOSITION

When surveyed during the 1980s and 1990s, American Jewry as a whole tended to be more dovish than the positions espoused by the Likud, despite the general lack of criticism for Likud positions. American Jewry tended not to see the question of territorial compromise or negotiations with the PLO in uncompromisingly ideological or hawkish terms. Rather they saw the issues in terms of maximizing Israeli security. While a majority of American Jews opposed negotiations with the PLO and a Palestinian state in the first half of the 1980s, that majority was reversed if evidence was provided of the PLO's peaceful intent.[44] So it was not really that surprising when most American Jews lined up behind the Oslo agreement.[45]

It has been suggested that American Jewish support for 'Land for Peace' is reflective of a typical American optimistic belief in the power of negotiations to yield results.[46] In this vein it is interesting to note that opinion surveys tended to show that while the majority of American Jews were dovish, this was most true of the less identifying and less involved sections of American Jewry. Correspondingly among the more involved sections of American Jewry, including many pro-Israel activists and those with the strongest sense of a particular cultural/religious Jewish identity, there was a significantly higher proportion of hawkish attitudes, which appeared to favour the Likud approach.[47]

One consequence of this was that when the dovish Labour government came to power in 1992, American Jewish public opposition to the Israeli government reached an unprecedented level of intensity. Not only was the taboo of publicly criticizing the Israeli government well and truly smashed, but American Jews actually lobbied against the democratically elected government on security-related issues. AIPAC Vice President Harvey Friedman declared that Rabin had *chutzpa* for suggesting that Israel might withdraw from the Golan, and after a derogatory reference to Yossi Beilin he was forced to resign. Neo-Conservatives, such as Norman Podhoretz, who had always argued against criticizing Israel during the Likud years reversed their position on the basis that it was legitimate to criticize Israel on security grounds, as opposed to 'moral' grounds. Moreover, some previously mainstream American Jews took this one step further as they lobbied Congress through Zionist organizations like Morton Klein's Zionist Organization of America (ZOA) and several think tanks in Washington – Frank Gaffney's Centre for Security Policy and the Jewish Institute of National Security Affairs (JINSA), for example – against Israel government policies which required Congressional support, such as aid to the Palestinian Authority and US troops on the Golan.

Why did this breakdown occur?

Until the Six Day War, American Jews tended to see Israel as a safe haven for Jewish refugees from other countries. Jews in the US supported Israel as an act of charity; Israel did not play a significant part in American Jewish identity. The Six Day War changed these attitudes. The run-up to the war, with the spectre of a Second Holocaust widely feared, had the effect of making American Jews feel separated from their fellow Americans, accentuating their particular Jewish identity. Following the war, the sense of Jewish solidarity engendered by the high threat perception prior to the war, coupled with pride in Israel its power and its victory, became central to a new more assertive form of American Jewish identity. In a sense support for Israel became the religion of American Jewry.[48] As Thomas Friedman put it, 'After the 1967 War, the perception of Israel in the mind of many American Jews shifted radically, from Israel as a safe Haven for other Jews to Israel as the symbol and carrier of (American) Jewish communal identity'.[49]

This new sense of American Jewish identity spawned a 'New Jewish Politics' (NJP) more aggressive and assertive than the traditional style of *Shtadlanut* politics, whose quiet compromising deferential style was deemed to have contributed to the Holocaust. According to Peter Medding, the credo of this new politics could be summed up as follows:

> The survival of Israel is at stake; the meaning of Jewish life everywhere is dependent on Israel; a threat to Israel's survival is a threat to Jews everywhere; Jews must be militant in acting to ensure Israel's survival; in acting to ensure Israel's survival, Jews are thereby acting to ensure their own survival and continuity; the response of non-Jews to Israel's struggle is indicative of their attitude to Jews in general; in the light of history, indifference to these concerns is as dangerous as outright anti-Semitism.[50]

The most important articulators of this New Jewish Politics were the Neo Conservatives led by Norman Podhoretz and *Commentary* magazine. They disassociated themselves from their former liberal universalist principles, became virulently anti-Communist and argued that Jews could not rely on anyone but themselves in a world where nations could have no friends, only interests.[51] They themselves had a significant influence on American politics during the Reagan administration, but the most powerful symbol of the actualization of the New Jewish Politics was the rise to power of AIPAC whose membership rose dramatically during the 1980s on the back of 'New Jewish Politics'.

The rise in American Jewish particularism which brought about the New Jewish Politics after the Six Day War matched the rise in Jewish Particularism that helped bring Likud to power in 1977.[52] While the centrality of the Holocaust to the NJP matched Israel's new civil religion and the outlook of Menachem Begin,[53] its emphasis on political assertiveness matched the thought of Jabotinsky.[54] In contrast, Prime Minister Rabin's declaration that 'the Siege' was over, Foreign Minister Peres's argument that Israel's security could not be guaranteed unilaterally but only through economic interdependence and a regional security pact, and Deputy Foreign Minister Beilin's belief in the importance of Israel being apart of the world community,[55] clashed with the fundamentals of the NJP. This new assertive American Jewish politics resonated more with Likud's defiant rhetorical style of politics than with Labour's optimistic progressive politics of compromise. This became apparent at AIPAC's annual policy conference in Washington in 1993. Israeli Ambassador Itamar Rabinovich told the 2400 participants that

> not just Arabs but also Israel would have to make compromises for peace. Only one delegate in the cavernous auditorium clapped. Sensing the awkward moment, Rabinovich recovered by saying: 'If it is hard to applaud the concessions we have to make, let us applaud the concessions the Arabs will have to provide'. The crowd roared.[56]

In essence the whole Rabin peace policy of conciliation clashed with the New Jewish politics whereby political assertiveness was deemed to be the key to security.

This tendency to favour Likud was compounded by the fact that during the 1980s Likud had built up a strong network of supporters in the American Jewish community including groups such as Americans for a Safe Israel and key leaders within the Presidents Conference, while Labour had concentrated on contacts with the State Department. Moreover, after the Oslo agreement with the PLO, Rabin's statements in favour of withdrawal from the Golan Heights and Israel's perceived softness on the issue of a united Jerusalem under Jewish sovereignty, American Jewry found that three of its core consensus positions which had developed under the Likud for the last ten years were broken by the country they were supposed to be supporting. People found it hard to sympathize with an Israeli government that proposed territorial concessions to the PLO and Syria, considering that for the previous 15 years the pro-Israel lobby had been arguing that such territorial concessions constituted a serious threat to the existence of Israel, as did the despotic Syrian and PLO leadership.

Not only did the Labour government's peace policy contradict the assertive orientation of the New Jewish politics, it also uncovered a deeper clash between the symbolic heroic special Israel of American Jewish consciousness and the real, pragmatic Israel which aspired to normality, peace and a quiet life. Large sections of active American Jewry wanted Israel to symbolize something special in terms of Jewish history, culture, and religion, whereas the Israelis were primarily concerned to advance the reality of the process of normalization in the Middle East. Thus for Rabin and his government the reality of the peace process superseded a symbolic UN vote on Jerusalem. Rabin was content to turn a blind eye to the largely symbolic issue of America not vetoing a UN resolution referring to Jerusalem as occupied territory. Instead, he preferred to use his good relations with the administration as a cover for creating 'facts on the ground' (settlement activity) in Jerusalem. This he believed would have a greater role in determining the final status of Jerusalem than any UN vote.[57] Whereas for American

Jews a UN vote on the status of Jerusalem was more central to their symbolic agenda.

The most vociferous opposition to the Labour government following the Oslo Accords came from the Orthodox Jewish community,[58] mainly based in New York. They perceived the Labour government as founded on secular Western materialistic values which they opposed. The aspiration to normalization was anathema to them as it symbolized collective assimilation and contradicted their basic concept of the Jewish people as a 'people that dwells alone'. They shared this orientation with many Orthodox Jews in Israel. This outlook coloured heavily the way they looked at the Oslo Accords. They saw the Oslo deal, particularly in the wake of subsequent terrorist attacks, as a symptom of the fact that Labour was unconcerned about Jewish lives in Israel.[59] They argued that the Oslo Accords could lead to a new Holocaust and compared the Rabin government to a 'Judenrat' handing over Jews to be killed by Arafat.[60] Many other Orthodox Jews' opposition to the Rabin government was supplemented by their belief that it is forbidden by Jewish law to cede territory in the Land of Israel.[61]

Indeed many of the most vociferous and extreme anti-government statements were made in the US and not Israel. On a visit to an Orthodox synagogue in New York City, Ambassador Rabinovich was called a traitor.[62] Moreover, it was an American rabbi who first publicly stated that 'Din Rodef' applied to Rabin.[63] Baruch Goldstein, perpetrator of the Hebron massacre, came from Brooklyn as did one of his political influences, Meir Kahane. Indeed, in the wake of the Goldstein Massacre, secular Israel came to view these American Jews as reviled fundamentalists, with Rabin even referring to some American Jewish rabbis as ayatollahs. Many Orthodox Jews and other identifying Jews opposed to the peace process live in New York, and it was no coincidence that two of the main congressmen who challenged the Rabin government policies in Congress, Republicans Senator Al D'amato, and Representative Benjamin Gilman, both represented New York.

Other Conservative Republican senators, such as Jesse Helms, who had been cultivated by Netanyahu and Likud figures in the 1980s, were also sympathetic to the Israeli opposition's agenda in Washington. Their domestic constituencies pushed them towards a pro-Israel view, but their stance was not closely tied to their relations with the American Jewish community. In fact, as Conservatives their domestic agenda was actually opposed by the majority of American Jewry, which was predominantly liberal in outlook. Nonetheless, Netanyahu was able to win them over by successfully emphasizing the idea of America and Israel as exceptional states, sister democracies that had to act vigourously with decisive military force against a terrorist threat emanating from the implacable anti-American dictatorships (Syria/PLO) surrounding Israel.[64] They too were sceptical of the Labour government's peace policy which involved concessions to former PLO terrorists who had been 'allied' with the 'Evil Empire'. Nor were they keen on supplying American aid to Arab dictatorship for the sake of peace, which to them sounded like 'appeasement' or worse, Détente. In addition, their fiscal conservatism had encouraged them to oppose US troops on the Golan and the extension of foreign aid to the Palestinian Authority (PA).[65] While the conservatives were uncomfortable with Labour's 'soft line' on security, Christian Zionists opposed territorial compromise for the same reason Gush Emunim and the religious Right did in Israel, namely that to do so would threaten a reversal of the Messianic process. In a broader sense, in the Christian fundamentalist theology of history, the Jewish people had a special role to play in the 'Second Coming'. Thus the expressed desire of the Israeli leadership to 'normalize Israel' was fundamentally at odds with their particular Christian vision.[66] In this vein Christian Zionist Jan Willen Van der Hoeven attacked Rabin's Land for Peace policy at an AIPAC policy conference.[67]

THE CHALLENGE TO LABOUR'S PEACE STRATEGY IN THE US

The final element in the anti-Labour coalition on Capitol Hill was the Israeli Likud activists Yossi Ben-Aharon, Yoram Ettinger, and Yigal Carmon, all of whom had been key government players during the Shamir years in the US. The team was an offshoot of a group set up by Netanyahu during the Shamir years to secretly raise funds from American Jews to help 'correct' Israel's image in the media.[68] While in opposition, they worked with groups sympathetic to the Likud in the United States as well as conservative Republican senators with whom they had established strong connections during their years in power. Although they were officially working without the sanction of Likud leader Benjamin Netanyahu, the Likud itself in the US actively criticized the Labour government. Ever since the Lebanon War, Likud had rejected the right of Labour and American Jews to criticize the Israeli government while in the United States. Now they were in opposition, the taboo was broken. Shamir criticized the Oslo Accords in a meeting with the Presidents Conference; Sharon declared that American Jews were welcome to criticize the Israeli government publicly; and other Likud figures toured US Jewish communities promoting the Likud line.[69]

However, the real shift was not so much the public criticism but the fact that former top Likud officials were openly lobbying against the Israeli government in Washington.[70] Following the Oslo Accords, Congress allowed the President to suspend the anti-PLO legislation and grant aid to the Palestinian Authority in return for periodic reports on

PLO compliance with its commitments in the DOP, in particular, to end terror. This agreement then formed the basis for the Middle East Peace Facilitation Act (MEPFA) which allowed this arrangement to continue for a year until June 1995. With the renewal of MEPFA due in June 1995, the opposition in America, in conjunction with the three Likud activists, undertook a serious campaign to stop the flow of American aid to the PA. They encouraged Congressional initiatives to set up separate Congressional committees to monitor PLO compliance. They hired a Washington public relations firm to discredit the PLO. Meanwhile, Netanyahu and Likud in Israel 'bombarded Congressmen's offices with faxes' attacking the Oslo Accords and the Palestinian Authority's record regarding implementation.[71] Likud MK Uzi Landau lobbied Congress against MEPFA and Senator Alfonse D'amato introduced a bill which sought to stop aid flowing to the PA altogether and instead give American aid for humanitarian causes.[72] Jesse Helms, apparently after talks with Ben-Aharon and the ZOA, introduced a bill which sought to tighten the terms of MEPFA by linking US aid to the PNC's cancellation of the Palestinian Covenant and the extradition of terrorists.[73] MEPFA did become law at the end of the 1996, but since then Helms has echoed Likud's doubts as to the PNC's actual revocation of the PLO Covenant, while Gilman's Committee has blocked $13 million in aid from reaching the PA.[74]

In response to the threat posed by Likud supporters in the US to Labour's coordinated policies with the administration over US troops on the Golan, American aid to the Palestinian Authority and Jerusalem, the Labour government recognized the importance of working with the Special Relationship and using *hasbara* in the Jewish community. Subsequently, Rabin spoke to congressmen personally to convince them that continued aid was an American and Israeli interest.[75] Meanwhile, Labour tried to curtail open opposition to the idea of US troops being stationed on the Golan in the event of an Israeli withdrawal.[76] However, on the whole there appeared to be a realization that the days when Israel could demand uncritical support from American Jewry were gone.[77] Instead the Israelis concentrated on trying to prevent criticism turning into alienation and political opposition. Consequently, the Labour party set up an American desk for the first time which arranged for English speakers to promote the Labour line in the Jewish community.[78] Israeli officials also began to seek a dialogue with Orthodox Jews in America.[79] Even Rabin, by now, recognized the political importance of diaspora Jewry and appointed an advisor for Diaspora Relations, a post he had pointedly left vacant since becoming Prime Minister. But it was only in the wake of the Rabin assassination that Peres made a serious effort to bridge the divide by appointing a dovish Orthodox rabbi, Yehuda Amital, to the Cabinet to help deal with the crisis.

CONCLUSIONS

Although Labour and Likud had opposite approaches to using the Special Relationship in the context of the peace process, both parties were guided by the same political calculation: the compatibility of their policy with that of the American administration. In addition, both parties made sense of their relationship with pro-Israel forces in the US and were influenced in that relationship, by the idea of *'Shlilat Hagalut'*. In the case of Likud, the concept helped explain why the pro-Israel lobby failed to defeat the President over loan guarantees and also helped map out a strategy to try and reverse that position. In the case of Labour, the idea helped explain why a 'Special Relationship' was apparently undesirable and hence led to its neglect. Indeed, it can be concluded that while the idea of the 'negation of the diaspora' encouraged Likud to overestimate the potential of the Special Relationship, it also led Labour to underestimate the importance of the Special Relationship.

One of the consequences of this was that while Likud actions were perceived by sections of American Jewry to have threatened the *Americanness* of their identity, Labour actions were perceived by sections of American Jewry as threatening to the *Jewishness* of their identity. It was the tension between communities, between Israel and the diaspora, focused around the idea of the 'negation of the diaspora' and over the meaning of 'Zionism' that was primarily behind American Jewish opposition to the Likud between 1989–92. In contrast, American Jewish opposition to the Labour government after 1992, manifest over the peace process, stemmed from a tension to be found across both communities, between those with, on the one hand, a more particularistic sense of Jewish identity, a strong perception of the Gentile world as basically antagonistic and a sense of Israel as something special, as opposed to those, on the other hand, with a more universalistic tendency within their Jewish identity, who do not believe that non-Jews are basically hostile and who tend to value the idea of Israel becoming a 'normal' country.[80]

This development may also herald another deeper change, a paradigm shift, in the terms of Israel's relationship with the American Jewish community and its other supporters in the US. In the past, on the American side, adherents of the Special Relationship were motivated to support Israel as a means of providing security for World Jewry after the Holocaust and as the symbol of American Jewish identity. However, for many among the younger generation of American Jews the Holocaust has ceased to provide a rationale for supporting Israel. The Jewish people no longer appear to be under existential threat, Israel is perceived as a normal country and if anything, it is the Palestinians who appear to be the underdogs.[81] Even the American Jewish leadership seems to be redirecting the focus of its attention away from Israel towards tackling very high rates of assimilation and 'Jewish continuity'. On the Israeli side, in the past, Israel did not value American Jewish culture and was primarily interested in American money and political support which was vital in a highly antagonistic international environment. Now, however, with the strengthening in Israel's international standing, its military and its economy, American civilian aid and Jewish charity is no longer felt to be as vital as it once was. Thus from both sides the old basis of the relationship seems to be deteriorating.

Some academics, notably David Vital, have argued for some time that a distancing between Israel and the diaspora is inevitable; extreme normalizationist and post-Zionist writers in Israel not only agree but see this as desirable.[82] However, before leaving office Shimon Peres and others began to address the problem by seeking to replace the survivalist NJP with a kind of Cultural Zionism akin to that proposed by Ahad Ha-am.[83] As Peres put it, 'Israel needs more *Yiddishkeit* (Judaism), the diaspora more Hebrew. Israel was an answer to Jewish tragedy and the Holocaust. Now it must attract people by choice... Israel must be a spiritual centre, where whatever is Jewish historically, universally and intellectually should be brought to Israel'.[84] Moreover, for the first time Israeli figures on the Right and the Left have spoken of the need for diaspora Jewry to invest in their own communities to ensure cultural survival and prevent complete assimilation.[85] To an extent, this concern is shrewd politics, with the end of the Cold War questioning the continued strategic rationale for a close relationship and with the memory of the Holocaust fading from mainstream American consciousness, the prevention of assimilation is the key to the maintenance of the Special Relationship as a political force at Israel's disposal in the long run.[86] But this shift in attitudes symbolizes more than just tactical awareness; it symbolizes a revolution. Previously Israeli political culture took the view that 'Israel was a value, the diaspora merely a fact', and that consequently, American Jewry was only of value if it made *Aliya* or helped Israel financially and politically. Now, in Israel there appears to be interest in a creative partnership with American Jewry in the interest of a meaningful Jewish continuity.

NOTES

1. G. Gruen, 'The Not So Silent Partnership: Emerging Trends in American Jewish–Israeli Relationships', in Gregory Mahler, ed., *Israel after Begin,* New York, 1990, p.209–32.
2. See L. Brandeis, 'The Jewish Problem and How to Solve It', in A. Herzberg, ed., *The Zionist Idea,* New York, 1984, p.520.
3. Y. Gorny, *The State of Israel in Jewish Public Thought,* London, 1994, p.109.
4. For details of this concept see C. Liebman and S. Cohen, *Two World of Judaism,* New Haven, 1990, pp.88–92. E. Don-Yehiya, 'Galut in Zionist Ideology and in Israeli Society', in E. Don-Yehiya, ed., *Religion and National Identity,* Contemporary Jewish Politics Vol.III, Ramat Gan, 1991.

5. M. Brecher, *The Foreign Policy System of Israel: Setting, Images, Process*, New Haven, 1972, p.232.
6. For details of the Pollard Affair when, Jonathan Pollard, an American Jew working for the US government was caught spying for Israel, see D. Schoenbaum, *The United States and the State of Israel*, Oxford, 1993, pp.314–19.
7. C. Shindler, *Swords into Ploughshares: Israelis and Jews in the Shadow of the Intifada*, London, 1991, pp.85–104; T. Friedman, *From Beirut To Jerusalem*, London, 1990, pp 451–91.
8. See the advice offered by leading AIPAC officials and the cable sent by Israeli Ambassador in Washington, Moshe Arad. In that cable Arad wrote to the Prime Minister: 'I implore you to reassess the grave repercussions which the law will have on relations between Israel and the United States *and as a direct consequence the ramifications on our own standing in the United States*', *Jerusalem Post*, 18 November 1988.
9. See Y. Harkabi, *Israel's Fateful Hour*, New York, 1988, pp.70–81.
10. Although the Conference was organized by Likudnik Ehud Olmert in conjunction with Labour hawk, Mota Gur, the Likud was the primary force behind the operation to end the PLO dialogue. In fact, Labour ministers in the National Unity government were prepared to listen to US reports of their conversations with the PLO in the hope that this might help advance the 1989 Israeli Peace Plan, whereas the Likud refused to listen to the reports.
11. *Washington Jewish Week*, 2 November 1989.
12. G. Frankel, *Beyond the Promised Land*, New York, 1994, pp.299–302.
13. Ibid., p.222. Thus in 1987 the American Jewish leadership rejected Shimon Peres's call to take Labour's side and support the London agreement even though a majority of the American Jewish public and leaders were closer to the Peres position. Shindler, *Israel, the Likud and the Zionist Dream*, London, 1993, p.231.
14. In November 1991 just before Shamir was set to address many Jewish audiences on a tour of America, an American Jewish Survey was deliberately brought out. It demonstrated that in contrast to Likud policy, 85% of the Jewish Community leadership opposed Shamir's policy of 'Not one inch' while over 77% favoured a settlement freeze and the eventual existence of a Palestinian state. See Y. Melman and D. Raviv, *Friends in Deed: Inside the U.S.–Israel Alliance*, New York, 1994, pp.432–33 and Frankel, *Beyond the Promised Land*, pp.222, 312.
15. *New York Times*, 21 February 1988; *Washington Jewish Week*, 16 March 1989, 10 October 1991; *Jerusalem Post*, 23 August 1990, 6 February 1992.
16. Cited in 'Israel', *Middle East Contemporary Survey 1989*, Tel-Aviv University, 1991, p.27.
17. Shindler, *Ploughshares into Swords*, p.142.
18. Ibid., p.245; Frankel, *Beyond*, p.226.
19. *Jerusalem Post*, 6 July 1990.
20. *American Jewish Yearbook 1992*, p.245.
21. Melman and Raviv, *Friends in Deed*, p.419. American Jewry, though split on the loan guarantees question, favoured silence on the settlements issue over a call for a settlement freeze and public opposition to the Shamir government. *American Jewish Yearbook 1993*, New York, p.239.
22. Frankel, *Beyond*, p.306; *Jerusalem Post*, 15 September 1991.
23. *Jerusalem Post*, 17 October 1991, 22 January 1992; Abraham Ben Zvi, *The United States and Israel*, New York, 1993, p.205.
24. *Jerusalem Post*, 13 September 1991.
25. Nimrod Novik, The *United States and Israel*, p.69.
26. Melman and Raviv, *Friends in Deed*, p.428.
27. *Jerusalem Report*, 10 October 1991.
28. Shindler, *Ploughshares into Swords*, p.143.
29. *Jerusalem Post*, 31 January 1992; Frankel, *Beyond*, p.306.
30. Gruen, 'Not So Silent Partnership', p.217.
31. Frankel, *Beyond*, p.225.
32. *Jerusalem Post*, 15 September 1991; Frankel, *Beyond*, p.229.
33. D. Horowitz, ed., *Yitzhak Rabin: Soldier for Peace*, London, 1996, p.157.
34. Melman and Raviv, *Friends in Deed*, p.344.
35. Horowitz, *Rabin*, p.157.
36. *New York Times*, 23 August 1992, p.2; *Ma'ariv*, 18 August 1992, p.3.
37. Horowitz, *Rabin*, p.159; *Jerusalem Post*, 22 October 1992, pp.2–3, 4 May 1993, p.1.

38. *Jewish Chronicle*, 18 November 1994, p.27.
39. Horowitz, *Rabin*, p.159.
40. *New York Times*, 1 February 1994, p.A3.
41. *NYT*, 20 February 1994, A39; Horowitz, *Rabin*, p.155.
42. *Jerusalem Post*, 21 March 1994, p.1.
43. *JP*, 7 April 1995, p.4.
44. Novik, *United States and Israel*, pp.71–4; *Jewish Chronicle*, 13 September 1996, p.8.
45. *Mideast Mirror*, 13 September 1995; *American Jewish Yearbook 1995*, p.157. Indeed, in 1996 a survey found that 51% of American Jews believed in Arafat's commitment to the peace process, and 63% supported a Palestinian state. *Jerusalem Report*, 3 October 1996, p.14.
46. Gruen, 'Not So Silent Partnership', p.238.
47. Novik, *The United States and Israel*, p.81; Gruen, 'Not So Silent Partnership', p.37–9; *Mideast Mirror*, 13 September 1995.
48. See J. Sacks, *Crisis & Covenant: Jewish Thought after the Holocaust*, Manchester, 1992, p.107; M. Beloff, 'The Diaspora and the Peace Process', in E. Karsh, ed., *Peace in the Middle East: The Challenge for Israel*, London, 1993, p.33.
49. T. Friedman, *From Beirut To Jerusalem*, London, 1990, p.454.
50. P. Medding, 'Segmented Ethnicity and the New Jewish Politics', in E. Mendelson, ed., *Jews and Other Ethnic Groups in a Multi-Ethnic Society*, New York, 1987, pp.38–9.
51. Gorny, *State of Israel*, pp.134–39.
52. See A. Rubinstein, *The Zionist Dream Revisited*, New York, 1984, pp.76–99; S. Sandler, *Land of Israel, State of Israel: Ethnonationalism in Israeli Foreign Policy*, Westport Connecticut, 1993.
53. C.S. Liebman and E. Don-Yehiya, *Civil Religion in Israel: Traditional Judaism and Political Culture in the Jewish State*, Berkeley, 1983; S. Sofer, *Begin: An Anatomy of Leadership*, New York, 1988, pp.103–13.
54. Gorny, *State of Israel*, p.139.
55. A. Klieman, 'New Directions in Israeli Foreign Policy', in Karsh, *Peace in the Middle East*, pp.96–117.
56. *Jerusalem Post*, 9 July 1993.
57. *JP*, 19 September 1995, p.9.
58. For polls confirming this trend see *Mideast Mirror*, 13 September 1995; *Jewish Chronicle*, 13 September 1995, p.8.
59. *Jewish Press*, 15 September 1995, p.14.
60. *Jewish Press*, 6 October 1993, p.16; *Los Angeles Times*, 9 September 1995; *Jerusalem Post*, 6 September 1995; *Jerusalem Report*, 19 October 1995, p.38; *Washington Post*, 14 June 1995, p.A32.
61. *Ma'ariv*, 11 September 1995, p.7.
62. *Yediot Aharonot*, 11 September 1995, p.1.
63. 'Din Rodef'– (The Law of the Pursuer) was the Halacha (Orthodox Jewish Law) which Yigal Amir (Rabin's assassin) cited as justification for his act. *Jerusalem Post*, 17 November 1995, p.11.
64. On Helms's 'conversion' to the pro-Israel cause see *Washington Post*, 8 March 1985. Helms's foreign policy advisor Dani Plekta, a fluent Hebrew speaker, is sympathetic to Netanyahu's position. *Jerusalem Report*, 26 June 1995, pp.36–7.
65. *Jerusalem Report*, 15 December 1994, pp.32–5. Although sympathetic to the Likud agenda, these Republicans were generally much less vociferous in their opposition to Labour's plans than Jewish groups.
66. Melman and Raviv, *Friends in Deed*, pp.349–61.
67. *American Jewish Yearbook, 1995*, p.15.
68. *Jerusalem Post*, 13 July 1995, p.4,
69. *JP*, 31 January 1994, p.7, 3 November 1995, p.4.
70. There had been previous suggestions by various Labour figures in the past asking American Jewry to support their peace policy, but not on anywhere near the same scale or in such an organized manner. See for example, Shindler, *Israel*, p.231.
71. Yigal Carmon and other figures sympathetic to the Likud in America supplied the American media with evidence of a 'speech in which Arafat had called for a Holy War, "Jihad"', and Gilman held Congressional committee hearings in which the PA's record on compliance was severely criticized. *Washington Post*, 10 July 1995; *Jerusalem Report*, 13

July 1995, p.4, 27 July 1995, p.11–12; *Jerusalem Post,* 22 July 1996; *Washington Jewish Week,* 24 August 1995.

72. *Jerusalem Report,* 27 July 1995, pp.11–12.
73. *Jerusalem Post,* 18 November 1994, p.3, 19 September 1995, p.2, 6 October 1995, p.10,
74. *Washington Post,* 1 November 1995; *Associated Press,* 12 March 1996, p.l; *Reuters,* 9 May 1996.
75. Rabin came to see the political utility of using limited Congress pressure as a lever to pressure the PLO to cooperate with Israel. Thus when MEPFA came up for renewal he backed Helms' amendment to link US aid to the PA to amending the Palestinian Covenant within six months of Palestinian elections, as stipulated in Oslo II. *Jerusalem Report,* 26 May 1995, p.36–7; *Ha-aretz,* 13 September 1995, p.4; *Jerusalem Post,* 6 October 1995, p.10.
76. *Jerusalem Report,* 24 August 1995, pp.32–3.
77. See the speech of Director General of the Foreign Ministry Uri Savir to the Presidents Conference about Oslo II. For the opposing view see speech of Labour Minister of Health Ephraim Sneh, *American Jewish Yearbook, 1995,* p.153.
78. The Foreign Ministry switched its strategy away from the mainstream American media and the promotion of the universalist vision of 'New Middle East', and instead sent generals and politicians to talk about how the Peace Process enhanced Israeli security in synagogues through the US during the High Holidays. *Jerusalem Post,* 11 January 1994, p.7, 4 September 1994, p.4, 14 February 1995, p.6; *Ha-aretz,* 11 September 1995, p.2.
79. *Washington Jewish Week,* 27 July 1995, p.27; *Yediot Aharonot,* 11 September 1995, p.1.
80. For evidence of the correlation between these orientations and attitudes towards the peace process in Israel see A. Arian, *Security Threatened: Surveying Israeli Opinion on Peace and War,* Cambridge, 1995, pp.161–86.
81. Gruen, *Not So Silent Partnership,* p.39. Contributions to the United Jewish Appeal following the Oslo Accords were half the 1990 figure when Israel had been under threat during the Gulf War. *Jerusalem Post,* 8 October 1993, p.7.
82. D. Vital, *The Future of the Jews: A People at the Crossroads?,* Cambridge, Mass., 1990.
83. *Jerusalem Post,* 13 November 1992, p.6, 9 November 1993, p.6. In this vein, A.B. Yehoshua suggested that World Jewry and Israel should form an Education Corps to act in the Third World. *Yediot Aharonot,* 29 January 1996.
84. *Jerusalem Post,* 9 April 1996, p.7.
85. *Jerusalem Report,* 8 August 1996, p.25.
86. A recent Jaffe Center Report asserted that with the end of the Cold War and the demise of the strategic rational for the Special Relationship, AIPAC and American Jewry were bound to become even more important in sustaining Congressional aid to Israel and thereby guaranteeing Israel's qualitative edge. Cited in *Jerusalem Post,* 4 January 1993.

ISRAEL AND ITS NEIGHBOURS

Arab Responses to
Yitzhak Rabin's Assassination

GIL FEILER

The election of the right-wing Benjamin Netanyahu as Israel's prime minister in May 1996 unleashed a spate of venomous personal attacks by the mass media throughout the Arab world, reminiscent of the darkest moments of the Arab–Israeli conflict. Interestingly enough, it was in Egypt, which spearheaded the Arab drive towards peace with the Jewish State some two decades ago, where Netanyahu was given the toughest ride, with vilification ranging from a madman to a warmonger to a new Hitler.

But if these fresh attacks can be attributed to fears of Netanyahu's reneging on the Oslo Accords, Arab responses to the assassination of Prime Minister Yitzhak Rabin in November 1995, on the altar of peace, were somewhat more puzzling. Broadly speaking, the Arab world displayed a wide range of reactions to the assassination, with emotions ranging from sympathy for Israel and hope for the continuation of the peace process on the part of Jordan and the Palestinian Authority, to declarations of satisfaction with the assassination and displays of pleasure among various Islamic elements in the refugee camps of Lebanon. Moreover, even in those countries which officially expressed sorrow for the murder it was possible to identify contrary feelings, primarily among political movements and organizations opposed to the peace process.

Based on Arab sources, primarily press editorials and commentaries in the electronic media, this essay will examine three levels of Arab reaction to the Rabin assassination: the official response, sentiments among opposition organizations, and popular reaction. The focus is on three aspects of Arab media coverage:

• Treatment of Yitzhak Rabin, the man;

• Discussion of the nature of Israeli society as a society which allowed the assassination to take place;

• Treatment of the possible impact of the assassination on the peace process.

Gil Feiler is Senior Lecturer in Political Studies at Bar-Ilan University and Executive Director of Info-Prod Research (Middle East) Ltd.

The dynamics of the reactions will be considered from the date of the murder over the following two months.

RABIN'S PERSONALITY

Yitzhak Rabin was portrayed during this period on the one hand as a hero of the peace process who paid for his beliefs with his life, and, on the other, as a 'terrorist', whose name was linked to some of the cruelest acts of violence perpetrated by Israel against the Arab people. This dual profile circulated, with variations in colour, throughout the Arab world, and against that background the official silence of Syria and Lebanon was prominent. The latter countries satisfied themselves with publishing factual accounts of the assassination without referring at all to Rabin, the man. A senior Syrian official even justified this approach by stating that Syria believed that peace was important to all the peoples of the area and should not be linked to specific individuals.[1]

The most enthusiastic official treatment of Rabin as a man and hero for peace came from Jordan. King Hussein, in his funeral eulogy of Rabin, referred to him in the same breath as his grandfather Emir Abdallah, who too had fallen in the attempt to bring the Arab–Jewish conflict to an end.[2] Egyptian President Husni Mubarak, in a press conference given before he left for the funeral, described Rabin as one of the architects of peace and compared him to the late Anwar Sadat.[3] The Chairman of the Palestinian Authority, Yasser Arafat, in an official announcement published after the murder, also expressed sorrow at the loss of a partner in the peace process.[4] The Foreign Minister of Turkey, in an announcement condemning and expressing regret over the murder, described Rabin as one of the bravest and most honest statesmen in the region, whose efforts on behalf of peace would always be honoured.[5] Some of the Gulf States, such as Oman and Qatar, reacted to the assassination with condemnations and expressions of sorrow and hope for the continuation and stabilization of the peace process.[6] Tunisia acted in a similar fashion.[7]

These official responses did not expressly consider the personality of Rabin, but their expressions of regret and the context in which they supported the continuation of the peace process reflected their positive perception of Rabin as someone who had worked for the advancement of peace.

Certain countries such as Iran and Libya, and elements opposed to the peace process in other countries, rejected this approach. In their view, Rabin was not a 'victim of peace', but a 'terrorist' who had committed a long line of crimes against the Palestinian and Arab peoples, and for whose death there was therefore no need to grieve.[8] The charges most often made against him were that he had led the policy of 'breaking the bones' of Palestinian children during the *intifada*, and that he had authorized the murder of Fathi Shkaki, leader of the Islamic Jihad, who was assassinated in Malta on 26 October 1995.[9] A number of news reports even stated that Rabin's assassination was a heavenly punishment for Shkaki's death.[10] Official spokesmen referred to additional 'crimes'. Thus, for example, the Islamic Action Front (Lebanon) charged Rabin with leading Israel's occupation drive in 1967; incarcerating Sheikh Ahmad Yassin, the spiritual leader of the HAMAS, in 1989; and being responsible for the deportation of about 400 HAMAS and Islamic Jihad activists to Lebanon in December 1992.[11] The Chairman of the Iranian Parliament even referred to Rabin's responsibility for the aborted assassination attempt on the Iranian consul in Argentina in October 1995.[12] Interestingly, officials of the Palestinian Authority, who were the alleged victims of the 'break their bones' policy, did not display the same desire to engage in historical recriminations with Rabin but preferred to emphasize his more recent contributions to peace.

It should be noted that the distribution referred to above between states which portrayed Rabin in a favourable light as a man of peace, who died at his post (Jordan, Egypt, the Palestinian Authority, Oman, Qatar and Tunisia) and states which reviled his memory as a criminal and terrorist (Libya and Iran) is accurate on the official level. However, an analysis of press reactions, in so far as they reflect opposition views and the views of the general public, reveals a more complex picture. On the whole, Islamic opposition elements throughout the Arab world expressed views which were close to those adopted in Libya and Iran, whereas among the general public in the different countries, the entire spectrum of views could be found, not simply acceptance of the official government line.

Thus, for example, certain Islamic elements in Jordan harshly criticized the eulogy delivered by King Hussein at Rabin's funeral. One Islamic leader, Layth Shabilat, was even arrested and accused of treason as a result of his criticism. Similarly, King Hussein attacked the press over a number of articles published in Jordanian weeklies, particularly in the Islamic weekly *al-Sabil*, where one headline read: 'One Less from the Stock of Murderers' and claimed that 'the Jordanians learned of the murder of Rabin with joy and the gift of sweets'. The weekly also gave prominent coverage to displays of joy among the Palestinian public.[13]

Other weeklies also exhibited happiness at Rabin's death and declared that historical justice had been done, though in many cases these articles were balanced by more moderate reports in other sections of the same newspaper. Thus, for example, the weekly *al-Ahali* published a column entitled 'Our mothers have wept much, now it is the turn of Leah Rabin, who should weep, clothe herself in black and learn the meaning of black',[14] whereas the main headline of the weekly *Sawt al-Mar'a*, proclaimed, inter alia, that 'the three bullets were... the first nail in the coffin of the Zionist entity'.[15] A good example of the ambivalent attitude to the event, seen among the Jordanian public, was provided by Jordanian parents who wished to name their new-born son after Yitzhak Rabin. While this desire was in line with the spirit of official sorrow in the country, the father was forced to fight in the Jordanian courts to enforce his right to call his son by this name and was even fired from his farming job as a result of this incident.[16] The Israeli Embassy in Jordan received numerous commiserating telephone calls and faxes from politicians and businessmen, but at the same time many among the lower economic classes – discussing the murder in cafes and in the street – felt no sorrow over Rabin's death. Surveys conducted by foreign news agencies revealed that in Egypt, Iran and the Palestinian Authority, the reaction of the general public was on the whole ambivalent. A survey conducted by the Iranian newspaper *Akhbar* showed that about 64 per cent of Iranians were pleased at Rabin's murder, although a higher percentage might have been expected in view of the official position taken in Iran.[17]

The two conflicting perceptions of Rabin's character could also be seen in the press of Kuwait and the United Arab Emirates. These countries did not issue individual official announcements but rather participated in a joint communiqué, issued by the foreign ministers of the Gulf Cooperation Council, condemning the assassination and hoping for the continuation of the peace process. Nevertheless, the UAE newspaper *al-Ittihad* published a caricature on 6 November 1995, two days after the murder, showing Rabin arriving at the portals of hell and telling the guardians of that place that 'I have come to you from Jerusalem the eternal capital of Israel'. Apart from the depiction of Rabin as someone suited to go to hell, the statement attributed to him seems to indicate that the 'eternal' capital of Israel is to share his fate. In Kuwait, *al-Siyasa* published an editorial on 7 November 1995, comparing Rabin to Sadat and describing the former as an important man of vision, though at the same time the newspaper published an article by one of its journalists justifying the murder as divine punishment for the attack on Fathi Shkaki.

In addition to blackening the name of Rabin by means of listing his 'crimes', Rabin was also accused of bringing about the circumstances leading to his own death. This responsibility for his own fate was supposed to be the result of his contribution to the strengthening of the Israeli settlers and extremists opposing the peace process. Rabin, it was alleged, fostered the settlers during the period of the *intifada* with the aim of creating a counterweight to the Palestinian uprising and was overly indulgent towards their opposition to the peace process; actions which ultimately backfired on him. This claim was made, inter alia, in articles in the prominent Egyptian newspaper *al-Ahram* and the Yemenite newspaper *al-Thawra*,[18] as well as in caricatures in various other newspapers. The Egyptian newspaper *Roz al-Yusuf* published a caricature portraying Rabin with a branch from 'the tree of terror' spearing his heart, and a watering can which he had previously used to water the tree, fallen at his feet. Another caricature, expressing the same sentiment, showed Rabin offering a fish to a crocodile representing violence, before being devoured by the same crocodile.

Interestingly enough, even among those reviling the memory of Yitzhak Rabin it was possible to distinguish an element of admiration for his character and for his standing with the Israeli public. The HAMAS spokesman in Jordan, Ibrahim Ghosha, described him as a strong man of principles and said that no Israeli leader could replace him,[19] whereas Ahmad Jibril, leader of the Popular Front for the Liberation of Palestine, described him as the cleverest statesman and therefore most dangerous to the Arabs.[20] Particular respect for Rabin, compared to other potential Israeli leaders, was also expressed in the Jordanian and Egyptian press. Al-Ahram portrayed him as the only man in the Labour Party who could have persuaded Israeli public opinion to accept the peace agreements,[21] whereas the Jordan Times stated that 'Israel had never had a leader like Mr. Rabin and it was not likely that it would ever have a leader like him in the future'.[22] One may assume that the prominent military component in Rabin's biography contributed to the admiration felt for him in the Arab world.

ISRAEL AS A SOCIETY WHICH ENABLED THE ASSASSINATION

The assassination afforded an opportunity to numerous Arab elements to criticize Israeli society and expose its (alleged) weaknesses to the rest of the world. Many argued that the murder should not be seen as an isolated incident, but rather as an action representative of the violent ethos underlying Israeli society. According to this view, Rabin himself fostered this ethos through his 'break their bones' policy for subduing the intifada: for years the Arabs and Palestinians were victims of Israeli violence and now the world as a whole had the opportunity to recognize this fact.

This approach was reflected in numerous sources, both in moderate countries and in countries advocating an extremist line. The differences in treatment of this aspect of the murder lay in the tone of the argument, namely, the extent to which it took on the form of slogans or propaganda or alternatively amounted to substantive criticism, as well as the extent to which the speaker was willing to discriminate when pointing the finger of blame at those he alleged were responsible for the murder.

Senior Iranian spokesmen of organizations opposed to the peace process adopted a propaganda-oriented approach and laid the blame on the 'Zionists' or Israeli people as a whole. The Speaker of the Iranian Parliament, Ali Akbar Nateq Nuri, stated that 'the Zionists had to learn that by using their terrorist methods they were exposing themselves to

comparable actions which could also happen to them'.[23] Likewise, a
senior Hizbullah activist in the Buqa area of Lebanon said that 'what
happened proves that the Israeli right and left are two sides of the same
coin. They are all murderers, criminals, and exploiters of terror and the
holy places'. He also pointed out that the Israelis had committed
multiple acts of slaughter against the Lebanese people.[24] A coarse and
anti-Semitic tone was also evident in the caricature published in the
newspaper al-Watan al-Arabi (Paris), portraying a diaspora Jew with a
long nose watering 'the flowers of extremism' sprouting from the head
of a small boy, who was stabbing him in the back.

The Egyptian government newspaper al-Ahram claimed that the
murder was the result of the 'religion of violence' worshipped in Israel
and that it represented the violent culture on which Israeli society is
based, and which Rabin symbolized.[25] Here too, the finger of blame was
pointed in an indiscriminate manner, but the fact that the allegation was
sociological in nature softened it somewhat compared to the comments
made by Iranian and Lebanese spokesmen, quoted above. The Egyptian
newspaper al-Wafd, too, wrote that the background to the murder was
the policy of violence followed by Israel, which encouraged the growth
of extremism.[26] The violent image of Israel in the eyes of the Egyptians
and the strengthening of this perception following the assassination
could also be seen in the caricatures of the time. One caricature
published in the Egyptian newspaper Roz al-Yusuf on 1 June 1996
showed an Israeli soldier, above whom appeared the word 'terrorist',
pointing his rifle towards a Lebanese citizen dressed in traditional Arab
garb, and defending himself with a saw. Below the drawing, the caption
read: 'Israeli violence still continues in southern Lebanon'. A second
caricature published in the same issue portrayed Rabin as the victim of
the violence which he himself had nurtured. The proximity of these
drawings hints that violence is deeply rooted in Israeli society but wears
a different garb internally and externally.

An exception to the approach governing the Egyptian press may be
seen in an article published about two months after the murder in the
Cairo journal al-Siyasa al-Duwaliyya. This article presented the murder
as an exceptional event in Israeli society and political culture, which
from its establishment had succeeded in preserving internal solidarity
and refraining from acts of violence within the country. The principal
significance attributed to the murder was actually the revelation of the
extent of opposition to the peace process among the Israeli public.[27]

Interestingly, this aspect of the assassination did not attract much
debate in the period immediately following its occurrence. The shift in
focus was apparently influenced by the period of time which elapsed
between the incident and the reaction to it, with the claims relating to
the exposure of the violent Israeli ethos almost being in the nature of an
emotional 'gut-reaction', which hardened in the course of time.

The *Jordan Times* also combined a measure of finger-pointing towards the extremist camp in Israel on the one hand and a more inclusive tone inspired by propaganda goals on the other. An editorial on 5 November 1995 stated that the murder was a reminder to the Arabs that Jewish terrorism which had been directed against Arabs for generations was still alive, and that care had to be taken against other signs of fanaticism on the part of those who believed in the notions of the 'promised land' and the 'chosen people'. A similar combination of views was expressed in an editorial published in the Jordanian newspaper *al-Ra'i* on 6 November 1995. It referred to the extremist elements in Israel as responsible for the murder – drawing attention to the fact that the assassination was committed during a peace rally in which 100,000 people had participated – and thereby indicating that the Israeli people as a whole should not be blamed; however, the article also characterized Israeli society as a society founded on hate and depravity and called for a re-examination of the educational system in Israel, which the article claimed was proved to have failed.

In this context, the comments of Palestinian speakers revealed a deeper understanding of Israeli realities. Saeb Arekat, Minister for Local Affairs in the Palestinian Authority, and Freih Abu Madin, Minister of Justice in the Palestinian Authority, laid the blame for the murder on Israeli settlers and extremists. Freih Abu Madin also pointed out that the directional shift of Israeli violence inward was the result of a society corrupted by occupation and founded on the exploitation of another people. These statements were similar to those published in the Egyptian press, though the tone was dominated less by stereotypes and bore a greater resemblance to internal criticism made by the Israeli left.[28]

Apart from the generalized claims regarding the violence characterizing Israeli society, speakers in various countries emphasized the use of this violence against the Arab people, in an effort to draw world attention to their plight. Thus, for example, Freih Abu Madin argued that the assassination should be seen within the context of the massacre at the Cave of the Patriarchs in Hebron and the killing of a Palestinian boy on 3 November 1995,[29] whereas the Lebanese Foreign Minister, Fares Buwayz, called for the world to focus on the daily violence wreaked by Israel in south Lebanon.[30] Cairo Radio, in a broadcast on 9 November 1995, tried to use the murder to support Egypt's demand for Israel's nuclear disarmament, arguing that the assassination proved that there are extremist elements in Israel, who presumably would not hesitate to use nuclear weapons if they ever got into government.[31]

Another element which could be discerned in Arab reactions to the murder, though one which was expressed less openly, was the call to rectify the unjust manner in which the world perceived Israel and the Jews compared to the perception of the Arab states and the Muslims. According to this view, the assassination exploded the myth glorifying Israel as 'the only democracy in the Middle East'. Political assassinations, known in the Arab states of the Middle East, could also occur in Israel.[32] The attempt by Israel to present itself as a tranquil and stable state was proven to be a mirage.[33] Moreover, the murder proved that terror and extremism were not the sole province of the Muslims. The Jews too were trying to torpedo the peace process.[34] A senior Hizbullah official complained that the world would not speak of 'Zionist terror' following the murder, but if the act had been committed by a Muslim the media would have been full of references to 'Islamic terror'.[35] A fundamentalist member of the Kuwaiti parliament, Khaled Adwa, said that the assassination proved that Jewish terror was the primary threat to peace in the Middle East.[36] The Egyptian newspaper al-Ahram wrote 'the Arabs feel a sense of relief that he was not killed by an Arab...',[37] a feeling also expressed among the Iranian public.[38] The sense of relief apparently arose out of the belief that the Jews were touched with the same evil spirit which was generally identified with the Arabs and Islam.

THE EXPECTED IMPACT OF THE ASSASSINATION ON THE PEACE PROCESS

The assassination intensified the dichotomy between the 'peace' and 'anti-peace' camps in the Arab world, as it provided an opportunity for many countries to express their support for the process, by issuing official proclamations or by sending representatives to attend Rabin's funeral. The countries opposed to the peace process, Iran and Libya, criticized the shift of the Arab world towards the West, as reflected by reactions to the murder, and attempted to establish an alternative dichotomy – the Arab and Islamic world against the West and Zionism. The assessments regarding the impact of the assassination on the continuation of the peace process were not uniform – some were of the opinion that the process would slow down, while others believed that it would in fact gain impetus.

In reacting to the assassination, many countries in the region gave public expression to their commitment to the peace process. Jordan, Egypt, the Palestinian Authority, Oman, Qatar and Tunisia published statements condemning the murder and expressing support for the peace process and hope for its continuation. A similar statement was issued by the Foreign Ministers of the Gulf Cooperation Council. Saudi Arabia and the United Arab Emirates did not publish official statements apart from the joint communiqué, although senior officials in both countries expressed similar sentiments to journalists working for Reuters.

Syria did not react to the murder officially, and the press reported it without commentary. Nevertheless, it called on Israel to spur the peace process while repeating its traditional demands.[39] Syrian Foreign Minister, Faruk al-Shara, said in a joint press conference with Britain's Foreign Minister, who was visiting Damascus on 8 November 1995, that Syria was committed to the peace process despite the murder and urged Israel's newly-appointed Prime Minister, Shimon Peres, to effect a breakthrough in negotiations.[40] Apparently, Syria decided to deliberately refrain from showing sympathy and too great an interest in events in Israel, but at the same time was cautious not to identify itself with the 'anti-peace' camp which was celebrating the murder. Lebanon, too, did not publish an official statement, but government ministers freely expressed their condemnations of Israel and its violent actions in South Lebanon.[41]

Contributing to the sharpening of the dichotomy between supporters of peace and its opponents was the publication of condemnations of the assassination by many of the countries referred to above, and the participation in Rabin's funeral by representatives of six Muslim countries: Jordan, Egypt, Morocco, Oman, Qatar, Mauritania and the Palestinian Authority, alongside leaders of the Western world. The existence of this dichotomy was emphasized in the speeches of Arab leaders. Hussein in his eulogy at the funeral gave it the clearest expression and called for the strengthening of the peace camp.[42] In a telephone conversation with US President Bill Clinton, following the murder, Egyptian President Mubarak declared his commitment to advancing the peace process and removing opportunities for opponents of the peace to torpedo it; he ensured that the contents of this conversation were brought to the attention of the Egyptian public.[43]

Contrary to these public expressions of support for the peace process, rejectionist states such as Iran and Libya did not publicly advertise their position following the assassination. One reason for this approach may have been that their opposition was in any event well-known, another that by deliberately ignoring the issue they emphasized their rejectionist stance. Thus, for example, a Radio Tehran report on the causes of the assassination noted that it took place during a 'gathering of Zionists' in Tel-Aviv, without referring to the fact that it was a rally in support of peace.[44] The reactions of these states focused on the personality of Rabin himself, as noted earlier.

At the same time, the Iranian media criticized the hypocrisy of the West in mourning Rabin, who was a criminal and not a 'victim of peace', while at the same time ignoring the heinous crimes committed against Muslims – the murder of Fathi Shkaki and the killing of Muslims in Bosnia.[45] This criticism was directed against the West, but was obviously also applicable to the Arab states which followed the same approach. It was most vociferously and explicitly voiced by Libya, which was the only Arab state to publish a statement declaring official gratification at the assassination. An editorial in the Libyan newspaper *al-Zahf al-Akhdar* concluded with the words: 'thank you Rabin, you have exposed them' – 'them' being the Arab leaders who, by participating in the funeral and showing grief over Rabin's death, had exposed their betrayal of the Arab nation and their willingness to humiliate themselves before and attempt to appease the Zionist entity.[46] In the view of these countries, the opposing camps are not 'supporters of peace' facing the 'enemies of peace', but Islam and Arabism facing the West and Zionism.

An apologetic editorial published in *al-Ahram* on 8 November 1995, responding to the spirit of the criticism at the excessive proximity of the Arabs to Israel and the West following the assassination, attempted to calm the Egyptian public and explain that Mubarak's participation at the funeral was essential to demonstrate solidarity with the peace camp in Israel at the time, but that the factors which had prevented him from visiting Israel in the past continued to prevail and Egypt was persevering with its demands for regional peace.[47]

Apart from asserting its position of principle towards the peace process, some concern was displayed at the possible practical repercussions of the murder for the continuation of the peace process. In the days following the murder this issue was not widely discussed, partly because of the need to 'digest' this unexpected incident and partly because not all the Arab speakers who reacted to the murder were in fact well-acquainted with the internal political scene in Israel.

One view expressed at this time was that the peace process would slow or stop altogether in the absence of Rabin, whose personality had been an important factor in its progress. On occasion, an express comparison was made in this context between Yitzhak Rabin and Shimon Peres, with the latter being described by most of the sources as less qualified to carry out the tasks needed to spur on the peace process. The Egyptian newspaper *al-Ahram* expressed fear that the peace process would be stopped because of the special place which Rabin had occupied in Israeli society, and which had enabled him to persuade Israeli public opinion to support the peace process.[48] The Lebanese Minister of Culture, Michel Idich, said that Rabin had succeeded in this task thanks to being both a 'dove' and a 'hawk', whereas Peres was solely a 'dove' and therefore less likely to succeed.[49] The HAMAS spokesman in Jordan, Ibrahim Ghosha, said that no leader in Israel could replace Rabin and that Peres was not as strong and determined as him.[50] Various persons pointed out that the murder had exposed the strength of the opposition to peace among the Israeli public.[51] Whereas the Egyptian newspaper *al-Sha'b* inferred from this that there would be difficulties in continuing the process,[52] Islamic members of parliament in Kuwait took the cynical view that in any event the peace was not driven by the people, but by the superpowers, and would therefore continue one way or another.[53] The possibility that the divisions inside Israel could spill over to violence and lead to the stopping of the peace process was also the subject of a caricature published in the newspaper *al-Sharq al-Awsat* on 12 December 1995, displaying the dove of peace hiding from gunfire directed from each side of the candelabra representing Israel. The symmetrical structure of the candelabra emphasizes the feeling that the real war is between the left and right in Israel.

In contrast, there were also assessments that the murder would actually spur the peace process. Some thought that Peres was in fact more likely to promote peace than Rabin; thus, for example, the Hizbullah spokesman in Beirut was of the opinion that the more dovish approach of Peres towards the process would impel it forward,[54] and the editor of the Egyptian weekly *al-Musawwar*, Makram Muhammad Ahmad, wrote that Peres conducted good negotiations and dialogue with the Palestinians, contrary to Rabin who had fought long and hard with himself before he could bring himself to agree to negotiate with Arafat. Similarly, a number of sources took the view that the weakening of the opposition in Israel following the murder would make it easier for the government of Israel to push forward the peace process.[55] On 7 November 1995, the East Jerusalem newspaper *al-Nahar* published an editorial brimming with optimism, to the effect that the murder had struck the Israeli right the hardest blow in its history and would result in the entire Israeli people coming together in support of Rabin's vision, as had occurred in the US following the murder of Kennedy.[56] More cautious optimism was expressed in an article published in the journal *al-Siyasa al-Duwaliyya* in January 1996. The writer noted the strengthening of the peace camp in Israel and the deep commitment of the Peres government to the peace process, but at the same time voiced fear that the position of supremacy which Israel was trying to assert in the negotiations with the Palestinians could lead to their failure.[57]

CONCLUSION

This essay has examined three different aspects of the Arab world's reaction to the assassination of Israel's Prime Minister Yitzhak Rabin. The conclusions which may be drawn from the above discussion are as follows:

• With regard to references to his personality – two opposing attitudes can be discerned. Countries supporting the peace process – Egypt, Jordan, the Palestinian Authority, the Gulf states, Morocco and Tunisia, officially expressed sorrow at his death and portrayed him as one of the pillars of the peace process, who paid for his convictions with his life. In contrast, states opposed to the process – Iran and Libya – as well as opposition movements in a variety of countries (some of which supportive of peace), portrayed him as a 'terrorist' and emphasized his responsibility for a range of 'crimes' against the Arab people, with the list headed by the 'break their bones' policy during the *intifada* and the order given to assassinate the leader of the Islamic Jihad, Fathi Shkaki.

Both the favourable and condemnatory approaches emphasized Rabin's biographical details and personality. The references were not only to 'the Prime Minister of Israel' who was murdered, but to Rabin – the man, his relations with various leaders, milestones in his life in so far as they were connected with the Arab world, and the unique role he filled in the peace process. Against this backdrop, the approach taken by Syria and Lebanon to refrain from any comment about Rabin the man, stood out and created the impression of estrangement and withdrawal linked to these countries' desire to preserve their unique status in terms of their attitude to the peace process – favouring neither the pro-peace nor anti-peace parties.

- The attitude to the future of the peace process following the assassination reflects the traditional distinction between the states supporting the process and the countries and elements opposing it. Egypt, Jordan, the Palestinian Authority, the Gulf states, and Tunisia expressed their support for the process following the murder, and six Muslim states, including Morocco, participated in Rabin's funeral. These steps sharpened the dichotomy between 'the peace camp' and 'the enemies of peace'. The main states opposing the peace – Iran and Libya – did not emphasize this opposition but focused on Rabin the man. At the same time their portrayal of the mourning displayed by Arab leaders as hypocritical and a form of appeasement of the West and the Zionist entity, seemed to be an attempt to revive the old dichotomy of Islam and Arabism against the West and Zionism. Syria again took a halfway approach by reiterating its traditional demands of Israel and calling for new impetus to be given the peace process, however, its formulations were substantive and tempered the link with Rabin's murder.

- There was no widespread discussion regarding preparations for the continuation of the peace process following the murder, perhaps because of the need to assimilate the fact of the assassination. Some evaluations talked of a slowdown of the peace process while others talked of it being given new impetus. Many of the former assessments relied on the relative importance and unique contribution of Rabin to the process, against the background of his personality and unique standing with the Israeli public.

- Contrary to the range of opinions concerning Rabin the man and the peace process, there was greater uniformity in reactions to Israeli society as nurturing the murderer. Such differences as existed were more in the tone of the charge than in its content. Editorials of various newspapers, including the official Egyptian *al-Ahram* and the *Jordan Times*, as well as statements published by the leaders of extremist groups and countries, declared that the murder had exposed the violent ethos on which Israeli society was founded, an ethos which until then had been reflected by acts directed against the Palestinians and Arab peoples. The murder thus reflected the boomerang effect of this ethos and exposed the real face of Israel to the world. It shattered the image of Israel as 'the only democracy in the Middle East' and undermined the myth of 'Islamic terror' torpedoing the peace process.

- It should be added that the range of views considered above on the national level, could also be seen within the general public in each country, and there was no complete identity between the official state reaction and popular feeling. A survey of Reuters reports reveals that in Egypt, Jordan, and the territories of the Palestinian Authority, where the leaders had expressed support for the peace process and Rabin, the reactions in the street were mixed and echoes could be heard of the extremist descriptions of Rabin as a 'terrorist' whose death was not a reason for regret. In contrast, a survey conducted by the Iranian newspaper *Akhbar* found that 64 per cent of Iranians were pleased at the murder, whereas the spirit of the official reaction would have led an observer to expect more widespread support for the murder.

- In some cases, the reactions of the opposition and public opinion in particular countries led to changes in the official reaction of the states in the period between the initial reaction and the later more considered pronouncements. In Jordan, where Islamic elements sharply criticized the warmth which King Hussein had demonstrated at the funeral, a tough line was taken against these critics and the state continued to pursue its original approach. In Egypt, however, the government newspaper *al-Ahram* cooled down the favourable tone taken towards Israel, as a reaction to the dissatisfaction felt among part of the Egyptian public after watching the well-attended Rabin funeral. Syria did not alter in any significant way the detached approach it had adopted from the outset, though it seems that the generally favourable world reaction, in the immediate aftermath of the murder, inspired it to place the emphasis on calling upon Israel to force a breakthrough in the peace negotiations.

An initial review of the Arab reaction to the Rabin assassination reveals therefore a varied and complex picture; future studies, focusing on reactions within a single Arab country, could undoubtedly shed light on additional aspects of this unique event.

NOTES

1. Issam Hamza, 'Syria Says Rabin Murder Will Not Change Peace Drive', *Reuters* (Damascus), 6 November 1995. This attitude was also reflected in Syria's reaction to the results of the elections held in Israel on 29 May 1996, when it was stated on Radio Damascus (31 May) that 'Syria does not gamble on a particular party and does not link its position regarding the peace to any particular person. Accordingly, the elections in Israel do not interest Syria'.
2. See the text of the eulogy in *Ma'ariv*, 7 November 1995.
3. Middle East News Agency (MENA, Cairo), in: Foreign Broadcasts Information Service (FBIS), Daily Report: Near East and South Asia, Supplement: Assassination of Israeli Prime Minister Yitzhaq Rabin, 6 November 1995, p.33 (hereinafter DR).
4. *Australian Review*, 17 November 1996.
5. *Turkey Today*, 4 November 1995.
6. WAKH, 5 November 1995, in: DR, 6 November 1995, pp.54–5.
7. *Ha-aretz*, 8 November 1995.
8. See the spokesman for the central command of Fatah's Central Committee, *Radio al-Quds*, 5 November 1995, in DR, 6 November 1995, p.46; *Jamahiriyya Arab News Agency* (JANA, Tripoli), 5 November 1995, in DR, 6 November 1995, p.55; JANA, 7 November 1995 (Reuters, 8 November 1995); editorial in the Libyan newspaper *al-Zahf al-Akhdar* of 10 November 1995; the Christian right-wing Lebanese newspaper *Nida al-Watan*, 6 November 1995.
9. Islamic Revolution News Agency (IRNA, Tehran), 4 November 1995, in DR, 6 November 1995, p.56; *Radio al-Quds*, 5 November 1995, in DR, 6 November 1995, p.44; HAMAS spokesman in Beirut in the *Voice of Tehran*, 5 November 1995, in DR, 6 November 1995, p.48; various officials in Amal and in Hizbullah in *Radio Beirut*, 5 November 1995, in DR, 6 November 1995, pp.52–3; spokesman for the Islamic Jihad in *Agence France Presse* (AFP, Paris), in DR, 6 November 1995, p.49; Ahmad Jibril in *Radio al-Quds*, 5 November 1995, in DR, 6 November 1995, p.46; announcement by the Islamic Action Front as published in DR, 6 November 1995, p.48; Hamza Mansur, spokesman for the opposition to peace bloc in Jordan, the leadership of which is Islamic, quoted in *Reuters*, 5 November 1995; Kujak, 'Hadith al-Madina' ('Talk of the Town'), *al-Siyasa* (Kuwait), 7 November 1995, p.28.
10. *Al-Siyasa* (Kuwait), ibid., article by Khaled al-Adwa, a fundamentalist member of parliament in Kuwait; IRNA, 4 November 1995, in DR, 6 November 1995, p.56, as well as the statements of the President of Iran Hashemi Rafsanjani, according to Middle East Economic Digest (MEED) 17 November 1995; *Radio al-Quds*, 5 November 1995, in DR 6 November 1995, p.44. A commentator on *Radio Iran* (on 6 November 1995), quoted in *Reuters*, even linked Yigal Amir's statement that he murdered Rabin by God's command to the punishment visited on Rabin by heaven for Shkaki's death. This view was echoed by other public personalities in Iran, see: Sharif Imam-Jomeh, 'Iranian Ambivalent Over Rabin Slaying', *Reuters* (Tehran), 7 November 1995.
11. The position of the Islamic Action Front as published in DR, 6 November 1995, p.48.
12. President of the Iranian Parliament, Natek al-Nuri, in *Islamic Republic of Iran Broadcasting* (Tehran), 5 November 1995, in DR 6 November 1995, p.58.
13. MEED, 20 November 1995; James Wyllie, 'Jordan – Vulnerabilities In The Peace Process', JIR, BIPAD, 1 May 1996. See also *al-Savil*, 6–12 November 1995.
14. *Al-Ahali*, 7 November 1996.
15. *Sawt al-Mar'a*, 7 November 1996.
16. 'Jordanian Succeeds in Naming Son Yitzhak Rabin', *Reuters*, 24 March 1996.
17. Samia Nakhoul, 'Official Egypt Mourns Rabin, Citizens in Two Minds', *Reuters* (Cairo), 5 November 1995; Rana Sabbagh, 'Jordanians Split Over Rabin Killing', *Reuters* (Amman), 5 November 1995; Taher Shriteh, 'Palestinians Watch Rabin Burial with Mixed Emotions', *Reuters* (Gaza), 6 November 1995; Sharif Imam-Jomeh, 'Iranians Ambivalent'.
18. *Al-Ahram*, 5 November 1995; *al-Thawra*, quoted in *Ha-aretz*, 8 November 1995.
19. *Jordan Times*, 6 November 1995.
20. *Radio Palestine*, 5 November 1995, in DR, 6 November 1995, p.47.
21. See quote in *Ha-aretz*, 8 November 1995.
22. *Jordan Times*, 5 November 1995, p.6.
23. AFP (Paris), 5 November 1995, in DR, 6 November 1995, p.58. For similar statements in Iran, see also Radio Tehran, 10 November 1995 (*Reuters*), and the proclamation issued by

the Islamic Jihad office in Tehran on 5 November 1995, in DR, 6 November 1995, p.49.
24. *Voice of the Oppressed People of Ba'al Beck*, 6 November 1995, in DR, 6 November 1995, p.54.
25. *Ha-aretz*, 8 November 1995.
26. *Al-Wafd*, 5 November 1995.
27. Ahmad Ibrahim Mahmud, 'Israel After Rabin: The Motives for Murder and the Chances of Armed Violence Developing', *al-Siyasa al-Duwaliyya*, January 1996, pp.213–19.
28. Saeb Arekat in *Radio Monte Carlo* (Paris), 5 November 1995, in DR, 6 November 1995, p.41; Freih Abu Madin's interview with *Voice of Jericho*, 5 November 1995, in DR, 6 November 1995, p.40–41. About four months after the murder, in March 1996, the Palestinian Ministry of Information published a booklet entitled 'The Assassination of Yitzhak Rabin From the Israeli Point of View'. The booklet attempts to review the background and motives for the murder and makes extensive references to Halachic rulings by the 'Rabbis of the settlements', extremist right-wing organizations in Israel, as well as the trial of Yigal Amir up to the date of publication. The booklet relies heavily on the Israeli press and contains numerous quotations. In the introduction the authors claim that the Israeli government shared responsibility for the assassination because of its soft-handed approach to the settlers, even after the massacre committed by Baruch Goldstein in the Tomb of the Patriarchs in Hebron. The publication of this booklet indicates the importance which the Palestinians attached to Rabin's murder. The angle from which the booklet is written points to an attempt on the part of the Palestinians to understand the trends within Israeli society. See al-Ja'bari, Jawad Sulayman, *Amaliyyat Ightiyal Ishaq Rabin fi al-Manzur al-Israili* (The Assassination of Yitzhak Rabin from the Israeli Point of View), Manshurat Wizarat al-A'lam al-Filastini, 1996.
29. *Voice of Jericho*, 5 November 1995, in DR, 6 November 1995, p.41.
30. *Radio Beirut*, 5 November 1995, in DR, 6 November 1995, p.52.
31. DR, 13 November 1995, p.8.
32. *Al-Nahar* (East Jerusalem), 5 November 1995; *Voice of Jericho*, 5 November 1995, in DR, 6 November 1995, p.42; article by Sana Saed in the weekly *al-Musawwar* (Egypt), 16 January 1996.
33. *Voice of Tehran*, 5 November 1995, in DR, 6 November 1995, p.60.
34. *Al-Ahram*, 5 November 1995; *Cairo Radio*, 9 November 1995, in DR, 6 November 1995, p.8; article by Mahmoud Sa'adni in *al-Musawwar*, 16 January 1996.
35. *Voice of the Oppressed People of Ba'al Beck*, 6 November 1995, in DR, 6 November 1995, p.54.
36. 'Kuwaitis Sharply Split Over Rabin Record', *Reuters*, 6 November 1995.
37. See the quotation in *Ha-aretz*, 8 November 1995.
38. Sharif Imam-Jomeh, 'Iranians Ambivalent'.
39. *Tishrin*, 6 November 1995.
40. Issam Hamza, 'Syria Says Quicker Peace 'Positive Reply' For Rabin', *Reuters* (Damascus), 8 November 1995.
41. See the comments of the Lebanese Foreign and Commerce Ministers in *Radio Beirut*, 5 November 1995, in DR, 6 November 1995, pp.52–3.
42. See *Ma'ariv*, 7 November 1995.
43. *Radio Cairo*, 5 November 1995, in DR, 6 November 1995, p.33.
44. *Voice of Tehran*, 5 November 1995, in DR, 6 November 1995, p.57.
45. See: AFP report from Tehran of 5 November 1995, and the IRIB broadcast from Tehran of the same date, in DR, 6 November 1995, p.58.
46. *Al-Zahf al-Akhdar*, 5 November 1995.
47. *Al-Ahram*, 8 November 1995.
48. See the quote in *Ha-aretz*, 8 November 1995.
49. AFP (Paris), 4 November 1995, in DR, 6 November 1995, p.54.
50. *Jordan Times*, 6 November 1995.
51. The Qatari newspapers: *Al-Watan*, 5 November 1995 and *Al-Raya*, 5 November 1995, as well as *al-Siyasa Al-Duwaliyya* from January 1996. See also the following two notes.
52. *Al-Sha'b*, 5 November 1995.
53. 'Rabin Death Shows Israel Shuns Peace – Kuwait MPs', *Reuters*, 5 November 1995.
54. *Voice of Tehran*, 5 November 1995, in DR, 6 November 1995, p.48.
55. *Al-Musawwar*, 16 January 1996.
56. *Al-Nahar*, 7 November 1995.
57. Ahmad Ibrahim Mahmud, 'Israel After Rabin: The Motives for Murder and the Chances of Armed Violence Developing', *al-Siyasa al-Duwaliyya*, January 1996, pp.218–19.

Rethinking Israel in the Middle East

ELIE PODEH

Despite Israel's geographic location at the heart of the Middle East, Israelis have generally been reluctant to view their country as part of the Middle East, whether politically, economically and culturally. This attitude has primarily stemmed from the hostility of the surrounding Arab states, which have refused to recognize the fact of Israel's existence. As a result, Israelis have long been convinced that reconciliation attempts are doomed to failure. Moreover, the historical, religious, cultural and linguistic differences between Israelis and Arabs have played an important role in further distancing Israel from the Middle East. Consequently, and one might add naturally, Israeli scholars have predominantly concentrated on the Arab–Israeli conflict, studying the Arab states through the prism of the 'other', while neglecting to discuss the non-conflictual aspects of Israel's role in Middle Eastern affairs.

This separation between Israel and the Middle East has been institutionalized by Israeli academia. The study of Israel has been largely excluded from the curriculum of the departments of Islamic and Middle Eastern History, being dealt with by departments of Jewish Studies, General History, Political Science, or, more recently, by specialized departments for Israel Studies. Likewise, various Israeli think-tanks on the Middle East do not consider the study of Israel as part of their agenda. Although the recent political changes in the region have produced several attempts to reassess Israel's foreign policy goals, none have thoroughly discussed the Jewish State's regional roles.[1]

The underlying assumption of this essay is that the separation between Israel and the Middle East has largely been unjustified. Notwithstanding its ostracism by the Arab states, Israel has played crucial roles in balancing and preserving the integrity of the Middle Eastern and Arab systems. These traditional roles, which may now alter with the successful consummation of the Arab–Israeli peace process, indicate that instead of analyzing 'Israel *and* the Middle East', one should rather speak of 'Israel *in* the Middle East'.

Elie Podeh is Lecturer in the Department of Islam and Middle Eastern Studies at the Hebrew University of Jerusalem and Research Fellow at the Truman Institute for the Advancement of Peace.

From an ethno-centric political viewpoint, Israel has been surrounded by three orbits: the Arab states and the Palestinians (or the PLO); the non-Arab and/or non-Muslim states and minorities in the Middle East; and the superpowers, the European and Third World states. Israel's urgent need for Western economic, political and military support, as well as the ramifications of the Arab–Israeli conflict, have caused it to 'leapfrog' the first two orbits, making Washington, London, Paris, and even Moscow the principal diplomatic arenas in a period when Jerusalem was boycotted by the Arab world and had only limited access – mostly behind the scenes – to states and minorities in the Middle East.

FIGURE 1

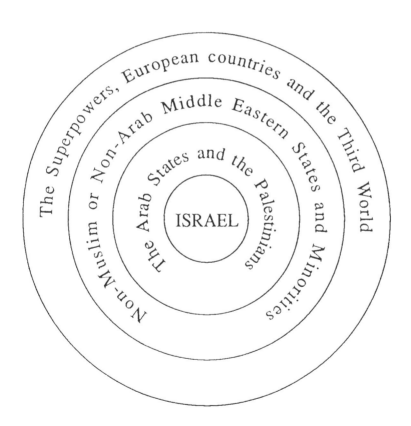

Israel is the only Middle Eastern state which has traditionally been excluded from political or economic coalitions in the region. As a result of the Arab–Israeli conflict, the Jewish State has been ostracized by the Arab world, while other countries preferred not to jeopardize their relations with the Arabs as a result of close association with Israel.[2] These unfortunate circumstances propelled Israel to search for a stable anchor by way of joining Western-led groupings, which would guarantee Israel's physical existence, breach the wall of Arab isolation, and grant Israel recognition as a regional actor in the Middle Eastern system on an equal footing with the Arab actors. It is in this context that one must look at Israel's various attempts, throughout the 1950s and 1960s, to become associated with Western defence organizations directed against the Soviet Union (the 'Middle East Command', the 'Middle East Defence Organization', and NATO), or political-economic groupings (the British Commonwealth, and the European Common Market).

While from a geographical point of view Israel's location in the Middle East is indeed undisputable, this is not as clear with regard to its political, economic and cultural situation. Political scientists find it a tiresome task to define Israel's place and role in the Middle East – a difficulty deriving from the country's isolation within the system, its economic ties with Europe and the United States, and its Western cultural orientation. Some have placed Israel in the 'Fourth World' – states for which a forced isolation determines their national security policy – the so-called 'pariah' or 'outcast' states, like Taiwan and South Africa.[3] Others go so far as to exclude Israel in their analysis of regional politics.[4] However, a closer examination would lead to the conclusion that Israel has played a central role in regional politics ever since its establishment.

ISRAEL IN THE MIDDLE EASTERN SYSTEM

One of the main problems in analyzing the Middle Eastern system is that the term 'Middle East' itself connotes an ill-defined geographical entity. There is unanimity among scholars about certain countries belonging to the regional 'core' (Egypt, Syria, Iraq, Jordan, Lebanon, etc.); however, the inclusion of certain other states in the periphery (the North African states, Turkey, Iran, Pakistan etc.) is still under debate.[5] The Middle East is not only a geographical unit; it is also considered to be a 'region' in the international system.[6] Leonard Binder was the first to suggest that the Middle East constitutes a separate 'region', or rather an 'international subordinate system' with characteristics and patterns of its own.[7] Cantori and Spiegel, Brecher and others contributed new definitions which reinforced Binder's argument.[8] The main division among the scholars here concerns the exact role played by the actors.

Emphasizing ethnic, linguistic, social and historical cohesion at the regional level leads to the placement of Arab states at the core, while the non-Arab states – Israel, Turkey and Iran – play a peripheral role. By contrast, focusing on the intensity of regional interactions (whether conflictual or cooperative) indicates that states involved in the Arab–Israeli conflict are among the region's main actors.[9] In either case, Israel is doubtlessly an integral part of the system.

The Middle Eastern system does not possess an ethnic identity or regional institutions of its own. It is cohesive neither from the political nor from the economic, social or cultural point of view. What makes it an entity is, more than anything else, the geographical proximity of its countries, and the existence of conflicts which are regional in nature.[10] True, the Western powers have looked at the Middle East as a strategic, political and economic system, subordinate to the global system. Most countries in the region, however, have not considered the Middle East to be the natural arena for their activities. For the Arab states, the inter-Arab system (see below) has been the main sphere; and Turkey, for its part, has looked to Europe and NATO. Thus, Israel and Iran have remained the only states hoping to find a place in regional politics, yet always rejected by the Arab majority.

At the time of its establishment, in the declaration of independence Israel's decision-makers called for cooperation with the neighbouring states and declared the Jewish State's readiness to 'do its share in a common effort for the advancement of the entire Middle East'.[11] The same motif recurred in the guidelines of the first Israeli government formed in March 1949. Among other things, it laid down that the country's foreign policy was to be based on 'working for a Jewish–Arab alliance (cooperation with the neighbouring countries in the economic, social, cultural and political fields) within the framework of the UN'.[12] Such language was to convey the impression of a consensus, within the leadership, on the question of Israel's place and role in the region. In reality, however, two schools of thought emerged, just as was the case over a number of other foreign and defence policy issues.[13] One, represented by David Ben-Gurion, head of the Jewish Agency and later the first Israeli prime minister, accorded priority to links with the West and with world Jewry over relations within the Middle East. The other view, represented by Moshe Sharett (Shertok), head of the Agency's political department and later Israel's first foreign minister, as well as by a number of 'Arabists' on the staff of the foreign ministry, argued that Israel's first priority was to make every conceivable effort for integration in the Middle East. Both agreed, however, on the importance of preserving Israel's Western cultural identity.[14]

The wall of Arab rejection which surrounded Israel after the 1948 War caused the country's policy-makers to 'discover' the second orbit, including Muslim non-Arab, countries (Turkey and Iran), Christian countries or states with a Christian identity (Ethiopia and Lebanon), and non-Arab ethnic minorities (like the Kurds and the Armenians). Even though relations with some of these had already been established by the Jewish Agency, it was only after 1948 that they acquired political significance.

While Turkey had voted against the establishment of the State of Israel in the UN vote of November 1947, Turkish–Arab hostility made an Israeli–Turkish *rapprochement* feasible. The fact that Ben-Gurion and some other Zionist leaders had studied in Istanbul University prior to the First World War and spoke Turkish well, probably added a psychological incentive for approaching Turkey. The latter was elected a member of the Palestine Conciliation Commission formed by the UN towards the end of 1948. In March 1949, Turkey declared its *de facto* recognition of Israel, and at the beginning of 1950 it became the first Muslim state to establish diplomatic relations with Israel. Eliyahu Sasson, head of the Foreign Ministry's Middle East department and a senior expert on Arab affairs, became minister in Ankara. Due to its isolation in the region, Israel used this post as a channel for a closer study of the Arab world.[15]

The second Muslim non-Arab state – Iran – also recognized Israel *de facto*, in March 1950, but was reluctant to establish formal diplomatic relations with it due to Arab sensitivities. However, it was precisely the lack of formal ties which opened secret avenues for close economic and subsequently, military cooperation. Back in 1949, Iran allowed Iraqi Jews heading for Israel to pass through its territory. Though the Iranian consulate in Tel-Aviv was closed down in 1952 due to internal difficulties, this did not affect economic cooperation between the two states. In 1953, Iran became one of the chief suppliers of crude oil to Israel. Due to the closure of the Suez Canal to Israeli ships or foreign vessels bound for Israel, the oil was shipped to Eilat and from there to Haifa through an overland pipeline. This cooperation became even closer during the 1950s and 1960s (see below).[16]

Further afield, Israel sought links with Christian Ethiopia. A mutual tradition links the two states, with the Ethiopian kings considering themselves descendants of King Solomon. Another point in common was the sense of isolation in facing the Muslim world; apart from Kenya, Ethiopia borders on Somalia and Djibouti – both Muslim and both members of the Arab League, though not ethnically Arab. The existence of a Jewish community (the Falashas) in Ethiopia provided yet another basis for cooperation.

Another target of Israeli policy-makers was the Christian-Maronite community of Lebanon. Relations with the Maronites and its religious establishment, grounded in the awareness of a common Jewish–Christian fate opposite the regional majority of Muslims, went back to the 1920s. It was this attitude which led the Maronite religious leaders to support the establishment of the State of Israel. These ties continued after 1949, especially with the Phalange movement.[17]

Following the Suez campaign in 1956, Israel attempted to tighten relations with Turkey, Iran and Ethiopia – a strategy that became known as the 'periphery policy'. This was intended to contain the Nasserist wave in the Middle East. Gamal Ahd al-Nasser's attempt to unite the Arab countries, as well as his collaboration with the Soviet Union, were seen as an imminent threat to the interests of the non-Arab, peripheral states. Israel, Turkey and Iran cooperated in particular in the fields of intelligence and security.[18] As the Nasserist threat faded, Turkey turned back to its major centre of activity in Europe. Cooperation between Israel, Iran and Ethiopia continued through the 1960s and well into the 1970s, but became exposed to hostile Muslim and Arab propaganda and was never formally institutionalized. Khomeini's revolution in Iran in 1979, and the growing Soviet influence in Ethiopia during the 1970s, brought down these two important pillars of Israel's regional policy.

ISRAEL AND THE ARAB SYSTEM

Within the Middle Eastern system operates an Arab system of states. It includes members of the Arab League, some of which are located on the periphery of the Middle East (the North African states, Sudan, and even Somalia and Djibouti which are ethnically non-Arab). In the view of members of the Arab system, the 'Middle East' is a term invented by the West to serve its own interests and split the Arab world by including non-Arab actors. Unlike the Middle Eastern system, the Arab system is not based primarily on geographic proximity, but rather on the sense of belonging to the 'Arab nation'. It has developed its own identity, stemming from its linguistic, cultural and historical heritage. Despite differences and rivalries among Arab states, and despite the inefficiency of the Arab League, the Arab system has evolved its own rules and patterns of behaviour.[19] Israel, though not an actor in the Arab system in the full sense of the word, has played an important role in the consolidation and the development of this system.

Traditionally, the Arabs have perceived Israel as a foreign enclave, serving the interests of Western imperialism. Its location in the midst of the Arab world, in this view, is meant to put a spoke in the wheels of Arab unity. While Turkey and Iran, being Muslim states, have been thought of as legitimate (though undesirable) regional actors, Israel has been considered an illegitimate actor, and its destruction was deemed inevitable.[20] Though the failure of the Arab world to 'liquidate' the 'Zionist entity' has contributed to a growing realization that Israel is a *fait accompli*, it has still been seen as an outside factor – *in* the region, but not *of* it. In the 1980s, two important Egyptian scholars, Bahgat Korany and Ali Dessouki, still spoke of Israel as 'ex-territorial' and mainly serving

Western interests.[21] Other Arab intellectuals have argued that Israel, being foreign to the region, presented an immediate danger to the Arab system.[22] Only recently, in the wake of the 1991 Gulf war, have there been signs that this attitude is beginning to change.[23]

Arab attempts to underrate Israel's importance and influence notwithstanding, the Jewish State did fulfill five roles – ostensibly contradictory, but in fact complementary – in the preservation, consolidation, and cohesion of the Arab system.

1. Unifying Factor

It is around Israel that Arab solidarity has consolidated on more than one occasion. This unity found expression in past Arab League decisions and joint Arab action – such as in the 1948 War, the Arab boycott, the Jordan water diversion scheme, the 1973 War, and the oil embargo. In other words: when an atmosphere militating for cooperation existed in the Arab world, Israel was a convenient point round which to close ranks.[24] The need for solidarity vis-à-vis Israel has also been a useful pretext for Arab leaders for evading other regional and local problems.

Since 1948, the attainment of Arab unity was closely linked with the elimination of Israel, because its existence became 'a physical barrier frustrating the realization of that unity'.[25] The ideology of pan-Arab groups (such as the al-Qawmiyyun al-Azab, or the Ba'th party) associated the liberation of Palestine with the liberation of the entire Arab world. A united Arab world was considered by these organizations to be the most efficient instrument in confronting Israel and Zionism. This, in turn, became an incentive in the search for unity. The early pioneers of the Palestinian national movement, too, believed that Arab unity was the only road leading to the 'liberation of Palestine'. True, the pan-Arab ideology was not formed against the background of the struggle with Israel, but that struggle prevented the collapse of the pan-Arab movement in the 1950s and the 1960s, when it was beset by personal and inter-Arab rivalries.[26]

2. Divisive Factor

The establishment of Israel disrupted the territorial continuity of the Arab world such as it had existed under the Ottoman Empire. The merger of Egypt and Syria in 1958 was taken as yet more proof that Israel was an obstacle to the free flow of goods and people across the Arab world. Yet at the same time Israel has been a strategic asset for both Syria and Jordan, serving as a buffer zone and protecting them from possible Egyptian encroachment.[27] In various attempts to reach an Israeli–Arab accommodation, the matter of restoring Arab territorial continuity has come up repeatedly – whether by means of Israel surrendering the Negev, or through a corridor linking the Gaza Strip and the West Bank. Such demands have been consistently turned down by Israel on security grounds.

Israel also became a divisive factor with regard to the 'unity of Arab ranks' (a phrase often used at the Arab League to connote solidarity and political coordination). Israel's very existence became a point of dispute between the 'radical' (Egypt until 1970, Syria, Iraq and Lybia) and the 'conservative' Arab states (such as the oil-rich states, Jordan and Morocco). Israel became a bone of contention between the two groups concerning the ways and means of action. Moreover, the 'radical' camp itself was divided over the nature of the action to be taken and its timing. In other words: Israel became a major factor in inter-Arab squabbles.[28]

The signing of the Israeli–Egyptian peace treaty in March 1979 caused the gravest rift the Arab world had seen thus far. Egypt – until then the standard-bearer of the Arab struggle against Israel – edged away from the 'confrontation ranks' and 'left the Arab trench'. It was expelled from the League, and most member states severed diplomatic relations with it. The current peace process has again accentuated Arab disunity by widening the gap between its advocates and its opponents.

In addition, Israel has been a divisive factor in the Arab system by opposing all Arab unity schemes, often seeking superpower support to this end. This was particularly true of the many Arab attempts to unite the Fertile Crescent (Iraq, Syria, Lebanon and Jordan).

3. Intrusive Factor

Just as superpowers intrude on regional sub-systems, so does Israel in the Arab system, though its interventions have remained at a lower level. On the whole Israeli decision-makers have been disinclined to interfere in Arab domestic affairs.[29] The dismal failure of Israeli intelligence in 1954 to cause an escalation in Egyptian–British tensions (the so-called 'security mishap') only served to reinforce such reluctance. Nonetheless, Israel has acted with some vigour to bolster the rule of the Maronites in Lebanon and of the Hashemites in Jordan. In so doing, it has contributed considerably, particularly in the case of Jordan, to preserving the territorial integrity and stability of two weak states which found it hard to fend off pressures from within and from the Arab system.[30] In Iraq, Israel's interference took a different form: it has supported the Kurds against the Sunni Arab ruling elite in Baghdad in the hope of reinforcing territorial irredentism and thus undermining the stability, perhaps even endangering the existence, of the Iraqi state.

4. Accelerating Factor

Israel at times has encouraged at least three political processes in the Arab world:

- Forming and dismantling of coalitions: Students of international relations differ in their assessments of exactly how instrumental Israel has been in this regard.[31] Nonetheless, it is agreed that Israel has been a crucial catalyst in forming and dismantling coalitions in the Arab world. Several wars, and the political developments that came in their wake, as well as the peace treaty with Egypt – all attest to the importance of Israel as a factor in Arab coalition-building.

• Consolidation of the Palestinian national movement: The very establishment of Israel, but especially the occupation of the West Bank and the Gaza Strip in 1967, helped to accelerate the consolidation of the Palestinian national movement. The incessant struggle against what, to the Palestinians, has been foreign domination became one of the central factors in forming their national experience, which subsequently led to the uprising of December 1987 (*intifada*). In addition, the Israeli recognition of the PLO in the 1993 Oslo Accord strengthened the latter's position within its constituency and in the Arab world.

• Promotion of local (*watani*) and pan-Arab (*qawmi*) legitimacy: The struggle of Arab leaders against Israel has been intended, *inter alia*, to deflect public opinion in their countries from the real, basic problems there. But it has also been intended to achieve a measure of legitimacy for their rule in the eyes of the masses. At the local level, leaders have been successful in mobilizing public opinion, in consolidating their grip on power, and in enhancing their prestige by responding to local pressures to take some action against Israel. At the regional level, Israel has played an important role in the overall struggle for hegemony in the Arab world. An Arab aspirant for leadership would de-legitimize his Arab rivals by accusing them of inaction against Israel. In particular, Egyptian President Abdal Nasser made use of the conflict with Israel as a lever in his struggle to establish Egyptian pan-Arab leadership. This has become a constant theme of inter-Arab politics, especially in the relations between Egypt, Iraq and Syria, reaching its peak during the 1990–91 Gulf crisis, when Saddam Hussein sought to justify his predatory move against Kuwait by portraying it as a bold first move towards the 'liberation of Palestine'.[32]

5. Balancing Factor

Though formally not an actor in the inter-Arab system, Israel has found itself in the role of balancer in the Arab system in the absence of structural checks and balances. Attempting to maintain the status-quo, Israel has opposed all Arab or Western schemes at territorial revisionism, especially among the confrontation states. Thus, Israel's constant opposition to Arab unity schemes (the Fertile Crescent or the Greater Syria plans) has been an attempt to maintain the existing balance of power – a target which has interestingly coincided with the wishes of several Arab leaders, such as the Saudi rulers. Israel's balancing position has been most evident with regard to Jordan and Lebanon: the menace to their territorial integrity and to the regional equilibrium – to Jordan in September 1970, to Lebanon ever since the beginning of the civil war in 1976 – has caused Israel to take military and political action in order to preserve the status quo. The destruction of the Iraqi nuclear reactor in 1981, though undertaken in the first place to remove a lethal threat to Israel, also helped to maintain the Arab balance of power; the possession of nuclear arms by Iraq would otherwise have had decisive ramifications for the Middle Eastern and Arab balance of power. It should be noted that in the eyes of US policy-makers, preserving the balance of power and stability in the region is one of the major tasks Israel is expected to fulfill in the post-Gulf War period.[33]

ISRAEL IN THE NEW MIDDLE EASTERN SYSTEM

The collapse of the Soviet Union, Iraq's invasion of Kuwait, and the lingering peace process between Israel, the PLO and the Arab states, have foreshadowed changes which are likely to lead to the following developments in the Middle East:

Greater Autonomy of the Middle East Regional Subsystem. The disintegration of the Soviet Union and the end of the Cold War may foreshadow a decrease in superpower involvement in regional sub-systems, a development that may lead to a greater autonomy of these sub-systems and to the emergence of regional leaders (see below). The rivalries between Britain and France in the first half of this century, and between the US and the USSR in the second half, has greatly affected the course of events in the Middle East (as well as in other sub-systems). The end of the Cold War provides greater leeway for local states to further their own regional interests. Currently, US involvement in Middle Eastern affairs is still significant, but domestic pressures as a result of economic difficulties may lead the US to reduce its foreign assistance and to decrease its involvement in Middle Eastern affairs.

A New Middle Eastern System?

The demarcation line dividing the Middle Eastern and the Arab systems will gradually be blurred. The line may not disappear altogether, since the existing cultural and linguistic differences will remain, but it may become less visible in light of common interests cutting across the two systems. This development might foreshadow the emergence of a new Middle Eastern system, with a new core and periphery, in which new patterns of behaviour would crystallize in the economic and political fields.[34]

Economically, there has hitherto been little, if any, economic cooperation between the two systems. Nor has there been any meaningful economic cooperation within the Arab system itself. The Arab Common Market (formed in 1964) did not take off. Later, three sub-regional organizations were set up, mainly to promote economic exchange: the Gulf Cooperation Council (GCC, 1981); the Arab Cooperation Council (ACC, 1989), comprising Egypt, Iraq, Jordan and Yemen; and the Arab Maghrib Union (AMU, 1989). However, the success of these organizations in the economic field has been less than satisfactory; moreover, the ACC virtually collapsed in the aftermath of the Gulf War.

While the gaps between the Israeli and the Turkish markets, on the one hand, and the Arab markets, on the other, are wider than ever, limited economic cooperation is certainly feasible. The gradual lift of the Arab boycott, mutual investments, a Middle East regional bank and possibly a Middle East common market are all ideas which are being explored now by politicians and businessmen alike. While the ostensible results of the Casablanca economic conference (November 1994) and the Amman economic conference (October 1995) were modest, this kind of activity might lead to greater economic cooperation in the future. Extensive economic cooperation with Israel may lead to certain hitherto peripheral states (in the Gulf and North Africa) playing a central role in the new system. This cooperation may expand and cover other fields as well, such as environmental issues, water resources and arms control.

Politically, the Arab–Israeli conflict has been one of the major – if not *the* major – sources of regional instability. Now, Israel, as well as other Middle Eastern states, faces two common dangers: that of 'fundamentalist radicalism', promoted by Iran and Sudan, and practised by such militant organizations as Hizbullah, HAMAS and the Islamic Jihad; and that of 'revolutionary radicalism', promoted by Saddam Hussein and Muammar Qaddhafi. Indeed, this is not the first occasion when Israel and several regional states find themselves threatened from the same quarter: the pan-Arab movement of the 1950s and 1960s was no less of a direct threat to Israel, Turkey, Iran and most Arab leaders.[35] The salient difference between the two periods is the wide recognition – whether direct or indirect – that Israel has gained from many Arab states. Nonetheless, the ability of Arab-Muslim governments to cooperate with the Jewish State in containing Muslim movements – however radical and extremist – is limited, at least as far as public opinion is concerned.

The Emergence of Regional Powers

The Middle East may see the emergence of local powers competing for regional hegemony. This development, as some scholars have argued, would be the result of the end of the Cold War and the disappearance of the bi-polar system. Consequently, the local, rather than foreign, powers are likely to set the regional agenda.[36] Yet the struggle for supremacy in the Arab world – Egypt and Iraq being its major protagonists – has been an old feature of Arab politics, which was recently reflected during the Iraqi invasion of Kuwait.[37] Recent developments in the Middle East may bring the non-Arab actors, Israel, Turkey and Iran – states with considerable military, economic, demographic and political capabilities – to join the quest for regional hegemony, thus challenging both Egypt's and Iraq's traditional leading roles in the Arab system. The struggle for hegemony will become fiercer the less the US interferes in the region.

New Core and Periphery

A new core and periphery may emerge in the new regional order. Turkey, hitherto at the periphery, may move to centre stage and become part of the core. Although Europe is still considered its main arena, Turkey may well become a pole of attraction for newly-emerging peripheral states, as well as an important actor in the struggle against the common threat of Islamic fundamentalism. Israel may also play a major role in the Middle East core, which, unlike in the past, will be a result of peaceful interactions. By contrast, Iran is likely to move into the position once filled by Israel: threatening the integrity and stability of the system from the inside – but also instrumental in its consolidation. Egypt, Iraq and Syria are among the Arab states most likely to play an important role in the new core. This, however, will largely depend on their ability to deal successfully with their own domestic problems. With the old periphery moving into the centre, a new periphery may emerge, including several remote and poor Arab states, as well as new Muslim republics. Based on their ethnic, cultural and linguistic affinities, these republics – contingent upon Russia's consent and goodwill – are likely to move either into the Turkish or the Iranian spheres of influence. Thus, the centre of activity, so long identified primarily with the Arab states, may gravitate in the direction of the non-Arab states, which will set the new regional agenda.

The Role of the Arab States

The Arab predicament following Iraq's invasion of Kuwait led Bernard Lewis to suggest that the Arab world may cease to function as a 'political entity'.[38] Paradoxically, however, the adverse developments in the Arab system may lead to renewed attempts at reconciliation and subsequently to increased cooperation. Such cooperation may well be more productive than in the past, if the resources hitherto invested in the conflict with Israel are allotted to new domestic projects. However, in the immediate future the Arab states seem more likely to struggle with their own vast domestic problems than take new risks in sharing Arab regional schemes. Furthermore, it would seem that the position of the Arab states in the Middle Eastern system is about to undergo a substantial change. Major Arab actors, including the so-called oil-rich countries, may find themselves playing greater roles due to the political and economic changes in the region.

Israel in the New Middle Eastern System

The processes described above have brought two important changes with regard to Israel's place in the Middle East. First, most Arab states have gradually come to recognize – whether explicitly or implicitly – that Israel is a major Middle Eastern political and strategic actor. No longer perceived necessarily as an enemy, this recognition may pave the way for Israel's participation, for the first time, in regional projects or alignments. Second, the demarcation line separating the two inner circles in Israeli foreign policy may disappear altogether. Israel may now find itself playing a central role in regional affairs with two optional policies: for one thing, it can turn its military superiority into political and economic hegemony as well. According to this scenario, Israel, which has long enjoyed military superiority in terms of nuclear and conventional weaponry, will now attempt to exploit the inability of the United States to project power effectively in the Middle East in order to achieve regional predominance. However, such a development is bound to be resented by the regional states and will undoubtedly exacerbate the already existing cultural differences.[39]

For another thing, Israel may act as *primus inter pares* among the states in the region. According to this scenario, Israel will become the linchpin in a system of economic, defence and communication networks between the Middle East and the West. Israel may also become a bridge linking the Arab East with the Arab West. Taking into account Arab sensitivities, Israel may associate itself – either overtly or covertly – with several Arab states against common regional threats posed mainly by Iran and other fundamentalist movements.

Israel's integration into the Middle Eastern system as *primus inter pares* would cause a substantial change in its regional position and its traditional roles in the system. First, Israel will no longer act as a unifying factor among the Arab states since the Arab–Israeli conflict will no longer top the Arab agenda. Secondly, it will play a divisive role should certain Arab states (such as Iraq or Libya) persist in their refusal to recognize its existence. Thirdly, Israel will no longer affect processes in the Arab world nor interfere in domestic developments in neighbouring states, except if they are powerful enough to threaten its stability. Finally, in all probability, Israel will continue to act – perhaps even with more vigour than in the past – as a balancing factor, aiming at maintaining the regional status quo.

Scholars are divided over Israel's strategic position in the aftermath of the Cold War. Lewis has categorically asserted that Israel's value as a strategic asset for the US ended with the demise of the Cold War. This change, in his view, was clearly manifested during the Gulf War, when Israel was irrelevant, some even said a nuisance.[40] Others claim that despite Israel's strategic marginality during the Gulf War, its military capabilities cannot be ignored and will be useful in preserving regional stability.[41] Assuming that domestic problems will cause the United States to reduce its interventions abroad, Washington policy-makers will have to rely on trustworthy regional powers. This may – perhaps unexpectedly – enhance Israel's position as a regional asset. But then overly close US–Israeli cooperation may make Israel suspect in the eyes of other – particularly Arab – actors; Israel will be conceived of as an instrument of the West, used to further its own interests in the Middle East.

The political, economic, and strategic incorporation of Israel into the region does not necessarily imply its cultural integration. Both its citizens and its neighbours think of it as part of 'Western Civilization' – unlike Arab culture which remains firmly anchored in Islam. All forms of concerted regional efforts must therefore be based on shared political and economic interests rather than on ideological or cultural affinities. Considerations based on the latter are more likely to remain obstacles than to become incentives for cooperation.

ACKNOWLEDGEMENT

The author would like to thank Moshe Ma'oz, Benny Miller, Ephraim Inbar, and David Tal for their helpful comments on an earlier version of the article. Please note that this article was finalized in 1995.

NOTES

1. See, for example: A. Klieman, 'New Directions in Israel's Foreign Policy', in E. Karsh, ed., *Peace in the Middle East: The Challenge for Israel*, London, 1994, pp.96–117; M. Porat, 'Israel and the New World Order', in T. Ismael and J. Ismael, eds, *The Gulf War and the New World Order*, Gainesville, 1994, pp.347–62; *War in the Gulf: Implication for Israel*, Report of a Jaffee Center Study Group, Boulder, 1992.
2. B. Reich, 'Israel', in E.A. Kolodziej and R.E. Harkavy, eds, *Security Policies of Developing Countries*, Lexington, 1982, p.213.
3. A. Klieman, *Israel's Global Reach: Arms Sales as Diplomacy*, Washington, 1985, pp.149–50. For further analysis of the 'pariah' state, see E. Inbar, *Outcast Countries in the World Community*, Monograph Series in World Affairs, Denver, 1985; idem, 'The Emergence of Pariah States in World Politics: The Isolation of Israel', *Korean Journal of International Studies*, Vol.XV (Winter 1983/84), pp.55–83.
4. I.W. Zartman, for example, termed Israel a 'thorn', which is 'in but not of the system'. See his 'Military Elements in Regional Unrest', in J.C. Hurewitz, ed., *Soviet–American Rivalry in the Middle East*, New York, 1969, p.1. J.P.Piscatori and R.K. Ramazani defined the Middle East as excluding Israel, but including all Arab states, Iran and Turkey, see 'The

Middle East', in W.J. Feld and K. Boyd, eds, *Comparative Regional Systems*, New York, 1980, p.275.

5. M. Hudson, 'The Middle East', in J. Rosenau *et al.*, eds, *World Politics: An Introduction*, New York, 1976, pp.468–70; N. Keddie, 'Is There a Middle East?', *International Journal of Middle East Studies*, Vol.4 (1973), pp.255–71.

6. B.M. Russet, *International Regions and the International System*, Chicago, 1967, Chapter 1.

7. L. Binder, 'The Middle East as a Subordinate International System', *World Politics*, Vol.10 (1958), pp.408–29.

8. L.J. Cantori and S.L. Spiegel, *The International Politics of Regions: A Comparative Approach*, Englewood Cliffs, 1970, pp.1–41; M. Brecher, *The Foreign Policy System of Israel: Setting, Images, Process*, London, 1972, Chapter 3; W.R. Thompson, 'The Regional Subsystem', *International Studies Quarterly*, Vol.17 (March 1973), pp.89–117; J.H. Lebovich, 'The Middle East: The Region as a System', *International Interaction*, Vol.12 (1986), pp.267–89; T.Y. Ismael, *International Relations of the Contemporary Middle East*, Syracuse, 1986, pp.5–10; Y. Evron, *The Middle East: Nations, Superpowers and Wars*, New York, 1975, Chapter 6.

9. See n.8, and: W.R. Thompson, 'Delineating Regional Subsystems: Visit Networks and the Middle Eastern Case', *International Journal of Middle Eastern Studies*, Vol.13 (1981), pp.215–16.

10. Y. Shimoni, 'Israel in the Pattern of Middle East Politics', *Middle East Journal*, Vol.4 (July 1950), p.278.

11. For the English version of the Declaration, see A.Z. Rubinstein, ed., *The Arab–Israeli Conflict: Perspectives*, New York, 1991, p.227–9.

12. *Shnaton Ha-memshala* (Government Yearbook), Jerusalem, 1950, p.38.

13. Brecher, *The Foreign Policy*, Chapter 12; I. Pappè, 'Moshe Sharett, David Ben-Gurion and the "Palestinian Option", 1948–1956', *Studies in Zionism*, Vol.7 (1986), pp.77–96; Y. Bar-Siman-Tov, 'Ben-Gurion and Sharett: Conflict Management and Great Power Constraints in Israeli Policy', *Middle Eastern Studies*, Vol.24 (July 1988), pp.330–56; A. Shlaim, 'Conflicting Approaches to Israel's Relations with the Arabs: Ben-Gurion and Sharett, 1953–56', *Middle East Journal*, Vol.37 (Spring 1983), pp.180–201.

14. On differences between Ben-Gurion and Sharett over this matter, see for example Knesset records for 15 November 1951; D. Ben-Gurion, *Mediniyut Ha-hutz* (Foreign Policy), Tel-Aviv, 1955, p.32; A. Ben-Asher, *Yahasei Hutz, 1948–1953*, (Foreign Relations, 1948–1953), Tel-Aviv, 1956, p.250.

15. A. Nachmani, *Israel, Turkey and Greece: Uneasy Relations in the East Mediterranean*, London, 1987, pp.3–4.

16. Sobhani Sohrab, 'The Pragmatic Entente: Israeli–Iranian Relations, 1948–1988', PhD Dissertation, Georgetown University, 1989; U. Bialer, 'The Iranian Connection in Israel's Foreign Policy – 1948–1951', *Middle East Journal*, Vol.39 (Spring 1985), pp.292–315; M.G. Weinbaum, 'Iran and Israel: The Discreet Entente', *Orbis*, Vol.18 (Winter 1975), pp.1070–87.

17. B. Morris, 'Israel and the Lebanese Phalange: The Birth of a Relationship, 1948–1951', *Studies in Zionism*, Vol.5 (1984), pp.125–44.

18. On Israel's periphery policy, see H. Eshed, *Mossad shel Ish Ehad: Reuven Shiloah, Avi Ha-modi'in Ha-israeli* (A One-Man Institution: Reuven Shiloah, Father of Israeli Intelligence), Tel-Aviv, 1988, pp.266–82; author's Interview with the late Yehoshafat Harkabi, former Head of the Military Intelligence, 16 February 1994.

19. J. Matar and Ali al-Din Hillal, *al-Nizam al-Iqlimi al-Arabi: Dirasa fi al-Alaqat al-Siyasiyya al-Arabiyya* (The Arab Regional Order: A Study in Arab Political Relations), Cairo, 1983, p.31. See also A. Taylor, *The Arab Balance of Power*, Syracuse, 1982, pp.7–21; P. Noble, 'The Arab System: Opportunities, Constraints and Pressures', in B. Korany and Ali H. Dessouki, eds, *The Foreign Policies of Arab States*, Cairo, 1984, pp.41–77.

20. On this point, see Y. Harkabi, *Arab Attitudes To Israel*, Jerusalem, 1970.

21. 'The Global System and Arab Foreign Policies: The Primacy of Constraints', in *The Foreign Policies of Arab States*, p.33.

22. Khair al-Din Haseeb et al., *The Future of the Arab Nation: Challenges and Options*, London, 1991.

23. See, for example: Nabil Abd al-Fattah, '*al-Arab wa-Nizam al-Sharq al-Awsat taht al-Tashkil*', ('The Arabs and the Emerging Middle East Order'), *al-Siyasa al-Duwaliyya*,

January 1993, pp.46–69; Lutfi al-Khouli, *Arab? Na'am. Wa-Sharq Awsatiyyun Aydan* ('Arabs? Yes, but Middle Easterners as well'), Cairo, 1994. Bassam Tibi noted that no collective security system was feasible without the participation of Israel, Turkey and Iran. See his *Conflict and War in the Middle East, 1967–91*, London, 1993, p.37.

24. M. Kerr, *The Arab Cold War: Gamal Abd al-Nasir and His Rivals*, New York, 3rd Ed., 1981, p.114.

25. N. Safran, *From War to War: Arab–Israeli Confrontation, 1948–1967*, New York, 1969, p.83.

26. Ibid., pp.86–7.

27. Ibid.

28. Lebovich, p.270.

29. Aharon Klieman argues that non-interference in Arab domestic affairs was one of four basic principles of Israeli foreign policy. See 'Zionist Diplomacy and Israeli Foreign Policy', *Jerusalem Quarterly*, No.11 (Spring 1979), p.105. Shlaim, on the other hand, holds that such interference was a constant feature of Israel's foreign policy, because of its desire to cause splits in Arab ranks. See 'Israeli Interference in Internal Arab Politics: The Case of Lebanon', in G. Luciani and G. Salame, eds, *The Politics of Arab Integration*, London, 1988, p.232.

30. G. Ben-Dor, *State and Conflict in the Middle East*, New York, 1983, p.208.

31. For two conflicting views, see: Y. Evron and Y. Bar-Siman-Tov, 'Coalitions in the Arab World', *Jerusalem Journal of International Relations*, Vol.I (Winter 1975), pp.71–91; G. Ben-Dor, 'Inter-Arab Relations and the Arab–Israeli Conflict', ibid., Summer 1976, pp.70–96.

32. On this theme, see the author's: *The Quest for Hegemony in the Arab World: The Struggle Over the Baghdad Pact*, Leiden, 1995.

33. See, for example, Martin Indyk, 'The Postwar Balance of Power in the Middle East', in J.S. Nye, and R.K. Smith, eds, *After the Storm: Lessons from the Gulf War*, New York, 1991, pp.83–5.

34. In this connection, see Lutfi al-Khouly, *Arab? Na'am. Wa-Sharq Awsatiyyun Aydan*, pp.51–8. He suggests, however, a wider definition for the term 'Middle East', including Pakistan, India and Bangaladesh, on the one hand, and Mediterranean countries, on the other, pp.57–8.

35. S.D. Walt, *The Origins of Alliances*, Ithaca, 1987, p.266.

36. D. Myres, ed., *Regional Hegemons: Threat Perception and Strategic Response*, Boulder, 1991, pp.vii–viii.

37. For an analysis of the Egyptian–Iraqi struggle for hegemony see Podeh, *The Quest for Hegemony*. For an analysis of this feature during the Gulf Crisis, see idem, 'One Year After Iraq's Invasion of Kuwait: The Ramifications of the Gulf Crisis on the Arab System', *Data and Analysis*, Tel-Aviv, 1991 (Hebrew).

38. B. Lewis, 'Rethinking the Middle East', *Foreign Affairs*, Vol.71 (Fall 1992), p.100.

39. On this option, see Z.T. Irwin, 'Israel: An Aspiring Hegemon', in D.J. Myers, ed., *Regional Hegemons*, pp.63–96.

40. Lewis, 'Rethinking the Middle East', pp.110–11.

41. *After the Storm: Challenges for America's Middle East Policy*, Report by the Washington Institute's Strategic Study Group (1991), pp.16–17.

Continuity and Change in Egyptian–Israeli Relations, 1973–97

KENNETH W. STEIN

For 25 years, tension, mistrust, and strain have characterized Egyptian–Israeli relations. Cairo and Jerusalem have made disagreeing with one another an art form. They have established and codified norms of disenchantment. Though coldness and uneasiness have marked their dialogue, and their treaty relationship has bent severely, it has never broken. Uniformity of Arab anti-Israeli feelings are passing to a series of separate Arab state attitudes towards Israel. In the meantime, Egypt and Israel are likely to continue to irk, confound, and disappoint each other. Their present frosty relationship not only reflects past chapters of disappointment and disillusionment, but contains competitive outlooks for how Middle Eastern nations and peoples might relate to one another.

Whether in bilateral relations or with regard to a variety of other Middle Eastern issues, Egypt and Israel retain unrealistic expectations of each other. The relationship has withstood a variety of long-standing attitudinal (mis)perceptions, regional and international political changes, and unanticipated governmental upheavals. Though both Jerusalem and Cairo regularly suspect the other of nefarious intentions about current and future military preparedness, neither country seeks a major confrontation with the other. Each believes that the other has not done enough to stimulate additional understanding and agreement between Israel and her Arab neighbours. Both are firmly committed not to anger the United States too much, too often, or to such a degree that economic and military assistance from Washington might be threatened or curtailed.

At a minimum, Egypt and Israel are obliged by treaty to have a non-belligerent physical relationship. However, neither is obliged or inclined to change the mutually distrustful emotional feelings that are the legacies from their rocky and disputatious past. For Egypt, Israel has not moved fast enough in returning to Arab control all territories taken in the June 1967 War and has been willing to impose its physical will on Arab lands and people. For Israel, Egypt has been all too slow to

Kenneth W. Stein is Professor of Middle Eastern History and Director of the Middle East Research Programme at Emory University, Atlanta, Georgia.

implement full normalization of diplomatic relations, too reluctant to tone down its verbal attacks against Israel, and too willing to foster Arab resistance to normalized relations with Israel. From the resilient continuity of their unfriendly affiliation, one discovers common and repetitive themes and therefore lessons that might be learned about Arab–Israeli relations in non-war environments.

PRAGMATIC ACCOMMODATIONS (1973–79)

Egypt and Israel feared each other as enemies prior to the October 1973 War. The war did little to alter attitudes of hatred or mistrust. It did however introduce the possibility that Israel's most trusted ally, the United States, might find a way to resolve the new and unsavory physical status quo. For Jerusalem and Cairo, conditions at the end of the war were almost intolerable. Egypt wanted its 15,000-strong Third Army saved from pending destruction at the hands of some vengeful Israeli generals; Israel wanted its POWs returned as quickly as possible. Pragmatic reality demanded that Cairo and Jerusalem consider trusting Washington, if not one another. The war – and Washington's interest, focus, and incessant urge to change the physical status quo – did nothing to change encrusted national attitudes each possessed of the other. Secretary of State Henry Kissinger's intervention evolved into shuttle diplomacy which in turn resulted in a step-by-step process resulting in negotiated agreements. American engagement in Egyptian–Israeli negotiations focused on territorial issues and changed physical realities on the ground in Sinai. For the next quarter century, US engagement in Arab–Israeli diplomacy focused on guaranteeing and supporting the concrete distance between Cairo and Jerusalem. Neither American presidents, nor their Secretaries of State, nor special Middle East envoys attempted to change each country's fundamental attitudes towards the other. Pragmatic accommodations dominated Egyptian–Israeli diplomacy because psychological attitudes were not susceptible to alteration. Most immediately, the status quo demanded reduction of American–Soviet brinkmanship in the Middle East, and the separation of entangled Egyptian and Israeli armies. American diplomacy concentrated on the timetables, distances, conditions, assurances, and degree of Israeli withdrawal from territories taken in the June 1967 War; it did not focus on defining the nature, depth, and manner in which Israel would receive peace in exchange. Asymmetrical concepts were embedded in US-sponsored, Israeli-sanctioned, and Egyptian-catalyzed Arab–Israeli diplomacy. Neither Israel's leaders nor its people ever doubted Egypt's legitimacy, sovereignty, and territorial integrity. On the contrary, Egypt's leaders and citizens were at best severely divided on Zionism's legitimate nature, the sovereignty of a Jewish State, and dimensions of Israel's borders. Israelis always concentrated on preserving security and seeking acceptance; Egyptians focused on restoring honour and sustaining prestige. Only Israelis could provide territory, only the Egyptians could provide peace.

Egyptian and Israeli Goals

Most of the core political objectives which Egypt and Israel imported into the October 1973 War survived it intact. Israel sought recognition by its neighbours. Egypt wanted to sustain its leadership role in the Arab state system. On non-Israeli-related matters, according to Egyptian President Anwar Sadat, 'the Arab world was divided before, during, after the October 1973 war'.[1] And on Israeli-related matters, Egypt's view was different from the rest. These cherished attitudes continued to be held alongside a new reality of negotiating with Washington. There was little in the functional discourse with Washington that forced either Egypt or Israel to change their core objectives. Above all, Cairo wanted Sinai's expeditious return to Egyptian sovereignty. To achieve that end, it needed positive relations with the United States. It also sought to obtain an undetermined but increasingly specific amount of military and financial assistance from Washington. To insure its domestic water requirements, Egypt needed positive and workable relations with Nile River riparian states. In addition, it sought to retain and sustain without much compromise its self-declared leadership in the Arab world. Under Sadat, Egypt vocally supported Palestinian self-determination and a 'comprehensive peace', but was willing to suspend those objectives when either delayed Egypt's primary interest of recovering all of Sinai. Cairo strongly advocated the land-for-peace formula (as it interpreted United Nations Security Council Resolution 242 of November 1967), which evolved into the framework of Arab–Israeli negotiations. Egypt never wavered from its interpretation that the Resolution's call for 'withdrawal of Israeli armed forces from territories taken in the recent conflict' meant withdrawal from *all* the territories. It retained its view that Israel was an aggressive usurper of Palestinian and Arab rights and needed to relinquish those rights (lands) as *a priority* to any consideration of accommodation. And if necessary, under the proper conditions and assurances, Egypt might agree to negotiate a non-resort-to-force agreement – or perhaps, if pushed, a non-belligerency agreement – with Israel. Israel brought into the October 1973 War a fear of the Arabs. Despite its military superiority, Israel lived with an extra historical chromosome. With the horrendous memory of the Holocaust ever-present in their minds, Israelis were consumed with survival and security. Their single most important external relationship was with Washington, because the United States helped protect their existence. In their not-so-friendly neighbourhood, Israelis wanted to achieve recognition, acceptance, and legitimacy from Arab capitals. In order to reduce the prospects for war with Arab states, they focused on building up their own military and finding ways to remove Egypt from the anti-Israel coalition like the one that was formed by its contiguous neighbours prior to the June 1967 War. Israel was willing to negotiate under the premises of UNSC Resolution 242 but only if it could determine what territories to return, over what period of time, and under what conditions. And in return, Israel wanted to exchange peace for land. It defined peace not as non-belligerency, but as a complete peace with full cultural, commercial, diplomatic, and political tentacles implied and applied. For Israel, peace included all the trappings of normal relations between states: tourism, business contracts between Egyptian and Israeli nationals, academic and scientific exchanges, unrestricted use of the Suez Canal, abandonment of the Arab economic boycott of Israel, and behaviour at international forums such as the United Nations and UNESCO, where Israel would not be attacked or berated.

Cairo's insistence on opening negotiations with the United States was an objective of the October 1973 War. In the years preceding the war, President Sadat wanted the US to help him restore Sinai to Egyptian sovereignty. He wanted Washington and Moscow to exert collective pressure on Israel to withdraw from all of Sinai and all of the other territories which Israel had won in the June 1967 War. Unlike Syria, Sadat had little intention of destroying Israel. After the 1973 War, he told the then Jordanian Foreign Minister, Zaid Rifa'i, that it was 'a war for movement not a war for liberation. For me, I [Sadat] would cross the canal and stop'.[2] By contrast, said Syria's Foreign Minister at the time, Abd al-Halim Khaddam, 'for Syria it was a war of liberation, not a war of movement; the objectives of the war were to liberate Golan and Sinai. The Syrian forces advanced according to the plan, the Egyptian forces, however, just passed the canal and stopped'.[3] Nabil al-Eraby, presently Egypt's Ambassador to the United Nations, who at the time worked in the Egyptian foreign ministry, recalled that Sadat entered the war 'not to attain military objectives, but to influence the political process'.[4] According to Joseph Sisco who was Assistant Secretary of State for Near Eastern Affairs at the time and his deputy, Roy Atherton, Sadat went to war because he could not get negotiations started otherwise. Said Sisco, 'the decision to go to war was precisely to get what he wanted, namely – a negotiation.[5]

The October War was Sadat's political key that would initiate, pursue, and sustain a diplomatic process. Apparently, Sadat never told Asad that he had only limited military objectives in the war. Sadat took an enormous political risk that he would succeed in taking Israel by surprise and not be dislodged from the east side of the canal by an Israeli counter-attack. He apparently did not contemplate a crushing Egyptian defeat, or even a threat of one; that the survival of his Third Army, surrounded by the Israelis halfway through the war, would make changing the status quo through negotiations so urgent and compelling; or that he would be tied as tightly, deeply, or quickly to American negotiating intervention as he was.

Egyptian–Israeli Interaction

Existentialist fear enveloped Israel during the war. Its fighting of the war was predicated on the notion of survival. Israeli leaders did not have diplomacy on their minds when they counter-attacked in the middle of the war, but rather retribution and retaliation. Trauma consumed the society. It took Israel a very long time after the 1973 War to believe that Sadat could be trusted. During that war, Israel was reluctantly pulled into US-sponsored negotiations with Egypt. Washington had resupplied Israel with much-needed weapons during the war and Israeli Prime Minister Golda Meir was somewhat obliged to listen to its premier superpower ally. She was also consumed with having Israeli POWs returned as soon as possible. Israel reluctantly trusted the American intervention in negotiating a satisfactory resolution to the war's aftermath: disengagement of troops, return of POWs, and putting trip-wires in place that would deter another Arab surprise attack against Israel or prevent the emergence of a Palestinian State. Meir possessed the notion that Kissinger would not do anything to sacrifice Israeli security; this contrasted with the reality that Kissinger had to preserve Washington's role as mediator. She trusted Kissinger, but not fully. For example, a week after the war ended, the US Secretary of State told Meir that if Israel did not cease jeopardizing the well-being of the surrounded Third Army, the United States would send supplies directly to them.[6]

Kissinger choreographed the December 1973 Geneva Middle East Peace conference so that an Egyptian–Israeli military disengagement agreement could emerge as a pre-cooked result of the conference. Sadat in January 1974 agreed with Israeli leaders on the number of Egyptian tanks that should remain on the east bank of the liberated Suez Canal, that relatively small amount of land Egypt took with great difficulty during the October War. Sadat astonished his Chief of Staff, General Muhammad Abd al-Ghani al-Gamasy, by accepting the presence of a very tiny compliment of Egyptian tanks there. According to Gamasy, Sadat told him, 'my dear general, we are talking about a long period of policy. Peace will not be hurt by 10 tanks, or 20 tanks, or 30 tanks. We are planning for peace *with the Americans [not the Israelis]*'.[7]

In the post-1973 War period Israeli leaders, especially Golda Meir, did not trust Sadat. For that matter neither Yitzhak Rabin, Menachem Begin, Yigal Allon nor Moshe Dayan trusted Sadat or his intentions. Every time Israel negotiated and signed another agreement with Egypt, every Israeli or American who came in contact with Sadat was asked the same question about his intentions: could he be trusted and was he sincere. Scepticism dominated Israeli decision-making about Egypt's intentions during and after the signing of the January 1974 and September 1975 disengagement agreements. Israeli scepticism regarding Sadat was sufficiently great that in March 1975 it was willing to sharpen differences with the United States. Rather than make additional territorial concessions in Sinai without obtaining the political agreement it sought with Egypt, Israel was willing to risk the possibility of US limitations on arms assistance and financial aid. Israel's strategic goal was a peace treaty with Egypt which implied Egypt's withdrawal from the Arab–Israeli conflict as an active military participant. From 1977 onwards, when he was Foreign Minister, Moshe Dayan always asked the question, 'Would Egypt sign a separate peace?' It is not clear whether Dayan fully understood that for Sadat, signing a separate peace with Israel did not mean that Egypt would jettison connections or leadership to the Arab world or support of the Palestinian cause. Israeli government scepticism about Sadat's intentions, or even clarity about what those intentions were, did not abate when President Jimmy Carter replaced Gerald Ford in 1977. Israel was prisoner to a concept that Arab leaders could not and would not make a true and real peace with Israel. Gamal Abdel Nasser had done his job well in terms of influencing Israeli doubts about trusting Arab leaders. Sadat's public diplomacy of disparaging Israel, but sporadic private attempts to reach agreements with it did little to instill among Israelis a sense of logic or trust in his behaviour. When Israeli leaders and their foreign ministry personnel had doubts about President Carter's attitudes towards Israel, when they developed chagrin about his public remarks about a Palestinian homeland or Israel's need to consider negotiating with the PLO, doubts about Sadat or his intentions could not be even addressed until they were certain that their relationship with Washington was on more solid ground.

After the Egyptian President's unexpected November 1977 trip to Jerusalem, Sadat felt offended that Begin did not reply in kind with a similar magnanimous gesture, like a public promise to withdraw from all of Sinai or remove the settlements there. Begin and Dayan were not interested in gestures, they were interested in trading land in Sinai for a peace treaty with Egypt but with little if any territorial withdrawals on the other fronts. Except for a few occasions, when Sadat and Begin met, they talked past each other. Their personalities clashed, causing a willing President Carter to become the intermediary between the two protagonists. In almost two weeks of negotiation at Camp David, Sadat and Begin only met twice. And when the two did meet in bilateral talks, tension characterized their relationship. That tension was repeatedly reinforced when Israeli and Egyptian negotiators met. Sadat's advisers were particularly reluctant to either advocate or support a separate agreement with Israel, especially one which did not explicitly spell out some guarantee for the Palestinians and withdrawal on other fronts.

American officials associated with Egyptian–Israeli negotiations were not only surprised at Sadat's visit to Jerusalem, but were equally dismayed at the surprises he presented them and his increasing willingness to reach something less than a comprehensive peace with the Israelis.

In the months before the September 1978 Camp David talks, Egyptian–Israeli relations were sour at best. Israeli officials did not trust either President Carter or his national security adviser, Zbigniew Brzezinski. Carter was intensely irritated with the slow pace of the Middle East peace negotiations. Sadat and Begin continued to be deeply distrustful of each other, and diplomatic exchanges between them continued to be sterile.[8] Carter invited Begin and Sadat to Camp David to resolve the crisis in relations between them. The atmosphere surrounding Egyptian–Israeli negotiations was anything but clear.

For Egypt and Israel, the Camp David Accords, the framework dealing with the Palestinians, was a written agreement, where both sides agreed to disagree. It was a signed agreement, witnessed by the United States, but contained profound distrust about what was intended, what was promised – the settlements, Jerusalem, etc. The Egyptians wanted 'linkage' between the Egyptian–Israeli treaty and progress towards Palestinian autonomy in the West Bank and Gaza. Begin rejected the concept of linkage. Just like the prelude to Camp David, at Camp David, and afterwards, there was mistrust between Egyptians and Israelis, differing interpretations of what needed to be accomplished and what was accomplished and promised at Camp David. At the Blair House talks in Washington in October 1978, initial optimism gave way to disputes over substance: timing of Israeli withdrawals, establishment of diplomatic relations, possibilities of revising a treaty after five years, US commitments to both sides, problems relating to Israel's demand for guaranteed oil supplies, and Egypt's request for a timetable for ending the Israeli military government in the West Bank and Gaza. President Carter had to intervene in the talks in Washington and again with a more dramatic presidential visit to Egypt and Israel in March 1979. Israeli leaders continued to mistrust American mediation; Cairo and Washington bristled over Israeli cabinet decisions to continue building settlements; tension and misunderstanding between Egypt and Israel did not abate.

In Article VI of the 26 March 1979 Egyptian–Israeli peace treaty, Israel insisted on a commitment from Egypt to make its treaty with Israel a diplomatic priority over previous agreed upon defence arrangements with the Arab world. But in Sadat's perception, having signed such a treaty with such an article did not remove Egypt from its natural Arab orbit. To be sure, Egypt was ostracized by an angry Arab world for much of the 1980s, but Egypt and Egyptians still saw themselves as integral if not central to the future of the Arab world.

On the other hand, Israel's priority remained detaching Egypt's strategic involvement in any future Arab–Israeli conflict. Israel remained focused on existence, defence, security, and fear of the next war. Israelis often doubted whether they were signing an agreement with an individual or a country; they had self-doubts about giving up Sinai, an asset of strategic depth, and about returning the oil fields and the airfields. But Israel and Israelis wanted and expected more. Sadat's historic trip, Egypt's recognition of Israeli existence, the signing of the Camp David Accords and the Egyptian–Israel peace treaty signified a breakthrough of enormous proportions and with equally enormous expectations of what would transpire next. Israel and Israelis wanted to believe that if the key psychological barrier was broken in terms of Arab (read Egyptian) negative attitudes towards the Jewish State, then peace would follow between Israel and its Arab neighbours. Those self-imposed and unrealistic expectations held by Israeli leaders and the Israeli public were met by disillusionment and profound reassessment about exchanging land for a hollow contextual peace.

For Egypt, its peace treaty with Israel was another interim agreement on the path towards total Israeli withdrawal from all of the territories taken in the June 1967 War, not merely the fulfillment of Sadat's goal of the return of Sinai to Egyptian sovereignty. Egypt fulfilled its goal of using diplomacy to liberate Sinai from Israeli control. Land was returned, but no one demanded that Egypt give Israel peace, at least the way Israelis defined it. Egypt's treaty relationship with Israel did mean its freedom from the costly conflict with Israel. It did not mean that Egypt was going to give up either its commitment to a comprehensive peace or stop advocating self-determination and an independent state for the Palestinians. Egypt's ability to promote these ends was temporarily truncated by the isolation placed on it by the remainder of the Arab world; yet neither Sadat's visit to Jerusalem, nor Begin's response with autonomy for the Palestinians, nor the signing of the Camp David Accords, nor the Egyptian–Israeli Peace Treaty changed the long-term objectives or perceptions in either Cairo or Jerusalem. A new dynamic of direct negotiations did occur; Washington reloaded its diplomatic guns with negotiating expertise, but a real long-term change in Egyptian–Israeli attitudes towards one another did not materialize.

Before Sadat's assassination in October 1981, Egypt and Israel set the precedents for their cold peace or cool normalization. Just a month after Sadat's visit to Jerusalem, Israeli Prime Minister Begin was personally hurt by the verbal epithets thrown at him in particular as a 'Shylock and a fascist'. Articles, anecdotes, and cartoons in the Egyptian press depicted Jews as immoral, hypocritical, unreliable, unmanly, intransigent, insecure, greedy, ill-intentioned, and chronically suspicious of everyone.[9] Begin appealed to Sadat directly and to his foreign ministers such as Muhammad Ibrahim Kamel in January 1978 to have such articles quashed.[10] For his own part, Begin was not averse to indicting the Egyptian media in public for its anti-semitic remarks, something he did at the Knesset within a week after rebuking Foreign Minister Kamel. When Israel invaded Lebanon in March 1978, the Egyptian daily *Akhbar al-Yawm*, described Begin as 'intransigent and defiant', and the invasion itself as a 'Hitlerite military adventure'.[11] Cairo's *al-Jumhuriyah* described the invasion as 'part of the Zionist attempt to annihilate the Palestinian people, whose principles were laid down by Herzl, and whom Begin has been one of the most efficient advocates since Dyar Yassin'.[12] Disputes about settlements and over the definition and application of Palestinian autonomy added fuel to a smouldering fire of dislike and animosity. In 1980, Israel's first ambassador to Egypt was socially boycotted and the Israeli embassy staff faced difficulties in renting apartments in Cairo. Almost no tourism from Egypt to Israel materialized and few commercial deals were negotiated. Academic and cultural exchanges were stillborn. Major professional associations in Egypt, like the lawyers, engineers, physicians, and General Federation of Trade Unionists formally boycotted agreements with Israel and banned participation in the normalization process. In a very public manner, Egyptian Deputy Prime Minister, Hassan al-Tuhami, called Jews 'treacherous and hypocritical' and said that it was not in vain that they were 'labeled such in history books and that Israel was a *shibh dawla* (quasi-state) doomed to disappear'.[13]

The very difficult and unsatisfactory autonomy talks which took place in 1979 and 1980 only added to the tension between Egyptians and Israelis. Each act of violence between Palestinians and Israelis became a reason to suspend or stop the autonomy talks; any unilateral Israeli action in the territories – from building settlements, to changing laws, to the deportation of Palestinians – rejuvenated Egyptian beliefs that Israel was not interested in comprehensive peace. In Israel, the media did not tire of charging Egypt of bad faith. In March 1980, whether true or not, reference to a 'secret document' emanating from the Egyptian foreign ministry was reported in the Israeli daily *Yediot Aharonot* which claimed that Egyptian officials were instructed to keep cooperation with Israel to a minimum.[14] In 1980, an Israeli foreign ministry report analyzing the normalization process said that there was 'an Egyptian tendency, particularly at the sub-presidential level, [to] deliberately slow down progress and the rate of normalization, and that progress could have been more substantial had the Egyptians been more forthcoming'.[15]

INSTITUTIONALIZING THE NORM OF DISTRUSTFUL RELATIONS (1979–1990s)

By the early 1980s, a pattern of Egyptian–Israeli bilateral behaviour had been established. Both Israel and Egypt believed that the other would not go to war. Both wanted to remain at least relatively close to Washington. The shift of the international community's preoccupation and regional concern to events in and around the Persian Gulf directed attention away from additional efforts to resolve outstanding issues of the Arab–Israeli conflict. Adamantly opposed to what Sadat had done, the Arab world had no interest in broadening Arab–Israeli negotiations. In the early 1980s, neither the Israeli, Egyptian, or American governments were prepared or able to give attention to broader issues unresolved from previous Egyptian–Israeli negotiations. Egypt and Israel had a negotiated treaty in which Israeli withdrawals were set to a timetable; in return Egypt provided diplomatic recognition. Egypt wanted to sustain its ties with the Arab world and Israel had grand expectations about full normalization with Egypt over a short period of time.

What is so remarkable is that the Egyptian–Israeli treaty withstood repeated disintegration from a series of events, each of which alone might have caused Cairo to at least suspend adherence to the treaty. Egypt never publicly offered to scrap its relationship with Israel. President Husni Mubarak's immediate priority was not his relationship with Israel, but Egypt's crying economic and infrastructure needs. Preparing for war again with Israel would have drained Egypt to the point of implosion. So for the next decade and a half, the Egyptian–Israeli treaty bent, but it did not break. Israeli actions against Arab targets and management of the Palestinians were sufficient for any Egyptian government to call into question adherence to the treaty. Israeli policies fuelled Egyptian domestic opposition to the treaty. Moreover, unfulfilled Egyptian expectations of a 'peace dividend' were met with disillusionment which carried over into general negative attitudes towards Israel. Besides the emotional issue of Israel's control over Jerusalem, more than a dozen non-bilateral issues presented themselves as volatile explosives, each separately and collectively capable of torpedoing the treaty. Egyptian reaction to Israeli-initiated events demonstrated that Cairo was not going to crawl under the Nile and forget its interests in the rest of the Arab world. Each of the following contributed to Egypt's distaste for Israeli leaders and its policies, receiving broad Egyptian governmental criticism and media outrage:

• Palestinian autonomy talks not reaching fruition
• Israel's bombing of the Iraqi nuclear reactor in June 1981
• Application of Israeli law to the Golan Heights in December 1981
• Israel's invasion of Lebanon in June 1982 and the Sabra and Shatilla Palestinian refugee camp massacres three months later
• Israel's prolonged presence and non-withdrawal from South Lebanon

- Continued growth and expansion of Jewish settlements
- The bombing of the PLO's Tunis headquarters in October 1985
- Israel's administration of the Palestinians in the West Bank and Gaza
- The outbreak and Israel's management of the Palestinian *intifada* in December 1987
- Soviet Jewish immigration (1988–91), seen as a threat to Palestinian demographic control of the West Bank
- The deportation of HAMAS activists to Lebanon in December 1992
- The killing of Palestinians in the Hebron mosque in February 1993
- The opening of the Western Wall tunnel in September 1996
- Delay in implementing an agreement on Hebron in 1996

These issues saw regular harsh criticism leveled at Israel and Israelis from the Egyptian press. Moreover, disputatious bilateral issues contributed to the reinforcement of Egyptian–Israeli mutual ill-will. These included the dispute over the land in Taba, Egyptian 'care' of Israeli nationals on Egyptian soil, and Egyptian characterization of the Israeli prime minister, Israelis, Zionists, and Jews.

Initially, in the autumn and winter of 1980, a whole series of positive exchange visits occurred between high-ranking Egyptian and Israeli officials. Sadat wanted to show Washington that his commitment to his treaty with Israel was intact. Israel had still to fulfill its obligation to withdraw from all of Sinai by April 1982. By the late spring of 1981, especially after Israel's bombing of the Iraqi nuclear reactor three days after a Begin–Sadat summit, Egyptian–Israeli cultural, trade, tourist, and commercial relations were put into deep freeze. Begin's re-election as prime minister in June 1981, Sadat's assassination in October, Israel's invasion of Lebanon in June 1982, and the massacre in the Palestinian refugee camps in Lebanon in September 1982, all intervened to work against developing a positive atmosphere in Egyptian–Israeli relations.

Egypt did not voluntarily recuse itself from the Arab world. Its isolation was imposed by angry Arab capitals. Repeated Arab world condemnation of its recognition of Israel influenced the Egyptian government to do the minimum in normalizing relations with Israel. But it also generated powerful motivation among Egyptians to show to their Arab brethren that the diplomatic process was the most advantageous to pursue if Israeli-held territories and assets were to be returned to Arab sovereignty. Constantly, Israeli leaders remained unsure about whether the exchange of oil and land could be balanced with the intangibles of peace. No American mediator monitored, rewarded, or punished either side for failing to change the psychology of mistrust. Israel pursued a security axiom towards the rest of the Arab world by implementing the obverse of the Golden Rule – 'Do Unto Others Before They Do Unto You'.

For the remainder of the decade and into the 1990s, the Egyptian government believed that its negotiations and treaty with Israel did not preclude vigorous and uninterrupted support for the Palestinian cause or stark opposition to Israeli policies applied to the Arab world or in the Golan Heights, West Bank, Jerusalem or Gaza territories. Likewise, Cairo did not relinquish any desire to play a significant or central role in the inter-Arab system.

In 1983, when asked about why one should sustain the E-I Treaty in 1983, President Mubarak said,

> What is the meaning of the annulment of the Camp David agreement?... Shall I return Sinai to Israel? ... It means the declaration of a state of war with Israel. If I want to declare a state of war, it is imperative for me to be militarily prepared. In other words, I should halt development and focus on the evolution of services. I should concentrate all my efforts on war. Who will foot the bill for war? The Arabs? I do not know. Suppose that we obtained the necessary funding from them – no less than L50–60 billion for armaments to enable the Army to stand its ground. Who will give me arms to fight Israel? The US will not give me arms to fight Israel. Furthermore, Europe also will not give me arms. [As for the Soviets, they]... will impose terms on us – and this is another matter...[16]

Addressing the connection between Egypt's Arab commitments and Cairo's relationship with Israel, Mubarak said in 1987,

> I would like to tell our brothers in Syria that the peace treaty is not against the Palestine question. When we sign a treaty we sign it because we are convinced of it. We did not and will not violate the [1950 Arab] Collective Defence Pact. We do not accept relinquishing one inch of land and will not negotiate over Palestine without the Palestinian people's representatives. But if someone asks me to violate Egypt's commitments and cancel the treaty, I will ask him to what use will this be to him and me? We are committed to peace and all the Arabs are committed to solving the issue peacefully.[17]

More specifically, Egyptian leaders linked progress on the Palestinian issue with progress in normalizing Egyptian attitudes and relations towards Israel. Not only was Egypt withholding progress in normalization with Israel, but in the 1980s it pressed Washington to upgrade the term 'legitimate rights' for the Palestinians to 'Palestinian self-determination'. Butros Ghali, the Egyptian Minister of State for Foreign Affairs, said in an interview in Cairo's *October* magazine on 20 July 1986 that 'relations between Egypt and Israel would not reach a stage of full normalization, quantitatively and qualitatively unless a comprehensive settlement of the Middle East crisis materializes'.

For Israelis, their relationship with Egypt in the 1980s fell far short of expectations. Cairo was in violation of Israel's deepest hope and expectation that a real, true, separate peace would restrain Egypt from advocating on behalf of other Arabs with territorial grievances against Israel. Despite the points already made about an absence of trust or goodwill flowing from Egypt to Israel, Israel had accomplished the task by 1979 of assuring itself at least for the intermediate future that Egypt would not be part of an Arab war coalition against Israel. Israel's main motivation for moving into Lebanon in 1982 was not meant to test Egypt's intentions on the linkage question – an Arab state was attacked by Israel, what would Egypt do? Israel's intention was to eradicate or destroy the PLO infrastructure in southern Lebanon.

As part of Egypt's view of Israel, the prolonged negotiation over the disputed land in Taba, a mere 1.29 sq km, added to Egyptian perceptions that Israel was a sly and untrustworthy negotiating partner. Resolution of the Taba dispute saw Cairo return its ambassador to Israel after a four year absence.

In characterizing Israel's harsh treatment of the Palestinians in 1986, the Egyptian media refered to it as 'expansionist and intransigent in nature' which made 'it a menace to the entire region'.[18] In criticizing Israeli Prime Minister Yitzhak Shamir personally, *al-Akhbar* said, 'Shamir's obstinacy and solitary position to the widespread support for the international conference signifies his desire to perpetuate the grave situation in the Middle East. His concept... indicates that riots, tension, and brutal acts of repression by Tel-Aviv's forces will continue'.[19] Typical of the continuing vitriolic condemnation of Israel and Israelis, the editorial in *al-Jumhuriyah* in September 1986 noted,

> Actually the various parties in Israel do not differ on the objective. They want more territorial expansion and they want to expel the Arabs and slaughter them and they want to cut off the heads which try to rise. They want the Arabs to be submissive sacrificial sheep without rights. They want them to work in silence without claiming any citizenship rights because they are regarded as living in the occupied territory temporarily. If a Jew can do the work done by an Arab then the latter is dismissed or killed.[20]

In the mid- and late 1980s, Israelis recoiled with anger as they witnessed on Egyptian soil repeated attacks against their citizens and diplomats. In August 1985, an Israeli diplomat was killed in Cairo; in October 1985 an Egyptian soldier killed five Israeli tourists, and then was hailed by some in the Egyptian press as a national hero; in March 1986 Israeli diplomats were attacked as they left the International Book Fair, and in February 1990 nine Israeli tourists were killed and 21 wounded in Sinai when masked men attacked an Israeli tourist bus.

With the outbreak of the Palestinian *intifada* in December 1987, a four-year winter blasted against Israel. Relentlessly, the Egyptian media vilified Israel and its leaders, comparing them to Nazis, the South African government, and equating Israel as barbaric, murderous, and blood-thirsty.[21] No nuance was employed by the Egyptian media in describing Israeli actions:

> As for those who planned to consolidate the Zionist entity on the land by deluding themselves that the Palestinian national personality would disappear through deportation and extermination, oppression and collective massacre – all these methods, which are more horrible than those of the Nazis and Fascists – their hopes collapsed in the face of Palestinian determination to lead a legitimate national struggle... Many of the illusions which served Israel in imposing its control over the Gaza Strip and West Bank cities have drowned in a sea of blood of children and youngsters.[22]

The occasion of Israel's handling of the Palestinian uprising, its embattled portrayal by the international media, and its reluctance to move forward towards a comprehensive peace was used by Egypt to support the Palestinians. Cairo indicted Israel for slowness in initiating Israeli–Palestinian talks and continuously voiced support for Palestinian statehood. Egypt did not withdraw its ambassador from Tel-Aviv as it had done after Israel's 1982 invasion into Lebanon, and Egyptian officials continued to meet with their Israeli counterparts; but the flow of traffic was distinctly from Israel to Egypt. Egypt picked its Israeli interlocutors, and though ministerial meetings were held with Likud party members, there was a clear preference to meet with Labour party stalwarts, or at least those who leaned towards a compromise with the Palestinians. Noticeably, President Mubarak refused to meet with Likud Prime Minister Shamir, because he felt such a meeting would be 'fruitless'.[23] From 1987 until after the convocation of the Madrid Middle East Peace Conference in October 1991, Egyptian sources leveled two distinctive kinds of censure against Israel. One emanated from official government circles. It focused on the procedure, substance, and possible outcomes of achieving a negotiated settlement between Israel and the Palestinians. It was mild in tone, but firm in policy preference. The second came from the secular and Islamic Egyptian press. It was viciously rancorous, hurling attacks against Israel, Israelis, Zionists, and Jews.

The Egyptian media provided a clear outline of Egypt's view of its peace with Israel and what should happen next in the peace process. Despite a very frosty relationship with the PLO in late 1989 and throughout 1990, Egypt did not diminish its commitment to Palestinian aspirations. Egyptian Minister of State for Foreign Affairs, Butros Ghali said in May 1991, 'We have recognized the PLO as the representative of the Palestinians. We do not always agree with it, we disagreed with its support for Saddam Hussein during the Gulf crisis, but a role is reserved for the PLO'.[24] And President Mubarak stated in July: 'The dialogue with the Palestinians is continuing and does not stop, because the Palestinian issue is not the exclusive province of Arafat or anyone else. It is an issue of the whole people, and Egypt has worked from the outset to ensure that the Palestinian issue is the issue of a people and a state, not a question of refugees'.[25]

In 1991, Egyptian Foreign Minister Amr Musa remarked that 'peace [with Israel] is no luxury, but a need'.[26] Egyptian Presidential adviser, Usama al-Baz said that 'most Arabs and Israelis realize that their future security does not lie in the acquisition of sophisticated weapons, ... but only through mutual recognition and coexistence... What poses a threat is certain policy lines, and not Israel's presence in the heart of the Arab world or the Arab presence around Israel'.[27] And in the prelude to the Madrid Conference, al-Baz said that 'talk about a final solution for the Palestinian problem has been postponed for the time being, because the Arab parties have accepted the principle of a gradual solution of the Palestinian issue'.[28] Sceptical Israeli analysts could easily conclude, as they have in 1997 from such remarks,[29] that long-term Egyptian objectives have been consistent in using diplomacy to bring Israel back to the June 1967 borders and thereafter resolve the question of Palestine through Israel's possible demise either territorially or demographically.

In interviews in April 1992, March 1994, and January 1995 President Mubarak reiterated that pragmatism motivates Egypt's relationship with Israel, that there is 'no alternative to diplomacy in the new world order'; that 'peace was made by Egypt, no one else' and that 'we regret not implementing Camp David... today 75 per cent of the occupied territories are covered by settlements. We had them in our hands without settlements'; and that 'if I cooperate strategically with Israel or anyone else, then it is because I have an interest'.[30]

Meanwhile, the Egyptian press attacked Israeli leaders and particularly Shamir in the most severest of anti-Semitic terms. The Egyptian paper, al-Musawwar titled an article, 'Shamir – Hitler number two, must go away before his loathsome crimes finish his own people off'.[31] A cartoon on the front cover of Ruz al-Yusuf portrayed Shamir in Nazi garb, decorated with both a swastika and the Star of David, raising his right arm in a Nazi salute and holding a club in his left.[32]

In the years before the Madrid Conference, President Mubarak, other leading Egyptian politicians and the media constantly criticized Shamir for tardiness, procrastination, foot-dragging, and inflexibility for refusing to consider going to an international conference. Egyptian vituperation did halt at the step of Israeli leaders; during 1991, Israel was variously accused in the Egyptian media of 'trying to harm Egyptian tourism and agriculture, undermining the Egyptian economy by the use of counterfeit dollars and society by drugs or AIDS, planning to deplete Egyptian water reserves, and using the Israel Academic Centre in Cairo for espionage purposes'.[33]

With Saddam Hussein's defeat in 1991, Egypt, having taken the lead Arab role in helping to organize the Arab part of the anti-Iraq international coalition, rode a heady crest. Egypt felt it was on the road to vindication with its choice of diplomacy rather than war with Israel. In the period from the end of the Gulf War through the meeting of the Madrid peace conference, Egyptian officials laid out their signposts for a comprehensive diplomatic solution to the Arab–Israel conflict.

Arab capitals that had never before considered joining the American-catalyzed diplomatic effort joined in the process. But the Gulf War itself, and its diplomatic aftermath witnessed only a temporary reduction in the intensity and frequency of anti-Israeli sentiment emanating from Cairo. Negative sentiment against any peace with Israel poured out after the Madrid conference, this time more frequently from Egyptian Muslim sources: 'Islam does not sanction peace with usurpers of Islamic lands and holy places... submission to the Zionist enemy... selling out the Palestine question... for the benefit of the Jews'.[34] The Egyptian fundamentalist Islamic press was full of hatred for Israel and Jews. Lamenting the Arab race to legitimize relations with Israel, Dr. Ahmad al-Malat, an Egyptian Muslim Brotherhood official, said in December 1994 that despite all the concessions Arabs have made to Israel, 'the "sense of *jihad*" is still very much alive in the heart of people who have opted for *jihad* until the Palestinian soil is liberated from the "dirt of the Jews". However, these *mujahidin* (strugglers) are now being accused of "terrorism and extremism" by Arafat, who wants to appease the Jews'.[35]

Until the election of Yitzhak Rabin in June 1992, the Egyptian media hurled invective after onslaught at Israeli leaders, especially the prime minister. Once Rabin replaced Shamir, the level and rate of invective directed at Israel, at least from official governmental circles and the secular Egyptian press, subsided noticeably. A week after he took office, Rabin visited Cairo, the first meeting that an Egyptian president had with an Israeli prime minister in six years; Mubarak promised a return visit to Israel (which came at Rabin's funeral in November 1995). A whole wave of Israeli politicians subsequently visited Egypt in 1992–93. Heightened Egyptian expectations that Rabin would make critical concessions to the Syrians and to the Palestinians did not materialize; anger resurfaced from official government circles and the Egyptian media. Egyptian impatience turned to angry criticism when Rabin expelled some 400 plus HAMAS activists in December 1992. In 1994 and 1995, Egypt maintained a vigorous advocacy against Israel. In censuring Israel's refusal to sign the Nuclear Proliferation Treaty in 1995, Egyptian Foreign Minister Musa had become a one-man protagonist indicting Israel almost daily for six months prior for its unqualified and uncompromising reluctance to sign the treaty.

Hollowness and anxiety continued to typify Israel's relationship with Egypt. Those feelings did nothing to diminish Israel's strategic preference for keeping Egypt out of any Arab circle contemplating the use of military force against her. Gradually, in public suppositions Israeli leaders articulated an Egyptian policy: Cairo was shaping a policy for keeping a minimum peace with Israel while seeking to preserve its central spot in the inter-Arab political system. Cairo would encourage Egyptian nationals to embrace Israel only gingerly if at all. In September 1989, the then Defence Minister Yitzhak Rabin remarked that President Mubarak had 'managed to prove to the Arab world specifically, but also to the entire world in general, that it is possible to return, and that Egypt can stand its own ground and attain a respectable place in the Arab and African world without giving up the peace agreement or the Israeli Embassy in Cairo and the fact that the Israeli flag flies over that city'.[36] Showing his displeasure with Egypt's stinginess in normalizing relations with Israel, the Director General of the Ministry of Defence, Major-General David Ivri, said in April 1992, 'The peace with Egypt is not peace, it is actually a cease-fire that has continued for 15 years; Mubarak has not created any Egyptian interest in Israel's continued existence'.[37] Defence Minister Moshe Arens repeated this charge, prompting Egyptian Foreign Minister Amr Musa to reply that such statements 'reflect stiffness of mind, disregard for ongoing world developments, and desire to abort the peace process as a whole'.[38]

In July 1991, Prime Minister Shamir gave his very negative estimate of relations with Egypt: 'Normalization [with Egypt]', he said,

> has sunk into oblivion; there is no normalization now. So many years after signing the peace treaty, there are no normal trade relations with Israel; there is no cultural cooperation; there is no Egyptian tourism to Israel. It is as if Israel and Egypt were not living in peace but were two absolute alien and estranged countries. This situation should come to an end.[39]

Yitzhak Rabin, certainly more understanding in his assessment, though no less critical of the slowness in Israel's normalization with Egypt, said just three months before his election as prime minister in June 1992: 'I am admittedly disappointed by the lack of satisfactory progress in normalizing ties between two countries at peace; however, I am also aware that the Egyptians have difficulties in promoting normalization before the peace process gathers momentum, especially in the Israeli–Palestinian sphere'.[40]

While 'official' Egypt did what was necessary to sustain a pragmatic and cool relationship with Israel, the Egyptian media was condemnatory of Israeli policies. Once the Oslo agreements were signed, Cairo shifted into a faster gear in pressuring Israel to be more forthcoming with the Palestinians. Gladly, Egypt took up the role of the major intermediary played by the Norwegians in achieving the Oslo Accords. Egypt became more than the main avenue for discussion for negotiating and implementing agreements; Cairo became the central advocate of the Palestinian view on negotiations with the Israel. At every possible juncture, Cairo accused Israel of tardiness in negotiations. The opening of bilateral and multilateral negotiations between and among Israel and its Arab neighbours after 1991 did little to diminish the barrage of negative epithets showered on Israel and Israelis.

Official Egypt continued to make the distinction between the need to sustain the minimum of substance demanded from the peace treaty relationship with Israel, regularly criticizing Israeli slowness in negotiating concessions for the Palestinians. In the aftermath of the February 1994 killing of Palestinians in Hebron, the official Egyptian media accused the Israeli government and its army of planning and executing the massacre.[41] By the end of 1994, Egypt hosted the tripartite summit of Syria and Saudi Arabia, primarily aimed at slowing the normalization of relations between Israel and other Arabs states. According to Deputy Foreign Minister Yossi Beilin, that summit and Egyptian goals reflected the existence of 'mixed feelings' about normalization.[42]

As the Oslo II Accords were signed in 1995, Egypt kept its lukewarm bilateral relationship with Israel. During that year, whether taking the lead from official Cairo or not, Dr. Yusuf al-Qardawi, an Egyptian Muslim scholar, staunchly advocated boycotting Israeli products. 'Zionist goods may not be bought', he claimed,

> Buying them should be deemed one of God's greatest prohibitions, for they are goods that come to us from an enemy who occupies our lands – al-Aqsa Mosque, Hebron, and other places – and who seizes and usurps lands. Boycotting them is the duty of all Muslims. Buying their goods is reprehensible.[43]

Particularly vexing for Cairo was the election of Benjamin Netanyahu as Israel's prime minister in May 1996. Gone from government was Egypt's preferred partner in negotiations, the Israeli Labour party. After the election, especially towards the end of August, Cairo increasingly berated Israel for not implementing the withdrawal from Hebron and then assigned total blame to the Netanyahu government for instigating the Palestinian–Israel violence that flowed from the opening of the Hasmonean Tunnel in Jerusalem in September 1996. Cairo increasingly became the central axis for influencing Arab attitudes and the pace of Arab normalization with Israel. This was a key mechanism for Mubarak to assert Egypt's role in inter-Arab politics. While Cairo hosted an economic conference in November 1996, which included Israeli participation, in the days prior to the conference President Mubarak linked the possible convocation of the conference and the level of Israel's participation in it to the Israeli government's conduct in negotiations with the Palestinians. Just prior, *not after* the conference, Egypt announced the arrest of two individuals (one of whom was an Israeli citizen) on suspicion of spying for Israel. In addition, in the days before the conference opened in early November the Egyptian press hurled epithets against Israel, its policies and leaders. Egypt's media expressed fear of an economic takeover of the region by Israel. Though the conference was held and Israelis participated, bilateral Egyptian–Israeli relations before, during, and after the conference were filled with tension.[44]

In late 1996 and early 1997, Egypt continued to mistrust Israeli intentions while Israel continued to chafe under Egyptian criticism from official governmental circles and from various elites. Opinion pieces written in the Israeli and Egyptian press typified those attitudes. Apart from Cairo's increasing willingness to stand behind a hardline Palestinian negotiating attitude towards Israel over the issue of Israel's military withdrawal from Hebron, Israeli commentator Ron Ben-Yishai, writing in November 1996 in *Yediot Aharonot*, noted that,

> all the Israeli intelligence bodies are certain that the Egyptians are still committed to peace with Israel – not out of the love of Zion, but because they wish to preserve strategic ties with the United States and the annual flow of billions of dollars from Washington... Egyptian opposition leaders have been demanding that Israel be dwarfed to its natural size; today it is official policy. Israeli intelligence has reached the conclusion that two important elements of this policy are the Egyptian support for a Palestinian State in the territories and the efforts to neutralize Israel's nuclear abilities.[45]

In January 1997, editorials in the Israeli daily *Ma'ariv* typified Israeli press consternation about the interfering and nefarious role Egypt was playing in the Hebron negotiations. These editorials called on the Israeli government to 'mark the negative role being played by Egypt in these talks', accused Cairo of 'sowing discord between Israel and the Palestinians', called Cairo's involvement in the negotiations 'arrogant interference' and argued that it was 'unacceptable that every move in the peace process will be conditional on the approval of President Mubarak'.[46]

However, Israel's strategic view to use Cairo as a focal point for normalization with the Arab world remained intact, as outlined by Dr. Dore Gold, Netanyahu's foreign policy adviser,

> ... Israel recognizes Egypt's primary role. For us, any media campaigns with Egypt disturb us and harm the peace process. What

we want is to build a positive relationship with Egypt, one that could become a model for other countries in the region, so that the peace process can be broadened. The worst thing that could happen is for the [Israeli] people to see the relationship with Egypt deteriorating. We do not want this to happen.[47]

With the Hebron agreement finalized in mid-January 1997, Cairo radio proudly noted that the 'signing of this agreement undoubtedly highlights the importance of Egypt's role and the efforts President Husni Mubarak has been making to achieve a just, lasting and comprehensive peace in the Middle East'.[48] Obviously Cairo relishes being the role model that Israel would like in the process of normalization, however in neither the content nor tone which Egypt demonstrates.

CONCLUSIONS AND REPEATED AXIOMS

After the October 1973 War, Egypt and Israel took the major step to remove war as a political and strategic option with the other. But in signing the March 1979 Peace Treaty, respective negative attitudes of each other have changed much more slowly. Deeply rooted scepticism of the other's intentions have only mildly dissipated. Israel's treaty with Egypt has not brought the normalization Israelis wanted; many Egyptians still do not accept Israel as a reality. But the Egyptian–Israeli treaty relationship based upon direct negotiations with American mediation opened the critical door to the Israel–PLO mutual recognition of September 1993 and the Jordanian–Israeli treaty in October 1994. Significantly for Israel, Sadat's policies and those pursued by Mubarak vis-à-vis Israel have destroyed the 'Israel hatred consensus' which had uniformly existed in the Arab world. No matter how difficult Israeli–Palestinian negotiations may be in the future or how angry Egypt is with Israel and vice-versa on a bilateral matter, the mode of communication is no longer all-out struggle and war, but still only angry verbal exchanges.

On the macro-level, there was an Arab–Israeli conflict based solely on armed struggle. For some Middle Eastern states and organizations, there still remains an uncompromising conflict with Israel; for others it is no longer a conflict but a matter of defining respective national relationships with Israel and defining Israel's future role in the Middle East. Sadat broke the uniform Arab consensus of isolating Israel. A quarter century after the October War, there are relatively frequent high-level exchanges between Arab and Israeli politicians and businessmen. Israeli tourists are found in numerous Arab capitals; Israeli and Arab academics and artists exchange visits and no longer meet just at neutral sites. Tensions are reduced over specific political issues and have in many cases generated a common Arab–Israeli cause towards curbing state-sponsored terrorism or creating lucrative and joint commercial ventures. The conferences in Amman, Cairo, and Casablanca have all aimed at developing economic foci and cooperative interchange between Arab, Israeli, and other businessmen. Today's discussion is not about saving an Egyptian army from annihilation or about the return of Israeli POWs; today's discussion is not about an Arab boycott of Israel, but how fast economic normalization with Israel should proceed.

On the micro-level, from the mind and from the words of 'official Egypt', Israel has done too little too slowly for the recognition that Sadat gave to Israel. Israel's pace in returning the territories taken in the June 1967 War and its policies towards the Palestinians, other Arabs, and in creating settlements in the West Bank, have increased Egyptian irritation towards Israel. Neither the Egyptian–Israeli peace treaty nor normalization as defined by 'official Cairo' or the media have greatly altered negative views of Israel or Israelis. An impression exists that there is some lessening in verbal attacks against Jews and Zionism, at least in terms of frequency. In disagreements between Israel and Arab sides over specific issues in Arab–Israeli negotiations, Egypt has willingly defended Arab positions. In part, Cairo has used the reinvigorated Arab–Israeli negotiating peace process to revalidate its credentials as the champion of 'Arab rights'. For example, as engaged defender of the Palestinian view in negotiations over the 1997 Hebron withdrawal agreement or as a 'bridge', messenger service, or interlocutor in negotiations between Israel and Syria, Egypt sustains the same positions advocated by Anwar Sadat prior to and after the October 1973 War: Israel's return of all the 1967 territories and the establishment of an independent Palestinian State.

Israelis remain highly disappointed that a change in Egyptian attitudes towards them has fallen significantly short of what were initially unrealistic expectations. Egyptian recognition did not bring the normalized relations that Israelis wanted. Likewise, the process of negotiations over tangible assets and their return has not significantly altered Egypt's emotional attitudes towards Israel and Israelis. Until 'official Cairo' and especially the print media make a concerted and systematic effort to tone down verbal attacks against Israel, strain and anxiety will remain integral to the relationship.

Israelis are slowly coming to the unwanted but reluctantly accepted realization that their relationship with Egypt will not be like the United States enjoys with Canada. Israelis may have to realize that what criticism they hear and read from Cairo, while highly objectionable and contrary to the spirit of normalization, may be necessary for the political management of Egyptian domestic constituencies. In the absence of war for a quarter century between Israel and Egypt, both countries are learning to administer core ingredients of mistrust and tension that still characterize their relationship.

CHARACTERISTIC AXIOMS OVER THE LAST QUARTER CENTURY

Talks, negotiations, and agreements held on the official level between
Israel and its Arab neighbours, including Egypt *do not change
necessarily or automatically negative emotional feelings and attitudes*
which Arabs, including Egyptians, may have for Israel. A signature does
not change feelings. Israelis did not understand that the Egyptian–Israeli
treaty was an interim agreement for Egypt's broader goal of a
comprehensive peace – which Cairo read as full Israeli withdrawal from
the 1967 territories and the establishment of an independent Palestinian
State with Jerusalem as its capital.

*Israel continues to feel that Egypt is inattentive to the realities of the
Middle East*, where there are still Arab and other Middle Eastern states
interested in Israel's destruction and therefore Israel must still wield
levers of power.

*Israel wrongly expects that concessions on bilateral procedures or
substance will change Arab attitudes positively towards Israel and
Israelis.* Returning tangible assets did not result in attitudinal changes.
Mutual mistrust and Israel's profound disappointment with what it saw
as meagre Egyptian attitudinal shifts, left the bilateral atmosphere
clouded by anger and recrimination. No guarantee exists that an
exchange of tangible assets will see a corresponding change in
psychological attitudes.

Israeli expectations remain too high. Israelis believe(d) that a separate
peace with Egypt would force a logical conclusion of normal diplomatic
relations. They believe(d) that detailed supervision and control of their
relations with neighbours through monitors, mechanisms of enforcement,
guarantees, and assurances will generate changes in attitudes towards Israel,
Israelis, Jews, Zionism, the presence of a Jewish State in the middle of the
Muslim world.

*On the formal level the treaty is meticulously preserved, but sharp
accusations through the media are the norm of normalization.*

A measure of Israeli scepticism remains: Is it Peace or Piece? After 18
years with a peace treaty with Egypt, Israelis are still sceptical about
Egypt's long-term intentions, and remain cautious about long-term
Egyptian objectives. One view holds that Egypt is pursuing a policy of
'phases', reducing Israel to its size of 1967, keeping relentless pressure
on Israel to reduce its territory, allow the Palestinians to develop a state,
and at some point in the next century, it will be possible for the Arab
world not to have peace with Israel, but a piece of Israel.

*Meaning of normalization, or its importance with Egypt has become
bifurcated in the minds of Israelis.* Attitudes of the general public differ
significantly from the Israeli military. In the years after 1979, Israel paid
very close attention to the level of normalization with Egypt. Would the
Egyptian–Israeli treaty hold? As Israel has broadened its relations with
other Arab states, the general public seems not to pay the same intense

attention to Egypt as it did when Egypt was the only country on non-war terms. Especially after the 1991 Gulf War and the beginning of the Madrid process, and all the more so after 1993, with the signing of the Oslo Accords between Israel and the PLO, Israelis in general did not take the temperature of the Egyptian–Israeli relationship as frequently as they did in the late 1970s and early 1980s. However, the Israeli military remains keenly attuned to evaluating Egyptian military capabilities and intentions, and the importance of Cairo staying out of a potential Arab war coalition against Israel.

Progress on other Arab–Israeli negotiation fronts does not guarantee warmer Egyptian attitudes towards Israel. Perhaps to the contrary, progress on other tracks has seen Egypt more stringent in a consistently relentless policy aimed at Israel's full withdrawal from all the territories won in the June 1967 War. And with various negotiations with Israel completed (Jordan) or in various stages of movement (Palestinians, Syria, and Lebanon) Egypt exerts efforts to limit the manner, breadth, and pace of real normalization with Israel.

As the final status talks draw closer and the clock goes on ticking, one might expect *even tenser times to come in the Egyptian–Israeli relationship.* In the hypothetical environment, what will Cairo do if the PLO, Syria, Lebanon, and Jordan are in treaty relationships with Israel? Will Cairo continue to fault Israel for doing less than it promised? But if negotiations do not transpire between Israel and other Arab states, or the PLO–Israeli negotiations continue to go like a car with only 4 of 8 cylinders working, Egypt will be able to keep its level of normalization low.

Israeli leaders believe that when Egypt 'rides' the Palestinian horse politically, it is merely reflecting Egypt's real negative intentions towards Israel. For a quarter century, Egypt's verbal war with Israel has not appreciatively dissipated; normalization has been systematically cool or cold. *For Egypt, normalization means not having the Egyptian–Israeli relationship deteriorate to something beyond non-war.* Among some in the Israeli establishment there is a belief that Egypt's peace with Israel is a sophisticated 'Trojan Horse'.

President Mubarak has evolved his policies into a political synthesis from both Sadat and Nasser. Vis-à-vis Israel, that has meant supporting the mechanism of diplomacy while insisting on Egypt's leadership role in inter-Arab affairs.

Significant regional and international changes affecting the political landscape of the Middle East have not greatly effected Egypt's attitude towards Israel or Israeli attitudes towards Egypt. Neither the demise of the Soviet Union, nor end of the Cold War in the Middle East, nor the Gulf War, nor even expansion of Arab–Israeli talks have altered attitudes or expectations of the other.

Egyptian opinion-makers have slowly come to the conclusion that there is a difference in policy options between Likud and Labour. However, the presence of the Labour party in office does not necessarily mean that shrill accusations against Israel have been or will be halted. *American support for Egypt has not waned because Cairo remains tough on Israel.* Egypt has learned that if it engages in an active fashion in prodding Arab states and the PLO to keep active negotiations with Israel going, then Washington will not pressurize it to tone down the antagonistic verbal assaults sent officially and unofficially in Israel's direction. Washington has not exhorted Egypt sufficiently to have Cairo change its public demeanour in opposing Israeli policies which it finds objectionable. *And there is no apparent interest or concerted effort on the part of the US to admonish or punish Egypt for using harsh language against Israel.*

US–Egyptian relations – Anwar Sadat intruded himself and Egypt strategically between the special US–Israeli relationship. Washington made its developing and positive relations with Egypt a stepping stone to better relations with the moderate Arab states, Camp David and the Egyptian–Israeli peace treaty notwithstanding. Though Egypt was Washington's most trusted Arab ally for more than two decades, that special relationship is losing its lustre as other Arab states and the Palestinians establish positive and strategic relations with the US. *Despite a quarter century of negotiations with Israel, Egypt retains resentment towards Washington because of its special relationship with Israel.*

There is an emerging Israeli–Egyptian competition for leadership in the Middle East. Cairo does not want to lose the role or opportunity to remain at the forefront of regional inter-Arab politics and a bridge, if not *the* bridge for Israeli entry and acceptance in the region. Israelis for their part want to by-pass Cairo's desired gate-keeper or bridging role.

NOTES

1. See interviews with President Anwar Sadat in *October* magazine, 12 and 26 March 1978, as quoted in *Foreign Broadcasts Information Service – Middle East and North Africa* (hereafter FBIS-MENA), 14 and 28 March 1978.
2. Author's interview with Zaid Rifa'i, 9 January 1993, Amman, Jordan.
3. Author's interview with Abd al-Halim Khaddam, 18 July 1993, Damascus.
4. Author's interview with Nabil al-Araby, 26 February 1993, Atlanta, Georgia.
5. Study Group on 'Lessons Learned From Arab–Israeli Negotiations', Remarks by Joseph Sisco and Roy Atherton (participants in Secretary of State Kissinger's 1973–76 'Shuttle Diplomacy'), United States Institute of Peace, Washington, D.C., 3 April 1991.
6. Edward R. F. Sheehan, *The Arabs, Israelis, and Kissinger: A Secret History of American Diplomacy in the Middle East*, New York, 1976, p.37.
7. Author's interview with General Muhammad Abd al-Ghani al-Gamasy, Chief of Operations of the Egyptian Armed Forces during the October 1973 War, 10 November 1992, Heliopolis, Egypt.
8. William B. Quandt, *Camp David: Peacemaking and Politics*, Washington, DC, 1986, p.206.

9. Colin Legum, ed. *Middle East Contemporary Survey* (hereafter MECS), Vol.II, 1977–78, New York, 1979, p.102.
10. Mohammed Ibrahim Kamel, *The Camp David Accords*, New York, 1986, pp.58–62.
11. *Akhbar al-Yawm*, 18 and 27 March 1978, or as quoted in FBIS-MENA, 22 and 31 March 1978 respectively.
12. *Al-Jumhuriyah*, 16 March 1978, or as quoted in FBIS-MENA, 17 March 1978.
13. Colin Legum, Haim Shaked, Daniel Dishon, eds, MECS, Vol.IV, 1979–80, pp.115–16. For the Tuhami interview with Muscat's, *al-Nahda*, see as published by the Middle East News Agency (MENA), Cairo, 5 April 1980 and quoted in this MECS, p.116.
14. *Yediot Aharonot*, 26 March 1980.
15. MECS, Vol.V, 1980–81, p.156.
16. Interview with Egyptian President Husni Mubarak in *al-Tadamun*, 5 November 1983, as quoted from MECS, Volume VIII, 1983–84, pp.380–81. For a similar attitude expressed by Mubarak, see his interview in *al-Ra'i al-Amm*, 8 October 1986.
17. Interview with Egyptian President Husni Mubarak, *al-Ittihad* (Abu Dhabi), 12 December 1987, as quoted in FBIS-NESA, 15 December 1987.
18. See *al-Akhbar*, 20 February and 8 April 1986.
19. Ibid., 25 November 1987.
20. Signed editorial by Muhammad al-Hayawan, *al-Jumhuriyah*, 3 September 1986.
21. See Itamar Rabinovich and Haim Shaked (eds), MECS, Vol.XI, 1987, p.351.
22. *Al-Akhbar*, 16 December 1987 and *al-Ahram*, 20 December 1987 as quoted from MECS, Vol.XI, 1987, p.351.
23. See *Yediot Aharonot*, 24 March 1989.
24. *Davar*, 15 May 1991, p.7.
25. *Al-Hayat* (London), 16 July 1991, p.5 as quoted in FBIS-NESA, 18 July 1991, p.8.
26. See Ami Ayalon, ed., MECS, Vol.XV, 1991, p.366.
27. *Davar*, 17 May 1991, p.14.
28. Remarks by Usama al-Baz, MENA, 26 July 1991 as quoted in FBIS-NESA, 5 August 1991.
29. See *Yediot Aharonot* (Sabbath supplement), 22 November 1996.
30. Remarks by Egyptian President Husni Mubarak as quoted from Egypt Radio Network, 30 April 1992, FBIS-NESA, 1 May 1992; quoted from MENA, 6 March 1994, by FBIS-NESA, 7 March 1994; Egypt Radio Network, 31 January 1995, as quoted in FBIS-NESA, 31 January 1995.
31. *Al-Musawwar*, 14 April 1989, as quoted in MECS, Vol.XIII, 1989, p.321.
32. MECS, Vol.XIII, 1989, p.321.
33. Ibid., Vol.XV, 1991, p.366.
34. Ibid., p.367.
35. See *al-Sha'b*, 29 November 1994 as quoted in FBIS-NESA, 7 December 1994.
36. Remarks by Israeli Defence Minister Yitzhak Rabin, *Jerusalem Domestic Service*, 22 September 1989, as quoted in FBIS-NESA, 22 September 1989, p.28.
37. *Jerusalem Post*, 14 April 1992.
38. Remarks by Egyptian Foreign Minister Amr Musa as quoted in FBIS-NESA, 16 April 1992.
39. Remarks by Israeli Prime Minister Yitzhak Shamir, as quoted from *Kol Israel*, 29 July 1991, FBIS-NESA, 29 July 1991.
40. *Davar* (Passover Supplement), 17 April 1992.
41. See Ami Ayalon and Bruce Maddy-Weitzman, eds, MECS, Vol.XVIII, 1994, p.278.
42. Ibid., p.279.
43. *Al-Sharq* (Doha), 25 August 1995, p.10, as quoted in FBIS-NESA, 14 September 1995, p.5.
44. See *Ma'ariv*, 11 November 1996.
45. *Yediot Aharonot* (Sabbath supplement), 22 November 1996.
46. *Ma'ariv*, 5, 12 January 1997. See for examples, *Yediot Aharonot*, 17 November 1996; *Ha-tzofe*, 16 December 1996; *Ha-aretz*, 5 January 1997.
47. Remarks by Dore Gold, 4 October 1996, taken from MBC (London), as quoted in FBIS-NESA, 4 October 1996.
48. Cairo Arab Republic Radio, 15 January 1997 as quoted in FBIS-NESA, 15 January 1997.

Myopic Vision: Whither Israeli–Egyptian Relations?

SHAWN PINE

The hosting of the 21 June 1996 Arab summit in Cairo, purportedly convened to mobilize Arab solidarity and develop a unified Arab response to the election of Likud's Benjamin Netanyahu as Israel's prime minister, should have been welcomed by Israel. After all, Egypt and Israel have a peace agreement that has existed for almost 20 years. Moreover, both countries are allied with the only remaining global hegemon, the United States.

However, the summit was not received by Israeli leaders as a positive event and generated consternation among many observers of the region. These concerns were precipitated by the harsh regional criticism of the results of the Israeli elections which preceded the meeting. This criticism had ominous undertones and harked back to the period in which the countries of the region attempted to isolate Israel. The Egyptians, rather than allay Arab concerns over the results of the elections, have taken a leading role in criticizing these results as a setback in the evolving peace process. Egyptian displeasure over the pace of the peace process under the Netanyahu-led government was underscored by threats to cancel a regional economic conference scheduled for November 1996. Egypt's harsh criticism of Israel surprised many observers considering that the first Arab–Israeli peace treaty, signed in 1979 between Egypt and Israel, had been reached with Israel's first Likud prime minister, Menachem Begin.

Yet Egypt's rhetoric and actions should not have come as a surprise. Any careful evaluation of Egyptian strategic interests, coupled with an examination of their expansive military buildup, makes an Egyptian–Israeli political, if not military, confrontation a viable prospect. This essay examines the current Egyptian–Israeli relationship in view of Egypt's regional strategic objectives and its perspectives towards Israel. It will also explore the implications for regional stability of the Egyptian military buildup, on the one hand, and the internal challenges posed by Islamic fundamentalism to the Egyptian regime, on the other.

Shawn Pine is a research student in International Relations at the Hebrew University of Jerusalem.

EGYPT'S STRATEGIC OBJECTIVES

Viewed in a wider context, the stream of unfriendly ranting emanating from Egypt since the Israeli 1996 election is nothing more than the latest manifestation of Egyptian hostility towards Israel, which can readily be understood in light of Egyptian regional strategic objectives. For the past decade, Egypt has been using the $2.1 billion annual aid from the United States, $1.3 billion of which is in military assistance, to modernize and expand its military forces in order to achieve two primary objectives. First, Egypt seeks to create a credible deterrent to counter regional conventional threats and re-establish itself as the leading Arab player.[1] The regional proliferation of Islamic fundamentalism has permeated Egypt and poses a threat to the stability of Husni Mubarak's regime. This threat is exacerbated by the geographical proximity of the Sudan, which became the leading African supporter of Islamic fundamentalism following the seizure of power by Lieutenant-General Omar al-Bashir on 20 June 1989. By hosting the June 1996 Arab summit, Egypt hoped to solidify its leadership over the 'conservative' Arab states and ameliorate tensions with revisionist regional states, by marshalling Arab forces against a common threat. In many respects, this was yet another effort in a long series of failed attempts to form a pan-Arab coalition against Israel; only now Egypt is (allegedly) leading this coalition towards peace with Israel rather than to war with the Jewish State, as it had done before. Second, Egypt hopes to strengthen its ties with the United States and weaken that country's support for Israel. For the last two decades Egypt has been in direct competition with Israel over diminishing American foreign assistance. The financial deficit has created domestic pressures within the United States to cut foreign aid, and since Israel and Egypt are by far the foremost recipients of this aid, accounting for some 42 per cent ($5.1 out of a total of $12 billion) of all US foreign assistance, they can readily expect a cut in the current level of support.[2]

Those who support maintaining current levels of US assistance to Egypt, while targeting Israel for future reductions, present at least three main arguments for their position:

- The collapse of the Soviet Union has diminished Israel's strategic value to the United States and has increased Egypt's importance for the simple reason that, as the largest Arab state, Egypt is more capable of exerting influence in the region and promoting US interests. This assessment is believed to have been vindicated during the 1991 Gulf War, when the refusal of the Arab states to condone Israeli military participation, even when faced with potentially existential threats, demonstrated the limited utility of Israel in furthering US regional strategic objectives in the post-Cold War era.

- Reductions in US assistance to Egypt will exacerbate its economic problems and might consequently increase domestic dissension to intolerable levels. It has been pointed out that US investment in Egypt has already exceeded $30 billion and that US regional interests would be adversely affected if Egypt were to succumb to the fundamentalist genie. Conversely, Israel's economy is believed to be thriving, and is far better poised than Egypt to withstand the economic reverberations of reduced US assistance.

- Arab attitudes towards Israel have improved to the extent that $3.1 billion of US annual aid to the Jewish State is no longer needed. Israel's peace treaties with Egypt and Jordan are believed to have ameliorated Arab–Israeli hostility to the point that the conventional justifications for maintaining Israel's qualitative military edge are no longer valid.

However intriguing, these arguments are totally misconceived. Formulation of any effective regional policy must be predicated upon reasonable expectations of regional stability. However, events in the Middle East have frequently made such expectations seem more like wishful thinking than careful analysis. The 1979 overthrow of the Iranian Shah and Iraq's 1990 invasion of Kuwait are just two examples of the instability that has plagued the region, and exemplify the problems confronting US policy-makers tasked with formulating a coherent regional policy. The historical instability of Middle Eastern regimes and/or states militates against creating a dependency upon them and strengthens the claims of Israel's supporters that Israel is the most, if not only reliable partner over the long term.

The historical record also demonstrates the circumscribed utility of US assistance in promoting regime stability. This is especially true in the case of Egypt, in which the influx of $2.1 billion in annual aid has done little to stem the proliferation of Islamic fundamentalism. The fact that much of this assistance is in military aid is only a partial explanation for this phenomenon.

Finally, it is a mistake to believe that the 1979 Israeli–Egyptian treaty has transformed these two historic enemies into friends.[2] Despite periodic convergence of interests, the relationship between Israel and Egypt has fallen far short of expectations and has been frequently characterized as a non-belligerency treaty, rather than a fully-fledged peace treaty.[3] Ironically, while many Western governments, and much of the Western media, have failed to recognize the superficiality of Israeli–Egyptian relations, Egyptian government officials and the intellectual elite have made no secret of their views concerning Israel.

EGYPTIAN PERSPECTIVES OF ISRAEL

According to Egyptian Brigadier-General Morad Dessouki, military expert at the al-Ahram Centre for Political and Strategic Studies, the

Egyptian government still views Israel as a regional enemy.[4] Dessouki's remarks were buttressed by Egyptian Defence Minister Muhammad Hussein Tantawi's statement that the September 1996 Egyptian military manoeuvre, dubbed 'Badr 96' and the largest in Egypt's history, was being conducted out of concern about Israel's non-conventional capabilities.[5] This stark prognosis was further underscored by the veteran political analyst, Muhammad Hassanein Heikal, who stated that Egypt rejected the concept of 'normalization' with Israel and that many Egyptian generals viewed the current situation as a temporary cease-fire.[6]

Manifestations of deteriorating Egyptian perceptions of Israel can be found in the vociferous anti-Israeli propaganda that has become common in the state-controlled media for quite some time. The Egyptian press, in clear violation of the 1979 peace treaty, has never desisted from routinely publishing anti-Israeli and anti-Jewish tracts. Equally forbidding have been attempts by Egypt to deter other states from establishing diplomatic and economic ties with Israel. Egypt has actively lobbied against US–Israeli assistance treaties, the 1995 Memorandum of Military Cooperation between Israel and Russia, as well as against Israeli–Turkish military cooperation agreements that were disclosed in June 1996.[7] Still another example of the deteriorating Israeli–Egyptian relationship is found in the erosion of Egyptian support for the continued presence of the multinational forces in the Sinai. As early as 18 November 1992 Egypt proposed that these forces be withdrawn from the peninsula,[8] and ever since has not deviated from the position that the multinational presence in the Sinai be significantly reduced, if not officially terminated, not least since they violate Egyptian sovereignty.[9]

These examples indicate that the 1979 peace treaty has failed to bring Israel the kind of peace it envisioned when returning the Sinai. The late Egyptian President Anwar Sadat's vision of expanded relations with Israel never came to fruition as, under the reign of his successor, Husni Mubarak, Egypt's intellectual, political, and economic elites continued to shun Israel as a regional actor.[10] Nor has the passage of time, or even the September 1993 Israel–Palestinian Declaration of Principles (DOP) improved Egyptian acceptance of Israel. Even President Mubarak admitted that the intelligentsia and the professionals in Egypt were as fanatically opposed to the acceptance of Israel as are the fundamentalist militants.[11] Outward manifestations of Egyptian rejection of Israel during this period include: the Egyptian Bar Association burning of American and Israeli flags on every anniversary of the signing of the 1979 peace treaty; the continued regular featuring of anti-Israel and anti-Semitic articles in Egyptian newspapers; and routine refusals by Egyptian teachers, student unions, medical professionals, and other grass-roots organizations to meet with Israeli counterparts for dialogue and cooperation. Moreover, Egypt has actively lobbied against Arab participation in joint working committees involving economic cooperation, water issues, and disarmament. A study of Egyptian university graduates, who were studying during the signing of the 1979 Egyptian–Israeli peace treaty, found that 92.8 per cent believed that Israel was an expansionist, aggressive state headed by terrorists.[12]

Rejection of Israel is not confined to Egypt's intellectual, political, and economic elites but permeates throughout the Egyptian population. An Egyptian public opinion poll showed that 98 per cent of the people opposed full normalization of relations with Israel. The same poll showed that 97 per cent opposed cultural ties, 96 per cent opposed economic ties, and that 92 per cent opposed normal tourist ties.[13] In light of this reality, the decade-long Egyptian military buildup takes on increased importance as the Egyptian military is much more capable of fulfilling Egyptian strategic military objectives than in any previous time, should the situation continue to deteriorate.

THE EGYPTIAN MILITARY BUILDUP

Since the early 1980s, Egypt has undertaken serious efforts to achieve conventional military parity with Israel, which has brought it closer than ever to the quantitative and qualitative level of the Israel Defence Forces (IDF).[14]

Conventional Buildup

Since the early 1980s, Egypt has completed two five-year plans, and has embarked on a third plan, to build, modernize and expand its military capabilities. The first five-year plan, which started in 1983, consisted of rebuilding Egypt's military infrastructure that was destroyed during the 1973 Arab–Israeli War. The primary focus of these efforts included the construction of new bases and communications systems. From 1988 to 1993, Egypt channelled funds into the air force by purchasing American F-16s and upgrading its command and control and air-defence capabilities. In the current five-year plan, the air force continues to receive priority. Egypt spends as much as 80 per cent of US military aid on the air force. As part of the 'Peace Vector Programme', the Egyptian air force has made four orders of F-16s, totalling 190 planes. About 130 F-16s have already arrived and the last batch, which will be assembled in Turkey, will start arriving around 1997.[15] Egypt has also obtained approval for the purchase of 21 F-16C aircraft.[16] Egypt's air-defence capabilities were greatly enhanced by the acquisition of 180 Hawk and 1,000 Hellfire II missiles.[17] Additionally, Egypt has been cooperating with the United States to develop an advanced C3I system that will assimilate data from air and ground sources into a single network so that aircraft and missile systems can engage multiple targets simultaneously.

Egypt has also enhanced its airborne early warning capabilities by taking delivery of five Grumman E-2C Hawkeyes. Today, Egypt has the largest air force in the Arab World, with about 550 fighting aircraft, more than half of which are of Western origin. The Egyptians are also acquiring a modern helicopter fleet. They have already received delivery of 24 Apaches (AH-64A), and are expected to take delivery of 12 more. These helicopters possess state-of-the-art night-flying equipment and carry up to 16 Hellfire anti-tank weapons and 38 rockets.[18]

The improvement of the Egyptian air force is not limited to combat planes. According to Israeli military analysts, this force has adopted Western command and control, attack techniques, support and aerial combat roles as well as training, most of it at US facilities. The Egyptians have also bought advance ordnance, avionics and accessories.[19]

In addition to its air force, Egypt has modernized its ground forces. Until the late 1970s, the Egyptian army comprised 10 divisions, only half of them either mechanized or armoured. Today, the army has 12 divisions, all but one of them either mechanized or armoured, and plans to field a total mechanized army by 2005. Egypt is now capable of fielding a modern mechanized military that can move with the speed and firepower equal to that of most modern armies. The mechanized divisions include 4500 armoured personnel carriers, the core of which consists of 2000 US M-113s. Egypt is also in the process of taking delivery of 611 Dutch YPR-765 armoured infantry fighting vehicles to replace its Soviet BMP arsenal.[20]

The Egyptian armoured corps has also undergone a serious reform. In the 1970s, this corps comprised almost exclusively Soviet tanks, the best of which was the T-62. Today, Egypt's armoured corps includes the most modern US tanks. First, Cairo acquired 850 M-60 A3s and formed two armoured divisions. After the 1991 Gulf War, the Egyptians began to assemble the US-made M1A1, which is widely regarded as one of the finest tanks in the world, under the 'Factory 200' programme. Egypt currently has 1100 M-60A3s, 1700 M-60A1s, and approximately 200 M1A1s. Eventually, Egypt plans to upgrade all M60A1 tanks to A3 standards.[21]

Additionally, Egypt is expanding its own domestic production of military armaments. The M1A1 'Factory 200' programme has been a major milestone in Egyptian efforts to achieve limited military self-sufficiency. Egypt obtained US approval in 1984 to build a giant factory to produce new tanks. Under the agreement, the Egyptians will assemble 524 M1A1 tanks and officials hope that will eventually rise to 1500 tanks. Six production cycles were established with each increment, increasing the level of technology from General Dynamics

Land Systems. The cost of this programme is estimated at $3.2 billion. The Egyptians will also produce the 120-mm cannon as well as an increasing number of parts for the tank. Egyptian officials say the goal is to make Cairo self-sufficient in tank production. Egypt has also substantially improved its anti-tank capability with the acquisition of 500 TOW-2 missiles and plans the purchase of additional 540 TOW launchers.[22]

Egypt has also taken steps to improve its navy. Here it has focused on upgrading its fleet of eight submarines acquired from China. Egypt has leased two former US Navy Knox class frigates and is expected to receive 10 ex-US Navy Seasprite ASW helicopters upgraded to SH-2G(E) standard. As part of its assimilation of Western technology, the navy holds joint manoeuvres with units of the American, French, British and Italian navies. Egypt is also modernizing four Chinese-built Romeo class submarines with improved weapon systems including Harpoon missiles, fire control systems and sonars.[23]

The result of this massive infusion of Western military technology, as reflected in the following tables, has been a marked decrease in Israel's qualitative advantage over Egypt in both armour and air power.

TABLE 1

EGYPTIAN–ISRAELI BALANCE OF FORCES

Main Battle Tanks

	1985–86 Total/HQ	1989–90 Total/HQ	1992–93 Total/HQ	1995–96 Total/HQ
Egypt	1750/350-	2425/785	3090/785	3500/1300
Israel	3600/850	3794/1200	3890/1450	4095/1430
Ratio	2.06/2.43	1.56/1.53	1.26/1.85	1.17/1.10

Combat Aircraft

	1985–86 Total/HQ	1989–90 Total/HQ	1992–93 Total/HQ	1995–96 Total/HQ
Egypt	504/50-	517/83	492/89	564/159
Israel	24 640/265	676/293	764/442	699/458
Ratio	1.2/5.3	1.3/3.53	1.55/4.97	1.24/2.88

Note: Israeli figures include aircraft in storage.

Source: Data taken from the IISS, *The Military Balance*. The definition of high quality was taken from the Jaffee Center for Strategic Studies, *The Middle East Military Balance 1995–96*, Boulder, 1996.

It is important to note that Israel's qualitative advantage over Egypt has deteriorated in practically every area of military armaments including armoured personnel carriers, precision guided munitions and attack helicopters. The results of this phenomenon are even more dramatic when a regional comparison of the Arab–Israeli quantitative/qualitative ratio is made. As shown in Table 2, Israeli qualitative edge over its Arab adversaries has clearly been eroded over the past decade.[24]

TABLE 2
ARAB–ISRAELI BALANCE OF FORCES

| | *Main Battle Tanks* | | | |
	1985–86 Total/HQ	1989–90 Total/HQ	1992–93 Total/HQ	1995–96 Total/HQ
Arab	12870/1450	14156/2153	12521/2903	14436/3983
Israel	3600/850	3794/1200	3890/1450	4095/1430
Ratio	3.57/1.70	3.78/1.79	3.22/2.00	3.53/2.78

| | *Combat Aircraft* | | | |
	1985–68 Total/HQ	1989–90 Total/HQ	1992–93 Total/HQ	1995–96 Total/HQ
Arab	1988/193	1940/261	2109/361	2125/392
Israel	640/265	676/293	764/442	699/458
Ratio	3.11/1.37	2.87/1.12	2.76/1.22	3.04/1.17

The results are even more compelling when comparing the current qualitative and quantitative differences to the October 1973 War. In that war, Israel was at roughly a 2:1 quantitative disadvantage in both main battle tanks and aircraft against its enemies. However, Israel was able to overcome this quantitative disadvantage due to its unequivocal qualitative superiority.[25] Today, the quantitative gap in both tanks and aircraft has grown to over 3:1, while Israel holds a negligible 1.17:1 qualitative advantage in combat aircraft and is at a 2.78:1 disadvantage in qualitative tanks.

This is not to say that Israel has lost its qualitative superiority vis-à-vis its neighbours. Israeli domestic production of high technology military avionics and armaments, and the US commitment to maintain Israel's qualitative edge will insure that a general qualitative gap in favour of Israel will continue in the foreseeable future. Still, the influx of Western technology into the Arab countries has at least two significant adverse ramifications for Israel. First, it will ensure a far smaller technological gap between Israel and its neighbours as compared to other periods.[26] This applies not only to the quality of major weapons systems at the armies' disposal: the influx of Western technology has dramatically increased the combat competency of the Arab soldier. The underlying premise dictating the production of many US weapons is the KISS principle (keep it simple, stupid). Under this principle, weapons are designed to be utilized by soldiers with negligible understanding of how these weapons may work. Today, weapons of extreme lethality can effectively be employed by soldiers who traditionally lacked the capability to effectively employ sophisticated equipment. Consequently, Israel's much heralded human qualitative edge is somewhat neutralized, as many of these weapons have made target acquisition, and therefore target destruction, much simpler. Moreover, the Arabs have closed this perceived qualitative gap due to a tremendous increase in the number of engineering and natural science graduates from Arab universities in the last two decades.[27] How this would relate on any future battlefield is open to speculation. However, it probably would significantly increase Israeli losses in any future conflict.

Second, the relative cost for Israel to maintain any qualitative gap is now much greater. Israel has generally maintained a high degree of technological advanced armaments. Consequently, each incremental gain in Israel's qualitative edge will cost that country substantially more in research and development costs. This will make the relative cost of each new system more expensive and will limit any attempt by Israel to maintain at present levels, or decrease the Arab quantitative advantage.

Technology returns tend towards an S shape: increasing performance for cost in its early growth phase, and diminishing returns during its later phase. As Israel precedes its neighbours along the S curve, its costs will increase faster if it desires to maintain a constant level of technological superiority.[28]

Consequently, Israel can maintain qualitative superiority only by devoting more resources from force structures to technology. Since Israel, as virtually every country, operates within well-defined budget constraints, it can maintain its qualitative advantage only at the expense of allowing the quantitative gap to increase.

This accounts for much of the alleged overt, and covert, Israeli intelligence activity that is currently being directed against US military arms manufacturers. Israel simply cannot afford the research and development costs involved in trying to maintain its tenuous qualitative advantage. The net result could be a further increase in the quantitative gap in favour of the Arab countries, as Israel attempts to maintain its dwindling qualitative edge.

NON-CONVENTIONAL BUILDUP

Egypt was one of the first countries to obtain nuclear-research capabilities when it purchased a small research reactor from the Soviet Union in the early 1960s. It is currently building a 300MW Chinese-made reactor that will have the capacity to manufacture four nuclear warheads a month. Additionally, Egypt is believed to be seeking joint nuclear weapons research with Syria and Saudi Arabia to defray the prohibitive costs and allow Egypt to continue its conventional buildup unabated. However, despite these achievements, it appears that Egypt has made the strategic decision to concentrate its efforts on increasing its conventional forces and non-conventional chemical and biological capabilities, rather than developing nuclear weapons.

Egypt is believed to have been working with Iraq for years on the production and stockpiling of chemical weapons. While the size of its arsenal is not known, it is probably similar to that of Iraq prior to the Gulf War. Chemical weapons are part of the Egyptian army's 'standard issue' and Egypt operates a chemical plant at Abu Za'abal.[29]

Egypt has also continued development of new delivery systems for its weapons. Cairo is working with the North Koreans to upgrade the Scud missile's range and accuracy. The project began as early as 1981, when Egypt transferred several Scud Bs to Pyongyang, violating the Egyptian treaty with Moscow. The Koreans then used reverse engineering to extend the range and improve the accuracy of the Scud B. The result has been the Scud C and Scud D, with ranges of 600 and 1000-kilometres respectively. It has been reported that Egypt has been given access to the new missiles.

The most ambitious Egyptian effort over the past decade has been the Condor missile project, with a range of 1000 kilometres. Conceived by Argentina, developed further by German scientists and financed by Iraq, the Condor resembled the US Pershing missile. Western intelligence sources say Egypt wanted the Condor to counter Israel's Jericho II missile, with a reported range of up to 1500 kilometres.[30]

IN THE FOOTSTEPS OF IRAN?

Even if the Israeli–Egyptian relationship had been the paradigm of inter-state harmony, the domestic under-currents operating within Egyptian society would be cause for Israeli alarm. Islamic violence in Egypt has reached perilous levels, leading some Western intelligence communities to question the medium- and long-term stability of the Mubarak regime.[31]

Since the late 1920s, when the Muslim Brethren movement was established by Hassan al-Banna, the Egyptian authorities have had to vie with the problem of religious fundamentalism. During the 1970s and the 1980s, the Muslim Brethren, ruthlessly suppressed in previous decades by Gamal Abdel Nasser, moderated their politics and were tolerated by Anwar Sadat and Husni Mubarak; they even took part in the Egyptian elections and did quite well. Yet relations with the authorities progressively deteriorated, and since 1992, when Islamic extremists announced their intention to overthrow the government and establish an Islamic state, over 900 people have died. In January 1995, following an unsuccessful assassination attempt on President Mubarak, the government intensified its campaign against the Brotherhood. In November 1995, 54 of the Brotherhood's organizers were sentenced by an Egyptian military court to sentences of three to five years. In January

1996, police arrested over 160 Brotherhood activists around the village of Minya.[32]

These actions prompted the Islamic groups to change tack and concentrate their efforts on targets outside Egypt. This change of venue gave them greater freedom of action and resulted in a number of immediate successes included the November 1995 assassination of Egypt's trade councillor at the UN mission in Geneva and suicide bombing of the Egyptian embassy in Islamabad.[33]

The disturbing aspect of this militant activity is that while the myriad of Islamic extremist groups reflect different nuances of Islam, they all share certain fundamental tenets, notably rejection of modernity as the negation of God's sovereignty and castigation of 'Westoxification' of Islam for having cast the Islamic world into a state of *jahiliyya* (pre-Islamic barbarity). These extremists believe that this state of *jahiliyya*, an extreme Hobbesian state of nature, is similar to the period preceding the Prophet Muhammad, and they reject the modern nation-state, the foremost manifestation of this state of affairs, as incompatible with Islam. As they see it, the panacea for this state of barbarity lies in the immediate overthrow of corrupt secular regimes and a return to the *Shari'a*.[34]

PROSPECTS FOR THE FUTURE

Despite Western fears concerning the stability of the Egyptian regime, President Mubarak has thus far managed to take the requisite steps to keep the situation under control. Consequently, the militants do not appear capable of toppling his regime in the short term.[35] However, given the unpredictability of such forces, especially against the backdrop of the ominous economic and demographic challenges confronting Egypt, the future ability of militant Islam to pose an existential threat to the Egyptian regime cannot be ruled out altogether. Should Egypt go the way of Iran and succumb to fundamentalist Islam, the Middle East would deteriorate into virtual chaos. US strategic interests in the region would be severely threatened as Israel, and the conservative Arab states, would be menaced.

Unfortunately, the decision of the United States to allow the Egyptian military buildup to far exceed its defence requirements reflects a myopic vision on the part of US regional policy-makers and their inability to learn from past experience. The fall of the Iranian Shah in 1979 should have taught the United States the inherent dangers of over-supporting non-democratic regimes in the region. A more prudent US foreign policy would have been to fully ensure Egypt's defensive capability against external threats, while insisting that most US assistance be earmarked for resolving Egypt's pressing social and economic problems in order to ameliorate the internal threat posed by

Islamic fundamentalism. Instead, the United States has provided Egypt with a potent military offensive force that is capable of posing an existential threat to all its neighbours.

As far as Israel is concerned, its experience of 'cold', if not 'hostile peace' with Egypt should dictate that it proceed with the utmost caution in future negotiations with its neighbours. While the outcome of the current peace process may determine the pace of deterioration in Israeli–Egyptian relations, it will have negligible impact on its overall direction. Egyptian resistance to regional assimilation of Israel will increase regardless of the outcome of the current peace process. Paradoxically enough, final agreements between Israel, the Palestinians and the Syrians may actually hasten the deterioration in Egyptian–Israeli relations by accelerating regional competition between the two countries and exacerbating Egypt's frustration with the loss of the pivotal role it had played since 1979 as a mediator between Israel and its Arab neighbours.

The failure of the 1979 Egyptian–Israeli peace treaty to fulfil Israeli expectations, and the current state of Egyptian–Israeli relations, should give Israel a respite in the conduct of future negotiations with the Syrians for three main reasons. First, President Asad has not shown anything remotely reminiscent of Anwar Sadat's commitment to peace, most vividly illustrated by Sadat's willingness to come to Jerusalem and make his case directly to the Israeli people. Unlike Sadat, Asad has rejected most ideas of normalizing relations with Israel, viewing peace as the price he has to pay for regaining the Golan Heights (in the absence of a military option) rather than as a positive development which serves Syria's real interests. This concept of peace is fundamentally different from that of Israel, indeed from the idea of peace *per se*, and should be more appropriately defined as non-belligerency rather than as peace.[36]

As with the post-Sadat Egyptian regime, Syrian rejection of the notion of 'real' peace with Israel is predicated as much on empirical self-interest as on ideology. Leaving aside Asad's difficulty (as a staunch pan-Arabist) to reconcile himself to Israel's existence, regional peace with Israel would have several detrimental effects for the Syrian regime. These include the marginalization of Syria in regional affairs following the loss of its role as 'spoiler'; the strengthening of Jordan at Syria's expense; the freeing of the Palestinians from Syrian influence; the weakening of the Syrian–Iranian axis with its attendant problems for Syria in Lebanon, and, finally, the transformation of Israel into a regional competitor against Syria.[37]

Last but not least, the assassination of Anwar Sadat in October 1981, and of Yitzhak Rabin 14 years later, demonstrate that even the best intentions can be derailed by an assassin's bullet. One can only speculate how Egyptian–Israeli relations would have evolved if Sadat had not been assassinated. What is clear, however, is that Sadat's commitment to normalization of relations with Israel was far deeper than that of his successor.

Consequently, even if Asad shared Sadat's commitment to peace, which he certainly does not, there is no way of ensuring that any peace agreement reached with him would survive his personal demise. However, the most important reason for Israeli caution is that its margin for error is far more restricted concerning withdrawal from the Golan Heights than it was in the Sinai. Unlike the Golan, the topography separating Egyptian–Israeli forces provides Israel with ample early warning should relations deteriorate towards military conflict. The time needed for Egyptian forces to traverse the Sinai desert would afford Israel the opportunity of defending itself while mobilizing its reserve forces. This luxury does not exist on the Golan. Even if Asad were to agree to demilitarizing the area down to Damascus – a highly unlikely prospect – Syrian tanks, should they achieve a strategic surprise, could still reach Israeli population centres within a few hours. Given this reality, the uncritical emulation of the Egyptian precedent would be a foolhardy move on Israel's part.

NOTES

1. Egyptian Defence Minister Muhammad Hussein Tantawi, *Jerusalem Post*, 11 March 1994.
2. For this all-too-common mis-characterization of the Egyptian–Israeli relationship see, for example, *Newsweek*, 17 June 1996, p.22.
3. This perception was articulated by Major-General David Ivri during his tenure as Director-General of Israel's Ministry of Defence, when he stated that 'peace with Egypt is not peace. It is actually a cease-fire that has continued for 15 years'. *Jerusalem Post*, 14 April 1992.
4. Ibid., 11 March 1994.
5. Tantawi's statements were quoted in the *Jerusalem Post*, 24 September 1996.
6. Yohanan Ramati, 'The Egyptian Threat to Israel', *Global Affairs*, Vol.8, No.2 (Spring 1993), p.88. The interview was reported as occurring on 18 May 1992.
7. See *Jerusalem Post*, 12 June 1996, and 8 December 1995.
8. Ramati, 'The Egyptian Threat', p.83.
9. Unnamed Western diplomat, *Jerusalem Post*, 11 March 1994.
10. Mosely Ann Lesch and Mark Tessler, *Israel, Egypt and the Palestinians: From Camp David to Intifada*, Indiana, 1989, p.62.
11. *Jerusalem Post*, 7 September 7 1995.
12. The study was conducted by Dr. Ahmad Zaree of al-Azhar University. His findings also revealed that 63% of those polled viewed Egyptian–Israeli normalization as a national security threat. *Jerusalem Post*, 3 March 1996. See also ibid., 17 May 1995 and 1 January 1996.
13. Ibid., 3 May 1995.
14. Egyptian Foreign Minister Amr Musa, *Jerusalem Post*, 11 March 1994.
15. Ibid.
16. *Jane's Defence Weekly*, 17 April 1996, p.3. Delivery of these aircraft is expected to begin in 1999 and be completed by the year 2000.
17. Ibid., 1 May 1996, p.8.
18. Ibid., 28 February 1996, p.23; International Institute for Strategic Studies, *The Military Balance 1995–1996*, London, 1996. Egypt was to take delivery of 24 AH-64s by the end of 1995.

19. *Jerusalem Post*, 11 March 1994.
20. *Jane's Defence Weekly*, 28 February 1996. p.22, 6 March 1996, p.23. These AIFVs include 304 YPR-765 PRIs mounted with a 25mm gun and coaxil 7.62mm machine-gun, and 210 YPR-765 PRAT-TOWs.
21. IISS, *The Military Balance 1995–1996*; *Jane's Defense Weekly*, 28 February 1996. p.23.
22. *Jane's Defence Weekly*, 28 February 1996. p.23; ibid., 21 February 1996, p.16.
23. Ibid., 28 February 1996. p.23.
24. Possible confrontation states include Iraq, Iran, Jordan, Saudi Arabia, and Syria. Anomalies in the tables are attributed to problems in collecting data in the aftermath of the Iran–Iraq and Persian Gulf Wars.
25. See Nadav Safran, *Israel: The Embattled Ally*, Cambridge, Mass., 1981, p.286.
26. This concern was raised as early as 1991. See Aharon Klieman and Reuven Pedatzur, *Rearming Israel: Defense Procurement Through the 1990s*, Boulder, 1991, pp.33–4.
27. Zeev Bonen, 'The Impact of Technology Developments on the Strategic Balance in the Middle East', in Jaffee Center for Strategic Studies, *The Middle East Military Balance, 1994*, Boulder, 1995, p.160.
28. Steven Canby, 'Military Doctrine and Technology', in *The Impact of New Military Technology*, The Adelphi Library 4, London, 1981. pp.37–40.
29. *Jerusalem Post*, 13 March 1989, 9 January and 12 April 1995.
30. Jaffee Center for Strategic Studies, *The 1994 Middle East Military Balance*, pp.231–4.
31. Concern about the Mubarak regime's ability to stem the rise of Islamic fundamentalism has been expressed on a number of occasions by US government officials. See, for example, *Jerusalem Post*, 23 August 1993, 24 February 1994.
32. EIU Country Report, *Egypt*, London, 1996, p.15.
33. Ibid., p.16.
34. Emanuel Sivan, 'The Islamic Republic of Egypt', *Orbis*, Vol.31, No.1, Spring 1987, p.46; idem, *Radical Islam: Medieval Theology and Modern Politics*, New Haven, 1985, pp.9, 46, 54.
35. This prognosis was articulated by Professor Shimon Shamir of Tel-Aviv University, former Israeli Ambassador to Egypt. See *Jerusalem Post*, 28 April 1993.
36. Moshe Ma'oz, 'Syrian–Israeli Relations and the Middle East Peace Process', *Jerusalem Journal of International Relations*, Vol.14, No.3 (September, 1992), p.13.
37. Barry Rubin, *Modern Dictators*, New York, 1987, pp.226–7.

DOCUMENTS

Protocol Concerning the Redeployment in Hebron

In accordance with the provisions of the Interim Agreement and in particular of Article VII of Annex I to the Interim Agreement, both Parties have agreed on this Protocol for the implementation of the redeployment in Hebron.

SECURITY ARRANGEMENTS REGARDING REDEPLOYMENT IN HEBRON

1. Redeployment in Hebron

The redeployment of Israeli Military Forces in Hebron will be carried out in accordance with the Interim Agreement and this Protocol. This redeployment will be completed not later than ten days from the signing of this Protocol. During these ten days both sides will exert every possible effort to prevent friction and any action that would prevent the redeployment. This redeployment shall constitute full implementation of the provisions of the Interim Agreement with regard to the City of Hebron unless otherwise provided for in Article VII of Annex I to the Interim Agreement.

2. Security Powers and Responsibilities

a. (1) The Palestinian Police will assume responsibilities in Area H-1 similar to those in other cities in the West Bank; and

(2) Israel will retain all powers and responsibilities for internal security and public order in Area H-2. In addition, Israel will continue to carry the responsibility for overall security of Israelis.

b. In this context – both sides reaffirm their commitment to honour the relevant security provisions of the Interim Agreement, including the provisions regarding – Arrangements for Security and Public Order (Article XII of the Interim Agreement); Prevention of Hostile Acts (Article XV of the Interim Agreement); Security Policy for the Prevention of Terrorism and Violence (Article II of Annex I to the Interim Agreement); Guidelines for Hebron (Article VII of Annex I to the Interim Agreement); and Rules of Conduct in Mutual Security Matters (Article XI of Annex I to the Interim Agreement).

3. Agreed Security Arrangements

a. With a view to ensuring mutual security and stability in the City of Hebron, special security arrangements will apply adjacent to the areas under the security responsibility of Israel, in Area H-1, in the area between the Palestinian Police checkpoints delineated on the map attached to this Protocol as Appendix 1 (hereinafter referred to as 'the attached map') and the areas under the security responsibility of Israel.

b. The purpose of the above-mentioned checkpoints will be to enable the Palestinian Police, exercising their responsibilities under the Interim Agreement, to prevent entry of armed persons and demonstrators or other people threatening security and public order, into the above-mentioned area.

4. Joint Security Measures

a. The DCO will establish a sub-office in the City of Hebron as indicated on the attached map.

b. JMU will operate in Area H-2 to handle incidents that involve Palestinians only. The JMU movement will be detailed on the attached map. The DCO will coordinate the JMU movement and activity.

c. As part of the security arrangements in the area adjacent to the areas under the security responsibility of Israel, as defined above, Joint Mobile Units will be operating in this area, with special focus on the following places:

(1) Abu Sneinah

(2) Harat A-Sheikh

(3) Sha'aba

(4) The high ground overlooking new Route No. 35.

d. Two Joint Patrols will function in Area H-1:

(1) a Joint Patrol which will operate on the road from Ras Jura to the north of the Dura junction via E-Salaam Road, as indicated on the attached map; and

(2) a Joint Patrol which will operate on existing Route No. 35, including the eastern part of existing Route No. 35, as indicated on the attached map.

e. The Palestinian and Israeli side of the Joint Mobile Units in the City of Hebron will be armed with equivalent types of weapons (Mini-Ingraham submachine guns for the Palestinian side and short M16s for the Israeli side).

f. With a view to dealing with the special security situation in the City of Hebron, a Joint Coordination Centre (hereinafter the 'JCC') headed by senior officers of both sides, will be established in the DCO at Har Manoah/Jabel Manoah. The purpose of the JCC will be to coordinate the joint security measures in the City of Hebron. The JCC will be guided by all the relevant provisions of the Interim Agreement, including Annex I and this Protocol. In this context, each side will notify the JCC of demonstrations and actions taken in respect of such demonstrations, and of any security activity, close to the areas under the responsibility of the other side, including in the area defined in Article 3(a) above. The JCC shall be informed of activities in accordance with Article 5(d)(3) of this Protocol.

5. The Palestinian Police

a. Palestinian police stations or posts will be established in Area H-1, manned by a total of up to 400 policemen, equipped with 20 vehicles and armed with 200 pistols, and 100 rifles for the protection of the police stations.

b. Four designated Rapid Response Teams (RRTs) will be established and stationed in Area H-1, one in each of the police stations, as delineated on the attached map. The main task of the RRTs will be to handle special security cases. Each RRT shall be comprised of up to 16 members.

c. The above-mentioned rifles will be designated for the exclusive use of the RRTs, to handle special cases.

d. (1) The Palestinian Police shall operate freely in Area H-1.

(2) Activities of the RRTs armed with rifles in the Agreed Adjacent Area, as defined in Appendix 2, shall require the agreement of the JCC.

(3) The RRTs will use the rifles in the rest of Area H-1 to fulfil their above mentioned tasks.

e. The Palestinian Police will ensure that all Palestinian policemen, prior to their deployment in the City of Hebron, will pass a security check in order to verify their suitability for service, taking into account the sensitivity of the area.

6. Holy Sites

a. Paragraphs 2 and 3(a) of Article 32 of Appendix 1 to Annex III of the Interim

Agreement will be applicable to the following Holy Sites in Area H-1:
  (1) The Cave of Othniel Ben Knaz/El-Khalil;
  (2) Elonei Mamre/Haram Er-Rameh;
  (3) Eshel Avraham/Balotat Ibrahim; and
  (4) Maayan Sarah/Ein Sarah.
b.   The Palestinian Police will be responsible for the protection of the above Jewish
Holy Sites. Without derogating from the above responsibility of the Palestinian
Police, visits to the above Holy Sites by worshippers or other visitors shall be
accompanied by a Joint Mobile Unit, which will ensure free, unimpeded and secure
access to the Holy Sites, as well as their peaceful use.

7. Normalization of Life in the Old City

a.   Both sides reiterate their commitment to maintain normal life throughout the
City of Hebron and to prevent any provocation or friction that may affect the
normal life in the city.
b.   In this context, both sides are committed to take all steps and measures necessary for
the normalization of life in Hebron, including:
  (1) The wholesale market – Hasbahe – will be opened as a retail market in which
goods will be sold directly to consumers from within the existing shops.
  (2) The movement of vehicles on the Shuhada Road will be gradually returned,
within 4 months, to the same situation which existed prior to February 1994.

8. The Imara

The Imara will be turned over to the Palestinian side upon the completion of the
redeployment and will become the headquarters of the Palestinian Police in the City
of Hebron.

9. City of Hebron

Both sides reiterate their commitment to the unity of the City of Hebron, and their
understanding that the division of security responsibility will not divide the city. In
this context, and without derogating from the security powers and responsibilities
of either side, both sides share the mutual goal that movement of people, goods and
vehicles within and in and out of the city will be smooth and normal, without
obstacles or barriers.

CIVIL ARRANGEMENTS REGARDING THE REDEPLOYMENT IN HEBRON

10. Transfer of Civil Powers and Responsibilities

a.   The transfer of civil powers and responsibilities that have yet to be transferred
to the Palestinian side in the City of Hebron (12 spheres) in accordance with Article
VII of Annex I to the Interim Agreement shall be conducted concurrently with the
beginning of the redeployment of Israeli military forces in Hebron.
b.   In Area H-2, the civil powers and responsibilities will be transferred to the
Palestinian side, except for those relating to Israelis and their property, which shall
continue to be exercised by the Israeli Military Government.

11. Planning, Zoning and Building

a.   The two parties are equally committed to preserve and protect the historic
character of the city in a way which does not harm or change that character in any
part of the city.
b.   The Palestinian side has informed the Israeli side that in exercising its powers

and responsibilities, taking into account the existing municipal regulations, it has undertaken to implement the following provisions:

(1) Proposed construction of buildings above two floors (6 meters) within 50 meters of the external boundaries of the locations specified in the list attached to this Protocol as Appendix 3 (hereinafter referred to as 'the attached list') will be coordinated through the DCL.

(2) Proposed construction of buildings above three floors (9 meters) between 50 and 100 meters of the external boundaries of the locations specified in the attached list will be coordinated through the DCL.

(3) Proposed construction of non-residential, non-commercial buildings within 100 meters of the external boundaries of the locations specified in the attached list that are designed for uses that may adversely affect the environment (such as industrial factories) or buildings and institutions in which more that 50 persons are expected to gather together will be coordinated through the DCL.

(4) Proposed construction of buildings above two floors (6 meters) within 50 meters from each side of the road specified in the attached list will be coordinated through the DCL.

(5) The necessary enforcement measures will be taken to ensure compliance on the ground with the preceding provisions.

(6) This Article does not apply to existing buildings or to new construction or renovation for which fully approved permits were issued by the Municipality prior to 15 January 1997.

12. Infrastructure

a. The Palestinian side shall inform the Israeli side, through the DCL, 48 hours in advance of any anticipated activity regarding infrastructure which may disturb the regular flow of traffic on roads in Area H-2 or which may affect infrastructure (such as water, sewage, electricity and communications) serving Area H-2.

b. The Israeli side may request, through the DCL, that the municipality carry out works regarding the roads or other infrastructure required for the well-being of the Israelis in Area H-2. If the Israeli side offers to cover the costs of these works, the Palestinian side will ensure that these works are carried out as a top priority.

c. The above does not prejudice the provisions of the Interim Agreement regarding the access to infrastructure, facilities and installations located in the city of Hebron, such as the electricity grid.

13. Transportation

The Palestinian side shall have the power to determine bus stops, traffic arrangements and traffic signalization in the City of Hebron. Traffic signalization, traffic arrangements and the location of bus stops in Area H-2 will remain as they are on the date of the redeployment in Hebron. Any subsequent change in these arrangements in Area H-2 will be done in cooperation between the two sides in the transportation sub-committee.

14. Municipal Inspectors

a. In accordance with paragraph 4.c of Article VII of Annex I of the Interim Agreement, plainclothes unarmed municipal inspectors will operate in Area H-2. The number of these inspectors shall not exceed 50.

b. The inspectors shall carry official identification cards with a photograph issued by the Municipality.

c. The Palestinian side may request the assistance of the Israel Police, through the DCL of Hebron, in order to carry out its enforcement activities in Area H-2.

15. *Location of Offices of the Palestinian Council*

The Palestinian side, when operating new offices in Area H-2, will take into consideration the need to avoid provocation and friction. Where establishing such offices might affect public order or security the two sides will cooperate to find a suitable solution.

16. *Municipal Services*

In accordance with paragraph 5 of Article VII of Annex I of the Interim Agreement, municipal services shall be provided regularly and continuously to all parts of the City of Hebron, at the same quality and cost. The cost shall be determined by the Palestinian side with respect to work done and materials consumed, without discrimination.

MISCELLANEOUS

17. *Temporary International Presence*

There will be a Temporary International Presence in Hebron (TIPH). Both sides will agree on the modalities of the TIPH, including the number of its members and its area of operation.

18. *Annex I*

Nothing in this Protocol will derogate from the security powers and responsibilities of either side in accordance with Annex I to the Interim Agreement.

19. *Attached Appendices*

The appendices attached to this Protocol shall constitute an integral part hereof.

Done at Erez checkpoint this 15th day of January 1997
Dan Shomron
for the Government of the State of Israel
Saeb Erekat
for the PLO

Appendices

APPENDIX 2, ARTICLE 5: AGREED ADJACENT AREA

The Agreed Adjacent Area ('AAA') shall include the following:
1. An area defined by a line commencing from AAA Reference Point (RP) 100, proceeding along old Route No. 35 until RP 101, continuing by a straight line to RP 102, and from there connected by a straight line to RP 103.
2. An area defined by a line commencing at RP 104, following a straight line to RP 105, from there following a line immediately westward of checkpoints 4, 5, 6, 8, 9, 10, 11, 12 and 13, and from there connected by a straight line to RP 106.
3. An area defined by a line connecting RPs 107 and 108, passing immediately northward of checkpoint 15.

APPENDIX 3, ARTICLE 12: LIST OF LOCATIONS

- The area of Al Haram Al Ibrahimi/the Tomb of the Patriarchs (including the military and police installations in its vicinity).
- Al Hisba/Abraham Avinu.
- Osama School/Beit Romano (including the military location in its vicinity).
- Al Daboya/Beit Hadasseh.
- Jabla Al Rahama/Tel Rumeida.
- The Jewish Cemeteries.
- Dir Al Arbein/The Tomb of Ruth and Yishai.
- Tel Al Jaabra/Givaat Avot Neighbourhood (including the police station in its vicinity).
- The Road connecting Al Haram Al Ibrahimi/the Tomb of the Patriarchs and Qiryat Arba.

Note for the Record

The two leaders met on 15 January 1997, in the presence of the US Special Middle East Coordinator. They requested him to prepare this Note for the Record to summarize what they agreed upon at their meeting.

MUTUAL UNDERTAKINGS

The two leaders agreed that the Oslo peace process must move forward to succeed. Both parties to the Interim Agreement have concerns and obligations. Accordingly, the two leaders reaffirmed their commitment to implement the Interim Agreement on the basis of reciprocity and, in this context, conveyed the following undertakings to each other:

Israeli Responsibilities
The Israeli side reaffirms its commitments to the following measures and principles in accordance with the Interim Agreement:

Issues for Implementation

1. Further Redeployment Phases
The first phase of further redeployments will be carried out during the first week of March.

2. Prisoner Release Issues
Prisoner release issues will be dealt with in accordance with the Interim Agreement's provisions and procedures, including Annex VII.

Issues for Negotiation

3. Outstanding Interim Agreement Issues
Negotiations on the following outstanding issues from the Interim Agreement will be immediately resumed. Negotiations on these issues will be conducted in parallel:
a. Safe Passage
b. Gaza Airport
c. Gaza port
d. Passages
e. Economic, financial, civilian and security issues
f. People-to-people

4. Permanent Status Negotiations
Permanent status negotiations will be resumed within two months after implementation of the Hebron Protocol.

Palestinian Responsibilities
The Palestinian side reaffirms its commitments to the following measures and principles in accordance with the Interim Agreement:

1. Complete the process of revising the Palestinian National Charter.

2. Fighting terror and preventing violence:
a. Strengthening security cooperation.
b. Preventing incitement and hostile propaganda, as specified in Article XXII of the Interim Agreement.
c. Combat systematically and effectively terrorist organizations and infrastructure.
d. Apprehension, prosecution and punishment of terrorists.
e. Requests for transfer of suspects and defendants will be acted upon in accordance with Article II(7)(f) of Annex IV to the Interim Agreement.
f. Confiscation of illegal firearms.

3. Size of Palestinian Police will be pursuant to the Interim Agreement.

4. Exercise of Palestinian governmental activity, and location of Palestinian governmental offices, will be as specified in the Interim Agreement.
The aforementioned commitments will be dealt with immediately and in parallel.

OTHER ISSUES

Either party is free to raise other issues not specified above related to implementation of the Interim Agreement and obligations of both sides arising from the Interim Agreement.

Prepared by Ambassador Dennis Ross at the request of Prime Minister Benjamin Netanyahu and Ra'ees Yasser Arafat.

Letter to be Provided by US Secretary of State Christopher to Benjamin Netanyahu at the Time of the Signing of the Hebron Protocol

Dear Mr. Prime Minister,
    I wanted personally to congratulate you on the successful conclusion of the 'Protocol Concerning the Redeployment in Hebron'. It represents an important step forward in the Oslo peace process and reaffirms my conviction that a just and lasting peace will be established between Israelis and Palestinians in the very near future.
    In this connection, I can assure you that it remains the policy of the United States to support and promote full implementation of the Interim Agreement in all of its parts. We intend to continue our efforts to help ensure that all outstanding commitments are carried out by both parties in a cooperative spirit and on the basis of reciprocity.

As part of this process, I have impressed upon Chairman Arafat the imperative need for the Palestinian Authority to make every effort to ensure public order and internal security within the West Bank and Gaza Strip. I have stressed to him that effectively carrying out this major responsibility will be a critical foundation for completing the implementation of the Interim Agreement, as well as the peace process as a whole.

I wanted you to know that, in this context, I have advised Chairman Arafat of U.S. views on Israel's process of redeploying its forces, designating specified military locations and transferring additional powers and responsibilities to the Palestinian Authority. In this regard, I have conveyed our belief, that the first phase of further redeployments should take place as soon as possible, and that all three phases of the further redeployments should be completed within twelve months from the implementation of the first phase of the further redeployments but not later than mid-1998.

Mr. Prime Minister, you can be assured that the United States' commitment to Israel's security is ironclad and constitutes the fundamental cornerstone of our special relationship. The key element in our approach to peace, including the negotiation and implementation of agreements between Israel and its Arab partners, has always been a recognition of Israel's security requirements. Moreover, a hallmark of U.S. policy remains our commitment to work cooperatively to seek to meet the security needs that Israel identifies. Finally, I would like to reiterate our position that Israel is entitled to secure and defensible borders, which should be directly negotiated and agreed with its neighbors.

Index

Abu Iyyad 127
Allenby, Sir Edmund 226
Allon, Yigal 202, 300
Algeria 205
American Jewish Committee (AJC) 241
American Jewry 239–59
American–Israel Public Affairs
    Committee (AIPAC) 241, 245–48,
    250–54
Amir, Yigal i, 28, 40
Anti Defamation League (ADL) 245–6,
    248
Aqaba 122
Arab boycott 286, 290
Arab Common Market 290
Arab Cooperation Council (ACC) 290
Arab–Israeli conflict 117–334
Arab League 117, 122, 125, 162, 285,
    287
Arafat, Yasser iii, v, vi, 23, 55, 59,
    117–18, 126–9, 130, 139, 147,
    158–64, 176, 180, 184, 193, 195–7,
    214–15, 220–21, 245–6, 255, 266,
    275
Arekat, Saeb 271
Arens, Moshe 10, 247, 312
Argentina 330
Armenians 284
Asad, Hafiz iii, 125, 126, 129–31, 173,
    229, 231, 233, 236, 238, 299, 333
Atherton, Roy 299
Ayyash, Yahya 160

Baker, James 126
Balfour Declaration (1917) 135
Ballistic missiles 235, 237
Bar-Lev line 120
Ba'th Party 122, 286
Barak, Ehud ii, 82, 87
al-Baz, Usama 310
Bedouins 89
Begin, Benny iv, 23
Begin, Menachem ii, iv, vi 9, 31, 121,
    123–4, 141, 172, 185, 202, 253,
    300–304, 306, 321

Beilin, Yossi 59, 250, 252, 253, 313
Ben-Aharon, Yossi 248, 256, 257
Ben-Gurion, David iv, 76, 88–9,
    240–242, 250, 283
Brandeis, Louis 241
Britain 228–9, 281, 282, 289
Brzezinski, Zbigniew 302
Bush, George 244–8

Cairo 117, 125, 296–9, 304–5, 307–19
Cairo Summit (1996) 316, 321–2
Camp David Accords vi, 138, 140–42,
    204, 207, 219, 301–3, 307, 310, 319
Carmon, Yigal 245, 256
Carr, Edward Hallett 134
Carter, Jimmy vi, 219, 243, 301
Casablanca Economic Conference
    (1994) 290, 316
China 329
Christopher, Warren 147, 251, 343–4
Circassians 89
Clinton, Bill 159, 201, 273
Cold War 119, 125, 133, 220, 289,
    291, 293, 318, 322

Damascus 225, 226, 233, 236
D'amato, Alfonse 255, 257
Dayan, Moshe 120, 202, 300–301
Declaration of Principles (DOP, 1993),
    see Oslo Accords/Process
Deri, Aryeh 18
Détente 249, 256
Dine, Tom 247
Dole, Robert 147, 251
Druckman, Haim 39
Druzes 89, 90–91

Eban Abba ii,
Egypt vi, 117, 118, 120–22, 125, 138,
    140–42, 149, 154, 156, 159, 162,
    172, 181, 204, 207, 218, 219, 226,
    227, 232, 233, 236, 282, 286, 288–9,
    291
    and peace with Israel 296–334
    military buildup 321–34

response to Rabin's assassination
    266–77
Eisenhower, Dwight 250
Eitan, Rafael 5, 12, 23, 108, 123
Eretz Israel iv, v, 29, 30–32, 35, 37, 38,
    41, 42, 43, 48–9, 58, 68, 104, 137,
    156, 157, 176, 179, 182, 183, 221
Ethiopia 78, 284–5
European Union 198, 282
Eyal 34, 177

Fahd, King 123
Fertile Crescent 226, 287–8
Fez 123, 219
First World War 227, 284
Ford, Gerald 301
Foxman, Abe 246
France 228–9, 281, 289
Frenkel, Jacob 22

Gaddafi, Mu'amar 125, 290
Gaffney, Frank 252
Galilee 228, 229, 234
Gamasy, Abd al-Ghani 300
Gaza Strip 38, 49, 56, 119, 120, 136,
    138, 139, 140–50, 155–63, 173, 175,
    179, 183, 198, 203, 205, 210, 216,
    220, 243, 286, 288, 302, 306–7
Geneva Peace Conference (1973) 300
Germany 62, 197–8, 330
Gesher Party 12, 13, 21, 61
Ghali, Butros 307, 309
Gilman, Benjamin 255, 257
Gingrich, Newt 147
Golan Heights iii, vi, 19, 49, 120, 121,
    130, 131, 136, 155–7, 225–38, 252,
    254, 257, 299, 305, 307, 332–3
Gold, Dore 314–15
Goldstein, Baruch 29, 39, 157, 199,
    255
Gorbachev, Mikhail 125, 126
Great Britain 135–6
'Greater Israel', see Eretz Israel
'Greater Syria' 288
Gulf Cooperation Council (GCC) 272,
    290
Gulf War (1991) 8, 10, 11, 78, 84,
    126–7, 220, 230, 237, 238, 244, 286,
    288, 293, 310–11, 313, 322
Gumayel, Bashir 123
Gush Emunim 28, 32, 37, 41, 48, 51,
    145, 256
Gush Etzion 18

Hadash Party 13

Haifa 157
HAMAS i, v, 37, 38, 39, 42–3, 118,
    127, 128, 156–61, 164, 172–4,
    179–80, 182, 184, 199, 209, 210,
    214–15, 221, 267, 269, 274, 290,
    306, 311
Hammer, Zevulun 15
Hartmann, David 42
Hashemites, see Jordan
Hebron 18, 23, 29, 38, 39, 43, 118,
    157, 159, 161, 177, 199, 251, 255,
    271, 306, 313, 314
    protocol v–vi, viii, 117, 129, 131,
        315–16, 337–44
Hecht, Abraham 33
Heikal, Muhammad Hassanein 324
Helms, Jesse 245, 257
Herzberg, Arthur 241
Herzl, Theodore 31, 304
Hizbullah 130, 270, 272, 275, 290
Holst, Johan Jorgen 140
Hussein, King 117, 266–7, 277
Hussein, Saddam 122, 126, 233, 236,
    288, 290, 310–11

Indyk, Martin 159
Intifada v, 37, 49, 51, 78, 82–3, 99,
    102–4, 106, 119, 124–5, 172, 195,
    202, 209–12, 214, 222, 239–40, 244,
    246, 266–9, 276, 288, 306, 308–9
Iran 122, 133, 194, 205, 209, 236,
    266–9, 272–3, 275–7, 282–5,
    290–92, 323, 330–32
Iran–Iraq War (1980–88) 118, 122–3,
    133, 233
Iraq 11, 78, 118, 122–3, 126–7, 194,
    205, 226, 230, 237, 282, 284,
    287–92, 306, 323
Islamic Jihad v, 118, 174, 182, 209,
    210, 214–15, 221, 267, 276
Israel
    and the Arab World 265–334
    and the diaspora 70–76, 239–59
    and Egypt vi, 118, 120–22, 125, 138,
        140–42, 172, 181, 204, 296–334
    and negotiations with the Palestinians,
        see Oslo Accords/Process
    and peace with Jordan 138–42
    and Syria 225–38
    and Turkey 282–5, 324
    and the United States 239–62, 296
    defence forces (IDF) 37, 56, 77–114,
        123–4, 173, 232–3, 325–9
    domestic politics i–vii,
    elections 3–24, 66–76, 128, 180

ethnic divisions 91–2
ideological schisms 28–65
national identity 47–76
new immigrants 93–5, 107
political system 3–24
religious fundamentalism 28–46,
177–8
War of Independence (1947–49) 204,
228–9, 232, 286
Israel be-Aliya Party 13, 15, 16, 18, 19,
20, 70, 72–3
Ivri, David 312

Jabotinsky, Ze'ev 68, 244, 253
Jaffa 157
Jakobovits, Immanuel 41
Jarring, Gunar 120
Jericho 56, 203, 220
Jerusalem iii, 17–18, 31, 36, 43, 49,
55, 66, 68, 74, 117, 133, 136, 141,
143–7, 148, 158, 161, 163, 176,
187–200, 205, 206, 208, 210, 213,
219, 251, 254–5, 257, 268, 275, 281,
296–7, 301–3, 305, 307, 313
Jewish diaspora 70–76, 239–59
Jibril, Ahmad 130
Jordan i, 53, 78, 117, 138, 139,
140–43, 147, 149, 156, 158, 172,
178, 189, 193, 194, 195, 204, 206,
211–13, 218–21, 226, 234, 265–9,
271–3, 275–7, 282, 286–7, 289–90,
299, 318, 323, 332
Jordan River/Valley 32, 138, 204, 206,
226, 227, 234, 286
Jordanian option iv, 53, 204, 206–7,
211–12, 219–20
Judea and Samaria (see also West Bank)
v, 29, 31, 40, 56, 68, 105, 117, 137,
175, 179, 183, 216

Kach 35, 36, 177
Kahane, Meir 35, 39, 42, 157, 255
Kamel, Muhammad Ibrahim 303–4
Kanafani, Marwan 147
Katsav, Moshe 248
Kenya 284
Khaddam, Abd al-Halim 299
Khalaf, Salah, see Abu Iyyad
Khomeini, Ruhollah 285
Kibbutz 32, 68, 107
Kissinger, Henry 297, 300
Klein, Morton 252
Knesset iii, vi, 3–24, 28, 38, 40, 53, 59,
69, 73, 88, 109, 162, 171, 174–6,
182, 184, 202, 213, 304

Kollek, Teddy 196
Kook, Rabbi Avraham Yitzhak Ha-
Cohen 30–31, 40
Kook, Rabbi Zvi Yehuda 31–3, 41
Kurds 284, 287
Kuwait 11, 118, 126–7, 268, 272, 274,
288–9, 291, 323

Labour Party i, ii, iii–vi, 3, 4, 6, 9, 13,
14, 20, 32, 38, 48, 50, 51–4, 66, 68,
74, 121, 128, 137, 171, 172, 175,
180, 197, 202, 239–40, 243, 249–59,
313, 319
Landau, Uzi 257
Lebanon 123–4, 125, 142–3, 147, 162,
220, 221, 228, 233, 234, 235, 266–7,
270–76, 284, 287, 289, 306, 318,
332
Lebanon War (1982) ii, 37, 41, 49, 84,
98, 106, 118–19, 123–4, 205, 206–7,
219, 246, 256, 304–6, 308–9
Levy, David 5, 10, 12, 20–22
Levy, Yitzhak 21, 23
Liberman, Avigdor 15
Libya 125, 194, 205, 266–7, 273–5,
287, 292
Likud Party i, ii, iv–vi, 4, 5, 6, 9,
10–24, 31, 38, 54, 56, 66, 70, 74,
117, 121, 125, 128, 129, 157, 161,
171, 176, 182, 202, 211, 239–40,
243–51, 253–54, 256–9, 309, 319,
321

Ma'aleh Edumim 18
Madrid Peace Conference (1991)
126–7, 129–30, 172, 211, 220, 231,
245, 250, 309–11, 313
Maimonides 37
Majali, Abd al-salam 194
Maksoud, Clovis 155
Mauritania 273
Mediterranean 226
Meir, Golda 300
MERETZ Party iv, 13, 51–4, 61, 68,
69, 74–5, 197
Meridor, Dan 11, 22, 23
Middle East Command 282
Moda'i, Yitzhak 11
Moledet Party iv, 10, 38
Morocco 273, 275, 287
Mount Hermon 225, 226
Mubarak, Husni 117, 162, 266, 273–4,
305, 307, 309–12, 315, 318, 322,
330–31
Musa, Amr 310–12

Muslim Bortherhood 311, 330–31

Nasser, Gamal Abdel 119–20, 234, 285, 288, 318, 330
Nateq-Nuri, Ali Akbar 269
National Religious Party (NRP) iv, 13, 14, 15, 16, 17, 18, 19, 21, 22, 23, 67, 68, 69, 71
Netanyahu, Benjamin i–iii, 38, 54, 61, 66, 67, 68, 70, 71, 74, 75–6, 105, 158, 161–3, 176, 184–5, 246, 256, 265, 313, 321
   and the peace process iv–viii, 117, 127–32, 201
   forming of government 3–24
'New Zionism' 49–54, 56
Nimr Darwish, Abdallah 59
North Atlantic Treaty Organization (NATO) 282, 283
North Korea 330

October 1973 War 32, 84, 101, 118, 120, 121, 218, 226, 229, 232, 233, 234, 237–8, 286, 297–301, 315–16, 328
Olmert, Ehud 11, 246
Oman 266–7, 272–3
Operation *Accountability* (1994) 84
Operation *Grapes of Wrath* (1996) 84, 193
Oslo Accords/Process i, iv–v, 33, 36, 38, 42–3, 47, 52, 54–9, 75, 77–8, 82, 104, 117–18, 127–85, 189–90, 201–3, 210–22, 255–9, 265–77, 288, 312–15, 318, 324
Ottoman Empire 286
Oz, Amos 123–4

Pakistan 282
Palestine Liberation Organization (PLO)/Palestinian Authority i, iii, vi, 47, 52, 55, 57, 82, 104, 119, 123–8, 130, 133, 139–40, 143, 147, 149, 156, 163, 171–3, 175–6, 178–80, 190–93, 201, 203–20, 240, 243–8, 250–52, 254–7, 265–7, 272–3, 275–7, 281, 286, 289, 301, 308–10, 315, 318–19
   covenant 128, 139–40, 173, 175, 180, 257
Palestinians v, vi, 29, 36, 37, 39, 43, 47, 48–54, 59, 69, 74, 78, 82, 100, 117–18, 124–7, 129, 131, 135, 136, 140–42, 145–8, 151–85, 187–99, 201–24, 266–9, 271, 281, 288, 298,

300–319
   'right of return' 18
   refugees 142–3, 148, 157
Pan-Arabism 118–21, 286–8
Peace Now 51
Peace Process (see also Oslo Accords/Process, Camp David Accords, Madrid Peace Conference) 239–62
Peres, Shimon i–iv, vi, 12, 40, 52–4, 57, 60, 66, 67, 69, 128, 130, 131, 160, 163, 171, 173–6, 178, 180–85, 193, 195, 197, 202, 250, 253, 273, 275
Podhoretz, Norman 252–3
Pollard, Jonathan 242
Popular Front for the Liberation of Palestine (PFLP) 156, 158, 269
Porat, Hanan 18
'Post-Zionism' 51–4, 58–60, 62–3, 74–6, 108, 259

Qatar 162, 266–7, 272–3
Quneitra 226, 234

Rabin, Yitzhak i, ii, iv, vi, 9, 28, 29, 33, 34, 36, 38, 40, 42, 43, 47, 52–3, 55, 59, 60, 66, 75, 77, 104, 127, 130, 131, 137–8, 140, 156, 163, 164, 171–8, 180–85, 201–24, 249–59, 265–77, 300, 311–12, 332
Rabinovich, Itamar 254, 255
Ramon, Haim iii
Reagan, Ronald 239, 243, 253
Reich, Seymour 247
Rifa'i, Zaid 299
Rubinstein, Amnon 40
Russia (see also Soviet Union) 291, 324

Sadat, Anwar 120–23, 133, 153–5, 219, 233, 266, 268, 298–303, 306, 315–16, 318–19, 324, 330, 332
Saudi Arabia 123, 127, 193, 250, 272, 289, 313, 329
Second World War 235
Sea of Galilee 225–6, 228–9
Shahak-Lipkin, Amnon 86, 87, 106, 109
Shamir, Yitzhak ii, iv, 8, 10, 11, 68, 171, 211, 242, 244–5, 247–9, 256, 308–12
Shammas, Anton 59
Shapira, Avraham 37
Shara, Farouq 273
Sharansky, Natan 16
Sharett, Moshe 283

Sharon, Ariel 5, 16, 20–22, 23, 24, 38, 123–4, 202, 247, 249, 256
Shas Party 13, 14, 15, 16, 17, 18, 19, 22, 23, 74
Shihabi, Hikmat 231
Shkaki, Fathi 267, 268, 273, 276
Shomron, Dan 82
Shultz, George 244
Sinai Campaign (1956) 250, 285
Sinai Peninsula vi, 42, 121, 138, 156, 227, 234, 237, 299, 301, 303, 306
Sisco, Joseph 299
Six Day War (1967) iii, 30–32, 49, 61, 101, 118–20, 127, 136, 137, 139, 145, 155, 195, 202, 218, 226, 229, 232, 233–4, 241, 252–3, 296–300, 303, 316
Somalia 285
South Africa 198, 282
Soviet Union 78, 93, 122, 123, 125, 188, 209, 220, 230, 233, 236, 249, 281, 289, 297, 318, 329
Sudan 285
Suez Canal 120, 121, 284, 299
Syria iii, vi, 57, 120, 122, 123, 125, 129–31, 143, 147, 157, 162, 173, 181, 205, 219, 220, 221, 225–38, 254, 256, 272–3, 282, 286–8, 291, 299, 307, 313, 318, 329, 332–3
  and the peace process iii, 125, 126, 129–31, 236–7
  invasion of Lebanon (1976) 233
  military potential 230–31
  response to Rabin's assassination 266, 276–7

Taba 138, 306, 308
Tantawi, Muhammad Hussein 324
Tel-Aviv 42, 43, 59, 66, 68, 146, 198, 245, 273, 284, 309
Thani, Hamad Bin Jasem 162
Thatcher, Margaret 62
Third Way Party 13, 15, 18, 19
Tibi, Ahmad 59
Tsomet Party 12, 13, 15, 176
Tuhami, Hassan 304

Tunis 205, 208, 221, 306
Tunisia 267, 272, 275–6
Turkey 266, 282–5, 290–91

United Arab Emirates 268, 272
United Nations 147, 196, 198, 229, 237, 254–5, 283, 284
  Emergency Force (UNEF) 121
  November 1947 Partition Resolution 48, 124
  Security Council Resolution 242 120, 124, 139, 144, 298–9
  Security Council Resolution 338 121, 124, 139, 144
  UNESCO 299
  UNRWA 148
United States ii, 55, 67, 124, 126, 130, 131, 147, 159, 162, 171, 172, 192, 196, 198, 208, 237, 281, 289, 291–3, 296–303, 305–7, 316, 319, 322–31
  the 'Special Relationship' 239–62
United Torah Judaism Party 13, 15, 16, 19, 20, 23, 24, 67

Vatican 188
Vietnam War 192
Vital, David 259

Weizman, Ezer 73, 162–3
West Bank (see also Judea and Samaria) v–vi, 28, 31, 34, 37, 38, 39, 49–50, 55–7, 59, 105, 117, 119, 121, 136–41, 144, 145, 147–9, 155–63, 175, 179, 182, 187, 198, 205, 211, 243, 286, 288, 302, 306–7, 316

Yassin, Ahmad 267
Yemen 120, 205, 268, 290
Yishuv 30
Yom Kippur War, see October 1973 War

Ze'evi, Rehavam 10, 11, 38
Zionism 28–33, 37, 44, 47–76, 78, 135, 138, 158, 198, 240–44, 256, 258–9, 297–8, 317
Zo Artzenu 37, 177

Cass series in Israeli History, Politics and Society

ISSN 1368-4795

Providing a multidisciplinary examination in all aspects, the series serves as a means of communication between the various communities interested in Israel: academics, policy-makers, practitioners, journalists and the informed public.

BETWEEN WAR AND PEACE
Dilemmas of Israeli Security
Edited by Efraim Karsh

This volume assesses the balance of opportunities and risks confronting Israel at this critical juncture in her history and offers possible solutions to her pressing dilemmas.

304 pages   1996   0 7146 4711 X cloth   0 7146 4256 8 paper

PEACE IN THE MIDDLE EAST
The Challenge for Israel
Edited by Efraim Karsh

As Israel grows closer to its loftiest ideal - contractual peace with its Arab neighbours - this book assesses the implications for Israel's political and economic systems, its national security and its regional and world standing.

176 pages   1994   0 7146 4614 8 cloth   0 7146 4141 3 paper

THE SHAPING OF ISRAELI IDENTITY
Myth, Memory and Trauma
Edited by Robert Wistrich and David Ohana

The essays in this volume examine in an original, provocative and critical perspective the fundamental myths, symbols and historical memories that have played an active role in shaping the development of Israeli society, in particular relating Zionism to the Jewish religious tradition, the reality of war, and the geopolitical isolation of Israel.

256 pages   1995   0 7146 4741 5 cloth   0 7146 4163 4 paper

U.S.-ISRAELI RELATIONS AT THE CROSSROADS
Edited by Gabriel Sheffer

The essays in this collection deal with, among other things, the general global setting and its implications for the U.S.-Israeli 'special relationship'.

256 pages   1997   0 7146 4747 0 cloth   0 7146 4305 X paper

REGIONAL SECURITY IN THE MIDDLE EAST
Past, Present and Future
Zeev Maoz

Middle Eastern politics of the 1990s has been characterized by a drive towards peace. However, whether the current drive for peace is successful or not will depend on several issues that have led to the collapse of past initiatives such as regional security, concession of territory and arms control. This book looks at the challenges presented by such problems, as well as providing practical advice on how risks of failure could be seized.

224 pages   1997   0 7146 4808 6 cloth   0 7146 4375 0 paper

MIDDLE EAST SECURITY
Prospects for an Arms Control Regime
Edited by Efraim Inbar and Shmuel Sandler

This collection of essays examines the obstacles to an effective arms control regime in the Middle East and assesses the prospects of overcoming them.

212 pages   1995   0 7146 4644 X cloth   0 7146 4168 5 paper

RELIGIOUS RADICALISM IN THE GREATER MIDDLE EAST
Edited by Bruce Maddy-Weitzman and Efraim Inbar

An in-depth analysis of religious radicalism in the Greater Middle East - a recently defined area encompassing the Middle East, Central Asia and North Africa.

272 pages   1997   0 7146 4769 1 cloth   0 7146 4326 2 paper

THE PFLP'S CHANGING ROLE IN THE MIDDLE EAST
Harold M Cubert

A ground-breaking history of the Popular Front for the Liberation of Palestine (PFLP), a violent Marxist faction within the Palestinian national movement.

248 pages   1997   0 7146 4772 1cloth   0 7146 4329 7 paper